## PART 6

### Five Common Sentence Errors

13. Revising Sentence Fragments  281
14. Revising Comma Splices and Fused Sentences  285
15. Revising Agreement Errors  288
16. Revising Awkward or Confusing Sentences  295
17. Revising Misplaced and Dangling Modifiers  300

## PART 7

### Sentence Grammar

18. Using Verbs Correctly: Form, Tense, Mood, and Voice  307
19. Using Pronouns Correctly  317
20. Using Adjectives and Adverbs Correctly  322

## PART 8

### Sentence Style

21. Writing Varied Sentences  329
22. Writing Emphatic Sentences  336
23. Writing Concise Sentences  341
24. Using Parallelism  346

## PART 9

### Using Words Effectively

25. Choosing Words  351
26. Using a Dictionary  359
27. A Glossary of Usage  363

## PART 10

### Understanding Punctuation

28. Using End Punctuation  379
29. Using Commas  382
30. Using Semicolons  392
31. Using Apostrophes  394
32. Using Quotation Marks  398
33. Using Other Punctuation Marks  405

## PART 11

### Understanding Spelling and Mechanics

34. Spelling  415
35. Capitalization  421
36. Italics  426
37. Hyphens  429
38. Abbreviations  432
39. Numbers  436

## PART 12

### College Survival Skills

40. Ten Habits of Successful Students  441
41. Developing Active Reading Skills  449
42. Writing Essay Exams  452
43. Writing about Literature  460
44. Designing Documents and Web Sites  475
45. Writing for the Workplace  491
46. Making Oral Presentations  504

## PART 13

### ESL

47. English for Speakers of Other Languages  515

Five Common Sentence Errors

Sentence Grammar

Sentence Style

Using Words Effectively

Understanding Punctuation

Understanding Spelling and Mechanics

College Survival Skills

ESL

Appendixes

# The Brief Handbook, *Fourth Edition*

## A Real Writer's Handbook

With the publication of its fourth edition, *The Brief Handbook*, by Laurie G. Kirszner and Stephen R. Mandell, continues its tradition of excellence and innovation, addressing the day-to-day needs of real students in contemporary classrooms.

With Chapter 40, "Ten Habits of Successful Students," the handbook is the first to introduce academic success as a core component of the text, addressing topics such as how to manage time, when and how to study, how to take advantage of college services, and how to become a lifelong learner. This new chapter introduces the "Academic Survival Skills" section, which offers advice and insights not available in other handbooks.

Since its first edition, *The Brief Handbook* has anticipated students' needs and preferences. The inaugural edition was the first to introduce a four-color design in a brief comb-bound handbook, making it easier for users to locate and access relevant material. The second edition moved research forward to Part 1, acknowledging its increasingly prominent role in first- and second-semester composition courses. In the third edition, Kirszner and Mandell were the first to include Frequently Asked Questions at the beginning of each part, enabling students to find answers to their questions even without knowledge of grammatical terminology.

Now, in its fourth edition, *The Brief Handbook* places a greater emphasis on technology and its effect on writing and research. Still, with all its innovations, *The Brief Handbook* retains its traditional strengths—practical and thorough coverage of writing with and without sources; numerous and varied models of student writing (more than in any other brief handbook); current, accurate, and easily accessible guides to documentation, grammar, mechanics, and usage; and extensive coverage of ESL and writing in the disciplines. With this combination of innovation and tradition, Kirszner and Mandell build on their long-standing reputation for helping college students to become better writers and to achieve academic and professional success.

# Ease of Use and an Open, Uncluttered Design

Tabbed dividers are designed to make part and chapter divisions easily and quickly accessible.

The front of each tabbed divider includes an overview of the chapters in that section, with page references for each chapter.

## PART 2

### Critical Thinking and Argumentation

**4 Thinking Critically  83**
  4a  Distinguishing Fact from Opinion  83
  4b  Evaluating Supporting Evidence  84
  4c  Detecting Bias  85
  4d  Understanding Inductive and Deductive Reasoning  86
  4e  Recognizing Logical Fallacies  88
**5 Writing Argumentative Essays  91**
  5a  Planning an Argumentative Essay  91
  5b  Using Evidence and Establishing Credibility  93
  5c  Organizing an Argumentative Essay  94
  5d  Writing an Argumentative Essay  96

*Critical Thinking & Argumentation 83 to 102*

## PART 2

### ? Frequently Asked Questions

**Chapter 4 Thinking Critically  83**
 • What is critical thinking?  83
 • How do I tell the difference between a fact and an opinion?  83
 • How do I detect bias in an argument?  85
 • What is an inference?  87
 • What is a logical fallacy?  88
 • What is a non sequitur?  88
 • How do I recognize post hoc reasoning?  88

**Chapter 5 Writing Argumentative Essays  91**
 • How do I know if a topic is suitable for argument?  91
 • What can I do to make sure I have an argumentative thesis?  92
 • How should I deal with opposing arguments?  92
 • How can I make sure I am being fair?  94
 • How should I organize my argumentative essay?  95

**URLs**  *Visit the following sites for answers to more FAQs*
**Critical Thinking (UMSL)**
  *http://www.umsl.edu/~klein/Critical_Thinking.html*
**Critical Thinking (Humboldt)**
  *http://www.humboldt.edu/~act/*
**Logic in Argumentation (Purdue)**
  *http://owl.english.purdue.edu/handouts/general/gl_argpapers.html*
**Logical Fallacies (or Errors in Thinking)**
  *http://www.intrepidsoftware.com/fallacy/toc.htm*
**Avoiding Common Errors in Logic and Reasoning (Princeton U.)**
  *http://web.princeton.edu/sites/writing//Handouts/logic&reason.pdf*
**Writing an Argument Paper (Muskingum College)**
  *http://muskingum.edu/~cal/database/writing.html#Argument*

*Critical Thinking & Argumentation 83 to 102*

The back of each tabbed divider includes Frequently Asked Questions for each chapter, with page references directing students to the answers. On the page, the answer to each FAQ is highlighted with a question mark icon so students can locate relevant information quickly.

**?**

URLs lead students to relevant Web sites.

## close*UP*

**When to quote** ?

- Quote when a source's wording or phrasing is so distinctive that a summary or paraphrase would diminish its impact.
- Quote when a source's words—particularly those of a recognized expert on your subject—will lend authority to your paper.
- Quote when paraphrasing would create a long, clumsy, or incoherent phrase or would change the meaning of the original.
- Quote when you plan to disagree with a source. Using a source's exact words helps to assure readers you are being fair.

### 6g Fine-Tuning Your Thesis

After you have finished your focused research and note taking, you must refine your tentative thesis into a carefully worded statement that expresses a conclusion your research can support. This **thesis statement** should be more precise than your tentative thesis, accurately conveying the direction, emphasis, and scope of your paper.

See 1c3

#### FINE-TUNING YOUR THESIS

| Tentative Thesis | Thesis Statement |
|---|---|
| Not all Americans have equal access to the Internet, and this is a potentially serious problem. | Although the Internet has changed our world for the better, it threatens to create two distinct classes—those who have access and those who do not. |

If your thesis statement does not express a conclusion your research can support, you will need to revise it. Reviewing your notes carefully, perhaps grouping information in different ways, may help you decide on a more suitable thesis. Or, you may try other techniques—for instance, using your research question as a starting point for additional brainstorming or freewriting.

119

*Close-up boxes* focus on issue of special concern to student writers.

Marginal "hyperlink" cross-references (which are keyed to blue underlined terms in the text) direct students to related discussions in other parts of the book.

---

#### ✓checklist Making a topic tree

- ✓ Review all your notes carefully.
- ✓ Decide on the three or four general categories of information that best suit your material.
- ✓ Write or type these categories across the top of a piece of paper.
- ✓ Review your notes again to select ideas and details that fall within each category.
- ✓ List each idea under a relevant heading, moving from general information to increasingly specific details as you move down the page.
- ✓ Draw lines to indicate relationships between ideas in each category.

As you accumulate additional material and as you review the material you have, you will add, delete, and rearrange the items on the branches of your topic tree. Your completed tree can help you develop a tentative thesis and organize supporting information in your essay.

#### (2) Understanding Thesis and Support

The essays you write for your college courses will have a thesis-and-support structure. As the diagram below illustrates, a **thesis-and-support essay** includes a **thesis statement** (which expresses the **thesis,** or main idea, of the essay) and the specific information that

| Introductory paragraph | ⟵ Thesis statement |
|---|---|
| Body paragraph | |
| Body paragraph | |
| Body paragraph | ⟵ Support |
| Body paragraph | |
| Concluding paragraph | |

14

*Checklists* reinforce key concepts.

---

**Note:** With your instructor's permission, you can also do **collaborative brainstorming**—that is, you can brainstorm with your classmates in small groups (either in person or electronically).

http://kirsznermandell.heinle.com

#### Generating ideas

Your computer can help you generate ideas. For example, you can set up a computer journal, and you can also use your computer for freewriting and brainstorming.

When you freewrite, try turning down the screen, leaving it blank to eliminate distractions and encourage spontaneity.

When you brainstorm, type your notes randomly. Then, after you print them out, you can add handwritten notes and graphic elements (arrows, circles, and so on) to indicate parallels and connections.

*Clustering* Clustering—sometimes called *webbing* or *mapping*—is similar to brainstorming. However, clustering allows you to explore your topic in a somewhat more systematic (and more visual) manner.

Begin making a cluster diagram by writing your topic in the center of a sheet of paper. Then, surround your topic with related ideas as they occur to you, moving outward from the general topic in the center and writing down increasingly specific ideas and details as you move toward the edges of the page. Eventually, following the path of one idea at a time, you create a diagram (often lopsided rather than symmetrical) that arranges ideas on spokes or branches radiating out from a central core (your topic). Nguyen Dao's cluster diagram appears on page 11.

*Asking Journalistic Questions* A more structured way of finding something to say about your topic is to ask questions. Your answers to these questions will enable you to explore your topic in an orderly and systematic fashion. Journalists often use the questions *What?*, *What?*, *Why?*, *Where?*, *When?*, and *How?* to assure themselves that they have explored all angles of a story. You can use these questions to see whether you have considered all aspects of your topic.

10

*Computer boxes,* identified by a special icon, highlight information that students will use as they write and revise.

V

## Unique Section on College Survival Skills

The comprehensive seven-chapter "College Survival Skills" section, unique among college handbooks, offers students the practical advice they need to achieve academic success. Chapters include "Ten Habits of Successful Students," "Developing Active Reading Skills," "Writing Essay Exams," "Writing about Literature," "Designing Documents and Web Sites," "Writing for the Workplace," and "Making Oral Presentations."

## PART 12

### College Survival Skills

**40 Ten Habits of Successful Students  441**
40a  Learn to Manage Your Time Effectively  441
40b  Put Studying First  442
40c  Be Sure You Understand School and Course Requirements  443
40d  Be an Active Learner in the Classroom  444
40e  Be an Active Learner Outside the Classroom  444
40f  Take Advantage of College Services  445
40g  Use the Library  445
40h  Use Technology  446
40i  Make Contacts—and Use Them  446
40j  Be a Lifelong Learner  447
**41 Developing Active Reading Skills  449**
41a  Previewing  449
41b  Highlighting  450
41c  Annotating  450
**42 Writing Essay Exams  452**
42a  Planning an Essay Exam Answer  452
42b  Developing a Thesis and a List of Points  454
42c  Writing and Revising an Essay Exam Answer  455
42d  Sample Essay Exam Answer  456
**43 Writing about Literature  460**
43a  Reading Literature  460
43b  Writing about Literature  462
43c  Sample Student Paper (without Sources)  464
43d  Sample Student Paper (with Sources)  468
**44 Designing Documents and Web Sites  475**
44a  Understanding Document Design  475
44b  Designing a Web Site  485
**45 Writing for the Workplace  491**
45a  Writing Business Letters  491
45b  Writing Letters of Application  493
45c  Designing Print Résumés  495
45d  Designing Scannable Résumés  498
45e  Writing Memos  500
45f  Writing E-Mail  502
**46 Making Oral Presentations  504**
46a  Getting Started  504
46b  Planning Your Speech  505
46c  Preparing Your Notes  506
46d  Preparing Visual Aids  507
46e  Rehearsing Your Speech  510
46f  Delivering Your Speech  510

College Survival Skills
441 to 512

---

Chapter **40**

## Ten Habits of Successful Students

As you have probably already observed, the students who are most successful in school are not always the ones who enter with the best grades. In fact, successful students have *learned* to be successful: they have developed specific strategies for success, and they apply those strategies to their education. If you take the time, you too can learn the habits of successful students and apply them to your own college education—and, later on, to your career.

1. Successful students manage their time.
2. Successful students put studying first.
3. Successful students understand what is required of them.
4. Successful students are active learners in the classroom.
5. Successful students are active learners outside the classroom.
6. Successful students use college services.
7. Successful students use the library.
8. Successful students use technology.
9. Successful students make contacts.
10. Successful students are lifelong learners.

### 40a  Learn to Manage Your Time Effectively

One of the most difficult things about college is the demands it makes on your time. It is hard, especially at first, to balance studying, course work, family life, friendships, and a job. But if you do not take control of your schedule, it will take control of you; if you do not learn to manage your time, you will always be struggling to catch up.

Fortunately, there are two tools you can use to help you manage your time: a personal organizer and a calendar. Of course, simply buying an organizer and a calendar will not solve your time-management problems—you have to *use* them. Moreover, you have to use them effectively and regularly.

441

The "College Survival Skills" section includes a new chapter, "Ten Habits of Successful Students," with helpful tips on managing time, taking notes, studying, using technology, and other essential topics.

# PART 3

## The Research Process

6  **The Research Process  105**
   6a  Choosing a Topic  106
   6b  Doing Exploratory Research and Formulating a
       Research Question  107
   6c  Assembling a Working Bibliography  108
   6d  Developing a Tentative Thesis  110
   6e  Doing Focused Research  110
   6f  Taking Notes  112
   6g  Fine-Tuning Your Thesis  119
   6h  Outlining, Drafting, and Revising  120
7  **Using and Evaluating Library Sources  126**
   7a  Doing Exploratory Library Research  126
   7b  Doing Focused Library Research  135
   7c  Evaluating Library Sources  141
   7d  Doing Research Outside the Library  144
8  **Using and Evaluating Internet Sources  147**
   8a  Understanding the Internet  147
   8b  Using the World Wide Web for Research  148
   8c  Using Other Internet Tools  155
   8d  Evaluating Internet Sources  158
   8e  Useful Web Sites  161
9  **Integrating Sources and Avoiding Plagiarism  164**
   9a  Integrating Source Material into Your Writing  164
   9b  Avoiding Plagiarism  169

Research
105 to 176

# The Research Process— Expanded

Research coverage has been significantly expanded and now includes topics such as balancing primary and secondary sources and using and evaluating both print and electronic sources.

Chapter **9**

## Integrating Sources and Avoiding Plagiarism

As you move through the research process and consult various sources, you take notes in the form of **paraphrase**, **summary**, or **quotation**. When your work is complete, these notes will be integrated into your research paper.

See 6c

### 9a  Integrating Source Material into Your Writing

Weave paraphrases, summaries, and quotations of source material smoothly into your discussion, adding your own analysis or explanation to increase coherence and to show the relevance of your sources to the points you are making. Remember that in your research paper, you are orchestrating a conversation among different speakers, and your own voice should dominate.

**closeUP**

**Integrating source material
into your writing**

?

To make sure your sentences do not all sound the same, experiment with different methods of integrating source material into your paper.
• Vary the verbs you use to introduce a source's words or ideas (instead of repeating *says* each time).

| | | |
|---|---|---|
| acknowledges | discloses | implies |
| suggests | observes | notes |
| concludes | believes | comments |
| insists | explains | claims |
| predicts | summarizes | illustrates |
| reports | finds | proposes |
| warns | concurs | speculates |
| admits | affirms | indicates |

164

Expanded coverage of plagiarism shows students how to avoid plagiarism when researching and writing.

MLA Style 10a

### Using MLA Style

the event, the date of the event, the forum (LinguaMOO, for example), the date of access, and the URL (starting with *telnet://*).

Guitar, Gwen. Online discussion of Cathy in Emily Brontë's <u>Wuthering
Heights</u>. 17 Mar. 1999. LinguaMOO. 17 Mar. 1999
<telnet://lingua.utdallas.edu:8888>.

**closeUP**

**Internet sources**

WARNING: Using information from Internet sources—especially newsgroups and online forums—is risky. Contributors are not necessarily experts, and frequently they are incorrect and misinformed. Unless you can be certain the information you are obtaining from these sources is reliable, do not use it. You can check the reliability of an Internet source by consulting the checklist Evaluating Internet Sources or by asking your instructor or reference librarian for guidance.

See 8d

*Sample MLA Works-Cited Entries:*
*Electronic Sources from a Subscription Service*
Subscription information services can be divided into those you subscribe to, such as America Online, and those that your college library subscribes to, such as InfoTrac, LexisNexis, and ProQuest Direct.
If the service you are subscribing to provides a URL, follow the examples in entries 43–53. If the subscription service enables you to use a keyword to access material, provide the keyword (following the date of access) at the end of the entry.

"Kafka, Franz." <u>Compton's Encyclopedia Online</u>. Vers. 3.0. 2000. America
Online. 8 June 2001. Keyword: Compton's.

If instead of using a keyword, you follow a series of topic labels, list them (separated by semicolons) after the word *Path*.

"Elizabeth Adams." <u>History Resources</u>. 11 Nov. 2001. America Online. 28 Apr.
2001. Path: Research; Biography; Women in Science; Biographies.

To cite information from an information service to which your library subscribes, include the underlined name of the database (if

199

The documentation section now includes three chapters, with separate chapters for MLA and APA coverage. The number of sample citations, particularly the models for citing electronic source material, has been increased.

## Chapter 2 Essay Patterns across the Disciplines

Chapter **2**

Essay Patterns across
the Disciplines

Writers have many options for arranging material within an
essay. The pattern of development you choose is determined by
your purpose, which in college writing is often stated in (or suggested by) your assignment.

Different academic disciplines have different assignments. For
example, if your assignment in a history course is to analyze the
events that led to the Spanish-American War, you would use a **cause-
and-effect** pattern; if your assignment in a political science course is
to evaluate the relative merits of two systems of government, you
would use **comparison and contrast**; if your assignment in a composition course is to reflect on an experience, you would use **narration**
or **description**; if your assignment in a literature course is to persuade readers that a literary work's reputation is not deserved, you
would use **exemplification**; and if your assignment in a chemistry
course is to write a lab report, you would use **process**. In each case,
of course, you have other options as well, and many essays combine
several patterns of development. (The same patterns used to structure essays can also be used as patterns of paragraph development.)

**2a** Writing Narrative Essays

A **narrative** essay tells a story by presenting events in chronological (time) order. Sometimes a narrative begins in the middle of a
story, or even at the end, and then moves back to the beginning.
Most narrative essays, however, move in a logical, orderly sequence
from beginning to end, from first event to last. Clear transitional
words and phrases (*later, after that*) and time markers (*in 1990, two
years earlier, the next day*) establish the chronological sequence and
the relationship of each event to the others.

**(1) Using Narration across the Disciplines**

You use narration in a variety of college writing situations—for
example, when you review a novel's plot, when you write a case

39

This new chapter includes eight full-length student essays, one for each rhetorical mode, along with information about college writing situations in which pattern mode is used.

## Chapter 46 Making Oral Presentations

This chapter offers tips for students preparing and delivering oral presentations. Special emphasis is placed on preparing visual aids, including advantages and disadvantages of computer presentation software, overhead projectors, posters, flip charts, and chalkboards or whiteboards.

Chapter **46**

Making Oral Presentations

At school and on the job, you may sometimes be called on to
make an oral presentation. In a college course, you might be
asked to explain your ideas, to defend your position, or to present
the results of your research. At work, you might be asked to discuss a process, propose a project, or solve a problem. Although
many people are uncomfortable about giving oral presentations,
the guidelines that follow can make the process easier and less
stressful.

**46a** Getting Started

Just as with writing an essay, the preparation phase of an oral
presentation is as important as the speech itself. The time you
spend on this phase will make your task easier later on.

*Identify Your Topic* The first thing you should do is to identify
the topic of your speech. Sometimes you are given a topic; at
other times, you have the option of choosing your own. Once
you have a topic, you should decide how much information, as
well as what kind of information, you will need.

*Consider Your Audience* The easiest way to determine what
kind of information you will need is to consider the nature of
your audience. Is your audience made up of experts or of people
who know very little about your topic? How much background
information will you have to provide? Can you use technical
terms, or should you avoid them? Do you think your audience
will be interested in your topic, or will you have to create interest? What opinions or ideas about your topic will the members of
your audience bring with them?

504

## Chapter 47 English for Speakers of Other Languages

Now with its own tabbed divider, this expanded chapter includes clear explanations of confusing rules and usages with numerous examples to help students understand the concepts. ESL material is also cross-referenced throughout the text.

See ESL 47a2

# PART 13

### ESL

**47 English for Speakers of Other Languages** 515
47a Nouns 516
47b Pronouns 519
47c Verbs 521
47d Adjectives and Adverbs 530
47e Prepositions 532
47f Word Order 535
47g Eliminating Wordiness 537
47h Commonly Confused Words 538

## New Integrated Technology
## Writer's Resources CD-ROM Version 2.0

**Description 2b**   Essay Patterns across the Disciplines

known as one of the most influential Irish-American men in the District of Columbia. Because he had grown up poor and had to work to put himself through law school, he was sympathetic to the poor and often went to great lengths to find them employment.

My maternal grandfather, a builder, was among the first to attempt to organize his fellow workers. Eventually, he became a union official for the AFL. He would have advanced much higher in the union if he had renounced Catholicism and joined the Masons, but he refused.

Conclusion   Many Irish immigrants in the late 1880s and early 1900s became priests, policemen, and blue-collar workers. That was as far as many of them could go because the anti-Irish prejudice that prevailed at this time severely limited their opportunities. In spite of some problems, however, many members of my family carved out good lives in this country.

**2b   Writing Descriptive Essays**

A **descriptive** essay communicates to readers how something looks, sounds, smells, tastes, or feels. The most natural arrangement of details in a description reflects the way you actually look at a person, scene, or object: near to far, top to bottom, side to side, or front to back. This arrangement of details is made clear by transitions that identify precise spatial relationships: *next to, near, beside, under, above,* and so on.

Note: Sometimes a descriptive essay does not have an explicitly stated thesis statement. In such cases, it is unified by a **dominant impression**—the effect created by all the details in the description.

**(1) Using Description across the Disciplines**

Description plays an important role in college writing. For example, technical reports, lab reports, case studies, and field notes all depend upon precise description. In addition, on a European history exam you might have to describe the scene of a famous battle, and in an American literature paper you might have to describe the setting of a play or novel. In other situations, too, description is

42

Throughout the text, marginal icons refer to the Writer's Resources CD-ROM Version 2.0. Writer's Resources CD-ROM Version 2.0 is an interactive multimedia program that teaches all aspects of grammar and writing. The program offers students complete rules and definitions, extensive examples, and numerous exercises and self-tests.

Writer's Resource CD-ROM

# The Brief Handbook
## Fourth Edition

Laurie G. Kirszner
*University of the Sciences in Philadelphia*

Stephen R. Mandell
*Drexel University*

**THOMSON**

**HEINLE**

Australia   Canada   Mexico   Singapore   Spain   United Kingdom   United States

THOMSON
HEINLE

# The Brief Handbook, Fourth Edition
*Laurie G. Kirszner, Stephen R. Mandell*

**Publisher:** Michael Rosenberg
**Acquisitions Editor:** Dickson Musslewhite
**Development Editors:** Julie McBurney,
Camille Adkins
**Sr. Production Editor:** Lianne Ames
**Director of Marketing:** Lisa Kimball
**Marketing Manager:** Katrina Byrd

**Manufacturing Manager:** Marcia Locke
**Compositor:** Carlisle Communications
**Project Manager:** Thistle Hill Publishing
Services
**Copyeditor:** Anne Lesser
**Cover/Text Designer:** Brian Salisbury
**Printer:** The Banta Corporation

**Library of Congress Cataloging-in-Publication Data**
Kirszner, Laurie G.
  The brief handbook / Laurie G. Kirszner,
Stephen R. Mandell.—4th ed.
    pm.  cm.
  Includes bibliographical references and index.
  ISBN 0-8384-0659-9
    1. English language—Rhetoric—Handbooks,
manuals, etc. 2. English language—Grammar—
Handbooks, manuals, etc. 3. Report writing—
Handbooks, manuals, etc. I. Mandell, Stephen R.
II. Title.

PE1408.K6745 2003
808'.042—dc21        2003049970

ISBN: 0-8384-0659-9
(InfoTrac® College Edition)

We would like to introduce you to the fourth edition of *The Brief Handbook*, a compact reference guide for college students that comes out of our experience as full-time teachers of writing with students much like yours. This handbook offers concise yet comprehensive coverage of the writing process, critical thinking and argumentation, research and documentation (including MLA, APA, Chicago, CSE, and COS styles), document design, common sentence errors, grammar and style, word choice, punctuation and mechanics, English for speakers of other languages, college survival skills, and many other useful topics. Despite its compact size, *The Brief Handbook* is more than just a quick reference; it can also serve as a two-semester classroom text and as a guide to writing in college and beyond.

## What makes *The Brief Handbook* so easy to use?

In preparing the fourth edition of *The Brief Handbook*, we have simplified complex material so students can understand it. We have also focused on making the text clear, useful, inviting, and easy to navigate. The book's many innovative design features, listed below, have helped us achieve these goals.

- An open, uncluttered design, the hallmark of *The Brief Handbook*, enables students to find information quickly and easily.
- A color-coded concise guide to the book appears on the inside front cover. Each of the book's three major sections—writing and research, grammar and style, punctuation and mechanics—has its own design color, and tabbed dividers in corresponding colors help students locate the section they need. (The MLA section is marked with a white tab.)
- Close-up boxes focus on special problems students frequently encounter with grammar, style, mechanics, and punctuation.
- Checklists that reinforce key concepts are distinguished by a checkmark icon.
- Boxed lists and charts set off other information that students are likely to turn to regularly.
- In the documentation sections, directories that list model citations for each documentation style help students locate the examples they need.

- Updated computer boxes throughout the book, identified by a special icon, highlight practical information students can use as they write and revise.
- Marginal "hyperlink" cross-references (keyed to blue underlined terms in the text) direct students to related discussions in other parts of the book.
- Hand-edited examples enable students to see revision and editing in action.
- Frequently asked questions (FAQs) are listed on the back of the section dividers. Each FAQ is cross-referenced to a page where the answer to the question is identified with a question mark icon. These FAQs address the problems that students encounter most often, and because they are phrased in students' own words, they enable them to find the answers they need without a knowledge of grammatical terminology. (A complete list of FAQs appears in the back of the book.)
- Electronic addresses (URLs) for relevant Web sites also appear on the section dividers, encouraging students to turn to the Internet to find additional information about the topics discussed in the text.

## What's new in the fourth edition of *The Brief Handbook*?

In this new edition, we resisted the temptation to change simply for the sake of change. Instead, we kept what instructors and students told us worked well, and we fine-tuned what we thought could work better. In addition, we expanded our coverage to include the material our students need to function in today's college classrooms and in today's world.

- New Chapter 2, "Essay Patterns across the Disciplines," includes eight model student essays, one for each rhetorical mode, along with practical advice about assignments and writing situations for which each essay pattern is suited.
- A comprehensive seven-chapter "College Survival Skills" section, unique among college handbooks, offers students the practical advice they need to achieve academic success. The survival skills section includes useful treatments of the specific skills students need to survive—and succeed—in college: reading texts, writing essay exams, writing about literature, designing Web sites and other documents, writing for the workplace, and making oral presentations.
- A new chapter, "Ten Habits of Successful Students," which opens the "College Survival Skills" section, includes tips on time

management, note taking, effective studying, using technology, and other essential topics.

- A new chapter, "Making Oral Presentations," gives students practical confidence-building skills that will help them with everything from simple oral reports to PowerPoint presentations.
- An extensively revised four-chapter research section now includes significantly expanded coverage of using and evaluating both library and Internet sources.
- The important issue of avoiding plagiarism is given considerably more thorough treatment.
- The treatment of documentation, in particular coverage of how to document electronic sources, has been significantly expanded and updated. The documentation section now extends over three chapters, with separate chapters devoted to MLA and APA coverage and an additional chapter covering Chicago, CSE (formerly CBE), and other documentation styles. The APA chapter now includes a new model student research paper, "Sleep Deprivation in College Students," and the MLA paper, "The Great Digital Divide," has been updated to reflect new developments on this issue.
- ESL coverage has been expanded to include even more of the problems in grammar and usage faced by students for whom English is a second language. In addition, the ESL chapter now has its own tabbed divider, and ESL cross-references now appear throughout the text.
- Coverage of document design includes a new section on designing Web sites and using graphics downloaded from the Internet.
- Additional close-up boxes and URLs have been added throughout the book.

### Ancillaries

The following materials are available for use with *The Brief Handbook*.

*Student Supplements:*

*The Brief Handbook* **Exercise Workbook**—Following the organization of *The Brief Handbook*, this printed workbook combines exercises with clear examples and explanations of grammar, usage, and writing to supplement the information in the handbook.

**Think About Editing: An ESL Guide for** *The Brief Handbook*—A self-editing manual for ESL writers, *Think About Editing* is designed to help intermediate to advanced students edit their writing for grammatical, structural, and usage correctness. The text is

Preface

prefaced with a correlation guide that links this book's units to corresponding sections in *The Brief Handbook.*

**The Brief Handbook Web Site**—The free companion Web site provides links, sample syllabi, quizzing and testing, a sample paper library, and other student and instructor resources.

**The Brief Handbook CD-ROM**—A fully interactive version of *The Brief Handbook,* this CD-ROM includes over 200 animated examples of the most important rules for writers and interactive versions of all the handbook exercises tied into a course-management system; where appropriate, exercises are automatically graded. In addition the CD contains the following features:

**An Online Workbook** Integrated into BCA, Thomson Learning's grade book, the online workbook component of *The Brief Handbook* CD-ROM enables professors to manage their students' workload easily while challenging students with excellent interactive exercises that complement the exercises in the handbook.

**Model Student Paper Library** This student paper library includes animated and interactive models tracing four student papers through the writing process. These student models demonstrate proper citation of MLA, APA, CMS, and CSE documentation styles, respectively. The library also provides interactive examples of the research process and online research activities. In addition, this resource contains student papers on each of the rhetorical modes as well as models of arguments based on the Aristotelean, Rogerian, and Toulmin methods of argumentation.

**Heinle InSite**—Heinle InSite is an online writing resource for students, instructors, and program administrators. Within one integrated program, students can submit papers, review and respond to peers' papers, and improve writing and grammar problems by linking directly to online handbook content. As a component of InSite's paper-portfolio service, an "originality" checker enables students to avoid plagiarism by checking their own drafts for properly quoted and paraphrased material prior to final submission.

Additionally, students can conduct online research with access to the InfoTrac® College Edition. Instructors using InSite can assign, view, and grade student papers and peer reviews and track all grades with a built-in course-management system. Program administrators can view and track student progress from an individual to a system-wide level.

**InfoTrac College Edition**—Indispensable to writers of research papers, InfoTrac College Edition offers students around-the-clock access to a database of more than 3,800 scholarly and popular sources with more than 10 million articles, providing information on almost any topic.

**Writer's Resources CD-ROM Version 2.0**—This CD-ROM contains more than 4,500 interactive exercises and activities, including many with animation and audio clips. A new section covers all stages of the writing process from prewriting to final draft, with students providing commentary on the writing process as they proceed through each stage. In addition, the CD-ROM can launch over 100 customized writing templates that guide the user through writing exercises in sentence, paragraph, and essay creation. More than an electronic exercise program, Writer's Resources helps students develop the skills necessary for choosing effective words, writing structurally balanced sentences, and developing detailed paragraphs as well as for writing a summary, an analysis, and an argumentative essay.

**Dictionaries**—The following dictionaries are available for a nominal price when bundled with *The Brief Handbook: The Merriam-Webster Dictionary, Merriam-Webster's Collegiate Dictionary,* Eleventh Edition, (2003), and *Heinle's Newbury House Dictionary of American English* with Integrated Thesaurus, Fourth Edition. The latter was created especially for ESL students.

*Instructor Supplements:*

**Instructor's Resource Guide**—Following the organization of the handbook, this resource guide includes instructor-oriented Frequently Asked Questions and URLs. Each chapter includes an introduction along with recommended readings, teaching strategies, and both individual/group and computer/Internet activities.

# Preface

**Heinle English Testing Center**—Built into Thomson Learning's BCA, the Heinle English Testing Center contains an Electronic Test Package and a Diagnostic Test Package. The Brief Electronic Test Package includes online testing correlated to *The Brief Handbook.* The Diagnostic Test Package contains sample TASP and CLAST tests that instructors can administer in a lab, at home, or in class; practice versions of the TASP and CLAST tests for students; and general diagnostic tests designed to help instructors and programs place students in the appropriate writing course.

## Acknowledgments

We begin at the beginning, by welcoming back Michael Rosenberg, publisher, and thanking him for his continued commitment to this book. We also thank Julie McBurney and Camille Adkins for helping to coordinate the project in its early stages and Dickson Musslewhite, acquisitions editor, for keeping things moving seamlessly along. Also at Heinle, we thank Lianne Ames, senior production editor, for her patience and skill, and Marita Sermolins, editorial assistant, for her constant willingness (and ability) to do whatever needed to be done. At Thistle Hill Publishing Services, we are grateful to Angela Urquhart and Andrea Archer for guiding the book through production. Finally, we thank our talented book designer, Brian Salisbury, for the beautiful new design.

In addition, we thank Patricia Arnott, *University of Delaware;* Scott Douglass, *Chattanooga State Technical Community College;* Melinda Lipani, *University of Texas at Austin;* Carol Sullivan, *Delaware Technical and Community College;* and Jessie Swigger, *University of Texas at Austin,* for their expert advice.

We are also grateful to the following colleagues who offered their advice in the form of reviews for this and previous editions:

Stephanie Batcos, *Berry College*
Rick Becker, *Illinois Central*
Susan Becker, *Illinois Central*
Sue Buck, *Florida Community College*
Dan Butcher, *Southeastern Louisiana University*
Henry Castillo, *Temple Junior College*
Penny Cefola, *California Lutheran University*
Laurie Chesley, *Grand Valley State University*

Victoria Cope, *St. Francis University*
Scott Douglass, *Chattanooga State Technical Community College*
Maurice Duperre, *Midlands Technical College*
Susan Fanetti, *Saint Louis University*
Darlynn Fink, *Clarion University of Pennsylvania*
Judith Funston, *SUNY Potsdam*
Barbara Gaffney, *University of New Orleans*
Joan Gagnon, *Honolulu Community College*
José Grave de Peralta, *University of Miami*
Marcia People Halio, *University of Delaware*
Eleanor Hansen, *Stockton State College*
Brooke Hessler, *Texas Christian University*
Dona Hickey, *University of Richmond*
Maureen Hoag, *Wichita State University*
Susan Hunter, *Kennesaw State University*
Susan Jackson, *Spartanburg Technical College*
Peggy Jolly, *University of Alabama at Birmingham*
Pamela Katzir, *Florida International University*
Brian Kennedy, *Cedarville College*
Pamela Kennedy-Cross, *Stockton State College*
Edis Kittrell, *Montana State University*
Lin Marklin, *Kellogg Community College*
John A. Matthew, *Ball State University*
Anne Maxham-Kastrinos, *Washington State University*
J. L. McClure, *Kirkwood Community College*
Peter Mortensen, *University of Kentucky*
Lee Newton, *Bradley University*
Thomas Otten, *Yale University*
Kathleen Parrish, *Niagara County Community College*
Judy Pearce, *Montgomery College*
John Pennington, *St. Norbert College*
Robert Perry, *Lock Haven University*
Robbie Pinter, *Belmont University*
Jill Pruett, *University of Florida*
Kathryn Raign, *University of North Texas*
Kathleen Raphael, *University of Texas at El Paso*
Jim Riser, *University of North Alabama*
Paul Rogalus, *Plymouth State College*
Laura Ross, *Seminole Community College*
Sandra S. Rothschild, *University of Arizona*
Gary Simmers, *Southern College of Technology*

# Preface

Anne Slater, *Frederick Community College*
Beverly Slaughter, *Brevard Community College*
Stephen Szilagyi, *University of Alabama in Huntsville*
Bonnie Tensen, *Seminole Community College*
Bob Whipple, *Creighton University*
Connie White, *Salisbury State University*

We would also like to thank our families—Mark, Adam, and Rebecca Kirszner and Demi, David, and Sarah Mandell—for being there when we needed them. And, finally, we each thank the person on the other side of the ampersand for making our collaboration work one more time.

Laurie G. Kirszner
Stephen R. Mandell
June 2003

# PART 1

# Writing Essays and Paragraphs

**1  Writing Essays   3**
  **1a**  Understanding the Writing Process   3
  **1b**  Planning   3
  **1c**  Shaping   12
  **1d**  Drafting and Revising   21
  **1e**  Editing and Proofreading   31

**2  Essay Patterns across the Disciplines   39**
  **2a**  Writing Narrative Essays   39
  **2b**  Writing Descriptive Essays   42
  **2c**  Writing Exemplification Essays   45
  **2d**  Writing Process Essays   48
  **2e**  Writing Cause-and-Effect Essays   50
  **2f**  Writing Comparison-and-Contrast Essays   53
  **2g**  Writing Division-and-Classification Essays   56
  **2h**  Writing Definition Essays   58

**3  Writing Paragraphs   62**
  **3a**  Writing Unified Paragraphs   62
  **3b**  Writing Coherent Paragraphs   64
  **3c**  Writing Well-Developed Paragraphs   68
  **3d**  Patterns for Paragraph Development   70
  **3e**  Writing Introductory and Concluding Paragraphs   76

# PART 1

## ? Frequently Asked Questions

**Chapter 1  Writing Essays    3**
- How do I find ideas to write about**?**   7
- How do I arrange ideas into an essay**?**   12
- How do I construct an outline**?**   19
- How do I revise a draft**?**   24
- How do I find a title for my paper**?**   33
- What should my finished paper look like**?**   35

**Chapter 2  Essay Patterns across the Disciplines    39**
- How do I decide which pattern to use to structure my essay**?**   39
- How do I organize a comparison-and-contrast essay**?**   54

**Chapter 3  Writing Paragraphs    62**
- When do I begin a new paragraph**?**   62
- What transitional words and phrases can I use to make my paragraphs flow**?**   66
- How do I know when I have enough information to support my paragraph's main idea**?**   68
- What is the best way to set up a comparison-and-contrast paragraph**?**   72
- How do I write a good introduction for my paper**?**   76
- How do I write an effective conclusion**?**   78

| URLs | *Visit the following sites for answers to more FAQs* |
|---|---|

**Strategies for Writing Thesis Statements (U. of Wisc.)**
*http://www.wisc.edu/writing/Handbook/thesis.html#Strategies*

**Outlining (Purdue)**
*http://owl.english.purdue.edu/handouts/general/gl_outlin.html*

**Proofreading (Bowling Green)**
*http://www.bgsu.edu/departments/writing-lab/goproofreading.html*

**Introductions, Conclusions, and Titles (George Mason U.)**
*http://www.gmu.edu/departments/writingcenter/handouts/introcon.html*

**Writing Transitions**
*http://www.unc.edu/depts/wcweb/handouts/transitions.html*

# Writing Essays

## 1a   Understanding the Writing Process

Writing is a constant process of decision making—of selecting, deleting, and rearranging material.

---

**THE WRITING PROCESS**

**Planning:** Consider your purpose, audience, and assignment; explore your topic.

**Shaping:** Decide how to organize your material.

**Writing:** Draft your essay.

**Revising:** "Re-see" what you have written; write additional drafts.

**Editing:** Check grammar, spelling, punctuation, and mechanics.

**Proofreading:** Check for typographical errors.

---

The neatly defined stages listed above communicate neither the complexity nor the flexibility of the writing process. These stages actually overlap: as you seek ideas, you begin to shape your material; as you shape your material, you begin to write; as you write a first draft, you reorganize your ideas; as you revise, you continue to discover new material. Moreover, these stages are repeated again and again throughout the writing process. During your college years and in the years that follow, you will develop your own version of the writing process and use it whenever you write.

## 1b   Planning

Writer's Resource CD-ROM

Planning your essay—thinking about what you want to say and how you want to say it—begins well before you actually start to record your thoughts in any organized way.

## (1) Determining Your Purpose

Your **purpose** is what you want to accomplish when you write. In general, you write to *express emotions,* to *inform,* or to *persuade.*

*Writing to Express Emotions* In diaries and journals, writers explore ideas and feelings to help them make sense of their experiences; in autobiographical memoirs and in personal e-mails, they communicate their emotions and reactions to others.

At the age of five, six, well past the time when most other children no longer easily notice the difference between sounds uttered at home and words spoken in public, I had a different experience. I lived in a world magically compounded of sounds. I remained a child longer than most; I lingered too long, poised at the edge of language—often frightened by the sounds of *los gringos,* delighted by the sounds of Spanish at home. I shared with my family a language that was startlingly different from that used in the great city around us.

(Richard Rodriguez, *Aria: A Memoir of a Bilingual Childhood*)

*Writing to Inform* In newspaper and magazine articles and in encyclopedia entries, writers report information, communicating to readers what they observe; in reference texts, instruction manuals, textbooks, and the like, they provide definitions and explain concepts or processes, trying to help readers see relationships and understand ideas.

Most tarantulas live in the tropics, but several species occur in the temperate zone and a few are common in the southern U.S. Some varieties are large and have powerful fangs with which they can inflict a deep wound. These formidable-looking spiders do not, however, attack man; you can hold one in your hand, if you are gentle, without being bitten. Their bite is dangerous only to insects and small mammals such as mice; for man it is no worse than a hornet's sting.

(Alexander Petrunkevitch, "The Spider and the Wasp")

*Writing to Persuade* In proposals, editorials, and position papers, writers try to convince readers to accept their position on an issue.

Testing and contact tracing may lead to a person's being deprived of a job, health insurance, housing, and privacy, many civil libertarians fear. These are valid and grave concerns. But we can find ways to protect civil rights without sacrificing public health. A major AIDS-prevention campaign ought to be accompanied by intensive public education about the ways the illness is *not* transmitted, by additional safeguards on data banks and by greater penalties for those who abuse HIV victims. It may be harsh to say, but the fact that an individual may suffer as a result of doing what is right does not make doing so less of an imperative.

(Amitai Etzioni, "HIV Sufferers Have a Responsibility")

Whenever you write, you may have one of these three general purposes—or, you may have other, more specific aims or a combination of purposes.

---

### ⟨✓⟩checklist Determining your purpose

*Is your purpose:*

| | |
|---|---|
| ✓ to express emotions? | ✓ to define? |
| ✓ to inform? | ✓ to satirize? |
| ✓ to persuade? | ✓ to speculate? |
| ✓ to explain? | ✓ to warn? |
| ✓ to evaluate? | ✓ to reassure? |
| ✓ to discover? | ✓ to amuse or entertain? |
| ✓ to analyze? | ✓ to take a stand? |
| ✓ to debunk? | ✓ to identify problems? |
| ✓ to criticize? | ✓ to suggest solutions? |
| ✓ to draw comparisons? | ✓ to define causes? |
| ✓ to make an analogy? | ✓ to predict effects? |

---

## (2) Identifying Your Audience

At different times, in different roles, you address different kinds of **audiences.** As you move through the stages of the writing process, you try to assess your readers' interests, educational level, biases, and expectations. This assessment determines not only the information you include but also your emphasis, the arrangement of your material, and the style or tone you adopt.

As a student, you most often write for an audience of one: the instructor who assigns the paper. Instructors expect correct information, specific support for general statements, standard grammar and correct spelling, logical presentation of ideas, and some stylistic fluency. If you are writing in your instructor's academic field, you can omit long overviews and basic definitions. Outside his or

5

her area of expertise, however, an instructor may need definitions, examples, and analogies.

Keep in mind that because different academic disciplines have their own document design formats, documentation styles, methods of reporting data, technical vocabularies, and stylistic conventions, instructors in different disciplines have somewhat different expectations.

> **✓checklist** **Identifying your audience**
> - ✓ Who will read your paper?
> - ✓ What are your audience's needs? expectations? biases? interests?
> - ✓ Does your audience need you to supply definitions? overviews? examples? analogies?
> - ✓ What does your audience expect in terms of style and tone? format? documentation style? methods of collecting and reporting data? use of formulas and symbols or specialized vocabulary?

## (3) Analyzing Your Assignment

Before you begin any writing task, you must know the exact requirements of your assignment. Ask questions, and be sure you understand the answers.

> **✓checklist** **Analyzing your assignment**
> - ✓ Has your instructor assigned a specific topic, or are you free to choose your own?
> - ✓ What is the word, paragraph, or page limit?
> - ✓ How much time do you have to complete your assignment?
> - ✓ Will you get feedback from other students or from your instructor? Will anyone review your drafts?
> - ✓ Does the assignment require research?
> - ✓ If the assignment requires a specific format, do you know what its conventions are?

## (4) Choosing a Topic

Although you are sometimes able to choose your own topic, more often you will be given a general assignment, which you must narrow to a **topic** that suits your purpose and audience.

# Planning

Planning 1b

## NARROWING AN ASSIGNMENT

| Course | Assignment | Topic |
| --- | --- | --- |
| American History | Analyze the effects of a social program on one segment of American society. | How did the G.I. Bill of Rights affect American servicewomen? |
| Psychology | Write a three- to five-page paper assessing one method of treating depression. | Animal-assisted therapy for severely depressed patients |
| Composition | Write about a problem you have encountered since you began college. | Confronting Asian-American stereotypes |

## (5) Finding Something to Say

Once you have a topic, you can begin to develop ideas for your paper, using one (or several) of the following strategies.

*Reading and Observing* As you read textbooks, magazines, and newspapers or browse the **Internet**, be on the lookout for ideas that relate to your topic, and make a point of talking informally with friends or family about it. Films, television programs, interviews, telephone calls, letters, and questionnaires can also provide material. But be sure your instructor permits such research—and remember to document ideas that are not your own. By doing so, you can avoid **plagiarism**.

See Ch.8

See 9b

*Keeping a Journal* Journals, unlike diaries, do more than simply record personal experiences and reactions. In a **journal** you explore ideas as well as record events and emotions; you think as you write, asking questions and drawing conclusions. You might, for example, explore your position on a political issue, try to solve an ethical problem, or trace the development of your thinking about an academic assignment.

*Freewriting* When you **freewrite,** you let yourself go and write *nonstop* about anything that comes to mind, moving as quickly as you can. Give yourself a set period of time—say, five minutes—and

7

don't stop to worry about punctuation, spelling, or grammar. This strategy encourages your mind to make free associations; thus, it can help you discover ideas that you aren't even aware you have. When your time is up, look over what you have written and underline, bracket, or star the most promising ideas. You can then use each of these ideas as the center of a focused freewriting exercise.

When you do **focused freewriting,** you zero in on your topic. Here too, you write without stopping to reconsider or reread, so you have no time to be self-conscious about style or form or to worry about the relevance of your ideas. At its best, freewriting can suggest new details, a new approach to your topic, or even a more interesting topic. Nguyen Dao, a student in a composition class, decided to write about Asian-American stereotypes, a problem he had encountered in college. His freewriting and focused freewriting exercises appear below.

### ✳ Freewriting (excerpt)

I really don't want to do this freewriting, but I have to—I'm being forced—I have no choice, but it seems stupid. If I have ideas they'll come and if not they won't. I don't see why I need an idea anyway—I wish she'd just say write about your summer vacation like they did in high school, and I'd write about Colorado last summer and the mountains and that lake I can't remember the name but we had a boat and I could see—This is too hard. I want to write about being Asian, but there weren't any Asians in that town on that lake. People looked at me like someone from outer space half the time. I wonder what they thought, or who they thought I was.

### ✳ Focused Freewriting (excerpt)

Being Asian in the Colorado mountains—wondering whether people thought I was a Japanese tourist—Asian cowboy—Asian hiker/athlete/mountain man. People never expect Asians to be athletes. Just engineers or violinists. Or maybe own fruit stands or be kung fu teachers. Being a teacher could be good for me—being a role model for kids, showing them other things to be.

# Planning

*Brainstorming* One of the most useful ways to accumulate ideas is brainstorming. This strategy encourages you to recall pieces of information and to see connections among them.

When you **brainstorm,** you list all the points you can think of that seem pertinent to your topic, writing down ideas—comments, questions, single words—as quickly as you can, without pausing to consider their relevance or trying to understand their significance. Your goal is to let one idea suggest another, so do nothing to slow down your momentum. Nguyen Dao's brainstorming notes appear below.

## BRAINSTORMING NOTES

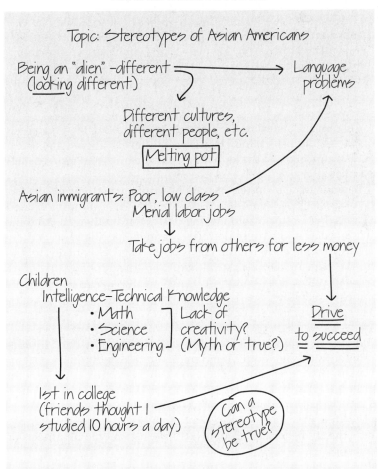

Topic: Stereotypes of Asian Americans

Being an "alien" –different (looking different) → Language problems

Different cultures, different people, etc.
Melting pot

Asian immigrants: Poor, low class
Menial labor jobs
↓
Take jobs from others for less money

Children
Intelligence–Technical Knowledge
• Math ⎤ Lack of
• Science ⎬ creativity?
• Engineering ⎦ (Myth or true?)

Drive to succeed

1st in college
(friends thought I studied 10 hours a day)

Can a stereotype be true?

**Note:** With your instructor's permission, you can also do **collaborative brainstorming**—that is, you can brainstorm with your classmates in small groups (either in person or electronically).

---

**http://kirsznermandell.heinle.com**

## Generating ideas

Your computer can help you generate ideas. For example, you can set up a computer journal, and you can also use your computer for freewriting and brainstorming.

When you freewrite, try turning down the screen, leaving it blank to eliminate distractions and encourage spontaneity.

When you brainstorm, type your notes randomly. Later, after you print them out, you can add handwritten notes and graphic elements (arrows, circles, and so on) to indicate parallels and connections.

---

*Clustering* **Clustering**—sometimes called *webbing* or *mapping*—is similar to brainstorming. However, clustering allows you to explore your topic in a somewhat more systematic (and more visual) manner.

Begin making a cluster diagram by writing your topic in the center of a sheet of paper. Then, surround your topic with related ideas as they occur to you, moving outward from the general topic in the center and writing down increasingly specific ideas and details as you move toward the edges of the page. Eventually, following the path of one idea at a time, you create a diagram (often lopsided rather than symmetrical) that arranges ideas on spokes or branches radiating out from a central core (your topic). Nguyen Dao's cluster diagram appears on page 11.

*Asking Journalistic Questions* A more structured way of finding something to say about your topic is to ask questions. Your answers to these questions will enable you to explore your topic in an orderly and systematic fashion. Journalists often use the questions *Who?*, *What?*, *Why?*, *Where?*, *When?*, and *How?* to assure themselves that they have explored all angles of a story. You can use these questions to see whether you have considered all aspects of your topic.

## CLUSTER DIAGRAM

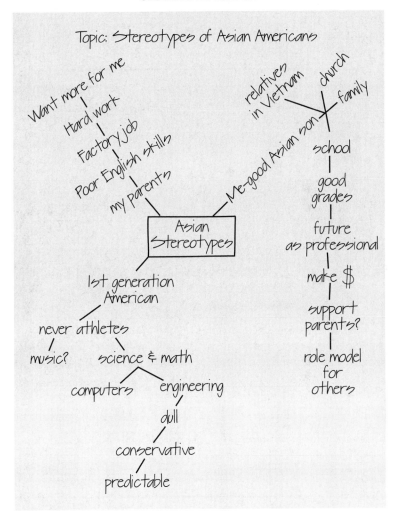

Topic: Stereotypes of Asian Americans

Want more for me
Hard work
Factory job
Poor English skills
my parents

relatives in Vietnam
church
family

Me-good Asian son

school
good grades
future as professional
make $
support parents?
role model for others

Asian Stereotypes

1st generation American

never athletes
music?
science & math
computers
engineering
dull
conservative
predictable

*Asking In-Depth Questions* If you have time, you can also ask a series of more focused questions about your topic. These questions can give you a great deal of information, and they may also suggest ways you can eventually shape your ideas into paragraphs and essays.

## IN-DEPTH QUESTIONS

| | |
|---|---|
| What happened?<br>When did it happen?<br>Where did it happen? | Suggest <u>narration</u> (your first day of school; Emily Dickinson's life) |
| What does it look like?<br>What does it sound like, smell like, taste like, or feel like? | Suggest <u>description</u> (of the Louvre; of a lab specimen) |
| What are some typical cases or examples of it? | Suggests <u>exemplification</u> (three infant day-care settings; four popular fad diets) |
| How did it happen?<br>What makes it work?<br>How is it made? | Suggest <u>process</u> (how to apply for financial aid; how a bill becomes a law) |
| Why did it happen?<br>What caused it?<br>What does it cause?<br>What are its effects? | Suggest <u>cause and effect</u> (events leading to the Korean War; results of Prohibition) |
| How is it like other things?<br>How is it different from other things? | Suggest <u>comparison and contrast</u> (of 1950s and 1960s music; of two paintings) |
| What are its parts or types?<br>Can they be separated or grouped?<br>Do they fall into a logical order?<br>Can they be categorized? | Suggest <u>division and classification</u> (components of the catalytic converter; techniques of occupational therapy; kinds of dietary supplements) |
| What is it?<br>How does it resemble and differ from other members of its class? | Suggest <u>definition</u> (What is Marxism? What is photosynthesis? What is romanticism?) |

## 1c  Shaping

Writer's
Resource
CD-ROM

### (1) Grouping Ideas: Making a Topic Tree

As you begin to see the direction your ideas are taking, you start to sift through these ideas and choose those you can use to build the most effective essay. At this point, you may find it useful to make a **topic tree,** a diagram that enables you to arrange material logically and to see relationships among ideas. Nguyen Dao's topic tree appears below.

## TOPIC TREE

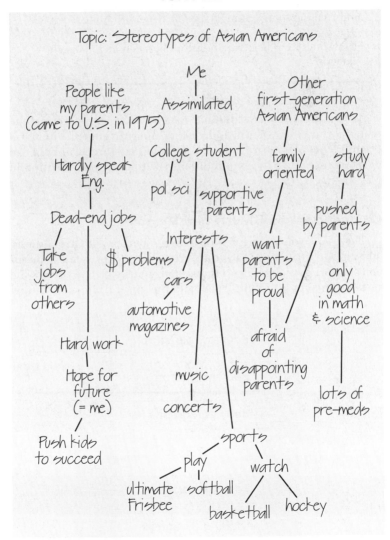

> ✓**checklist** **Making a topic tree**
> ✓ Review all your notes carefully.
> ✓ Decide on the three or four general categories of information that best suit your material.
> ✓ Write or type these categories across the top of a piece of paper.
> ✓ Review your notes again to select ideas and details that fall within each category.
> ✓ List each idea under a relevant heading, moving from general information to increasingly specific details as you move down the page.
> ✓ Draw lines to indicate relationships between ideas in each category.

As you accumulate additional material and as you review the material you have, you will add, delete, and rearrange the items on the branches of your topic tree. Your completed tree can help you develop a tentative thesis and organize supporting information in your essay.

## (2) Understanding Thesis and Support

The essays you write for your college courses will have a thesis-and-support structure. As the diagram below illustrates, a **thesis-and-support essay** includes a **thesis statement** (which expresses the **thesis,** or main idea, of the essay) and the specific information that

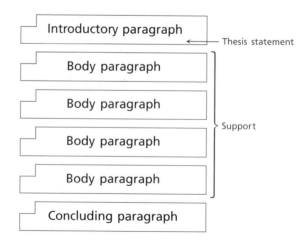

explains and develops that thesis. Your essay will eventually consist of several paragraphs—an **introductory paragraph**, which introduces your thesis; a **concluding paragraph**, which gives your essay a sense of completion, perhaps restating your thesis; and a number of **body paragraphs,** which provide the support for your essay's thesis.

See 3e1

See 3e2

## (3) Stating Your Thesis

An effective thesis statement has four characteristics.

1. *An effective thesis statement should clearly communicate your essay's main idea.* It tells your readers not only what your essay's topic is, but also how you will approach that topic and what you will say about it. Thus, your thesis statement reflects your essay's **purpose**.

2. *An effective thesis statement should be more than a general subject, a statement of fact, or an announcement of your intent.*

   Subject: Intelligence tests

   Statement of Fact: Intelligence tests are used for placement in many elementary schools.

   Announcement: The paragraphs that follow will show that intelligence tests may be inaccurate.

   Thesis Statement: Although intelligence tests are widely used for placement in many elementary schools, they are not always the best measure of a student's academic performance.

3. *An effective thesis statement should be carefully worded.* Your thesis statement—usually expressed in a single concise sentence—should be direct and straightforward, including no vague, abstract language, overly complex terminology, or unnecessary details that might confuse or mislead readers. Moreover, effective thesis statements should not include phrases like "As I will show," "I hope to demonstrate," and "It seems to me," which weaken your credibility by suggesting that your conclusions are based on opinion rather than on reading, observation, and experience.

4. *Finally, an effective thesis statement should suggest your essay's direction, emphasis, and scope.* Your thesis statement should not make promises that your essay will not fulfill. It should suggest the major points you will cover, the order in which you will introduce them, and where you will place your emphasis (as the following thesis statement does).

15

Effective Thesis Statement: Widely ridiculed as escape reading, romance novels are becoming increasingly important as a proving ground for many first-time writers and, more significantly, as a showcase for strong heroines.

This thesis statement tells readers that the essay to follow will focus on two major new roles of the romance novel; it also suggests that the role of the romance as escapist fiction will be treated briefly. This effective thesis statement, as the diagram below shows, also indicates the order in which the various ideas will be discussed.

Discussion of romance formulas; general settings; plots and characters     **Thesis statement:** Widely ridiculed as escape reading, romance novels are becoming increasingly important as a proving ground for many never-before-published writers, and, more significantly, as showcases for strong heroines. — *Introduction*

Romance novels as escape reading

Romance novels as outlets for unpublished writers

Romance novels as showcases for strong heroines

Romance novels as showcases for strong heroines, continued — *Body*

Review of major points; summary of recent trends in romance novels — *Conclusion*

close**UP**

### Stating your thesis

Try to avoid vague, wordy phrases—*centers on, deals with, involves, revolves around, has a lot to do with, is primarily concerned with,* and so on. Be direct and forceful.

The real problem in our schools ~~does~~ is not ~~revolve around~~ the absence of nationwide goals and standards; the problem is ~~primarily concerned with~~ the absence of resources with which to implement them.

> ✓ **checklist** Stating your thesis
>
> ✓ Does your thesis statement clearly communicate your essay's main idea? Does it suggest the approach you will take toward your material? Does it reflect your essay's purpose?
> ✓ Is your thesis statement more than a subject, a statement of fact, or an announcement of your intent?
> ✓ Is your thesis statement carefully worded?
> ✓ Does your thesis statement suggest your essay's direction, emphasis, and scope?

## (4) Revising Your Thesis Statement

The thesis statement that you develop as you plan your essay is only tentative. As you write and rewrite, you may modify your essay's direction, emphasis, and scope several times; if you do so, you must reword your thesis statement as well. Notice how the following tentative thesis statement changed as the writer moved through successive drafts.

Tentative Thesis Statement (*rough draft*): Professional sports can easily be corrupted by organized crime.

Revised Thesis Statement (*final paper*): Although supporters of legalized sports betting argue that organized crime cannot make inroads into professional sports, the way in which underworld figures compromised the 1919 World Series suggests the opposite.

### Using original phrasing

One of the simplest kinds of thesis statements to write is also one of the dullest and most mechanical: the "three points" (or "four reasons" or "five examples") thesis. This thesis statement enumerates each of the specific points to be discussed ("Hot air ballooning is an exciting sport for three reasons: x, y, and z"), and the paper that follows goes on to cover each of these points, using the same tired language: "The first reason hot air ballooning is so exciting is x"; "Another reason is y"; "The most important reason is z." This kind of formulaic thesis statement can be a very useful strategy for a rough draft, but as you revise, try to substitute fresher, more interesting, and more original language.

## (5) Using a Thesis Statement to Shape Your Essay

See
Ch.2 &
3d

The wording of a thesis statement can suggest not only a possible order and emphasis for an essay's ideas, but also a specific **pattern of development**: narration, description, exemplification, process, cause and effect, comparison and contrast, division and classification, or definition. Remember, though, that a pattern of development is never imposed on your essay; it emerges naturally during the course of the writing process. (Patterns of development can also shape the individual body paragraphs of your essay.)

### USING A THESIS STATEMENT TO SHAPE YOUR ESSAY

| Thesis Statement | Pattern of Development |
|---|---|
| As the months went by and I grew more and more involved with the developmentally delayed children at the Learning Center, I came to see how important it is to treat every child as an individual. | Narration |
| Looking around the room where I had spent my childhood, I realized that every object I saw told me I was now an adult. | Description |
| The risk-taking behavior that characterized the 1990s can be illustrated by the increasing interest and involvement in such high-risk sports as mountain biking, ice climbing, skydiving, and bungee jumping. | Exemplification |
| Armed forces basic training programs take recruits through a series of tasks designed to build camaraderie as well as skills and confidence. | Process |

| | |
|---|---|
| The exceptionally high birthrate of the post–World War II years had many significant social and economic consequences. | Cause and Effect |
| Although people who live in cities and people who live in small towns have some obvious basic similarities, their views on issues like crime, waste disposal, farm subsidies, and educational vouchers tend to be very different. | Comparison and Contrast |
| The section of the proposal that recommends establishing satellite health centers is quite promising; unfortunately, however, the sections that call for the creation of alternative educational programs, job training, and low-income housing are seriously flawed. | Division and Classification |
| Until quite recently, most people assumed rape was an act perpetrated by a stranger, but today's wider definition encompasses acquaintance rape as well. | Definition |

## (6) Preparing an Outline

An **outline** is a blueprint for an essay. A **formal outline** indicates both the order of the ideas you will explore and the relationship of those ideas to one another. An **informal outline** is less detailed, but it too arranges your essay's main points and supporting ideas in an orderly way to guide you as you write. Nguyen Dao's informal outline appears on the following page.

## ❊ *Sample Informal Outline*

Asian-American Stereotypes

Thesis Statement: As an Asian American, I am frequently a victim of ethnic stereotyping, and this has been a serious problem for me.

Stereotypes of Asian immigrants

    —Poor English

    —Can't use skills and education here

    —Low-paid jobs

        —Sacrifice for children

        —Take from U.S. citizens

Stereotypes of children of Asian immigrants

    —Hard workers

    —Study hard

        —Pushed by parents

    —Focus on math and science

        —Premed

Stereotypes applied to me

    —Science major

    —Forced to study all day

        —No social life

---

### ✓checklist Preparing an informal outline

See
1c1

✓ Copy down the categories and subcategories from your **topic tree**.
✓ Arrange the categories and subcategories in the order in which you plan to discuss them.
✓ Expand the outline with additional material from your notes, adding any new points that come to mind.

**Constructing a formal outline**

For a short paper, an informal outline is usually sufficient. For a long or complex essay, however, you will need to construct a formal outline like the one that accompanies the student research paper in Chapter 10.

- Outline format should be followed strictly.
  - I. First major point of your paper
    - A. First subpoint
    - B. Next subpoint
      - 1. First supporting example
      - 2. Next supporting example
        - a. First specific detail
        - b. Next specific detail
  - II. Second major point
- Each heading should have at least two subheadings.
- Outline should include the paper's thesis statement.
- Outline should cover only the body of the essay.
- Headings should be concise and specific.
- Headings of the same rank should be grammatically parallel.

**Note:** A formal outline can be a *topic* outline or a *sentence* outline. In a **topic outline,** each entry is a word or short phrase; in a **sentence outline,** each entry is a complete sentence.

**http://kirsznermandell.heinle.com**

**Constructing a formal outline**
If you use your computer to construct a formal outline, set your tabs so you can easily format the various levels of the outline. Once you begin outlining, some computer programs will automatically arrange what you type in outline format.

## 1d Drafting and Revising

Writer's Resource CD-ROM

Inexperienced writers often do little more than change a word here and there, correct grammatical or mechanical errors, or make their papers neater. Experienced writers, however, expect revision to involve a major reworking of their papers, so they are willing to rethink a thesis statement or even to completely rewrite and rearrange an entire essay. (You can see how this revision process operates in the three drafts of Nguyen Dao's essay about Asian-American stereotypes that appear in this chapter.)

## (1) Writing a Rough Draft

Because its purpose is really just to get your emerging ideas down on paper so you can react to them, a rough draft usually includes false starts, irrelevant information, and seemingly unrelated details. Try not to see this absence of focus and order as a problem. You will generally write several drafts of your essay, so you should expect to add or delete words, to reword sentences, to rethink ideas, to reorder paragraphs—even to take an unexpected detour that may lead you to a new perspective on your topic.

To facilitate such extensive revision, leave plenty of room on the page so you can add material or rewrite. If you type, triple-space. If you write, skip lines (and be sure to use only one side of a sheet of paper so you can cut and paste freely without destroying material on the other side of the page). To streamline your revision process, try using symbols—arrows, circles, boxes, numbers, and so on— that will signal various operations to you.

The rough draft that follows includes Nguyen Dao's handwritten revisions on his typed rough draft.

### ✳ Rough Draft with Handwritten Revisions

*The unique characteristic of American culture is its genuine desire to understand & embrace the wide range of traditions and values of its people.*

The United States prides itself on being the "melting pot" of the world, *—a nation where diverse cultures intermingle to form a unique and enlightened society.* However, in reality, the abundance of different cultures in America often causes misunderstandings and even conflicts within the society. These misunderstandings and conflicts result from the society's lack of knowledge about other cultures. *Still, as* ~~As~~ an Asian American, I am frequently a victim of ethnic stereotyping, *people keep trying to make me something I'm not, and this is a* ~~and this has been a~~ serious problem for me.

# Drafting and Revising

It has been within the last twenty years or so that the United States has seen a large rise in the number of Asian immigrants. First-generation immigrants are seen as an underclass of poor ^people who struggle in low paying jobs so that their children will have a better future. Many accuse immigrants of accepting ~~less~~ lower pay for their work than ^other American citizens are ~~the established majority is~~ willing to accept, thus putting the established majority out of work. While it is true that most newly arrived Asians do seek low paying, low-skill jobs, they are just following the same ~~trend~~ road that other immigrant groups followed when they first arrived in the ~~U.S.~~ United States. *The Irish who escaped the potato famines came to the U.S. without many advanced skills. To this day, many Latinos come to the US in search of a better life with little more than the shirts on their backs.* Because the first generation of Asian Americans ^my parents included have poorly developed skills in English, they are forced into jobs which do not require ~~these skills~~ English. Many Asians received degrees from institutions in their native countries or received advanced training of some kind but cannot use those skills in the United States. *Therefore, they have no choice but to accept whatever low-paying job they can get—not to steal jobs from others, but to survive.*

^*Along with the view of the first-generation Asian Americans as low-skilled workers comes the notion that* Asian-American children are ~~seen as~~ hard workers who are pushed by their families to succeed. Asian children are seen as intelligent, but only in ^terms of scientific and technical knowledge. The media likes to point ~~to the facts~~ out that most Asians succeed only in ~~the~~ math, science, and engineering ~~fields~~ and that ~~there is an inordinate~~ a great number of Asian college students who identify themselves as "premed." ^*What the media seems to forget is that other immigrant groups also seem to prize success above all else.*

In my personal experience, in college, many of my friends assume that I am either a science or an engineering major and that my parents force me to study five to ten hours a day. They believe that I sacrifice all my free time and social life in pursuit of a high grade point average. *My friends are quite surprised when I tell them that I take drawing classes and that I am majoring in political science not as a stepping-stone into law school, but as a study of man & society.* ~~In fact, I am a political science major. I also like to go to basketball games, listen to music,~~ and read automotive magazines, ~~just like other~~

*continued on the following page*

*continued from the previous page*

college students I know. My parents do encourage me to do well in school because they see that education is a stepping stone to social class mobility; however, I am lucky because my parents do not push me in one direction or another as many of my Asian friends' parents do. Many of my friends do not realize that just two or three generations ago, their parents and grandparents were going through the same process of social adjustment that all immigrants endure. It is important to remember that *most people don't* ~~not all Asians~~ fit into *these cultural stereotypes.* *For example, not all Asians fit* the overachieving, success-oriented stereotype. When any child comes from an economically disadvantaged background, many times they must sacrifice their academic pursuits in order to support their families. Also, as Asians, particularly the children, become more integrated into the society, the traditional Asian values of hard work & familial obligations will certainly clash with the American pursuits of recreation & individualism. The resolution of that conflict will add yet another facet to the complexity of America's society.

This practice of assuming people of similar ethnic backgrounds share certain traits is certainly not limited to Asian Americans. African-American students complain people expect them to be athletes, to like rap music, to be on scholarship, to be from single-parent families, even to be gang members. Athletes say people expect them to be dumb jocks, to drink a lot, and to mistreat their girlfriends. Latinos say people assume their parents are immigrants and that they speak Spanish better than English. Business majors say people think they're politically conservative and not creative. Engineering students are expected to be dull & wear pocket protectors. Women are supposed to be weak in math & science. Overweight people are expected to be class clowns. In fact, my friends (of all ethnic groups) buy their clothes where I do, & we listen to the same music & laugh at the same jokes. But outsiders don't know this. They have different expectations for each of us, & these expectations are based on culture, not ability.

## ❓ (2) Using Specific Revision Strategies

Everyone revises differently, and every writing task demands a slightly different process of revision. Four strategies in particular can help you revise at any stage of the writing process.

See
1c6

*Using a Formal Outline* Making a **formal outline** of a draft can help you check the structure of your paper and reveal whether points are irrelevant, poorly placed, or missing. This strategy is especially helpful early in revision, when you are reworking the larger structural elements of your essay.

http://kirsznermandell.heinle.com

**Revising**

Because it can be much more difficult to see errors on the computer screen than on hard copy, it is a good idea to print out every draft so you can revise on paper rather than on the screen, making revisions by hand on your typed draft and then returning to the computer to type these changes into your document. If you do revise directly on the computer screen, be very careful not to delete any information that you may need later; instead, move such material to the end of your document so you can assess its relevance later on and retrieve it if necessary. As you type your drafts, get into the habit of including notes to yourself in parentheses or brackets, perhaps highlighting your comments and questions in boldface or italic type.

*Doing Collaborative Revision* Instead of trying to imagine an audience, you can address a real audience, doing **collaborative revision** by asking a friend, classmate, or family member to read your draft and comment on it, either in person or in an e-mail conversation. Collaborative revision can also be more formal. Your instructor may conduct the class as a workshop, assigning students to work in groups to critique other students' essays or having students exchange essays and write evaluations, in person or electronically. (The checklists on pages 26–28 can be useful for collaborative revision as well as for revision that you do on your own.)

*Using Instructors' Comments* Instructors frequently make comments on your papers to suggest changes in content or structure. Such comments may ask you to add supporting information or to arrange paragraphs differently within the essay, or they may recommend stylistic changes, such as using more varied sentences. Instructors' comments may also question your logic, suggest a more explicit thesis statement, ask for clearer transitions, or propose a new direction for a discussion. Although you may disagree with some of these suggestions, you should consider your instructor's comments seriously.

Also take note of any correction symbols that correspond to those on the inside back cover of this handbook. With these symbols, your instructor may direct you to explanations and illustrations of particular stylistic, grammatical, or mechanical problems.

Instructors also comment on your papers in one-on-one conferences. (If a face-to-face conference is hard to schedule, your instructor may agree to answer questions and offer feedback via e-mail.)

---

**✓checklist** Getting the most out of a conference

✓ **Make an appointment.** If you are unable to keep your appointment, be sure to call or e-mail your instructor to reschedule.

✓ **Review your work carefully.** Before the conference, reread your notes and drafts and go over all your instructor's comments and suggestions. Make all the changes you can on your draft.

✓ **Bring a list of questions.** Preparing a list in advance will enable you to get the most out of the conference in the allotted time.

✓ **Bring your paper-in-progress.** If you have several drafts, you may want to bring them all, but be sure you bring any draft that has your instructor's comments on it.

✓ **Take notes.** As you discuss your paper, write down any suggestions that you think will be helpful so you won't forget them when you revise.

✓ **Participate actively.** A successful conference is not a monologue; it should be an open exchange of ideas.

---

*Using Checklists* The following four checklists parallel the revision process, moving in stages from the most global concerns to the most specific. As your familiarity with the writing process increases and you are better able to assess the strengths and weaknesses of your writing, you may want to add questions of your own to these checklists. You can also use your instructor's comments to help you tailor the checklists to your own needs.

---

**✓checklist** Revising the whole essay

✓ Are thesis and support logically related, with each body paragraph supporting your thesis statement? **(See 1c2)**

✓ Is your thesis statement clearly and specifically worded? **(See 1c3)**

✓ Have you discussed everything promised in your thesis statement? **(See 1c3)**

✓ Have you presented your ideas in a logical sequence? Can you think of a different arrangement that might be more appropriate for your purpose? **(See 1c6)**

✓ Is your essay's pattern of development consistent with your assignment and purpose? **(See Ch. 2)**

✓ Do clear transitions between paragraphs allow your readers to follow your essay's structure? **(See 3b2)**

---

## ✓checklist Revising paragraphs

✓ Does each body paragraph have one main idea? **(See 3a)**
✓ Are topic sentences clearly worded and logically related to the thesis? **(See 3a1)**
✓ Are your body paragraphs developed fully enough to support your points? **(See 3c)**
✓ Does your introductory paragraph arouse interest and prepare readers for what is to come? **(See 3e1)**
✓ Does each body paragraph have a clear organizing principle? **(See 3b1)**
✓ Are the relationships of sentences within paragraphs clear? **(See 3b2–4)**
✓ Are your paragraphs arranged according to familiar patterns of development? **(See 3d)**
✓ Does your concluding paragraph sum up your main points? **(See 3e2)**

## ✓checklist Revising sentences

✓ Have you strengthened sentences with repetition, balance, and parallelism? **(See 22c and 22d)**
✓ Have you avoided overloading your sentences with too many clauses? **(See 23c)**
✓ Have you used correct sentence structure? **(See Chs. 13 and 14)**
✓ Have you placed modifiers clearly and logically? **(See Ch. 17)**
✓ Have you avoided potentially confusing shifts in tense, voice, mood, person, or number? **(See 16a 1–4)**
✓ Are your sentences constructed logically? **(See 16b–d)**
✓ Have you used emphatic word order? **(See 22a)**
✓ Have you used sentence structure to signal the relative importance of clauses in a sentence and their logical relationship to one another? **(See 22b)**
✓ Have you avoided wordiness and eliminated unnecessary repetition? **(See 23a–b)**
✓ Have you varied your sentence structure? **(See 21a)**
✓ Have you combined sentences where ideas are closely related? **(See 21b1)**

See ESL
47g

## ✓checklist Revising words

✓ Is your level of diction appropriate for your audience and your purpose? **(See 25a)**

✓ Have you selected words that accurately reflect your intentions? **(See 25b1)**

✓ Have you chosen words that are specific, concrete, and unambiguous? **(See 25b3–4)**

✓ Have you enriched your writing with figures of speech? **(See 25d)**

✓ Have you eliminated jargon, neologisms, pretentious diction, clichés, ineffective figures of speech, and offensive language from your writing? **(See 25c and 25e)**

Nguyen Dao's next draft incorporates the rough draft's handwritten revisions and includes comments made by an instructor to guide his future revisions.

## SECOND DRAFT WITH INSTRUCTOR'S COMMENTS

The Danger of Stereotypes

The United States prides itself on being the "melting pot" of the world—a nation where diverse cultures intermingle to form a unique and enlightened society. However, in reality, the abundance of different cultures in America often causes misunderstandings and even conflicts within the society. These misunderstandings result from the society's lack of knowledge about other cultures. The unique characteristic of American culture is its genuine desire to understand and embrace the wide range

*Can you sharpen the thesis so it takes a stand? Why is stereotyping a problem?*

of traditions and values of its people. Still, as an Asian American, I am a victim of ethnic stereotyping: people keep trying to make me something I'm not, and this is a serious problem for me.

*Wordy – see 23a*

It has been within the last twenty years or so that the United States has seen a large rise in the number of Asian immigrants. First-generation immigrants are seen as an underclass of poor people who struggle in low-paying jobs so that their children will have a better future. Many are angry at immigrants, accusing them of accepting lower pay for their work than other American citizens are willing to accept, thus putting the established majority out of work. *Good background. But you might condense* ⟨¶s 2 & 3 a *bit. You're wandering from your topic.*

While it is true that most newly arrived Asians do seek low-paid, low-skill jobs, they are just following the same road that other immigrant groups followed when they first arrived in the United States. The Irish who escaped the potato famines came to the United States without many advanced skills. To this day, many Latinos come to the United States in *cliché (see 25c4). Also — you may be guilty of stereotyping here.* search of a better life with little more than the shirts on their backs. Because the first generation of Asian Americans, my parents included, have poorly developed skills in English, they are forced into jobs which do not require English. Many Asians received degrees from institutions in their native countries or received advanced training of some kind but *pronoun ref.—see 19c2* cannot use ⟨those⟩ skills in the United States. Therefore, they have no choice but to accept whatever low-paying job they can get—not to steal jobs from others, but to survive.

Along with the view of the first-generation Asian Americans as low-skilled workers comes the notion that Asian-American children are hard workers who are pushed by their families to succeed. Asian children are seen as intelligent, but only in terms of scientific and technical knowledge. The media like⟨s⟩ to point to the facts that most Asians succeed only in math, science, and engineering and that a great number of Asian college *agreement — see 15a6* students identify themselves as "premed." What the media seem⟨s⟩ to *(Media-plural; medium-singular)* forget is that other immigrant groups also seem to prize success above all else.

*continued on the following page*

*continued from the previous page*

*Wordy — see 23a*

In my personal experience, in college, many of my friends assume

that I am either a science or an engineering major ant that my parents

force me to study five to ten hours a day. The believe that I sacrifice all my

free time and social life in pursuit of a high grade point average. My friends

are really surprised when I tell them that I take drawing classes and that

I am majoring in political science—not as a stepping-stone into law school,

but as a study of (man) and society. *sexist language*
*See 25e2*

*Are you sure you need all this? Your focus in this paper is on ethnic*

This practice of assuming people of similar ethnic backgrounds share

certain traits is certainly not limited to Asian Americans. African-American

*(specifically Asian) stereotypes, remember?*

students complain people expect them to be athletes, to like rap music,

to be on scholarship, to be from single-parent families—even to be gang

members. Athletes say people expect them to be dumb jocks, to drink a

lot, and to mistreat their girlfriends. Latinos say people assume their

parents are immigrants and think they speak Spanish better than

English. Business majors say people think they're politically conservative

and not creative. Engineering students are expected to be dull and wear

pocket protectors. Women are supposed to be weak in math and

science. Overweight people are expected to be class clowns. In fact, my

friends (of all ethnic groups) buy their clothes where I do, and we listen

to the same music and laugh at the same jokes. But outsiders don't

know this. They have different expectations for each of us, and these

expectations are based on culture, not ability.

*good point — but wordy (see 23a)*

It is important to remember that most people do not fit these

cultural stereotypes. For example, not all Asians fit into the overachieving, success-oriented stereotype. When any (child) comes from an economically

← *agreement—see 15b*

disadvantaged background, many times (they) must sacrifice their academic

pursuits in order to support their families. Also, as Asians, particularly the

children, become more integrated into the society, the traditional Asian

values of hard work and familial obligations will certainly clash with the

American pursuits of recreation and individualism. The resolution of that

conflict will add yet another facet to the complexity of America's society.

*Are you sure this is what you want to leave your readers with? It doesn't really address your essay's main point.*

*I like what you've done here, but something important is still missing. You really do need more examples from your own experience. Also, think about this question before our conference on Tuesday: exactly why are the stereotypes you enumerate so harmful, so damaging? This idea needs to be developed in some detail (it's really the heart of your paper), and it should certainly be addressed in your thesis statement and conclusion as well.*

# 1e   Editing and Proofreading

Writer's
Resource
CD-ROM

After you have revised your rough draft to your satisfaction, two additional steps remain: *editing* and *proofreading* your paper.

When you **edit,** you concentrate on grammar and spelling, punctuation and mechanics. You will have done some of this work as you revised previous drafts of your paper, but now your *focus* is on editing. Approach your work as a critical reader would, reading each sentence carefully.

http://kirsznermandell.heinle.com

## Using spell checkers and grammar checkers

Spell checkers and grammar checkers can make the process of editing and proofreading your papers a lot easier. Remember, though, that both have limitations. Neither a spell checker nor a grammar checker is a substitute for careful editing and proofreading.

- **Spell checkers** A spell checker simply identifies strings of letters it does not recognize; it does *not* distinguish between homophones or spot every typographical error. For example, it does not recognize *there* in "They forgot <u>there</u> books" as incorrect, nor does it spot a typo that produces a correctly spelled word, such as *word* for *work* or *thing* for *think*. Moreover, a spell checker may not include every technical term, proper noun, or foreign word you may use.
- **Grammar checkers** Grammar checkers are not always accurate. For example, they may identify a long sentence as a run-on when it is in fact grammatically correct, and they generally advise against using passive voice—even in contexts where it is appropriate. Moreover, grammar checkers do not always supply answers; often, they ask questions—for example, whether *which* should be *that* or *which* preceded by a comma—that you must answer. In short, grammar checkers can guide your editing, but you yourself must always be the one who decides when a sentence is (or is not) correct.

After you have completed your editing, print out a final draft and **proofread,** rereading every word carefully to make sure you did not make any errors as you typed. Also make sure the final copy of your paper conforms to your instructor's format requirements.

## Choosing a title ?

When you are ready to decide on a title for your essay, keep these criteria in mind.

- A title should be descriptive, giving an accurate sense of your essay's focus. Whenever possible, include one or more of the key words and phrases that are central to your paper.
- A title's wording can echo the wording of your assignment, reminding you (and your instructor) that you have not lost sight of it.
- Ideally, a title should arouse interest, perhaps by using a provocative question or a quotation or by taking a controversial position.

Assignment: Write about a problem faced on college campuses today.

Topic: Free speech on campus

Possible titles:

Free Speech: A Problem for Today's Colleges (echoes wording of assignment and includes key words of essay)

How Free Should Free Speech on Campus Be? (provocative question)

The Right to "Shout 'Fire' in a Crowded Theater" (quotation)

Hate Speech: A Dangerous Abuse of Free Speech on Campus (controversial position)

---

http://kirsznermandell.heinle.com

## Editing and proofreading

- As you edit and proofread, try looking at only a small portion of text at a time. If your software allows you to split the screen or create another window, create one so small that you can see only one or two lines of text at a time.

*continued on the following page*

*continued from the previous page*

- Use the *search* or *find* command to look for words or phrases in usage errors you commonly make—for instance, confusing *it's* with *its*, *lay* with *lie*, *effect* with *affect*, *their* with *there*, or *too* with *to*. You can also uncover <u>sexist language</u> by searching for words like *he*, *his*, *him*, or *man*.

See
25e2

- Finally, keep in mind that neatness does not equal correctness. The computer's ability to produce neat-looking text can disguise flaws that might otherwise be readily apparent. Take special care to ensure that spelling and typographical errors do not slip by.

The annotated paper that follows is the final draft of Nguyen Dao's essay, which you first saw on pages 22–24. It incorporates the suggestions made by his instructor on the second draft (pages 28–31).

Dao 1

?

Nguyen Dao

Professor Cross

English 101

10 October 2002

My Problem: Escaping the Stereotype of the

"Model Minority"

The United States prides itself on being a nation where di- Introductory verse cultures intermingle to form a unique and enlightened soci- paragraph presents ety. However, in reality, the existence of so many different cultures basic back- in America often causes misunderstandings within the society. ground These misunderstandings result from most people's lack of knowl- edge about other cultures. The unique characteristic of American culture is its genuine desire to understand and embrace the wide range of traditions and values of its people. Still, as an Asian American, I am frequently confronted with other people's ideas about who I am and how I should behave. Such stereotypes are not just limiting to me, but also dangerous to the nation because Thesis they challenge the image of the United States as a place where statement people can be whatever they want to be.

Within the last twenty years, the United States has experi- First body enced a sharp rise in the number of Asian immigrants, and these paragraph: Common immigrants, and their children, are stereotyped. First-generation stereotypes immigrants are seen as an underclass of poor people who strug- applied to Asian gle in low-paying jobs, working long hours so that their children will Americans have a better future. Along with the view of the first-generation Asian Americans as driven, low-skilled workers comes the notion

Dao 2

that all Asian-American children are hard workers who are pushed by their families to succeed. Asian children are seen as intelligent, but only in terms of scientific and technical knowledge. The media like to point out that most Asians succeed only in math, science, and engineering and that a disproportionately large number of Asian college students identify themselves as premed. What the media seem to forget is that many other immigrant groups also value success. In a larger sense, America has always been seen as the land of opportunity, where everyone is in search of the American dream.

Second body paragraph: Stereotypes applied to student himself

Many of my college friends assume that I am some kind of robot. They think I must be either a science or an engineering major and that my parents force me to study many hours each day. They believe that I sacrifice all my free time and social life in pursuit of a high grade point average. Naturally, these assumptions are incorrect. My friends are really surprised when I tell them that I take drawing classes and that I am majoring in political science—not as a stepping-stone into law school, but as a foundation for a liberal arts education. They are also surprised to find that I am not particularly quiet or shy, that I do not play a musical instrument, and that I do not live in Chinatown. (I don't know why this surprises people; I'm not even Chinese.)

Third body paragraph: Negative effects of stereotypes on student

I try to see these stereotypes as harmless, but they aren't. Even neutral or positive stereotypes can have negative consequences. For example, teachers have always had unreasonably high expectations for me, and these expectations have created pressure for academic success. And even though teachers

Dao 3

expect me to do well, they only expect me to excel in certain areas. So, they have encouraged me to take AP math and science classes, try out for band, sign up for an advanced computer seminar, and join the chess club. No one has ever suggested that I (or any other Asian American I know) pursue athletics, creative writing, or debating. I spent my high school years trying to be what other people wanted me to be, and I got to be pretty good at it.

I realize now, however, that I have been limited and that similar stereotypes also limit the options other groups have. The law says we can choose our activities and choose our careers, but things do not always work out that way. Often, because of long-held stereotypes, we are gently steered (by peers, teachers, bosses, parents, and even by ourselves) in a certain direction, toward some options and away from others. We may have come a long way from the time when African Americans were expected to be domestics or blue-collar workers, Latinos to be migrant farmers or gardeners, and Asians to be restaurant workers. But at the college, high school, and even elementary school level, students are expected to follow certain predetermined paths, and too often these expectations are based on culture, not interests or abilities.

Fourth body paragraph: Negative effects of stereotypes on society

Most people do not fit these cultural stereotypes. For example, not all Asians fit into the overachieving, success-oriented mold. When children come from an economically disadvantaged background, as the children of some recent Asian immigrants do, they must work hard and study hard. But this situation is only temporary. Even as Asian children become more assimilated into

Conclusion

Dao 4

American society, they retain the traditional Asian values of hard work and family obligations—but they also acquire the American drive for individualism. I know from my own experience that the stereotypes applied to Asians are not accurate. In the same way, people of other ethnic groups know that the cultural stereotypes applied to them are not valid. My problem is not just <u>my</u> problem because ethnic and cultural stereotypes are never harmless. Whenever someone is stereotyped, that person has fewer choices. And freedom to choose our futures, to be whoever we want to be, is what the United States is supposed to be all about.

# Chapter 2

# Essay Patterns across the Disciplines

Writers have many options for arranging material within an essay. The pattern of development you choose is determined by your **purpose**, which in college writing is often stated in (or suggested by) your assignment.

See
1b1

Different academic disciplines have different assignments. For example, if your assignment in a history course is to analyze the events that led to the Spanish-American War, you would use a **cause-and-effect** pattern; if your assignment in a political science course is to evaluate the relative merits of two systems of government, you would use **comparison and contrast;** if your assignment in a composition course is to reflect on an experience, you would use **narration** or **description;** if your assignment in a literature course is to persuade readers that a literary work's reputation is not deserved, you would use **exemplification;** and if your assignment in a chemistry course is to write a lab report, you would use **process.** In each case, of course, you have other options as well, and many essays combine several patterns of development. (The same patterns used to structure essays can also be used as **patterns of paragraph development**.)

**?**

See
3d

## 2a   Writing Narrative Essays

Writer's
Resource
CD-ROM

A **narrative** essay tells a story by presenting events in chronological (time) order. Sometimes a narrative begins in the middle of a story, or even at the end, and then moves back to the beginning. Most narrative essays, however, move in a logical, orderly sequence from beginning to end, from first event to last. Clear transitional words and phrases (*later, after that*) and time markers (*in 1990, two years earlier, the next day*) establish the chronological sequence and the relationship of each event to the others.

### (1) Using Narration across the Disciplines

You use narration in a variety of college writing situations—for example, when you review a novel's plot, when you write a case study, when you summarize your employment history in a letter of application for a job, when you present background on a history examination, when you recount personal experiences in a journal, or when you write an autobiographical essay.

Any assignment that asks you to *tell, trace, summarize the events, present the background,* or *outline* may call for narration. Here are some typical assignments that might suggest narrative writing.

- *Trace* the events that led the Food and Drug Administration to ban thalidomide in this country. (Public health paper)
- *Summarize* the incidents that immediately preceded the French Revolution. (History exam)
- *Present some background* to show why nineteenth-century British workers were receptive to the ideas of social reformers like Robert Owen. (Political science exam)
- *Outline* the plot of Jane Austen's novel *Sense and Sensibility.* (English literature quiz)

## (2) Student Essay: Narration

The following student essay was written by Gary McManus for a sociology course. The instructor asked each student to interview a relative and to write a brief family history based on the interview.

### My Family History

Introduction (identifies subject; gives background)    On October 7, I interviewed my father, John McManus, about my family history. Although he knew more about his own ancestors than my mother's, he was able to give me valuable details about both sides of my family. The family history, as I have reconstructed it, shows me that although some of my relatives experienced the financial hardships and

Thesis statement    prejudice common to many other immigrants, many members of my family were lucky enough to achieve success.

Events presented in sequence    My grandmother on my father's side was born in Newry, Ireland, in poverty caused by the potato famine. When she was a child, her father, a sea captain, took his family to Liverpool, England, so he could find work. While in England, my grandmother McManus was constantly teased by the English children because of her Irish-Catholic ancestry. When she

**40**

# Writing Narrative Essays

was eighteen, she came alone to the United States to visit a distant cousin in Baltimore, Maryland. At the time, she had no way of knowing that she would never return home. In Baltimore, she met her future husband, and they were married a year later.

My grandfather McManus was born and raised in the Baltimore area and came from a well-to-do family. His uncle invented the bottle cap (before this, people used corks) and was president of the Crown Cork and Seal Bottle Company. One of my grandfather's aunts was a judge in juvenile court in Boston—no minor achievement for a woman in the late 1880s. Another of his uncles was an architect who designed several of Boston's churches. He had trouble getting other commissions, however, because of discrimination against the Irish. At that time, it was common in Boston to see signs in shop windows saying "Workers needed—N.I.N.A." (No Irish Need Apply). As an officer in the U.S. Army, my grandfather McManus fought in the Spanish-American War in the Philippines in the 1890s and later during the Boxer Rebellion in China. During his military career, he served under both General Arthur MacArthur and his son General Douglas MacArthur.

**Narrative continues** During World War I, from 1918 to 1919, a terrible influenza epidemic killed millions worldwide and hundreds of thousands in the United States. So many people died that there were not enough gravediggers to bury the dead. Squads of men would go from house to house in many cities on the east coast, collecting the bodies of those who had died. Two of my grandparents' children died from influenza during the epidemic. One son only six years old died early one day just after sunrise, and later that evening their two-year-old daughter died in her sleep.

**Shift to mother's family** My mother's family settled in Irish neighborhoods in Washington, D.C., where my great-grandfather, John Howard, owned a livery stable. His son, my great-uncle Lee, was a U.S. attorney and judge who was known as one of the most influential Irish-American men in the District of Columbia. Because he had grown up poor and had to work to put himself through law school, he was sympathetic to the poor and often went to great lengths to find them employment.

My maternal grandfather, a builder, was among the first to attempt to organize his fellow workers. Eventually, he became a union official for the AFL. He would have advanced much higher in the union if he had renounced Catholicism and joined the Masons, but he refused.

Conclusion      Many Irish immigrants in the late 1880s and early 1900s became priests, policemen, and blue-collar workers. That was as far as many of them could go because the anti-Irish prejudice that prevailed at this time severely limited their opportunities. In spite of some problems, however, many members of my family carved out good lives in this country.

## 2b   Writing Descriptive Essays

Writer's
Resource
CD-ROM

A **descriptive** essay communicates to readers how something looks, sounds, smells, tastes, or feels. The most natural arrangement of details in a description reflects the way you actually look at a person, scene, or object: near to far, top to bottom, side to side, or front to back. This arrangement of details is made clear by transitions that identify precise spatial relationships: *next to, near, beside, under, above,* and so on.

> **Note:** Sometimes a descriptive essay does not have an explicitly stated thesis statement. In such cases, it is unified by a **dominant impression**—the effect created by all the details in the description.

### (1) Using Description across the Disciplines

Description plays an important role in college writing. For example, technical reports, lab reports, case studies, and field notes all depend upon precise description. In addition, on a European history exam you might have to describe the scene of a famous battle, and in an American literature paper you might have to describe the setting of a play or novel. In other situations, too, description is

necessary—for example, for presenting your reactions to a painting or a musical composition.
The following assignments are typical of those you may encounter.

- Describe the structures you observed during your dissection of the reproductive system of the fetal pig. (Biology laboratory manual)
- Describe William Penn's plan for the city of Philadelphia (architecture quiz)
- Write an essay in which you describe one character in the novel *The Color Purple*. (American literature paper)
- Describe Titian's use of color in his *Madonna with Members of the Pesaro Family*. (Art history exam)

## (2) Student Essay: Description

Barbara Quercetti, a student in a composition course, wrote this essay in response to an assignment asking her to describe a place that had made a strong impression on her. She based her descriptive essay largely on her own firsthand observations of her subject. (Factual details reflect the notes she took during a guided tour of the site.)

A Newport Mansion

Introduction (historical overview)    Located on Ochre Point Avenue in Newport, Rhode Island, The Breakers is a mansion presently owned by the Preservation Society of Newport County. The mansion was built in 1895 for Cornelius Vanderbilt, the financier who accumulated the renowned Vanderbilt fortune. This house, like other Newport mansions, was used only during the three summer months, when the Newport social season was at its peak. The architect, Richard Morris Hunt, modeled The Breakers after an Italian Renaissance Palace. Presently, The Breakers is one of Newport's most popular tourist attractions because its extravagant architecture and opulent decor call up a time of lost elegance.

Thesis statement

View of exterior    As visitors approach the grounds of the mansion, they see enormous black wrought iron gates that are thirty feet high at the center point and weigh seven tons. The arched top of the gates is decorated with very elaborate scrollwork, and this arch pattern is repeated throughout the exterior and interior of the mansion. To either side of the gates are two twenty-foot-high square posts, each with a black wrought-iron lantern also decorated with scrollwork. The buff Indian limestone that is used for the posts is also used for the facade of The Breakers.

View of exterior, continued

Standing in front of the mansion, visitors see that although none of the faces of The Breakers is identical, each relates to the others. The first story of each exterior wall is made up of a series of arches, with the interior of each arch inlaid with ceramic tiles. Supporting the arches are round columns with Greek Ionic capitals. Each facade is three complete stories high, except for the east side, which has a terrace above the second-story level. This terrace is one of three that give a panoramic view of the Atlantic Ocean. The other two terraces are located on the north side of The Breakers. One, at the first-story level, extends out to the garden area. The other terrace is above the first-story level. The south face of the mansion has a semicircular protrusion that forms an open one-story foyer. The entire building is decorated with ornate figures sculpted by Karl Bitter.

View of interior: Great Hall

As visitors enter The Breakers, they see that the interior is as exquisite as the exterior. The first room visitors encounter is the Great Hall or reception room, which is also decorated with intricately carved stone and marble. The Great Hall rises nearly fifty feet and is the largest room in any of the Newport mansions. Its ceiling is covered with geometric patterns of fourteen-karat-gold gilding that run over the entire surface. There are eight chandeliers, each suspended by a single metal rod. The second story of the room is an open balcony with a black wrought-iron railing that repeats the scrollwork pattern of the entrance gates. The railing is divided into sections by two-story-high square stone columns with Ionic capitals. These Greek Ionic columns are similar to those used on the exterior of the mansion. The railing continues along the side of the royal red carpeted stairs to the first floor. Surrounding the room is a series of arches, each situated between two of the two-story-high columns. Floor-length royal red tie-back draperies hang inside the arches. The wood parquet floor is covered with Persian area rugs, and potted ferns at the base of each column add a touch of greenery to the room.

View of interior: dining room

Walking through the Great Hall, visitors come to an equally impressive dining room that is also two full stories high. Lavish decorations fill the room, which is lined with two-story-high columns with arches in between. The columns are red alabaster with bronze Corinthian capitals. As in the Great Hall, royal red tie-back draperies hang inside the arches. Above each arch is a gilded cornice around which is a ceiling arch containing life-sized sculptured figures. Four huge crystal chandeliers hang down the length of the room. On the west wall, there is only one arch, and this outlines a blue carved Venetian marble fireplace. The room is richly furnished with antique European furniture, and the wood parquet floor is covered with Persian carpets. A solid oak dining table ten feet by ten feet square dominates the center of the room.

Conclusion

The Newport social season is now part of America's past, and so are the individuals who spent millions for a summer residence. But The Breakers remains one of the grandest mansions of the area. Now a tourist

Restatement of thesis

attraction, it retains its popularity because it stands as a reminder to us of a time when America was rapidly expanding and life in Newport was a good deal more extravagant than it is today.

# 2c   Writing Exemplification Essays

Writer's Resource CD-ROM

**Exemplification** essays support a thesis statement with a series of specific examples (or, sometimes, with a single extended example). These examples can be drawn from personal observation or experience or from the facts and opinions you gather through research. Within the essay, examples are linked to one another and to the thesis statement with clear transitional words and phrases: *the first example, another reason, in addition, finally,* and so on.

## (1) Using Exemplification across the Disciplines

Exemplification is basic to most college writing assignments. In fact, any time you are called upon to give a specific example of a more general principle, you use exemplification. The following assignments are typical of those you may encounter.

- Discuss three examples of *film noir.* (Film midterm)
- Write an essay in which you illustrate the following statement by the literary critic John Tytell: "Although the Beat movement lacked any shared platform such as the Imagist or surrealist manifestoes, it nonetheless cohered as a literary group." (Literature paper)
- In what ways does existentialism confront the problem of personal action in a universe devoid of purpose? (Philosophy final)
- Discuss four technological advances that took place during the Renaissance. (History of science paper)
- Identify and discuss three examples that Glazer and Moynihan give to support their thesis that in New York City and in much of the United States, the melting pot does not exist. (Sociology midterm)

## (2) Student Essay: Exemplification

The following paper on a life-changing accident was written for a health psychology course by Felicia Marianni, who supports her thesis statement with a variety of examples from her own experience.

A New Experience

Introduction    The ability to see is not often thought of as a privilege. In fact, in daily life, it is rarely even acknowledged. Unlike most other people, however, I understand how important sight is because I recently lost part of my vision because of my own carelessness. Impatient to remove my contact lenses one evening, I borrowed an unmarked bottle of solution that was lying on a shelf in the dorm bathroom. Unaware that the liquid was not saline but hydrogen peroxide, I woke up the next morning with my eyes stinging. I had chemically burned both eyes, causing hemorrhaging. Fortunately, the damage turned out to be both minimal and temporary. I did not lose my sight completely; I only lost clarity—that is, the ability to see distinct, sharp lines. I was not isolated in a world of blackness or of lights and shadows. I was able to see colors. Nevertheless, my world was

**Thesis statement** "fuzzy," and this caused a lot of problems that adversely affected my feelings of security and of self.

**First group of examples** Problems that I had never anticipated coping with now plagued me. For example, reading even for short periods of time strained my eyes and gave me headaches. I could not recognize my friends from a distance of more than a couple of feet. Friends thought I was behaving rudely if I didn't stop to chat, unaware that if I had recognized them, I certainly would have stopped to say hello. Stairways became dangerous, for it was difficult to determine where one step ended and the next began. Sometimes, in the evening after a rainy afternoon, I could not determine whether a dark area in front of me was a puddle or just a shadow, and I must have looked strange to onlookers who saw me skirt a pool of darkness as if I were afraid to get my feet wet.

**Second group of examples** Not only did letters in a book and human faces become distorted, but the beauty of nature did, too. As the hours and the days passed, I missed being able to see clear outlines of trees against the sky; all I could see was something greenish fading to brown as it neared the ground. I longed to see separate blades of grass rather than a mass of green beside the grayish strip that I knew to be pavement. If I heard a bird chirping, I was not able to find the source of the sound. I missed shapes of clouds shifting and changing above me. When it rained, I could not see reflections in puddles.

**Third group of examples** I also missed being able to see the cityscape that I had learned to integrate into my field of experience. After my accident, I could no longer discern the sharp edges of the sides of the buildings; instead, I saw a large reddish blur instead of a red-brick building. The beauty of the arching skeleton of a bridge had turned into a jumble of disconnected shapes. I was aching to see the real features of the people hurrying around me and the intricate architecture of public statues. But none of this was possible.

Conclusion          After a week and a half of limited vision, I recovered. My first reaction to "seeing again" was disbelief. When I went outside and looked around, my vision was still blurred, but this time with tears. Now, I appreciate every new day that I can wake up and put in my contact lenses, or put on

Restatement  my glasses, to see everything clearly. But the world will never look as
of major     beautiful to me as it did when I saw it anew for the first time.
point

## 2d  Writing Process Essays

Writer's
Resource
CD-ROM

A **process** essay explains how to do something or how something works. It presents a series of steps in strict chronological order, using transitional words such as *first, then, next, after this,* and *finally* to link steps in the process.

Some process essays are **instructions,** providing all the specific information that enables readers to perform a procedure themselves. Instructions use commands and the present tense. **Process explanation** essays simply explain the process to readers, with no expectation that they will actually perform it. These process essays may use first or third person and past tense (for a process that has been completed) or present tense (for a process that occurs regularly).

### (1) Using Process across the Disciplines

Academic situations frequently call for process explanations and sometimes for instructions. In scientific and technical writing, you may describe how an apparatus works or how a procedure is carried out. Occasionally, you may even write a set of instructions telling your readers how to duplicate your procedure. In the humanities, you might have to write a proposal for a research paper

# Writing Process Essays

in which you explain how you plan to carry out your research. Here are some typical assignments that call for a process pattern of development.

- Explain how an amendment is added to the Constitution. (Political science quiz)
- Review the stages that each of the Old English long vowels went through during the Great Vowel Shift. (Examination in history of the English language)
- Outline the steps in the process of mitosis. (Biology lab quiz)
- Write a set of instructions that outlines a treatment plan for a patient complaining of lower back pain. (Physical therapy paper)

## (2) Student Essay: Process

Richard Patrone, a student in a course in animal biology, submitted the following laboratory report. In writing up his experiment, he was careful to provide an exact record of what he did in order to give readers the information they would need to understand his procedure.

### Background

Introduction  Based on the postulation that pollen contains an anticarcinogenic principle that can be added to food, an experiment was set up in which female mice, fed with pollenized food, were checked for delays in the appearance of spontaneous mammary tumors. Mice used in the study were bred from a subline of the $C_3H$ strain, which develops palpable tumors at between 18 and 25 weeks of age.

### Procedure

Steps in the process  First, 10 mice were set aside as controls, to be fed only unpollenized food (Purina Laboratory Chow). Next, the pollen suspension was prepared: one gram of bee-gathered pollen was ground and then mixed with 50 ml of distilled water. Two different mixtures were then prepared with this pollen suspension. One mixture consisted of 6 lb of food with a 36 ml dosage of pollen suspension (1 part pollen per 3,800 parts food), and one consisted of 6 lb of lab chow with an 8 ml dosage of suspension

**49**

(1 part pollen per 120,000 parts food). Each of these two mixtures was then fed to a different group of 10 mice. The mice were weighed weekly, and the amount of food eaten was recorded. As soon as estrus began, vaginal smears of each mouse were made daily and examined microscopically for the presence of cornified cells.

Results

Conclusion  The experimental results indicated that the development of mammary tumors in $C_3H$ mice was delayed 10 to 12 weeks with the ingestion of pollenized food.

# 2e  Writing Cause-and-Effect Essays

Writer's
Resource
CD-ROM

**Cause-and-effect** essays explore causes or predict or describe results; sometimes a single cause-and-effect essay does both. Because cause-and-effect relationships are often quite complex, clear, specific transitional words and phrases such as *one cause, another cause, a more important result, because,* and *as a result* are essential.

## (1) Using Cause and Effect across the Disciplines

Many of your course assignments call for writing that examines causes, predicts effects, or does both. Language like "How did X affect Y?" "What were the contributing factors?" "Describe some side effects," "What caused X?" "What were the results of X?" and "Why did X happen?" suggests cause-and-effect writing. Here are some typical assignments.

- Identify and explain some factors that contributed to the stock market crash of 1987. (Economics essay)
- Describe some of the possible side effects of dialysis. (Nursing exam)
- How have geologic changes affected the productivity of Pennsylvania soil? (Agronomy project)
- What factors led to the wave of eastern European immigration to this country at the end of the nineteenth century? (American history exam)
- How did Ernest Hemingway's experiences during World War I influence his writing? (American literature paper)

## (2) Student Essay: Cause and Effect

Michael Liebman wrote the essay that follows for a class in elementary education. The assignment was "Identify the causes of a social problem of concern to both parents and educators, and analyze the effects of this problem, making some recommendations about how the problem can be solved." Michael decided to examine the positive and negative effects on children of being left on their own after school.

### The Latchkey Children

Introduction (States primary cause: working parents)

In recent years, the expanding economy and wider employment opportunities for women have combined to lead more and more mothers of school-aged children to return to work. In fact, more than half of the mothers of school-aged children are now employed, and the two-paycheck family has become the norm. As a result, many children are now left unsupervised between 3 and 6 p.m. every day. The lack of much-needed after-school programs has left some families in cities and suburbs alike

Thesis statement

with no other alternative but to leave the children on their own and hope for the best. Luckily, many of the children seem to manage very well.

Negative effects

The negative effects of the latchkey trend are fairly easily perceived. Many parents' firm rules—don't use the stove, don't open the door for anyone, don't let telephone callers know you are alone—have made some children (especially those without siblings) fearful and jittery. These children may also become very lonely in an empty house or apartment. Because many working parents do not allow their children's friends to visit when no adult is present, their children may spend hours with no company but the television set. A lonely, frightened child turning to the TV for comfort and companionship is a common stereotype of the latchkey child.

Other possible negative effects

The latchkey phenomenon has the potential to have some even more disturbing effects on children. Parents and teachers worry that unattended children will be more vulnerable to violent crimes, especially sexual assaults and kidnapping. They also fear the children will be unable to protect themselves in case of fire or other disaster. Parents have been concerned as well that young adolescents left alone will be free to experiment with sex, drugs, and alcohol. But these fears have not been substantiated by statistical data.

First positive effect        Surprisingly enough, in fact, many positive results have actually been observed—positive both for the children and parents involved and for our society as a whole. One such positive result has been the response of the many schools across the country that have instituted courses in "survival skills." In these courses, boys and girls as young as ten learn such skills as cleaning, cooking, and sewing; consumerism; safety and first aid; and how to care for younger siblings. The focus of the home economics courses in these schools has changed as the students' needs have, and the trend toward these "domestic survival courses" seems to be spreading.

Second positive effect        Perhaps the most significant positive effect has been a subtle one: the emotional strengths so often observed in the latchkey children. As they learn to fend for themselves, and take pride in doing so, their self-esteem increases. Educators cite these children as more self-reliant, more mature, more confident; parents add that they are also more cooperative around the house. Of course it is still too early to tell whether the latchkey trend will produce a generation of more independent, self-reliant adults, but it is certainly a possibility.

Conclusion        Clearly, the latchkey syndrome has negative as well as positive results, but the answer is not to have parents leave the workforce. For the majority of working parents, especially in single-parent families, working is an economic necessity. Parents should be able to remain employed, and most of their children will benefit—though some, inevitably, will suffer. The best solution would be the continued development of government-subsidized programs to meet the needs of the latchkey child. Most important among these would be supervised after-school programs, perhaps utilizing school buildings and facilities. Communities and private industry can also contribute—the former by establishing networks of "block parents" and information and referral services, the latter by offering "flextime" as an option for working parents. Most latchkey children are managing quite well, but their lives and their parents' lives can—and should—be made a lot easier.

## 2f  Writing Comparison-and-Contrast Essays

Writer's
Resource
CD-ROM

**Comparison-and-contrast** essays explain how two subjects are alike or different; sometimes a single comparison-and-contrast essay examines both similarities and differences. The two subjects being compared or contrasted must have a clear **basis for comparison;** that is, they must have qualities or elements in common that make the comparison or contrast logical. Similarities and differences are identified with appropriate transitional words and phrases, such as *similarly* and *likewise* for comparison and *however* and *in contrast* for contrast. These transitions can also signal movement from one subject to another.

### (1) Using Comparison and Contrast across the Disciplines

Instructors often ask you to use comparison and contrast in answering examination questions.

- Compare and contrast the Neoclassic and Romantic views of nature. (Literature)
- Discuss the similarities and differences of the insanity defenses for murder under the M'Naghten test and the Durham rule. (Criminology)
- What are the advantages and disadvantages of load and no-load mutual funds? (Personal finance)
- Examine the benefits and liabilities of team-taught and individual teacher-centered classrooms. (Educational methods)
- How did Darwin and Lamarck differ on the subject of mutability of the species? (Biology)

Each of these assignments provides you with cues that tell you how to treat your material. Certain words and phrases—*compare and contrast, similarities and differences, advantages and disadvantages,* and *benefits and liabilities*—indicate that you should use comparison and contrast to structure your answer.

Many other situations also call for comparison and contrast. For example, if your supervisor on a work-study project asked you to write a report discussing the feasibility of two types of insulation, cellulose and urethane foam, you would use comparison and contrast to organize your ideas.

## (2) Student Essay: Comparison and Contrast

**?**

See 3d6

See 3d6

When asked by his composition instructor to compare any two subjects, Alan Escobero, a professed expert on arcade games, used a **point-by-point comparison** to present his ideas—that is, he alternated between subjects, making a point about one subject and then making a comparable point about the other subject. (A **subject-by-subject comparison** treats one subject in full and then moves on to discuss the other subject in full.)

Arcade Wars

Introduction    Long ago, in a time more innocent than ours, pinball aficionados were content to while away the hours watching silver balls bounce frenetically through a maze of bumpers and flashing lights. That, of course, was in the pre-Space Invader era, before solid-state technology revolutionized the coin-operated game industry and challenged pinball machines with computerized video games. Currently, pinball and video games are locked in deadly combat in arcades across the country for dominance of a multi-

Thesis statement    million-dollar market. How this battle will be won or lost depends, to a great extent, on how enthusiasts react to two entirely different game formats.

History (Pinball machines)    Pinball machines have a long history. They can be traced back to a popular nineteenth-century game that was played on a table and was similar to pool. The original pinball game, a board with a coin chute and variations on the placement of holes, went through a swift period of change. New machines had new scoring and play attraction features.

# Writing Comparison-and-Contrast Essays

Pinball games as we now know them got their start in the late 1930s and within a few years developed into the flippers, bumpers, and flashing lights we know today.

**History (Video games)** Video games had their start in the solid-state technology that was a spinoff of the space program and computer research. The first video game, called Pong, appeared in 1972 and had a television screen and a handheld control. This simple machine, which at first was viewed by pinball manufacturers as a curiosity, eventually revolutionized the industry and prepared the way for the games that followed. Current video games combine intellectual strategies with realistic visual effects.

**Players (Pinball machines)** Pinball players are mainly young males. Players who talk about how they feel playing pinball say that they get great satisfaction from beating the machine. Some say that pinball challenges their skill and enables them to beat a machine on its own terms. Obviously the game provides a release of frustration, a challenge, and an opportunity to win—all very important. It also stimulates the senses with buzzers, gongs, voices, and electronic effects. One habitual player sums up the attraction of pinball games when he says, "When you play, nothing else counts. It's just you and the machine."

**Players (Video games)** Computerized video games attract a different type of player, as a trip to a downtown arcade any weekday at lunchtime will show. Standing beside the usual crowd of teenagers are groups of young executives. This is not surprising, for video games draw players into a world that lets their imaginations run wild. They can give players the sense of piloting a starship or the thrill of snowboarding down a realistic mountain trail. The most popular—for example, Tekkan, Mace, and Mortal Kombat—allow players to work out their most violent and aggressive fantasies.

**Conclusion** It is too soon to tell who will win the technological war that is presently being fought in arcades. The stakes are high, for a good machine can take

in hundreds of dollars a week. Presently, both pinball and video game de-
signers are planning new and spectacular games. But even the most
eager pinball players believe that video games will eventually triumph.
Pinball is still a game of silver balls being bounced by flippers and
bumpers, but video games are constantly evolving as computer technology develops. Possibly the most important difference between the two is
that when you play a pinball machine, you only push around a ball, but
when you play a video game, you fight for a galaxy.

## 2g   Writing Division-and-Classification Essays

A **division-and-classification** essay **divides** (breaks a subject into
its component parts) and **classifies** (groups individual items into
categories). Division and classification are closely related
processes. For example, when you *divide* the English language into
three historical categories (Old English, Middle English, Modern
English) you can then *classify* examples of specific linguistic characteristics by assigning them to one of these three historical periods. Transitional words and phrases help to distinguish categories
from one another: *one kind, another group, a related category, the most
important component.*

### (1) Using Division and Classification across
### the Disciplines

You divide and classify information every time you write an academic paper: you *divide* your subject into possible topics, you
*classify* your notes into categories, and you *divide* your paper into
paragraphs.

Division and classification are also called for in specific academic situations. For example, when you study a laboratory animal, you may arrange your observations in categories that reflect
the animal's systems: digestive, circulatory, nervous, and so on.
When you write a book review, you may organize your information
into sections devoted to plot, the author's previously published
works, and your evaluation of the book you are reviewing. Assignments like the following are typical of the many that call for
division and classification.

# Writing Division-and-Classification Essays

- The English language is constantly in the process of acquiring new words. Write an essay in which you classify some of the many examples of these coinages and adaptations into at least five distinct categories. (History of language midterm)
- Discuss recurrent themes in James Baldwin's novels, short stories, and essays. (American literature research paper)
- Analyze the workings of the federal court system, paying special attention to the relationship between the lower courts, the appellate courts, and the Supreme Court. (Take-home exam in American government)
- Write a detailed report analyzing the possible roles of each member of the management team during the proposed reorganization of the credit department. (Business management report)
- Explain in general terms how the most common orchestral instruments are classified, making sure you provide examples of instruments in each group. (Introduction to music quiz)

## (2) Student Essay: Division and Classification

Robin Twery used division and classification to structure the following written version of an **oral presentation** she gave to her public speaking class. Before writing out her speech, she made an informal outline that enabled her to establish categories and clarify the relationship of one category to another. (Information was adapted from notes she took in her geology class.)

See Ch. 46

Classes of Rocks

Introduction (Lists categories)    To most people, rocks are distinguished from one another only by size: some are big; others are little. But actually, rocks are divided into three general classes: igneous rocks, sedimentary rocks, and metamorphic rocks.

First category    Igneous rocks were once molten rock; now they have cooled down and solidified. Igneous rocks, like the one I'm holding up now, may be intrusive or extrusive. Intrusive igneous rocks, in their molten state, forced their way into other rocks and cooled and hardened there, sometimes forming very large masses called batholiths. These batholiths are frequently made up of granite, a crystalline rock. Some other intrusive igneous rocks can form between other rocks in the form of sills or dikes.

Other igneous rocks are extrusive; that is, they are formed when molten rock is driven out onto the surface of the earth to cool and harden. The molten rock that flows along the earth's surface is lava. The bits of molten rock that are extruded into the air solidify in the air and fall to the ground in the form of volcanic ash and cinder.

Second category
Sedimentary rocks are formed when other rocks break apart. Pieces of rock, borne by water or wind, are deposited in the form of sediments. After a time, these particles are consolidated into rock. Sedimentary rocks may be classified according to the size of the grains of which they are composed, ranging from coarse gravel to finer sand, silt, or clay to fine lime and marl. As you can see in this picture, sedimentary rocks are usually deposited in layers (strata), with the oldest sediments on the bottom and the most recent on top.

Third category
The final category, metamorphic rock, has been subjected to great heat and pressure. Metamorphic rocks have been buried under other rocks so that their structures and their mineral components have been altered by the weight of the layers above and the high temperatures to which they are exposed under the earth. An example of a metamorphic rock is the crystalline rock called gneiss, which is now being passed around the room.

Conclusion
The next time you take a walk, you can look for igneous, sedimentary, and metamorphic rocks. Now that you know that not all rocks are alike, I hope you will look at them in a different way.

# 2h Writing Definition Essays

Writer's Resource CD-ROM

A **formal definition** includes the term being defined, the class to which it belongs, and the details that distinguish it from the other members of its class.

(term)                  (class)                 (details)
Carbon is a nonmetallic element occurring as diamond, graphite, and charcoal.

# Writing Definition Essays

A **definition** essay develops a formal definition with narration, description, exemplification, process, cause and effect, comparison and contrast, or division and classification—or any combination of these patterns. In addition, it may examine the origin of a term by using an **analogy** or by using negation (telling what a term is *not*).

See 3d6

## (1) Using Definition across the Disciplines

In academic writing, you must define your terms to demonstrate to your audience that you know what you are talking about and to clarify crucial concepts or terms. Following are some typical assignments calling for definition.

- What is the WPA? (American history quiz)
- The villanelle in French and American poetry (Literature paper)
- Define either the Organic or the International school of modern architecture. (Architecture exam)
- What is a colluvial soil? (Agronomy quiz)
- Define the school of painting known as Fauvism, paying particular attention to the early work of Matisse. (History of art midterm)
- Identify and define four of the following: anorexia, autism, schizophrenia, agoraphobia, paranoia, manic depression, dyssymbolia. (Psychology quiz)

## (2) Student Essay: Definition

In response to the American history **exam question** "Choose one early-twentieth-century American social or political movement and briefly discuss its purpose, its leading supporters, and their social or political contribution," Suzanne Bohrer chose to write on the muckrakers. In defining the term *muckraker*, she decided to include a formal definition, provide a brief explanation of the term's origin, and expand the basic definition to discuss the movement's role in American social and political history.

See Ch. 42

Introduction
(Includes
formal
definition
and origin
of term)

Muckrakers were early-twentieth-century reformers whose mission was to look for and uncover political and business corruption. The term muckraker, which referred to the "man with a muckrake" in John Bunyan's Pilgrim's Progress, was first used in a pejorative sense by Theodore

Roosevelt, whose opinion of the muckrakers was that they were biased and overreacting. The movement began about 1902 and died down by 1917.

**Thesis statement** Despite its brief duration, however, it had a significant impact on the political, commercial, and even literary climate of the period.

**First point—movement's influence reflected in magazines** Many popular magazines featured articles whose purpose was to expose corruption. Some of these muckraking periodicals included The Arena, Everybody's, The Independent, and McClure's. Lincoln Steffens, managing editor of McClure's (and later associate editor of American Magazine and Everybody's), was an important leader of the muckraking movement. Some of his exposés were collected in his 1904 book The Shame of the Cities and in two other volumes, and his 1931 autobiography also discusses the corruption he uncovered and the development of the muckraking movement. Ida Tarbell, another noted muckraker, wrote a number of articles for McClure's, some of which were gathered in her 1904 book The History of the Standard Oil Company.

**Second point—movement's influence reflected in fiction of D. G. Phillips** Muckraking appeared in fiction as well. David Graham Phillips, who began his career as a newspaperman, went on to write muckraking magazine articles and eventually novels about contemporary economic, political, and social problems, such as insurance scandals, state and municipal corruption, shady Wall Street dealings, slum life, and women's emancipation.

**Third (and most important) point—movement's influence reflected in The Jungle** Perhaps the best known muckraking novel was Upton Sinclair's The Jungle, the 1906 exposé of the Chicago meatpacking industry. The novel focuses on an immigrant family and sympathetically and realistically describes their struggles with loan sharks and others who take advantage of their innocence. More important, Sinclair graphically describes the brutal working conditions of those who find work in the stockyards. Sinclair's description of the main character's work in the fertilizer plant is particularly gruesome; at the novel's end, this man turns to socialism.

Conclusion   With the muckrakers featured prominently in fiction, magazines, and newspapers—especially the New York <u>World</u> and the Kansas City <u>Star</u>—some results were forthcoming. Perhaps the most far-reaching was the pure-food legislation of 1906, supposedly a direct result of Roosevelt's reading of <u>The Jungle</u>. In any case, the muckrakers helped to nourish the growing tradition of social reform in America.

## ✓checklist) Essay patterns across the disciplines

✓ **Narration**   Have you discussed enough events to enable readers to understand what occurred? Have you supported your thesis statement with specific details?

✓ **Description**   Have you supplied enough detail about what things look like, sound like, smell like, taste like, and feel like? Will your readers be able to visualize the person, object, or setting that your essay describes?

✓ **Exemplification**   Have you presented enough examples to support your essay's thesis? If you have used a single extended example, will readers understand how it supports the essay's thesis?

✓ **Process**   Have you presented enough steps to enable readers to understand how the process is performed? Is the sequence of steps clear? If you are writing instructions, have you included enough explanation—as well as reminders and warnings—to enable readers to perform the process efficiently and safely?

✓ **Cause and Effect**   Have you identified enough causes (subtle as well as obvious, minor as well as major) to enable readers to understand why something occurred? Have you identified enough effects to show the significance of the causes and the impact they had?

✓ **Comparison and Contrast**   Have you supplied a sufficient number of details to illustrate each of the subjects in the comparison? Have you presented a similar number of details for each subject?

✓ **Division and Classification**   Have you presented enough information to enable readers to identify each category and distinguish one from another?

✓ **Definition**   Have you presented enough detail (examples, analogies, and so on) to enable readers to understand the term you are defining and to distinguish it from others in its class?

# Chapter 3

# Writing Paragraphs

A **paragraph** is a group of related sentences, which may be complete in itself or part of a longer piece of writing.

> ### ✓ checklist When to paragraph
>
> ? ✓ Begin a new paragraph whenever you move from one major point to another.
>
> ✓ Begin a new paragraph whenever you move your readers from one time period or location to another.
>
> ✓ Begin a new paragraph whenever you introduce a new step in a process or sequence.
>
> ✓ Begin a new paragraph when you want to emphasize an important idea.
>
> ✓ Begin a new paragraph every time a new person speaks.
>
> ✓ Begin a new paragraph to signal the end of your introduction and the beginning of your conclusion.

Writer's
Resource
CD-ROM

## 3a Writing Unified Paragraphs

A paragraph is **unified** when it develops a single idea. Each paragraph should have a **topic sentence** that states the main idea of the paragraph; the other sentences in the paragraph support that idea.

### (1) Using Topic Sentences

Usually, a topic sentence comes at the beginning of a paragraph, where it tells readers what to expect.

<u>I was a listening child, careful to hear the very different sounds of Spanish and English.</u> Wide-eyed with hearing, I'd listen to sounds more than words. First, there were English (*gringo*) sounds. So many words were still unknown that when the butcher or the lady at the drugstore said something to me, exotic polysyllabic sounds would bloom in the midst of their sentences. Often the speech of people in public seemed to me very loud, booming with confidence. The man behind the counter would literally ask, "What can I do for you?" But

# Writing Unified Paragraphs

by being so firm and so clear, the sound of his voice said that he was a *gringo;* he belonged in public society.

(Richard Rodriguez, *Aria: A Memoir of a Bilingual Childhood*)

Occasionally, the topic sentence may appear at the end of a paragraph, particularly when a writer needs to lead readers gradually to a controversial or surprising conclusion.

These sprays, dusts and aerosols are now applied almost universally to farms, gardens, forests, and homes—nonselective chemicals that have the power to kill every insect, the "good" and the "bad," to still the song of the birds and the leaping of fish in the streams, to coat the leaves with a deadly film, and to linger on in soil—all this though the intended target may be only a few weeds or insects. Can anyone believe it is possible to lay down such a barrage of poisons on the surface without making it unfit for life? They should not be called "insecticides," but "biocides."

(Rachel Carson, "The Obligation to Endure")

## (2) Testing for Unity

Each sentence in a paragraph should support the main idea stated in the topic sentence. In the following paragraph, the italicized sentences do not support the main idea.

Not Unified:

One of the first problems students have is learning to use a computer. All students were required to buy a computer before school started. Throughout the first semester, we took a special course to teach us to use a computer. *My notebook computer has a large memory and can do word processing and spreadsheets. It has a large screen and a DVD drive. My parents were happy that I had a computer, but they were concerned about the price. Tuition was high, and when they added in the price of the computer, it was almost out of reach. To offset expenses, I got a part-time job in the school library.* By the end of the first week of the course, I was convinced that I would never be able to work with my computer.

(Student Writer)

To unify this paragraph, the writer deleted the sentences about his parents' financial situation and the computer's characteristics, keeping only those details related to the main idea and adding other relevant details.

Unified:

One of the first problems I had as a college student was learning to use my computer. All first-year students were required to buy a computer before school started. Throughout the first semester, we took a special course to teach us to use the computer. In theory, this system sounded fine, but in my case it was a disaster. In the first place, the closest I had ever come to a computer was the handheld calculator I used in math class. In the second place, I could not type. And to make matters worse, many of the people in my computer orientation course already knew how to operate a computer. By the end of the first week of the course, I was convinced that I would never be able to work with my computer.

### Topic sentences

In some situations, you may not need a topic sentence. For example, sometimes a topic sentence stated in one paragraph covers a subsequent paragraph as well. Also, in some narrative or descriptive paragraphs an explicit topic sentence may seem forced or artificial.

## 3b  Writing Coherent Paragraphs

Writer's
Resource
CD-ROM

A paragraph is **coherent** when all its sentences are logically related to one another. You can achieve coherence by arranging details according to an organizing principle and by using transitional words and phrases, parallel constructions, and repeated key words and phrases.

### (1) Arranging Details

Even if all a paragraph's sentences are about the same subject, the paragraph lacks coherence if the sentences are not arranged according to a general organizing principle—that is, in *spatial, chronological,* or *logical order.*

**Spatial order** establishes the perspective from which readers view details. For example, an object or scene can be viewed from top to bottom or from near to far. Spatial order is central to de-scriptive paragraphs.

See
3d2

**Chronological order** presents details in time sequence, using transitional words and phrases that establish the sequence of events—*at first, yesterday, later,* and so on. Chronological order is central to **narrative paragraphs** and **process paragraphs**.

See
3d1;
3d4

# Writing Coherent Paragraphs

Logical order presents details or ideas in terms of their logical relationships to one another. The ideas in a paragraph may move from *general* to *specific,* as in the conventional topic-sentence-at-the-beginning paragraph, or the ideas may progress from *specific* to *general,* as they do when the topic sentence appears at the end. A writer may also choose to begin with the *least important* idea and move to the *most important.*

## (2) Using Transitional Words and Phrases

Transitional words and phrases clarify the relationships among sentences by establishing the spatial, chronological, and logical connections within a paragraph. The following paragraph, which has no transitional words and phrases, illustrates just how important transitions are.

Paragraph without Transitional Words and Phrases:

Napoleon certainly made a change for the worse by leaving his small kingdom of Elba. He went back to Paris, and he abdicated for a second time. He fled to Rochefort in hope of escaping to America. He gave himself up to the English captain of the ship *Bellerophon.* He suggested that the Prince Regent grant him asylum, and he was refused. All he saw of England was the Devon coast and Plymouth Sound as he passed on to the remote island of St. Helena. He died on May 5, 1821, at the age of fifty-two.

It is certainly not impossible to determine the relationship among these sentences. The topic sentence clearly states the main idea of the paragraph, and the rest of the sentences support this idea. However, not only is the paragraph choppy, but it also is difficult to understand. Because of the lack of transitional words and phrases, readers cannot tell exactly how one event relates to another. Notice how much easier it is to read this passage once transitional words and phrases (such as *after, finally, once again,* and *in the end)* have been added to indicate the order in which events occurred.

Paragraph with Transitional Words and Phrases:

Napoleon certainly made a change for the worse by leaving his small kingdom of Elba. <u>After Waterloo,</u> he went back to Paris, and he abdicated for a second time. <u>A hundred days after</u> his return from Elba, he fled to Rochefort in hope of escaping to America. <u>Finally,</u> he gave himself up to the English captain of the ship *Bellerophon.* <u>Once again,</u> he suggested that the Prince Regent grant him asylum, and <u>once again,</u> he was refused. <u>In the end,</u> all he saw of England was the Devon coast and Plymouth Sound as he passed on to the remote island of St. Helena. <u>After six years of exile,</u> he died on May 5, 1821, at the age of fifty-two.

(Norman Mackenzie, *The Escape from Elba*)

## FREQUENTLY USED TRANSITIONAL WORDS AND PHRASES

**To Signal Sequence or Addition**

| | |
|---|---|
| again | furthermore |
| also | in addition |
| besides | moreover |
| first . . . second . . . third | one . . . another |
| | too |

**To Signal Time**

| | |
|---|---|
| afterward | later |
| as soon as | meanwhile |
| at first | next |
| at the same time | now |
| before | soon |
| earlier | subsequently |
| finally | then |
| in the meantime | until |

**To Signal Comparison**

| | |
|---|---|
| also | likewise |
| by the same token | similarly |
| in comparison | |

**To Signal Contrast**

| | |
|---|---|
| although | nevertheless |
| but | nonetheless |
| despite | on the contrary |
| even though | on the one hand . . . on the |
| however | other hand |
| in contrast | still |
| instead | whereas |
| meanwhile | yet |

**To Introduce Examples**

| | |
|---|---|
| for example | specifically |
| for instance | thus |
| namely | |

**To Signal Narrowing of Focus**

| | |
|---|---|
| after all | in particular |
| indeed | specifically |
| in fact | that is |
| in other words | |

**To Introduce Conclusions or Summaries**

| | |
|---|---|
| as a result | in summary |
| consequently | therefore |
| in conclusion | thus |
| in other words | to conclude |

**To Signal Concession**

| | |
|---|---|
| admittedly | naturally |
| certainly | of course |
| granted | |

**To Introduce Causes or Effects**

| | |
|---|---|
| accordingly | since |
| as a result | so |
| because | then |
| consequently | therefore |
| hence | |

## (3) Using Parallel Structure

**Parallelism**—the use of matching words, phrases, clauses, or sentence structures to express similar ideas—can help increase coherence in a paragraph.

See 24a

Note in the following paragraph how parallel clauses (sentences that begin with "He was _____") link Thomas Jefferson's accomplishments.

Thomas Jefferson was born in 1743 and died at Monticello, Virginia, on July 4, 1826. During his eighty-four years, he accomplished a number of things. Although best known for his draft of the Declaration of Independence, Jefferson was a man of many talents who had a wide intellectual range. He was a patriot who was one of the revolutionary founders of the United States. He was a reformer who, when he was governor of Virginia, drafted the Statute for Religious Freedom. He was an innovator who drafted an ordinance for governing the West and devised the first decimal monetary system. He was a president who abolished internal taxes, reduced the national debt, and made the Louisiana Purchase. And finally, he was an architect who designed Monticello and the University of Virginia.

(Student Writer)

## (4) Repeating Key Words and Phrases

Repeating **key words and phrases**—those essential to meaning—throughout a paragraph connects the sentences to one another and to the paragraph's main idea.

The following paragraph repeats the key word *mercury* to help readers focus on the subject.

Mercury poisoning is a problem that has long been recognized. "Mad as a hatter" refers to the condition prevalent among nineteenth-century workers who were exposed to mercury during the manufacturing of felt hats. Workers in many other industries, such as mining, chemicals, and dentistry, were similarly affected. In the 1950s and 1960s there were cases of mercury poisoning in Minamata, Japan. Research showed that there were high levels of mercury pollution in streams and lakes surrounding the village. In the United States, this problem came to light in 1969 when a New Mexico family got sick from eating food tainted with mercury. Since then, pesticides containing mercury have been withdrawn from the market, and chemical wastes can no longer be dumped into the ocean.

(Student Writer)

### Coherence between paragraphs

The methods you use to establish coherence within paragraphs may also be used to link paragraphs in an essay. In addition, you can use a transitional paragraph as a bridge between two paragraphs.

## 3c Writing Well-Developed Paragraphs

A paragraph is **well developed** when it includes all the support—examples, statistics, expert opinion, and so on—that readers need to understand and accept the main idea.

At first glance, the following paragraph may seem well developed.

From Thanksgiving until Christmas, children are bombarded with ads for violent toys and games. Toy manufacturers persist in thinking that only toys that appeal to children's aggressiveness will sell. Despite claims that they (unlike action toys) have educational value, video games have increased the level of violence. The real question is why parents continue to buy these violent toys for their children.

(Student Writer)

Upon closer observation, however, it becomes clear that the paragraph does not contain enough support to convince readers that children are "bombarded with ads for violent toys and games."

The following revision includes specific examples that support the topic sentence.

| | |
|---|---|
| Topic sentence | From Thanksgiving until Christmas, children are bombarded with ads for violent toys and games. Toy manufacturers persist in thinking that only toys that appeal to |
| Specific examples | children's aggressiveness will sell. <u>One television commercial praises the merits of a commando team that attacks and captures a miniature enemy base. Toy soldiers wear realistic uniforms and carry automatic rifles, pistols, knives, grenades, and ammunition. Another commercial shows laughing children shooting one another with plastic rocket fighters and tanklike vehicles.</u> Despite claims that they (unlike action toys) have educational value, video games have increased the level of violence. <u>The most popular video |
| Specific examples | games involve children in strikingly realistic combat situations. One game lets children search out and destroy aliens from outer space in underground tunnels. Other best-selling games graphically simulate hand-to-hand combat on city streets.</u> The real question is why parents continue to buy these violent toys and games for their children. |

## Well-developed paragraphs

Keep in mind that it is not length that determines whether a paragraph is well developed. The amount and kind of support you need depends on your audience, your purpose, and the scope of your paragraph's main idea.

- *Identify your audience.* Will readers be familiar with your subject? Given the needs of your audience, is your paragraph well developed?
- *Identify your purpose.* Should the paragraph give readers a general overview of your topic, or should it present detailed information? Given your purpose, is your paragraph well developed?
- *Identify your paragraph's main idea.* Do you need to explain it more fully? Do you need another example, a statistic, an anecdote, or expert opinion? Given the complexity and scope of your main idea, is your paragraph well developed?

# 3d    Patterns for Paragraph Development

Writer's
Resource
CD-ROM

See
Ch. 2

The pattern of a paragraph—*narration, description,* and so on—like the pattern of an entire <u>essay</u>, reflects the way a writer arranges ideas to express ideas most effectively.

## (1) Narration

**Narrative** paragraphs tell a story. Transitional words and phrases move readers from one time period to another.

> My academic career almost ended as soon as it began when, three weeks after I arrived at college, I decided to pledge a fraternity. By midterms I was wearing a straw hat and saying "Yes, sir" to every fraternity brother I met. When classes were over, I ran errands for the fraternity members, and after dinner I socialized and worked on projects with the other people in my pledge class. In between these activities, I tried to study. Somehow I managed to write papers, take tests, and attend lectures. By the end of the semester, though, my grades had slipped, and I was exhausted. It was then that I realized that I wanted to be popular, but not at the expense of my grades and my future career. At the beginning of my second semester, I dropped out of the fraternity and got a job in the biology lab. Looking back, I realize that it was then that I actually began to grow up.
>
> (Student Writer)

## (2) Description

**Descriptive** paragraphs convey how something looks, sounds, smells, tastes, or feels. Transitional words and phrases clarify spatial relationships.

> When you are inside the jungle, away from the river, the trees vault out of sight. It is hard to remember to look up the long trunks and see the fans, strips, fronds, and sprays of glossy leaves. Inside the jungle you are more likely to notice the snarl of climbers and creepers round the trees' boles, the flowering bromeliads and epiphytes in every bough's crook, and the fantastic silk-cotton tree trunks thirty or forty feet across, trunks buttressed in flanges of wood whose curves can make three high walls of a room—a shady, loamy-aired room where you would gladly live, or die. Butterflies, iridescent blue, striped, or clear-winged, thread the jungle paths at eye level. And at your feet is a swath of ants bearing triangular bits of green leaf. The ants with their leaves look like a wide fleet of sail-

ing dinghies—but they don't quit. In either direction they wobble over the jungle floor as far as the eye can see. I followed them off the path as far as I dared, and never saw an end to ants or to those luffing chips of green they bore.

(Annie Dillard, "In the Jungle")

### (3) Exemplification

**Exemplification** paragraphs use specific illustrations to clarify a general statement. Some exemplification paragraphs, like the following, use several examples to support the topic sentence (others may develop a single extended example).

Illiterates cannot travel freely. When they attempt to do so, they encounter risks that few of us can dream of. They cannot read traffic signs and, while they often learn to recognize and to decipher symbols, they cannot manage street names which they haven't seen before. The same is true for bus and subway stops. While ingenuity can sometimes help a man or a woman to discern directions from familiar landmarks, buildings, cemeteries, churches, and the like, most illiterates are virtually immobilized. They seldom wander past the streets and neighborhoods they know. Geographical paralysis becomes a bitter metaphor for their entire existence. They are immobilized in almost every sense we can imagine. They can't move up. They can't move out. They cannot see beyond. Illiterates may take an oral test for drivers' permits in most sections of America. It is a questionable concession. Where will they go? How will they get there? How will they get home? Could it be that some of us might like it better if they stayed where they belong?

(Jonathan Kozol, *Illiterate America*)

### (4) Process

**Process** paragraphs describe how something works, presenting a series of steps in chronological order. The topic sentence identifies the process, and the rest of the paragraph presents the steps involved.

Members of the court have disclosed, however, the general way the conference is conducted. It begins at ten A.M. and usually runs on until later afternoon. At the start each justice, when he enters the room, shakes hands with all others there (thirty-six handshakes altogether). The custom, dating back generations, is evidently designed to begin the meeting at a friendly level, no matter how heated the intellectual differences may be. The conference takes up, first, the applications for review—a few appeals, many more petitions for cer- tiorari. Those on the Appellate Docket, the regular paid cases, are considered first, then the pauper's applications on the Miscella- neous Docket. (If any of these are granted, they are then transferred to the Appellate Docket.) After this the justices consider, and vote on, all the cases argued during the preceding Monday through Thursday. These are tentative votes, which may be and quite often are changed as the opinion is written and the problem thought through more deeply. There may be further discussion at later con- ferences before the opinion is handed down.

(Anthony Lewis, *Gideon's Trumpet*)

### Instructions

When a process paragraph presents instructions to enable readers to actually perform the process, it is written in the present tense and in the <u>imperative mood</u>: "*Remove* the cover . . . and *check* the valve."

See
18c

## (5) Cause and Effect

**Cause-and-effect** paragraphs explore why events occur and what happens as a result of them.

The main reason that a young baby sucks his thumb seems to be that he hasn't had enough sucking at the breast or bottle to sat- isfy his sucking needs. Dr. David Levy pointed out that babies who are fed every 3 hours don't suck their thumbs as much as babies fed every 4 hours, and that babies who have cut down on nursing time from 20 minutes to 10 minutes . . . are more likely to suck their thumbs than babies who still have to work for 20 minutes. Dr. Levy fed a litter of puppies with a medicine dropper so that they had no chance to suck during their feedings. They acted just the same as babies who don't get enough chance to suck at feeding time. They sucked their own and each other's paws and skin so hard that the fur came off.

(Benjamin Spock, *Baby and Child Care*)

## (6) Comparison and Contrast

**Comparison-and-contrast** paragraphs examine the similarities and differences between two subjects. Comparison emphasizes similarities, whereas contrast emphasizes differences.

Comparison and contrast can be organized in one of two ways. One strategy is to compare the subjects **point by point:** the paragraph alternates points about one subject with comparable points about the other subject.

There are two Americas. One is the America of Lincoln and Adlai Stevenson; the other is the America of Teddy Roosevelt and the modern superpatriots. One is generous and humane, the other narrowly egotistical; one is self-critical, the other self-righteous; one is sensible, the other romantic; one is good-humored, the other solemn; one is inquiring, the other pontificating; one is moderate, the other filled with passionate intensity; one is judicious and the other arrogant in the use of great power.

(J. William Fulbright, *The Arrogance of Power*)

Other paragraphs, **subject-by-subject** comparisons, treat one subject completely and then move on to the other subject. In the following paragraph, notice how the writer shifts from one subject to the other with the transitional word *however.*

First, it is important to note that men and women regard conversation quite differently. For women it is a passion, a sport, an activity even more important to life than eating because it doesn't involve weight gain. The first sign of closeness among women is when they find themselves engaging in endless, secretless rounds of conversation with one another. And as soon as a woman begins to relax and feel comfortable in a relationship with a man, she tries to have that type of conversation with him as well. However, the first sign that a man is feeling close to a woman is when he admits that he'd rather she please quiet down so he can hear the TV. A man who feels truly intimate with a woman often reserves for her and her alone the precious gift of one-word answers. Everyone knows that the surest way to spot a successful long-term relationship is to look around a restaurant for the table where no one is talking. Ah . . . now *that's* real love.

(Merrill Markoe, "Men, Women, and Conversation")

An **analogy** is a special kind of comparison that explains an unfamiliar concept or object by likening it to a familiar one. Here an author uses the behavior of people to explain the behavior of ants.

Ants are so much like human beings as to be an embarrassment. They farm fungi, raise aphids as livestock, launch armies into wars, use chemical sprays to alarm and confuse enemies, capture slaves. The families of weaver ants engage in child labor, holding their larvae like shuttles to spin out the thread that sews the leaves together for their fungus gardens. They exchange information ceaselessly. They do everything but watch television.

(Lewis Thomas, "On Societies as Organisms")

## (7) Division and Classification

**Division** paragraphs take a single item and break it into its components.

The blood can be divided into four distinct components: plasma, red cells, white cells, and platelets. Plasma is 90 percent water and holds a great number of substances in suspension. It contains proteins, sugars, fat, and inorganic salts. Plasma also contains urea and other by-products from the breaking down of proteins, hormones, enzymes, and dissolved gases. In addition, plasma contains the red blood cells that give it color, the white cells, and the platelets. The red cells are most numerous; they get oxygen from the lungs and release it in the tissues. The less numerous white cells are part of the body's defense against invading organisms. The platelets, which occur in almost the same number as white cells, are responsible for clotting.

(Student Writer)

**Classification** paragraphs take many separate items and group them into categories according to qualities or characteristics they share.

Charles Babbage, an English mathematician, reflecting in 1830 on what he saw as the decline of science at the time, distinguished among three major kinds of scientific fraud. He called the first "forging," by which he meant complete fabrication—the recording of observations that were never made. The second category he called "trimming"; this consists of manipulating the data to make them look better, or, as Babbage wrote, "in clipping of little bits here and there from those observations which differ most in *excess* from the mean and in sticking them on to those which are too small." His third category was data selection, which he called "cooking"—the choosing of those data that fitted the researcher's hypothesis and the discarding of those that did not. To this day, the serious discussion of scientific fraud has not improved on Babbage's typology.

(Morton Hunt, *New York Times Magazine*)

## (8) Definition

**Definition** paragraphs develop the formal definition with other patterns, defining *happiness,* for instance, by telling a story (narration), or defining a diesel engine by telling how it works (process).

The following paragraph begins with a straightforward definition of *gadget* and then cites an example.

A gadget is nearly always novel in design or concept and it often has no proper name. For example, the semaphore which signals the arrival of the mail in our rural mailbox certainly has no proper name. It is a contrivance consisting of a piece of shingle. Call it what you like, it saves us frequent frustrating trips to the mailbox in winter when you have to dress up and wade through snow to get there. That's a gadget!

*(Smithsonian)*

---

**✓checklist Developing paragraphs**

✓ **Narration**  Do you present enough explanation to enable readers to understand the events you discuss? Do you support your main idea with descriptive details?

✓ **Description**  Do you supply enough detail about what things look like, sound like, smell like, taste like, and feel like? Will your readers be able to visualize the person, object, or setting that your paragraph describes?

✓ **Exemplification**  Do you present enough individual examples to support your paragraph's main idea? If you use a single extended example, is it developed in enough detail to enable readers to understand how it supports the paragraph's main idea?

✓ **Process**  Do you present enough steps to enable readers to understand how the process is performed? Is the sequence of steps clear? If you are writing instructions, do you include enough information—including reminders and warnings—to enable readers to perform the process?

✓ **Cause and Effect**  Do you identify enough causes (subtle as well as obvious, minor as well as major) to enable readers to understand why something occurred? Do you identify enough effects to show the significance of the causes and the impact they had?

✓ **Comparison and Contrast**  Do you supply a sufficient number of details to illustrate and characterize each of the subjects in the comparison? Do you present a similar number of details for each subject? Do you discuss the same or similar details for each subject?

✓ **Division and Classification**  Do you present enough information to enable readers to identify each category and distinguish one from another?

✓ **Definition**  Do you present enough support (examples, analogies, descriptive details, and so on) to enable readers to understand the term you are defining and to distinguish it from others in its class?

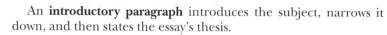

## 3e  Writing Introductory and Concluding Paragraphs

Writer's
Resource
CD-ROM

### (1) Introductory Paragraphs

An **introductory paragraph** introduces the subject, narrows it down, and then states the essay's thesis.

> Christine was just a girl in one of my classes. I never knew much about her except that she was strange. She didn't talk much. Her hair was dyed black and purple, and she wore heavy black boots and a black turtleneck sweater, even in the summer. She was attractive—in spite of the ring she wore through her left eyebrow—but she never seemed to care what the rest of us thought about her. Like the rest of my classmates, I didn't really want to get close to her. It was only when we were assigned to do our chemistry project together that I began to understand why Christine dressed the way she did.
>
> (Student Writer)

To arouse an audience's interest, writers may vary this direct approach by using one of the following introductory strategies.

---

**STRATEGIES FOR EFFECTIVE INTRODUCTIONS**

**Quotation or Series of Quotations**

When Mary Cassatt's father was told of her decision to become a painter, he said: "I would rather see you dead." When Edgar Degas saw a show of Cassatt's etchings, his response was: "I am not willing to admit that a woman can draw that well." When she returned to Philadelphia after twenty-eight years abroad, having achieved renown as an Impressionist painter and the esteem of Degas, Huysmans, Pissarro, and Berthe Morisot, the *Philadelphia Ledger* reported: "Mary Cassatt, sister of Mr. Cassatt, president of the Pennsylvania Railroad, returned from Europe yesterday. She has been studying painting in France and owns the smallest Pekingese dog in the world." (Mary Gordon, "Mary Cassatt")

**Question or Series of Questions**

Of all the disputes agitating the American campus, the one that seems to me especially significant is that over "the canon." What should be taught in the humanities and social sciences, especially in introductory courses? What is the place of the

---

classics? How shall we respond to those professors who attack "Eurocentrism" and advocate "multiculturalism"? This is not the sort of tedious quarrel that now and then flutters through the academy; it involves matters of public urgency. I propose to see this dispute, at first, through a narrow, even sectarian lens, with the hope that you will come to accept my reasons for doing so. (Irving Howe, "The Value of the Canon")

**Definition**

Moles are collections of cells that can appear on any part of the body. With occasional exceptions, moles are absent at birth. They first appear in the early years of life, between ages two and six. Frequently, moles appear at puberty. New moles, however, can continue to appear throughout life. During pregnancy, new moles may appear and old ones darken. There are three major designations of moles, each with its own unique distinguishing characteristics. (Student Writer)

**Unusual Comparison**

Once a long time ago, people had special little boxes called refrigerators in which milk, meat, and eggs could be kept cool. The grandchildren of these simple devices are large enough to store whole cows, and they reach temperatures comparable to those at the South Pole. Their operating costs increase each year, and they are so complicated that few home handymen attempt to repair them on their own. Why has this change in size and complexity occurred in America? It has not taken place in many areas of the technologically advanced world (the average West German refrigerator is about a yard high and less than a yard wide, yet refrigeration technology in Germany is quite advanced). Do we really need (or even want) all that space and cold? (Appletree Rodden, "Why Smaller Refrigerators Can Preserve the Human Race")

**Controversial Statement**

Something had to replace the threat of communism, and at last a workable substitute is at hand. "Multiculturalism," as the new menace is known, has been denounced in the media recently as the new McCarthyism, the new fundamentalism, even the new totalitarianism—take your choice. According to its critics, who include a flock of tenured conservative scholars, multiculturalism aims to toss out what it sees as the Eurocentric bias in education and replace Plato with Ntozake Shange and traditional math with the Yoruba number system. And that's just the beginning. The Jacobins of the multiculturalist

*continued on the following page*

*continued from the previous page*

movement, who are described derisively as P.C., or politically correct, are said to have launched a campus reign of terror against those who slip and innocently say "freshman" instead of "freshperson," "Indian" instead of "Native American" or, may the Goddess forgive them, "disabled" instead of "differently abled." (Barbara Ehrenreich, "Teach Diversity—with a Smile")

**Introductory paragraphs**

Avoid introductions that simply announce your subject ("In my paper, I will talk about Lady Macbeth") or that undercut your credibility ("I don't know much about alternative energy sources, but I would like to present my opinion about the subject").

**✓checklist Revising introductions**

✓ Does your introduction include your essay's thesis statement?

✓ Does it lead naturally into the body of your essay?

✓ Does it arouse your readers' interest?

✓ Does it avoid statements that simply announce your subject or that undercut your credibility?

## (2) Concluding Paragraphs

A **concluding paragraph** typically begins with specifics—reviewing the essay's main points, for example—and then moves to more general statements. Whenever possible, it should end with a sentence readers will remember.

As an Arab-American, I feel I have the best of two worlds. I'm proud to be part of the melting pot, proud to contribute to the tremendous diversity of cultures, customs and traditions that makes this country unique. But Arab-bashing—public acceptance of hatred and bigotry—is something no American can be proud of.

(Ellen Mansoor Collier, "I Am Not a Terrorist")

Writers may also use one of the following concluding strategies.

## STRATEGIES FOR EFFECTIVE CONCLUSIONS

**Prediction**

Looking ahead, [we see that] prospects may not be quite as dismal as they seem. As a matter of fact, we are not doing so badly. It is something of a miracle that creatures who evolved as nomads in an intimate, small-band, wide-open-spaces context manage to get along at all as villagers or surrounded by strangers in cubicle apartments. Considering that our genius as a species is adaptability, we may yet learn to live closer and closer to one another, if not in utter peace, then far more peacefully than we do today. (John Pheiffer, "Seeking Peace, Making War")

**Opinion**

A piece of writing is never finished. It is delivered to a deadline, torn out of the typewriter on demand, sent off with a sense of accomplishment and shame and pride and frustration. If only there were a couple more days, time for just another run at it, perhaps then. . . . (Donald Murray, "The Maker's Eye: Revising Your Own Manuscripts")

**Quotation**

When we let freedom ring, when we let it ring from every village and every hamlet, from every state and every city, we will be able to speed up that day when all of God's children, black men and white men, Jews and Gentiles, Protestants and Catholics, will be able to join hands and sing in the words of the old Negro spiritual, "Free at last! Free at last! Thank God almighty, we are free at last!" (Martin Luther King, Jr., "I Have a Dream")

### Concluding paragraphs

Avoid concluding paragraphs that introduce new points or go off in new directions. Because it is your last word, a weak or uninteresting conclusion detracts from an otherwise strong essay. Do not just repeat your introduction in different words, and do not apologize or in any way cast doubt on your concluding points ("I may not be an expert" or "At least this is my opinion").

**✓checklist** **Revising conclusions**

✓ Does your conclusion sum up your essay, perhaps by reviewing the essay's main points?

✓ Does it end memorably?

✓ Does it do more than repeat the introduction?

✓ Does it avoid apologies?

# PART 2

# Critical Thinking and Argumentation

**4   Thinking Critically   83**
    **4a**   Distinguishing Fact from Opinion   83
    **4b**   Evaluating Supporting Evidence   84
    **4c**   Detecting Bias   85
    **4d**   Understanding Inductive and Deductive Reasoning   86
    **4e**   Recognizing Logical Fallacies   88

**5   Writing Argumentative Essays   91**
    **5a**   Planning an Argumentative Essay   91
    **5b**   Using Evidence and Establishing Credibility   93
    **5c**   Organizing an Argumentative Essay   94
    **5d**   Writing an Argumentative Essay   96

# PART 2

## ? Frequently Asked Questions

**Chapter 4  Thinking Critically   83**
- What is critical thinking? 83
- How do I tell the difference between a fact and an opinion? 83
- How do I detect bias in an argument? 85
- What is an inference? 87
- What is a logical fallacy? 88
- What is a non sequitur? 88
- How do I recognize post hoc reasoning? 88

**Chapter 5  Writing Argumentative Essays   91**
- How do I know if a topic is suitable for argument? 91
- What can I do to make sure I have an argumentative thesis? 92
- How should I deal with opposing arguments? 92
- How can I make sure I am being fair? 94
- How should I organize my argumentative essay? 95

| **URLs** | *Visit the following sites for answers to more FAQs* |
|---|---|

**Critical Thinking (UMSL)**
*http://www.umsl.edu/~klein/Critical_Thinking.html*

**Critical Thinking (Humboldt)**
*http://www.humboldt.edu/~act/*

**Logic in Argumentation (Purdue)**
*http://owl.english.purdue.edu/handouts/general/gl_argpapers.html*

**Logical Fallacies (or Errors in Thinking)**
*http://www.intrepidsoftware.com/fallacy/toc.htm*

**Avoiding Common Errors in Logic and Reasoning (Princeton U.)**
*http://web.princeton.edu/sites/writing//Handouts/logic&reason.pdf*

**Writing an Argument Paper (Muskingum College)**
*http://muskingum.edu/~cal/database/writing.html#Argument*

Chapter **4**

# Thinking Critically

As you read and write essays, you should think very carefully about the ideas they present. This is especially true in **argumentative essays**—those that take a stand on a debatable topic. Although some writers of argumentative essays try their best to be fair and balanced, others are less scrupulous. They attempt to convince readers by using emotionally charged language, by emphasizing certain facts over others, and by intentionally using flawed logic. For this reason, it is particularly important that you approach arguments *critically:* that you learn to distinguish facts from opinions, that you evaluate supporting evidence, that you learn to detect bias, and that you understand some basic principles of inductive and deductive reasoning.

See Ch. 5

## 4a Distinguishing Fact from Opinion

A **fact** is a verifiable statement that something is true or that something occurred. An **opinion** is a conclusion or belief that can never be substantiated beyond any doubt and is, therefore, debatable.

Fact: Measles is a potentially deadly disease.

Opinion: All children should be vaccinated against measles.

An opinion may be *supported* or *unsupported*.

Unsupported Opinion: All children in Pennsylvania should be vaccinated against measles.

Supported Opinion: Despite the fact that an effective measles vaccine is widely available, several unvaccinated Pennsylvania children have died of measles each year since 1992. States that have instituted vaccination programs have had no deaths in the same time period. For this reason, all children in Pennsylvania should be vaccinated against measles.

As these examples show, supported opinion is more convincing than unsupported opinion. Remember, however, that supporting evidence can only make a statement more convincing; it cannot turn an opinion into a fact.

## Kinds of supporting evidence

### Examples

The American Civil Liberties Union is an organization that has been unfairly characterized as left wing. It is true that it has opposed prayer in the public schools, defended conscientious objectors, and challenged police methods of conducting questioning and searches of suspects. However, it has also backed the anti-abortion group Operation Rescue in a police brutality suit and presented a legal brief in support of a Republican politician accused of violating an ethics law.

### Statistics

A recent National Institute of Mental Health study concludes that mentally ill people account for more than 30 percent of the homeless population (27). Because so many homeless people have psychiatric disabilities, the federal government should seriously consider expanding the state mental hospital system.

### Expert Testimony

Clearly no young soldier ever really escapes the emotional consequences of war. As William Manchester, noted historian and World War II combat veteran, observes in his essay "Okinawa: The Bloodiest Battle of All," "the invisible wounds remain" (72).

## 4b  Evaluating Supporting Evidence

See
5b1

The more reliable the supporting evidence—examples, statistics, or expert testimony—the more willing readers will be to accept a statement. No matter what kind of evidence writers use, however, it must be *accurate, sufficient, representative,* and *relevant.*

Evidence is likely to be **accurate** if it comes from a trustworthy source. Such a source quotes *exactly* and does not present remarks out of context. It also presents examples, statistics, and expert testimony fairly, drawing them from other reliable sources.

For evidence to be **sufficient,** a writer must present an adequate amount of evidence. It is not enough, for instance, for a writer to cite just one example in an attempt to demonstrate that most poor women receive adequate prenatal care. Similarly, the opinions of a single expert, no matter how reputable, are not enough to support this idea.

Detecting Bias

Writers should also select evidence that is **representative** of a fair range of sources and viewpoints; they should not choose evidence that supports their arguments and ignore evidence that does not. In other words, they should not permit their biases to govern their choice of evidence. For example, a writer who is arguing that Asian immigrants have had great success in achieving professional status in the United States must draw from a range of Asian immigrant groups—Vietnamese, Chinese, Japanese, Indian, and Korean, for example—not just one.

Finally, evidence must be **relevant**—that is, it must apply to the case being discussed. For example, you cannot support the position that the United States should send medical aid to developing nations by citing examples that apply just to our own nation's health-care system.

## 4c Detecting Bias

A **bias** is a tendency to think a certain way. Writers are biased when they base conclusions on preconceived ideas rather than on evidence. As a result, they see what they want to see and always select evidence that supports one conclusion over another.

### Detecting bias

Look for the following kinds of bias when you evaluate an argument.

- *A writer's stated beliefs* In a recent article, a writer declared herself to be a strong opponent of childhood vaccinations. This statement should alert you to the fact that the writer probably will likely *not* present a balanced view of the subject.
- *Sexist or racist statements* A writer who assumes all engineers are male or all nurses are female reflects a clear bias. A researcher who assumes certain racial or ethnic groups are intellectually superior to others is also presenting a biased view.
- *Slanted language* **Slanted language** is language that contains value judgments. Some writers use slanted language to influence readers' reactions. For example, a newspaper article that states "The politician gave an impassioned speech" gives one impression; the statement "The politician delivered a *diatribe*" gives another.

*continued on the following page*

*continued from the previous page*

- *Tone* The **tone** of a piece of writing indicates a writer's attitude toward readers or toward his or her subject. An angry or excessively apologetic tone should alert you to the possibility that the writer is overstating or understating his or her case.
- *Choice of evidence* As you read, try to evaluate a writer's use of supporting evidence. Frequently, the examples, statistics, or experts included in a piece of writing reveal the writer's bias. For example, a writer may include only examples that support a point and leave out examples that may contradict it.

# 4d  Understanding Inductive and Deductive Reasoning

Arguments must be based on **logical reasoning.** The two most common methods of reasoning, *induction* and *deduction,* often occur together in a single argument.

## (1) Using Inductive Reasoning

**Inductive reasoning** moves from specific facts, observations, or experiences to a general conclusion. Writers use inductive reasoning when they address a skeptical audience that requires a lot of evidence before it will accept a conclusion. You can see how inductive reasoning operates by studying the following list of statements, which focuses on the relationship between SAT scores and admissions at one liberal arts college.

- The SAT is an admission requirement for all applicants.
- High school grades and rank in class are also examined.
- Nonacademic factors such as sports, activities, and interests are taken into account as well.
- Special attention is given to the applications of athletes, minorities, and children of alumni.
- Fewer than 52 percent of applicants for a recent class with SAT verbal scores between 600 and 700 were accepted.
- Fewer than 39 percent of applicants with similar math scores were accepted.

## Inductive and Deductive Reasoning

- Approximately 18 percent of applicants with SAT verbal scores between 450 and 520 and about 19 percent of applicants with similar SAT math scores were admitted.

After reading the statements above, you can use inductive reasoning to conclude that although important, SAT scores are not the single factor that determines whether a student is admitted.

### Inductive reasoning

No matter how much evidence is presented, an inductive conclusion is never certain, only probable. An inductive conclusion is an **inference**, a statement about the unknown based on what is known. The more observations you make, the narrower the gap between your observations and your conclusion.

**?**

### (2) Using Deductive Reasoning

**Deductive reasoning** moves from a generalization believed to be true or self-evident to a more specific conclusion. Writers use deductive reasoning when they address an audience that is more likely to be influenced by logic than by evidence. The process of deduction has traditionally been illustrated with a **syllogism,** a three-part set of statements or propositions that includes a **major premise,** a **minor premise,** and a **conclusion.**

Major Premise: All books from that store are new.
Minor Premise: These books are from that store.
Conclusion: Therefore, these books are new.

The major premise of a syllogism makes a general statement that the writer believes to be true. The minor premise presents a specific example of the belief that is stated in the major premise. If the reasoning is sound, the conclusion should follow from these two premises. (Note that no terms are introduced in the conclusion that have not already appeared in the major and minor premises.) The strength of a deductive argument is that if readers accept the premises, they usually grant the conclusion.

# 4e Recognizing Logical Fallacies

**?** **Fallacies** are flawed arguments. A writer who inadvertently uses logical fallacies is not thinking clearly or logically; a writer who intentionally uses them is trying to deceive readers. Learn to recognize fallacies—to challenge them when you read and to avoid them when you write.

---

## GUIDE TO LOGICAL FALLACIES

- **Hasty Generalization** Drawing a conclusion based on too little evidence

  The person I voted for is not doing a good job in Congress. Therefore, voting is a waste of time. (One disappointing experience does not warrant the statement that you will never vote again.)

- **Sweeping Generalization** Making a generalization that cannot be supported, no matter how much evidence is supplied

  Everyone should exercise. (Some people, for example those with severe heart conditions, might not benefit from exercise.)

- **Equivocation** Shifting the meaning of a key word during an argument

  It is not in the public interest for the public to lose interest. (Although clever, the shift in the meaning of the term *public interest* clouds the issue.)

**?**
- **Non Sequitur (Does Not Follow)** Arriving at a conclusion that does not follow logically from what comes before

  Kim Williams is a good lawyer, so she will make a good senator. (Just because Kim Williams is a good lawyer, it does not follow that she will make a good senator.)

- **Either/Or Fallacy** Treating a complex issue as if it has only two sides

  Either we institute universal health care, or the health of all people will decline. (Good health does not necessarily depend on universal health care.)

**?**
- **Post Hoc** Establishing an unjustified link between cause and effect

  The United States sold wheat to Russia. This must have caused the price of wheat to rise. (Other factors, unrelated to the sale, could have caused the price to rise.)

---

- **Begging the Question** (circular reasoning) Stating a debatable premise as if it were true

  Stem-cell research should be banned. How can anything good come from something so inherently evil? (Where is the evidence that stem-cell research is "inherently evil"?)

- **False Analogy** Assuming that because things are similar in some ways, they are similar in other ways

  When forced to live in crowded conditions, people act like rats. They turn on each other and act violently. (Both people and rats might dislike living in crowded conditions, but unlike rats, most people do not necessarily resort to violence in this situation.)

- **Red Herring** Changing the subject to distract readers from the issue

  Our company may charge high prices, but we give a lot to charity each year. (What does charging high prices have to do with giving to charity?)

- **Argument to Ignorance** Saying that something is true because it cannot be proved false, or vice versa

  How can you tell me to send my child to a school where there is a child who has AIDS? After all, doctors can't say for sure that my child won't catch AIDS, can they? (Just because a doctor cannot prove the speaker's claim to be false, it does not follow that the claim is true.)

- **Bandwagon** Trying to establish that something is true because everyone believes it is true

  Everyone knows that eating candy makes a child hyperactive. (Where is the evidence to support this claim?)

- **Argument to the Person** (*Ad Hominem*) Attacking the person and not the issue

  Of course the congressman supports increases in the defense budget. He worked for a defense contractor before he was elected to Congress. (By attacking his opponent, the speaker attempts to avoid the issue.)

- **Argument to the People** Appealing to people's prejudices

  Because foreigners are attempting to overrun our shores, we should cut back on immigration. (By exploiting prejudice, the speaker attempts to avoid the issue.)

> **✓ checklist Thinking critically**
>
> ✓ What point is the writer making? What is stated? What is suggested?
>
> ✓ Do you agree with the writer's ideas?
>
> ✓ Are the writer's points supported primarily by fact or by opinion? Does the writer present opinion as fact?
>
> ✓ Does the writer offer supporting evidence for his or her statements?
>
> ✓ What kind of evidence is provided? How convincing is it?
>
> ✓ Is the evidence accurate? sufficient? representative? relevant?
>
> ✓ Does the writer display any bias? If so, is the bias revealed through language, tone, or choice of evidence?
>
> ✓ Does the writer present a balanced picture of the issue?
>
> ✓ Are any alternative viewpoints overlooked?
>
> ✓ Does the writer omit pertinent examples?
>
> ✓ Does the writer use valid reasoning?
>
> ✓ Does the writer use logical fallacies?
>
> ✓ Does the writer oversimplify complex ideas?
>
> ✓ Does the writer make reasonable inferences?
>
> ✓ Does the writer represent the ideas of others accurately? fairly?
>
> ✓ Does the writer distort the ideas of others or present them out of context?

# Chapter 5

# Writing Argumentative Essays

For most people, the true test of their critical thinking skills comes when they write an **argument,** which takes a position on an issue and uses logic and evidence to convince readers. The goal of an argument is to change the way readers think—and, sometimes, to cause them to take action.

## 5a    Planning an Argumentative Essay

Writer's
Resource
CD-ROM

### (1) Choosing a Debatable Topic

Because an argumentative essay attempts to change the way people think, it must focus on a **debatable topic,** one about which reasonable people disagree. Factual statements—those about which people do not disagree—are therefore not suitable for argument.

Fact:  Many countries hold political prisoners.

Debatable Topic:  The United States should not trade with countries that hold political prisoners.

Some topics—such as "The Need for Gun Control" or "The Effectiveness of the Death Penalty"—have been written about so much that you will probably not be able to say anything interesting about them. Such topics usually inspire uninteresting essays that add little or nothing to a reader's understanding of an issue. Instead of relying on a tired topic, choose one that enables you to contribute something to the debate.

Be sure your topic is narrow enough so that you can write about it within the page limit you have been given. Remember, though, that you will have to develop your own ideas and present supporting evidence while also pointing out the strengths and weaknesses of opposing arguments. If your topic is too broad, you will not be able to cover it in enough detail.

### (2) Developing an Argumentative Thesis

After you have chosen a topic, your next step is to state your position in an **argumentative thesis,** one that takes a strong stand.

See
1c2

One way to make sure your **thesis statement** actually does take a stand is to formulate an **antithesis,** a statement that takes an arguable position opposite from yours.

Thesis: Term limits would improve government by bringing fresh faces into office every few years.

Antithesis: Term limits would harm government because elected officials would always be inexperienced.

**Note:** Be careful to use precise language in your thesis statement, avoiding vague and judgmental words such as *wrong, bad, good, right,* and *immoral.*

**?**

## Developing an argumentative thesis

You can determine whether or not your thesis is argumentative by asking the following questions:

- Is your thesis one with which reasonable people might disagree?
- Does your thesis attempt to change people's ideas or actions?
- Can you think of arguments against your thesis?
- Can your thesis be supported by evidence?
- Does your thesis statement make clear to readers what position you are taking?

## (3) Considering Your Audience

See
1b2

As you plan your essay, keep a specific **audience** in mind. Are your readers unbiased observers or people deeply concerned about the issue? Can they be cast in a specific role—concerned parents, victims of discrimination, irate consumers—or are they so diverse that they cannot be categorized? Are they likely to be sympathetic or hostile to your position? Although you may never be able to convince hostile readers that your conclusion is valid, you may be able to get these readers to acknowledge the strength of your argument.

**?** ## (4) Refuting Opposing Arguments

As you develop your argument, you must also **refute**—that is, disprove—opposing arguments by showing that opposing views are

92

untrue, unfair, illogical, unimportant, or irrelevant. In the following paragraph, a student refutes an argument against her position that Sea World should not keep whales in captivity.

Of course some will say Sea World only wants to capture a few whales, as George Will points out in his commentary in *Newsweek*. However, Will downplays the fact that Sea World wants to capture a hundred whales, not just "a few." And after releasing ninety whales, Sea World intends to keep ten for "further work." At hearings in Seattle last week, several noted marine biologists went on record as condemning Sea World's research program.

**Note:** When you acknowledge an opposing view, do not distort or oversimplify it. This tactic, called creating a **straw man,** can seriously undermine your credibility.

> **http://kirsznermandell.heinle.com**
>
> ### Refuting opposing arguments
> Construct a table with your computer, making two columns. Label the first column *Arguments Against* and the second column *Refutations*. In the first column, list all the arguments you can think of against your position. In the second column, list your refutations of these arguments. When you are finished, cross out the weakest opposing arguments and consider the ones that are left. In your essay, concede the strength of any particularly compelling arguments against your position; then, use arguments of your own to refute them.

## 5b   Using Evidence and Establishing Credibility

### (1) Using Evidence

Most arguments are built on **assertions**—claims you make about a debatable topic—backed by **evidence**—supporting information, in the form of examples, statistics, or expert opinion. Only statements that are *self-evident* ("All human beings are mortal"), true by *definition* (2 + 2 = 4), or *factual* ("The Atlantic Ocean separates England and the United States") need no proof. All other kinds of assertions require supporting evidence.

**Note:** If you use words or ideas that are not your own, be sure to use proper <u>documentation</u>.

See
Chs.
10–12

### (2) Establishing Credibility and Being Fair

In order to convince readers, you must prove you have **credibility**—in other words, that you are someone they should listen to. Readers will also judge your argument on the basis of its **fairness.**

> **✓checklist** Establishing credibility
>
> *FIND COMMON GROUND*
> ✓ Identify the various sides of the issue.
> ✓ Identify the points on which you and your readers agree.
> ✓ Work these areas of agreement into your argument.
>
> *DEMONSTRATE KNOWLEDGE*
> ✓ Include relevant personal experiences.
> ✓ Include relevant special knowledge of your subject.
> ✓ Include the results of any relevant research you have done.
>
> *MAINTAIN A REASONABLE TONE*
> ✓ Avoid talking down to or insulting your readers.
> ✓ Use moderate language, and qualify your statements.

**?** **✓checklist** Being fair

> ✓ Do not distort evidence.
> ✓ Do not misrepresent opponents' views by exaggerating them and then attacking this extreme position.
> ✓ Do not change the meaning of a statement by focusing on certain words and ignoring others.
> ✓ Do not select only information that supports your case and ignore information that does not.
> ✓ Do not use inflammatory language calculated to appeal to the emotions or prejudices of readers.

Finally, even if readers see you as credible and fair, they will not accept your argument unless it is logical. Revise carefully to be sure you have avoided <u>logical fallacies</u>.

See
4d

Writer's
Resource
CD-ROM

## 5c  Organizing an Argumentative Essay

In its simplest form, an argument consists of a thesis statement and supporting evidence. However, argumentative essays frequently contain additional elements calculated to win audience approval and to overcome potential opposition.

## ELEMENTS OF AN ARGUMENTATIVE ESSAY

### Introduction

The **introduction** of your argumentative essay orients your readers to your subject. Here you can show how your subject concerns your audience, establish common ground with your readers, or explain how your subject has been misunderstood.

See
3e1

### Background

In this section, you may present a brief summary of past events, an overview of others' opinions on the issue, definitions of key terms, or a review of basic facts.

### Thesis Statement

Your **thesis statement** can appear anywhere in your argumentative essay. In many cases, you state your thesis in your introduction. However, in highly controversial arguments—those to which your audience might react negatively—you may postpone stating your thesis until later in your essay, when you have prepared readers to accept it.

See
1c3

### Arguments in Support of Your Thesis

Here you present your points and the evidence to support them. Most often, you begin with your weakest argument and work up to your strongest. If all your arguments are equally strong, you might begin with ideas with which your readers are familiar (and therefore likely to accept) and then move on to relatively unfamiliar ideas.

### Refutation of Opposing Arguments

If the opposing arguments are relatively weak, refute them after you have made your case. However, if the opposing arguments are strong, concede their strengths and then discuss their limitations before you present your own points.

### Conclusion

Most often, the **conclusion** restates the major arguments in support of your thesis. Your conclusion can also summarize key points, restate your thesis, reinforce the weaknesses of opposing arguments, or underscore the logic of your position. Many writers like to end their arguments with a strong last line, such as a quotation or a statement that sums up the argument.

See
3e2

### Using transitions with argumentative essays

Argumentative essays should include transitional words and phrases to indicate which paragraphs are arguments in support of the thesis (*because, for example, given*); which are refutations of opposing positions (*although, certainly, granted, of course*); and which are conclusions (*in conclusion, therefore, in summary*). These transitional words and phrases send important signals that help readers follow the progression of the argument.

Writer's
Resource
CD-ROM

## 5d Writing an Argumentative Essay

The following essay includes many of the elements discussed above. The student writer was asked to write an argumentative essay, drawing her supporting evidence from her own knowledge of the subject as well as from other sources.

# Writing an Argumentative Essay

Samantha Masterton

Professor Wade

English 102

15 March 2002

The Returning Student:

Older Is Definitely Better

After graduating from high school, young people must decide **Introduction** what they want to do with the rest of their lives. Many graduates (often without much thought) decide to continue their education uninterrupted, and they go on to college. This group of teenagers makes up what many see as the typical first-year college student. Recently, however, this stereotype has been challenged by an influx of older students into American colleges and universities. Not only do these students make a valuable contribution to the schools they attend, but they also present an alternative to young people who go to college simply because it is the thing to do. A few years **Thesis** off between high school and college can give many—perhaps **statement** most—students the life experience they need to appreciate the value of higher education.

The college experience of an eighteen-year-old is quite different **Background** from that of an older student. The typical teenager is often concerned with things other than cracking books—going to parties, dating, and testing personal limits, for example. Although the maturation process from teenager to adult is something we must all go through, college is not necessarily the appropriate place for this to occur. My experience as an adult enrolled in a university has convinced me that many students would benefit from delaying entry into college.

Masterton 2

I almost never see older students cutting lectures or not studying. Most have saved for tuition and want to get their money's worth, just as I do. Many are also balancing the demands of home and work to attend classes, so they know how important it is to do well.

Generally, young people just out of high school have not been challenged by real-world situations that include meeting deadlines and setting priorities. Younger college students often find themselves hopelessly behind or scrambling at the last minute simply because they have not learned how to budget their time. Although success in college depends on the ability to set realistic goals and organize time and materials, college itself does little to help students develop these skills. On the contrary, the workplace—where reward and punishment are usually immediate and tangible—is the best place to learn such lessons. Working teaches the basics that college takes for granted: the value of punctuality and attendance, the importance of respect for superiors and colleagues, and the need for establishing priorities and meeting deadlines.

The adult student who has gained experience in the workplace has advantages over the younger student. In general, the older student enrolls in college with a definite course of study in mind. As Laura Mansnerus observes in her article "A Milieu Apart," for the older student, "college is no longer a stage of life but a place to do work" (17). For the adult student, then, college becomes an extension of work rather than a place to discover what work will be. This greater sense of purpose is not lost on college instructors. Dr. Laurin Porter, assistant professor of English at the University of Texas at Arlington, echoes the sentiments of many of

*Margin annotations:*

Argument in support of thesis

Support: examples

Argument in support of thesis

Support: expert opinion

# Writing an Argumentative Essay

Masterton 3

her colleagues when she says, "Returning older students, by and large, seem more focused, more sure of their goals, and more highly motivated."

Given their age and greater experience, older students bring more into the classroom than younger students do. Eighteen-year-olds have been driving for only a year or two, have just gotten the right to vote, and usually have not lived on their own. In contrast, the older student has generally had a variety of real-life experiences. Most have worked for several years; many have started families. Their years in the "real world" have helped them to become more focused and more responsible than they were when they graduated from high school. As a result, they are better prepared for college. Thus, they not only bring more into the classroom, but also take more out of it.

Of course, postponing college for a few years is not for everyone. There are certainly some teenagers who have a definite sense of purpose and a maturity well beyond their years, and these individuals might benefit from an early college experience so that they can get a head start on their careers. Charles Woodward, a law librarian, went to college directly after high school, and for him the experience was positive. "I was serious about learning, and I loved my subject," he said. "I felt fortunate that I knew what I wanted from college and from life." For the most part, though, students are not like Woodward; they graduate from high school without any clear sense of purpose. For this reason, it makes sense for most students to stay away from college until they are mature enough to benefit from the experience.

*Margin annotations:*

Argument in support of thesis

Support: examples

Refutation of opposing argument

Support: expert opinion

Masterton 4

**Refutation of opposing argument**

Granted, some older students do have difficulties when they return to college. Because these students have been out of school so long, they may have trouble studying and adapting to the routines of academic life. Some older students may even feel ill at ease because they are in class with students who are many years younger than they are and because they are too busy to partici-

**Support: example**

pate in extracurricular activities. As I have seen, though, these problems soon disappear. After a few weeks, older students get into the swing of things and adapt to college. They make friends, get used to studying, and even begin to participate in campus life.

**Conclusion**

All things considered, higher education is wasted on the young, who are either too immature or too unfocused to take advantage of it. Taking a few years off between high school and college would give younger students the breathing room they need to

**Support: statistics**

make the most of a college education. According to a 1991 study, 45 percent of the students enrolled in American colleges in 1987 were twenty-five years of age or older (Aslanian 57), and these

**Support: expert opinion**

numbers, according to Dr. Porter, have since grown. These older students have taken time off to serve in the military, to get a job, or to raise a family. Many have traveled, engaged in informal study, and taken the time to grow up. By the time they get to college, they have defined their goals and made a commitment to achieve them. It is clear that postponing college for a few years can result in a better educational experience for both students and teachers. As

**Quotation sums up argument**

Dr. Porter says, when the older student brings more life experience into the classroom, "everyone benefits."

Masterton 5

Works Cited

Aslanian, Carol B. "The Changing Face of American Campuses."
USA Today Magazine May 1991: 57–59.

Mansnerus, Laura. "A Milieu Apart." New York Times 4 Aug. 1991,
late ed.: A7.

Porter, Laurin. E-mail to the author. 23 Feb. 2002.

Woodward, Charles B. Personal interview. 25 Feb. 2002.

Works Cited
begins new
page

## ✓ checklist  Writing argumentative essays

✓ Is your topic debatable?
✓ Does your essay develop an argumentative thesis?
✓ Have you considered the opinions, attitudes, and values of your audience?
✓ Have you identified and refuted opposing arguments?
✓ Are your arguments logically constructed?
✓ Have you supported your assertions with evidence?
✓ Have you documented all material that is not your own?
✓ Have you established your credibility?
✓ Have you been fair?
✓ Have you avoided logical fallacies?
✓ Have you provided your readers with enough background information?
✓ Have you presented your points clearly and organized them logically?
✓ Have you written an interesting introduction and a strong conclusion?

# PART 3

## The Research Process

**6   The Research Process   105**
   **6a**   Choosing a Topic   106
   **6b**   Doing Exploratory Research and Formulating a
            Research Question   107
   **6c**   Assembling a Working Bibliography   108
   **6d**   Developing a Tentative Thesis   110
   **6e**   Doing Focused Research   110
   **6f**   Taking Notes   112
   **6g**   Fine-Tuning Your Thesis   119
   **6h**   Outlining, Drafting, and Revising   120

**7   Using and Evaluating Library Sources   126**
   **7a**   Doing Exploratory Library Research   126
   **7b**   Doing Focused Library Research   135
   **7c**   Evaluating Library Sources   141
   **7d**   Doing Research Outside the Library   144

**8   Using and Evaluating Internet Sources   147**
   **8a**   Understanding the Internet   147
   **8b**   Using the World Wide Web for Research   148
   **8c**   Using Other Internet Tools   155
   **8d**   Evaluating Internet Sources   158
   **8e**   Useful Web Sites   161

**9   Integrating Sources and Avoiding Plagiarism   164**
   **9a**   Integrating Source Material into Your Writing   164
   **9b**   Avoiding Plagiarism   169

# PART 3

## ? Frequently Asked Questions

**Chapter 6 The Research Process   105**
- How do I plan a research project?   105
- How do I keep track of my sources?   108
- What format should I use for taking notes?   114
- What is the difference between a paraphrase and a summary?   117
- When should I quote the source?   119

**Chapter 7 Using and Evaluating Library Sources   126**
- Why should I use the library's electronic resources? Why can't I just use the Internet?   132
- What online databases should I use?   140
- How do I evaluate the books and articles that I get from the library?   141
- What is the difference between a scholarly publication and a popular publication?   143

**Chapter 8 Using and Evaluating Internet Sources   147**
- What is the best way to do a keyword search?   150
- How do I choose the right search engine?   152
- How can I evaluate the information on a Web site?   158
- How do I know if I can trust an anonymous Web source?   159

**Chapter 9 Integrating Sources and Avoiding Plagiarism   164**
- How do I avoid saying "he said" or "she said" every time I use a source?   164
- What exactly is plagiarism?   169
- Is there anything I do not have to document?   170
- How can I make sure that readers will be able to tell the difference between my ideas and those of my sources?   173

**URLs**   *Visit the following sites for answers to more FAQs*

**General Research Tips/Strategies**
*http://www.jtasd.k12.pa.us/highschool/library/LibraryWebQuest*

**Researchpaper.com**
*http://www.researchpaper.com/*

**Academic Libraries—U.S. (searchable)**
*http://sunsite.berkeley.edu/Libweb/usa-acad.html*

**Plagiarism**
*http://www.indiana.edu/~wts/wts/plagiarism.html*

# Chapter 6

# The Research Process

Research is the systematic investigation of a topic outside your own knowledge and experience. However, doing research means more than just reading about other people's ideas. When you undertake a research project, you become involved in a process that requires you to **think critically**, evaluating and interpreting the ideas explored in your sources and formulating ideas of your own.

See Ch 4

Not so long ago, searching for source material meant spending long hours in the library flipping through card catalogs, examining heavy reference volumes, and hunting for books in the stacks. Technology, however, has dramatically changed the way research is conducted. The wiring of school and community libraries means that today, students and professionals engaged in research find themselves spending a great deal of time in front of a computer, particularly during the exploratory stage of the research process. Note, however, that although the way in which research materials are stored and accessed has changed, the research process itself has not. Whether you are working with **print sources** (books, journals, magazines) or **electronic resources** (online catalogs, databases, the Internet), in the library or at your home computer, you need to follow a systematic process.

See 7a4

## THE RESEARCH PROCESS

| Activity | Date Due | Date Completed |
|---|---|---|
| Choose a Topic, **6a** | | |
| Do Exploratory Research and Formulate a Research Question, **6b** | | |
| Assemble a Working Bibliography, **6c** | | |
| Develop a Tentative Thesis, **6d** | | |
| Do Focused Research and Take Notes, **6e–f** | | |
| Fine-Tune Your Thesis, **6g** | | |

*continued on the following page*

*continued from the previous page*

| Activity | Date Due | Date Completed |
|---|---|---|
| Outline Your Paper **6h1** | _____ | _____ |
| Draft Your Paper **6h2** | _____ | _____ |
| Revise Your Paper **6h3** | _____ | _____ |

## 6a   Choosing a Topic

The first step in the research process is finding a topic to write about. In many cases, your instructor will help you choose a topic, either by providing a list of suitable topics or by suggesting a general subject area—for example, a famous trial, an event that happened on the day you were born, a problem on college campuses. Even in these instances, you will still need to choose one of the topics or narrow the subject area: decide on one trial, one event, one problem.

If your instructor prefers that you select a topic on your own, you must consider a number of possible topics and weigh both their suitability for research and your interest in them. You decide on a topic for your research paper in much the same way you decide on a topic for a short essay: you read, brainstorm, talk to people, and ask questions. Specifically, you talk to friends and family, coworkers, and perhaps your instructor; read magazines and newspapers; take stock of your interests; consider possible topics suggested by your other courses (historical events, scientific developments, and so on); and, of course, search the Internet. (Your search engine's **subject guides** can be particularly helpful to you as you look for a promising topic or narrow a broad subject.)

See
8b2

As you look for a suitable topic, keep the following guidelines in mind.

**✓checklist) Choosing a research topic**

✓ **Are you genuinely interested in your research topic?** Remember that you will be deeply involved with the topic you select for weeks—perhaps even for an entire semester. If you lose interest in your topic, you are likely to see your research as a tedious chore rather than as an opportunity to discover new information, new associations, and new insights.

✓ **Is your topic suitable for research?** Topics limited to your personal experience and those based on value judgments are not suitable for research. For example, "The superiority of Freud's work to Jung's" might sound promising, but no amount of research can establish that one person's work is "better" than another's.

✓ **Are the boundaries of your research topic appropriate?** A research topic should be neither too broad nor too narrow. "Julius and Ethel Rosenberg: Atomic Spies or FBI Scapegoats?" is far too broad a topic for a 10-page—or even a 100-page—treatment, and "One piece of evidence that played a decisive role in establishing the Rosenbergs' guilt" would probably be too narrow for a 10-page research paper. But how one newspaper reported the Rosenbergs' espionage trial or how a particular group of people (government employees or college students, for example) reacted at the time to the couple's 1953 execution might work well.

✓ **Can your topic be researched in a library to which you have access?** For instance, the library of an engineering or business school may not have a large collection of books of literary criticism; the library of a small liberal arts college may not have extensive resources for researching technical or medical topics. (Of course, if you have access to the Internet or to specialized databases, your options are greatly increased.)

## 6b Doing Exploratory Research and Formulating a Research Question

Doing **exploratory research**—searching the Internet and looking through general reference works such as encyclopedias, bibliographies, and specialized dictionaries (either in print or online)—helps you to get an overview of your topic. Your goal is to formulate a **research question,** the question you want your research paper to answer. A research question helps you to decide which sources to seek out, which to examine first, which to examine in depth, and which to skip entirely. (The answer to your research question will be your paper's <u>thesis statement</u>.)

See 1c2–5

# 6c  Assembling a Working Bibliography

As soon as you begin your exploratory research, you begin to assemble a **working bibliography** for your paper. (This working bibliography will be the basis for your <u>works-cited list</u>, which will include all the sources you cite in your paper.)

See 10a2

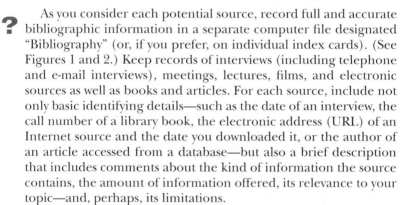

**close UP**

## Assembling a working bibliography

As you record bibliographic information for your sources, include the following information:

**Book** Author(s); title (underlined or in italics); call number (for future reference); city of publication; publisher; date of publication; brief description

**Article** Author(s); title of article (in quotation marks); title of journal (underlined or in italics); volume number; date; inclusive page numbers; electronic address (if applicable); date downloaded (if applicable); brief description

**?** As you consider each potential source, record full and accurate bibliographic information in a separate computer file designated "Bibliography" (or, if you prefer, on individual index cards). (See Figures 1 and 2.) Keep records of interviews (including telephone and e-mail interviews), meetings, lectures, films, and electronic sources as well as books and articles. For each source, include not only basic identifying details—such as the date of an interview, the call number of a library book, the electronic address (URL) of an Internet source and the date you downloaded it, or the author of an article accessed from a database—but also a brief description that includes comments about the kind of information the source contains, the amount of information offered, its relevance to your topic—and, perhaps, its limitations.

As you go about collecting sources and building your working bibliography, be careful to monitor the quality and relevance of all the materials you examine. Making informed choices early in the research process will save you a lot of time in the long run, so don't collect a large number of sources first and assess their usefulness later. Resist the temptation to check out every book that mentions your subject, photocopy page after page of perhaps only marginally useful articles, or download material from every electronic source to which you have access. After all, you will eventually have to read all these sources and take detailed notes on them. If you have too many sources, you will be overwhelmed, unable to remember why a particular idea or a certain article seemed important. For more on evaluating library sources, **see 7c;** for guidelines on evaluating Internet sources, **see 8d.**

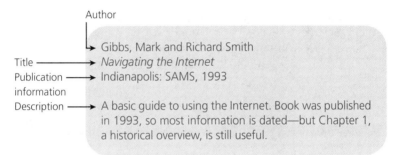

Author

Gibbs, Mark and Richard Smith
Title → *Navigating the Internet*
Publication → Indianapolis: SAMS, 1993
information
Description → A basic guide to using the Internet. Book was published in 1993, so most information is dated—but Chapter 1, a historical overview, is still useful.

**Figure 1** *Information for Working Bibliography (in Computer File)*

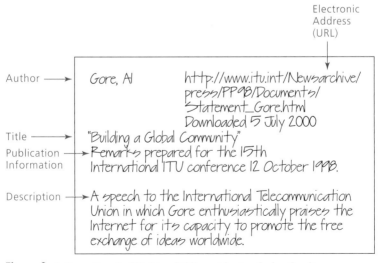

Electronic
Address
(URL)

Author → Gore, Al    http://www.itu.int/Newsarchive/
press/PP98/Documents/
Statement_Gore.html
Downloaded 5 July 2000
Title → "Building a Global Community"
Publication → Remarks prepared for the 15th
Information    International ITU conference 12 October 1998.
Description → A speech to the International Telecommunication
Union in which Gore enthusiastically praises the
Internet for its capacity to promote the free
exchange of ideas worldwide.

**Figure 2** *Information for Working Bibliography (on Index Card)*

# 6d   Developing a Tentative Thesis

Your **tentative thesis** is a preliminary statement of what you think your research will support. This statement, which you will eventually refine into a **thesis statement**, should be the tentative answer to your research question.

*See 6g*

---

**DEVELOPING A TENTATIVE THESIS**

| Subject Area | Topic | Research Question | Tentative Thesis |
|---|---|---|---|
| Computers and society | The Internet's effect on American society | Do all Americans have equal access to the Internet? | Not all Americans have equal access to the Internet, and this is a potentially serious problem. |

---

Because it suggests the specific direction your research will take as well as the scope and emphasis of your argument, the tentative thesis you come up with at this point can help you generate a list of the main points you plan to develop in your paper. This list of points can help you narrow the focus of your research so you can zero in on a few specific categories to explore as you read and take notes.

Tentative Thesis:   Not all Americans have equal access to the Internet, and this is a potentially serious problem.

- Give background about the Internet; tell why it is important
- Identify groups that do not have access to the Internet
- Explain problems this creates
- Suggest possible solutions

# 6e   Doing Focused Research

Once you have decided on a tentative thesis and made a list of the points you plan to explore in your paper, you are ready to begin your focused research. When you do **focused research,** you look for the specific information—facts, examples, statistics, definitions, quotations—you need to support your points.

## (1) Reading Sources

As you look for information, try to explore as many sources, and as many different viewpoints, as possible. It makes sense to examine more sources than you actually intend to use. This strategy will enable you to proceed even if one or more of your sources turns out to be biased, outdated, unreliable, superficial, or irrelevant—in other words, unusable. Exploring different viewpoints is just as important. After all, if you read only those sources that agree on a particular issue, it will be difficult for you to develop a balanced viewpoint of your own.

As you explore various sources, try not to waste time reading irrelevant material; instead, try to evaluate each source's potential usefulness to you as quickly as possible. For example, if your source is a book, skim the table of contents and the index; if your source is a journal article, read the abstract. Then, if an article or a section of a book seems potentially useful, photocopy it for future reference. Similarly, when you find an online source that looks promising, resist the temptation to paste it directly into a section of your paper-in-progress. Instead, print it out (or send it to yourself as an e-mail attachment) so you can evaluate it further later on. (For information on evaluating library sources, **see 7b;** for information on evaluating Internet sources, **see 8c.**)

## (2) Balancing Primary and Secondary Sources

During your focused research, you will encounter both **primary sources** (original documents and observations) and **secondary sources** (interpretations of original documents and observations).

### PRIMARY AND SECONDARY SOURCES

| Primary Source | Secondary Source |
|---|---|
| Novels, poems, plays, films | Criticism |
| Diaries, autobiographies | Biography |
| Letters, historical documents, speeches, oral histories | Historical commentary |
| Newspaper articles | Editorials |
| Raw data from questionnaires or interviews | Social science articles; case studies |
| Observations/experiments | Scientific articles |

For many research projects, primary sources are essential, but secondary sources, which provide scholars' insights and interpretations, are also valuable. Remember, though, that the further you get from the primary source, the more chances exist for inaccuracies caused by researchers' inadvertent misinterpretations or distortions.

## 6f Taking Notes

As you locate information in the library and on the Internet, you take notes to keep a record of exactly what you found and where you found it. Each piece of information you record in your notes (whether summarized, paraphrased, or quoted from your sources) should be accompanied by a short descriptive heading that indicates its relevance to one of the points you will develop in your paper. Because you will use these headings to guide you as you organize your notes, you should make them as specific as possible. Labeling every note for a paper on the "digital divide" created by the Internet digital divide or Internet, for example, will not prove very helpful later on. More focused headings—dangers of digital divide or government's steps to narrow the gap, for instance—will be much more useful.

Also include brief comments that make clear your reasons for recording the information and identify what you think it will contribute to your paper. These comments (enclosed in brackets so you will know they express your own ideas, not those of your source) should establish the purpose of your note—what you think it can explain, support, clarify, describe, or contradict—and perhaps suggest its relationship to other notes or other sources. Any questions you have about the information or its source can also be included in your comment.

Finally, each note should fully and accurately identify the source of the information you are recording. You need not write out the complete citation, but you must include enough information to identify your source. For example, Gibbs and Smith 5 would be enough to send you back to your working bibliography card or file, where you will be able to find the complete documentation for Mark Gibbs and Richard Smith's book *Navigating the Internet*. (If you use more than one source by the same author, you need a more complete reference.)

112

# Taking Notes

## (1) Managing Source Information

When you take notes, your goal is flexibility: you want to be able to arrange and rearrange information easily and efficiently as your paper takes shape. If you take notes on your computer, type each piece of information under a specific heading rather than listing all information from a single source under one general heading. If you take notes by hand, you may decide to use the time-tested index-card system. If you do, write on only one side of the card, and be sure to use a separate index card for each piece of information rather than running several ideas together on a single card. (See Figures 3 and 4.)

---

**http://kirsznermandell.heinle.com**

### Taking notes

Note-taking software can make it easy for you to record and organize information, allowing you to enter notes (quotations, summaries, paraphrases, or your own comments), pictures, or tables; to sort and categorize your material; and even to print out the information in order on computerized note cards. If you do not have access to such software, type each note under an appropriate heading, and divide notes from one another with extra space or lines. Then, you will be able to sort notes into categories as well as to add and delete bits of information and to experiment with different sequences of ideas.

---

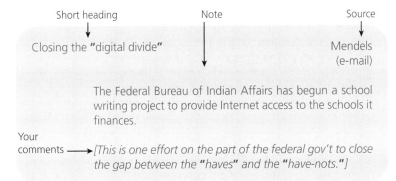

Short heading    Note    Source

Closing the "digital divide"    Mendels
                (e-mail)

The Federal Bureau of Indian Affairs has begun a school writing project to provide Internet access to the schools it finances.

Your comments ⟶ *[This is one effort on the part of the federal gov't to close the gap between the "haves" and the "have-nots."]*

**Figure 3** *Notes (in Computer File)*

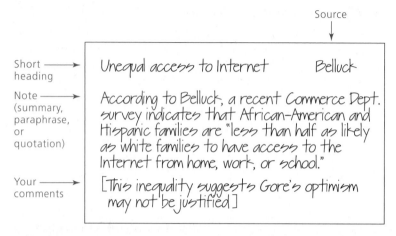

**Figure 4** *Notes (on Note Card)*

**? ✓checklist Taking notes**

✓ **Identify the source of each piece of information clearly and completely.** Even if the source is sitting on your bookshelf or stored in your computer's hard drive, include full source information with each note.

✓ **Include everything now that you will need later** to understand your note—names, dates, places, connections with other notes—and to remember why you recorded it.

✓ **Distinguish quotations from paraphrases and summaries and your own ideas from those of your sources.** If you copy a source's words, place them in quotations marks. (If you take notes by hand, circle the quotation marks; if you type your notes, put the quotation marks in boldface.) If you write down your own ideas, enclose them in brackets—and, if you are typing, italicize them as well. These techniques will help you eliminate accidental **plagiarism** in your paper.

See Ch 9

✓ **Put an author's comments into your own words whenever possible,** summarizing and paraphrasing material as well as adding your own observations and analyses. Not only will this strategy save you time later on, but it will also help you understand your sources and evaluate their usefulness now, when you still have time to find additional sources if necessary.

✓ **Copy an author's comments accurately,** using the exact words, spelling, punctuation marks, and capitalization.

### Photocopies and computer printouts

Making photocopies and printing out sections of electronic sources that you have downloaded can be useful, time-saving strategies, but photocopies and computer printouts are no substitute for notes. In fact, copying information is only the first step in the process of taking thorough, careful notes on a source. You should be especially careful not to allow the ease and efficiency of copying to encourage you to postpone decisions about the usefulness of your information. Remember, you can easily accumulate so many pages that it will be almost impossible to keep track of all your information.

Also keep in mind that photocopies and printouts do not have the flexibility of notes you take yourself because a single page of text may include information that should be earmarked for several different sections of your paper. This lack of flexibility makes it difficult for you to arrange source material into any meaningful order.

Finally, remember that the annotations you make on photocopies and printouts are usually not focused or polished enough to be incorporated directly into your paper. You will still have to paraphrase and summarize your source's ideas and make connections among them. Therefore, you should approach a photocopy or printout just as you approach any other print source—as material that you will read, highlight, annotate, and then take notes about.

---

**✓ checklist** **Working with photocopies and computer printouts**

✓ Record full and accurate source information, including the inclusive page numbers, URL, and any other relevant information, on the first page of each copy.

✓ Clip or staple together consecutive pages of a single source.

✓ Do not copy a source without reminding yourself—*in writing*—why you are doing so. In pencil or on removable self-stick notes, record your initial responses to the source's ideas, jot down cross-references to other works or notes, and highlight important sections.

✓ Photocopying can be time consuming and expensive, so try to avoid copying material that is only marginally relevant to your paper.

✓ Keep photocopies and printouts in a file so you will be able to find them when you need them.

## (2) Summarizing, Paraphrasing, and Quoting

Although it may seem like a sensible strategy, copying down the words of a source is the least efficient way to take notes. Experienced researchers know that a better strategy is to take notes that combine summary and paraphrase with direct quotation. By doing so, they make sure they understand both the material and its relevance to their research. This understanding makes it possible for them to synthesize borrowed material with their own ideas in an original and coherent piece of writing.

*Summarizing Sources* A **summary** is a brief restatement, in your own words, of a source's main idea. When you summarize a source, you condense the author's ideas into a few concise sentences. You do *not* include your own opinions or interpretations of the writer's ideas.

*Original Source*

Today, the First Amendment faces challenges from groups who seek to limit expressions of racism and bigotry. A growing number of legislatures have passed rules against "hate speech"—[speech] that is offensive on the basis of race, ethnicity, gender, or sexual orientation. The rules are intended to promote respect for all people and protect the targets of hurtful words, gestures, or actions.

Legal experts fear these rules may wind up diminishing the rights of all citizens. "The bedrock principle [of our society] is that government may never suppress free speech simply because it goes against what the community would like to hear," says Nadine Strossen, president of the American Civil Liberties Union and professor of constitutional law at New York University Law School. In recent years, for example, the courts have upheld the right of neo-Nazis to march in Jewish neighborhoods; protected cross-burning as a form of free expression; and allowed protesters to burn the American flag. The offensive, ugly, distasteful, or repugnant nature of expression is not reason enough to ban it, courts have said.

But advocates of limits on hate speech note that certain kinds of expression fall outside of First Amendment protection. Courts have ruled that "fighting words"—words intended to provoke immediate violence—or speech that creates a clear and present danger are not protected forms of expression. As the classic argument goes, freedom of speech does not give you the right to yell "Fire!" in a crowded theater. (Sudo, Phil. "Freedom of Hate Speech?" *Scholastic Update* 124.14 [1992]: 17–20.)

## Summary

The right to freedom of speech, guaranteed by the First Amendment, is becoming more difficult to defend. Some people think stronger laws against the use of "hate speech" weaken the First Amendment, but others argue that some kinds of speech remain exempt from this protection (Sudo 17).

*Paraphrasing Sources* A summary conveys just the general sense of a source; a **paraphrase** is a detailed restatement, in your own words, of all a source's important ideas—but not your opinions or interpretations of those ideas. In a paraphrase, you not only indicate the source's main points, but also its order, tone, and emphasis. Consequently, a paraphrase can sometimes be as long as the source itself.

---

### ✓ checklist Summarizing a source

✓ Reread your source until you understand its main idea.
✓ Write your summary, using your own words and phrasing. If you quote a distinctive word or phrase, use quotation marks.
✓ Add appropriate documentation.

---

Compare the following paraphrase with the summary of the same source above.

## Paraphrase

Many groups want to limit the right of free speech guaranteed by the First Amendment to the Constitution. They believe this is necessary to protect certain groups of people from "hate speech." Women, people of color, and gay men and lesbians, for example, may find that hate speech is used to intimidate them. Legal scholars are afraid that even though the rules against hate speech are well intentioned, such rules undermine our freedom of speech. As Nadine Strossen, president of the American Civil Liberties Union, says, "The bedrock principle [of our society] is that government may never suppress free speech simply because it goes against what the community would like to hear" (qtd. in Sudo 17). People who support speech codes point out, however, that certain types of speech are not protected by the First Amendment—for example, words that create a "clear and present danger" or that would lead directly to violence (Sudo 17).

## ✓ checklist  Paraphrasing a source

✓ Reread your source until you understand its key points.
✓ List the key points in the order in which they appear in the source.
✓ Write your paraphrase, following the order, tone, and emphasis of the original. Use your own words and phrasing; if you quote a distinctive word or phrase, use quotation marks.
✓ Add appropriate documentation.

## close **UP**

### Summarizing and paraphrasing sources

When you summarize or paraphrase, be sure to familiarize yourself with your source before you begin to write, and then try not to look at it again until you are finished. Use language and syntax that come naturally to you, and be careful not to duplicate the wording or sentence structure of the source. If you cannot think of a synonym for an important word or phrase, place it in quotation marks.

See ESL
47f4

*Quoting Sources* When you <u>quote</u>, you copy an author's remarks exactly as they appear in a source, word for word and punctuation mark for punctuation mark, enclosing the borrowed words in quotation marks. As a rule, you should not quote extensively in a research paper. The use of numerous quotations interrupts the flow of your discussion and gives readers the impression that your paper is just an unassimilated collection of other people's ideas.

**When to quote**

- Quote when a source's wording or phrasing is so distinctive that a summary or paraphrase would diminish its impact.
- Quote when a source's words—particularly those of a recognized expert on your subject—will lend authority to your paper.
- Quote when paraphrasing would create a long, clumsy, or incoherent phrase or would change the meaning of the original.
- Quote when you plan to disagree with a source. Using a source's exact words helps to assure readers you are being fair.

## 6g   Fine-Tuning Your Thesis

After you have finished your focused research and note taking, you must refine your tentative thesis into a carefully worded statement that expresses a conclusion your research can support. This **thesis statement** should be more precise than your tentative thesis, accurately conveying the direction, emphasis, and scope of your paper.

See 1c3

### FINE-TUNING YOUR THESIS

**Tentative Thesis**

Not all Americans have equal access to the Internet, and this is a potentially serious problem.

**Thesis Statement**

Although the Internet has changed our world for the better, it threatens to create two distinct classes—those who have access and those who do not.

If your thesis statement does not express a conclusion your research can support, you will need to revise it. Reviewing your notes carefully, perhaps grouping information in different ways, may help you decide on a more suitable thesis. Or, you may try other techniques—for instance, using your research question as a starting point for additional brainstorming or freewriting.

**119**

# 6h Outlining, Drafting, and Revising

Keeping your thesis in mind, you are now ready to outline your supporting points and draft your paper.

## (1) Outlining

Before you write your rough draft, make an outline. At this point, you need to make some sense out of all the notes you have accumulated, and you do this by sorting and organizing them. By identifying categories and subcategories of information, you begin to see your paper take shape and are able to construct an outline that reflects this shape.

A formal outline is different from the list of main points you tentatively plan to develop in your paper. A **formal outline** includes all the points you will develop and indicates not only the exact order in which you will present your ideas but also the relationship between main points and supporting details.

**Note:** The outline you construct at this stage is only a guide for you to follow as you draft your paper; you are likely to change it as you draft and revise. The final outline, you may be required to prepare after your paper is complete will reflect what you have written and serve as a guide for your readers. An example of a formal outline appears with the sample MLA research paper in **10c.**

---

**✓checklist** Preparing a formal outline

✓ Write your thesis statement at the top of the page.

✓ Review your notes to make sure each note expresses only one general idea. If this is not the case, recopy any unrelated information, creating a separate note.

✓ Check that the heading for each note specifically characterizes that note's information. If it does not, change the heading.

✓ Sort your notes by their headings, keeping a miscellaneous file for notes that do not seem to fit into any category. Irrelevant notes, those unrelated to your paper's thesis, should be set aside (but not discarded).

✓ Check your categories for balance. If most of your notes fall into one or two categories, rewrite some of your headings to create narrower, more focused categories. If you have only one or two notes in a category, you may need to do additional research or treat that topic only briefly (or not at all).

✓ Organize the individual notes within each group, adding more specific subheads to your headings as needed. Arrange your notes in an order that highlights the most important points and subordinates lesser ones.

✓ Decide on a logical order in which to discuss your paper's major points.

✓ Construct your formal outline, using divisions and subdivisions that correspond to your headings. Be sure each heading has at least two subheadings; if one does not, combine it with another heading. (Outline only the body of your paper, not your introduction and conclusion.) Follow outline format strictly.

    I. First major point of your paper
       A. First subpoint
       B. Next subpoint
          1. First supporting example
          2. Next supporting example
             a. first specific detail
             b. next specific detail
    II. Second major point

✓ Review your completed outline to make sure you have not placed too much emphasis on a relatively unimportant idea, ordered ideas illogically, or created sections that overlap with others.

---

**http://kirsznermandell.heinle.com**

## Outlining

Before you begin writing, create a separate word-processing file for each major section of your outline. Then, copy your notes into these files in the order in which you intend to use them. You can print out each file as you need it and use it for a guide as you write.

## (2) Drafting

When you are ready to write your **rough draft,** arrange your notes in the order in which you intend to use them. Follow your outline as you write, using your notes as needed. As you draft, jot down questions to yourself, and identify points that need further clarification (you can bracket those ideas or print them in boldface on a typed draft, or you can write them on self-stick notes).

See
1d1

Leave space for material you plan to add, and bracket phrases or whole sections that you think you may later decide to move or delete. In other words, lay the groundwork for a major revision. Remember that even though you are guided by an outline and notes, you are not bound to follow their content or sequence exactly. As you write, new ideas or new connections among ideas may occur to you. If you find yourself wandering from your thesis or outline, check to see whether the departure is justified.

As your draft takes shape, each paragraph will probably correspond to one major point on your outline. Be sure to supply transitions between sentences and paragraphs to show how your points are related. To make it easy for you to revise later on, triple-space your draft. Be careful to copy source information fully and accurately on this and every subsequent draft, placing the documentation as close as possible to the material it identifies.

**http://kirsznermandell.heinle.com**

**Drafting**
You can use a split screen or multiple windows to view your notes as you draft your paper. You can also copy the material that you need from your notes and then insert it into the text of your paper. (As you copy, be especially careful that you do not unintentionally commit plagiarism.)

See 9b

*Shaping the Parts of the Paper* Like any other essay, a research paper has an introduction, a body, and a conclusion. In your rough draft, as in your outline, you focus on the body of your paper. Do not spend time planning an introduction at this stage; your ideas will change as you write, and you will want to revise your opening and closing paragraphs later to reflect those changes.

See 3e1

In your **introduction,** you identify your topic and establish how you will approach it. Your **introduction** also includes your thesis statement, which expresses the position you will support in the rest of the paper. Sometimes the introductory paragraphs briefly summarize your major supporting points (the major divisions of your outline) in the order in which you will present them. Such a preview of your thesis and support provides a smooth transition into the body of your paper. Your introduction can also present an overview of the problem you will discuss or summarize research already done on your topic. In your rough draft, however, an undeveloped introduction is perfectly acceptable; in fact, your thesis statement alone can serve as a placeholder for the more polished introduction that you will write later.

As you draft the **body** of your paper, indicate its direction with strong **topic sentences** that correspond to the divisions of your outline.

> Today, many people believe the Internet has ushered in a new age, one in which this instant communication will bring people closer together and eventually even eliminate national boundaries.

You can also use **headings** if they are a convention of the discipline in which you are writing.

*Reactions from Public Officials*

> Many public officials recognize the potential danger of the "digital divide," and they are taking steps to narrow the gap.

Even in your rough draft, carefully worded headings and topic sentences will help you keep your discussion under control.

The **conclusion** of a research paper often restates the thesis. This is especially important in a long paper because by the time your readers get to the end, they may have lost sight of your paper's main idea. Your **conclusion** can also include a summary of your key points, a call for action, or perhaps an apt quotation. In your rough draft, however, your concluding paragraph is usually very brief.

*Working Source Material into Your Paper* In the body of your paper, you evaluate and interpret your sources, comparing different ideas and assessing conflicting points of view. As a writer, your job is to draw your own conclusions, blending information from various sources into a paper that coherently and forcefully presents your own original viewpoint to your readers.

Be sure to **integrate source material** smoothly into your paper, clearly and accurately identifying the relationships among various sources (and between those sources' ideas and your own). If two sources present conflicting interpretations, you must be especially careful to use precise language and accurate transitions to make the contrast apparent (for instance, "Although Gore is optimistic, recent studies suggest . . ."). When two sources agree, you should make this clear (for example, "Like Belluck, Gates believes . . ." or "Commerce Department statistics confirm Gates's point"). Such

**123**

phrasing will provide a context for your own comments and conclusions. If different sources present complementary information about a subject, blend details from the sources *carefully*, keeping track of which details come from which source, to reveal the complete picture.

## (3) Revising

A good way to start revising is to check to see that your thesis statement still accurately expresses your paper's central focus. Then, make an outline of your draft, and compare it with the outline you made before you began the draft. If you find significant differences, you will have to revise your thesis statement or rewrite sections of your paper. The checklists in 1d2 can guide your revision of your paper's overall structure and its individual paragraphs, sentences, and words.

---

**✓checklist** Revising a research paper

✓ Should you do more research to find support for certain points?
✓ Do you need to reorder the major sections of your paper?
✓ Should you rearrange the order in which you present your points within those sections?
✓ Do you need to add section headings? Transitional paragraphs?
✓ Have you **integrated source material** smoothly into your paper?
✓ Do you introduce source material with **identifying tags**?
✓ Are quotations blended with paraphrase, summary, and your own observations and reactions?
✓ Have you avoided **plagiarism** by carefully documenting all borrowed ideas?
✓ Have you analyzed and interpreted the ideas of others rather than simply stringing those ideas together?
✓ Do your own ideas—not those of your sources—define the focus of your discussion?

See 9a
See 9a1
See 9b

http://kirsznermandell.heinle.com

### Revising

When you finish revising your paper, copy the file that contains your working bibliography, and insert it at the end of your paper. Delete any irrelevant entries, and use the bibliographic information to help you compile your works-cited list. (Make sure the format of the entries on your works-cited list conforms to the documentation style you are using.)

### Preparing a final draft

Before you print out the final version of your paper, **edit and proofread** hard copy of your outline and your works-cited list as well as of the paper itself. Next, consider (or reconsider) your paper's title. It should be descriptive enough to tell your readers what your paper is about, and it should create interest in your subject. Your title should also be consistent with the purpose and tone of your paper. (You would hardly want a humorous title for a paper about the death penalty or world hunger.) Finally, your title should be engaging and to the point—and perhaps even provocative. Often a quotation from one of your sources will suggest a likely title.

See
1e

When you are satisfied with your title, read your paper through again, proofreading for grammar, spelling, or typing errors you may have missed. Pay particular attention to parenthetical documentation and works-cited entries. (Remember that every error undermines your credibility.) Once you are satisfied that your paper is as accurate as you can make it, print it out one last time. Then, fasten the pages with a paper clip (do not staple the pages or fold the corners together), and hand it in.

**Note:** A variety of different Web sites may be useful to you as you go through the research process. Some of these are mentioned in this chapter; for a more complete list see *The Brief Handbook* Web site, http://kirsznermandell.heinle.com.

# Chapter 7

# Using and Evaluating Library Sources

## 7a Doing Exploratory Library Research

Even though the Internet has changed the nature of research, the traditional place to begin your paper remains the same—the library. Modern college libraries offer you access to many of the print and electronic resources (some suitable for **exploratory research,** others for **focused research**) that you cannot get anywhere else—even on the Internet. You can begin your exploratory research in the library by consulting encyclopedias, dictionaries, and bibliographies; it is also the place to find the many specialized resources you will use during focused research—for example, periodical indexes, articles, and books.

During exploratory research, your goal is to find a **research question** for your paper. You begin this process by searching your library's **online catalog** for information about your topic. You then look at general reference works and consult the library's electronic resources.

See 6b
See 6e
See 6c

---

**(✓)checklist  Before you start library research**

✓ Know your library's physical layout.
✓ Take a tour of the library if one is offered.
✓ Familiarize yourself with the library's holdings.
✓ Find out if the library has a guide to its resources.
✓ Meet with a librarian if you have questions.
✓ Be sure you know the library's hours.
✓ Find out if you can access some of the library's resources through your own computer at home or in your dorm room.

---

### (1) Using Online Catalogs

Most college and university libraries—and a growing number of regional and community libraries—have abandoned print cataloging systems in favor of **online catalogs**—computer databases that list all the books, journals, and other materials held by the library.

You access an online catalog (as well as the other electronic resources of the library) by going to one of the computer terminals located throughout the library and typing in certain words or phrases—*search terms* or *options*—that enable you to find the information you need. If you have never used an online catalog, ask a reference librarian for help.

When you search the online catalog for information about your topic, you may conduct either a *keyword search* or a *subject search*. (Later on in the research process, when you know more precisely what you are looking for, you can search for a particular source by entering its title or author.)

*Conducting a Keyword Search* When you carry out a **keyword search,** you enter into the online catalog a term or terms associated with your topic. The computer then retrieves any catalog entries that contain those words. The more precise your search terms are, the more specific and useful the information you will retrieve. (Combining keywords with AND, OR, and NOT allows you to narrow or broaden your search. This technique is called conducting a **Boolean search.**)

See 7a4

---

**✓checklist Keyword do's and don'ts**

When conducting a keyword search, remember the following hints:

✓ Use precise, specific keywords to differentiate your topic from similar topics.

✓ Enter both singular and plural keywords when appropriate—*the printing press* and *printing presses*, for example.

✓ Enter both abbreviations and their full-word equivalents (for example, *U.S.* and *United States*).

✓ Remember to try variant spellings (for example, *color* and *colour*).

✓ Don't use too long a string of keywords. (If you do, you may retrieve irrelevant material.)

---

*Conducting a Subject Search* When you carry out a **subject search,** you enter specific subject headings into the online catalog. The subject categories in a library are most often arranged according to headings established in the five-volume manual titled *The Library of Congress Subject Headings,* sometimes referred to as the "big red books," which are held at the reference desk of your library. Although it may be possible to guess at a subject heading, your search will be more successful if you consult these volumes to help you identify the exact wording you need.

### Keyword searching vs. subject searching

*Keyword Searching*
- Searches many subject areas
- Any significant word or phrase can be used
- Retrieves large number of items
- May retrieve many irrelevant items

*Subject Searching*
- Searches only a specific subject area
- Only the specific headings listed in the *Library of Congress Subject Headings* can be used
- Retrieves small number of items
- Retrieves few irrelevant items

http://kirsznermandell.heinle.com

## Using your library's Web site

Many college and university libraries have their own Web sites that enable users to access their online catalogs and other electronic resources from a dorm room or from any computer connected to the Internet. Ask at your library for the URL and password.

You can also browse the online catalogs of major research libraries, such as the Library of Congress, the New York Public Library, or the list of academic libraries maintained by the University of California. Although you will not be able to access subscription-only databases or indexes, searching a research library's catalog can give you an overview of the sources available for your topic and the bibliographic information you can use if you want to request material via **interlibrary loan**.

See
7b4

## (2) Browsing

**Browsing** through the books in your library can help you narrow your topic to a research question. Once you know the classification system your library uses, you can browse through its shelves with a better sense of what materials are there and where they are located.

### Library materials

*The Circulating Collection*
- Books (hardback and paperback)—novels, essay collections, biographies, and so on
- Periodicals—newspapers, magazines, and journals
- CDs, audiotapes, and videotapes—music, films, speeches, and so on
- Large-print books and Books-on-Tape

*The Reference Collection*
- Dictionaries, encyclopedias, handbooks, and atlases provide facts and background information
- Bibliographies and indexes tell you what source material is available for the subject you are researching
- Special subject guides help you find detailed information quickly

*The Dewey Decimal Classification System* Some public libraries, as well as some smaller college libraries, arrange books according to the **Dewey Decimal Classification System** (DDC). This organizational system arranges all holdings in the library into ten broad areas and then assigns them numbers.

### Dewey Decimal subject numbers

000–099   General knowledge
100–199   Philosophy
200–299   Religion
300–399   Social sciences

*continued on the following page*

*continued from the previous page*

| | |
|---|---|
| 400–499 | Language |
| 500–599 | Pure sciences |
| 600–699 | Technology (applied sciences) |
| 700–799 | Fine arts |
| 800–899 | Literature |
| 900–999 | History |

This means that if you are working on a science-related topic, browsing through the books on the 500 shelves may help you find useful information about your topic.

*The Library of Congress Classification System* Another classification system is the **Library of Congress Classification System** (LC). Because the Library of Congress in Washington, D.C., contains almost every book ever published in the United States, it uses a flexible system that can accommodate an ever-growing base of knowledge. Most large public libraries and large college and university libraries now use this cataloging system.

### Library of Congress Classification System

| | |
|---|---|
| A | General works |
| B | Philosophy, psychology, and religion |
| C–F | History |
| G | Geography, anthropology, recreation |
| H | Social science |
| J | Political science |
| K | Law |
| L | Education |
| M | Music |
| N | Fine arts |
| P | Language and literature |
| Q | Science |
| R | Medicine |
| S | Agriculture |
| T | Technology |
| U | Military science |
| V | Naval science |
| Z | Bibliography and library sciences |

## (3) Consulting General Reference Works

**General reference works,** which provide a broad overview of a particular subject, can be helpful when you are exploring possible research topics. You can learn key facts and specific terminology as well as find dates, places, and people. In addition, general reference works often include bibliographies that you can use later on when you do focused research. The following kinds of reference works, many of which are available in electronic form as well as print, are useful for exploratory research.

### General reference works

*General Encyclopedias* Many general multivolume encyclopedias are available in electronic format. For example, *The New Encyclopaedia Britannica* is available on CD-ROM and DVD as well as on the World Wide Web at <http://www.britannica.com>.

*Specialized Encyclopedias, Dictionaries, and Bibliographies* These specialized reference works contain in-depth articles focusing on a single subject area.

*General Bibliographies* General bibliographies list books available in a wide variety of fields.

> *Books in Print.* An index of authors and titles of books in print in the United States. The *Subject Guide to Books in Print* indexes books according to subject area.
>
> *The Bibliographic Index.* A tool for locating bibliographies.

*General Biographical References* Biographical reference books provide information about people's lives as well as bibliographic listings.

*Living Persons*

> *Who's Who in America.* Gives concise biographical information about prominent Americans.
>
> *Who's Who.* Collects concise biographical facts about notable British men and women.
>
> *Current Biography.* Includes articles on people of many nationalities.

*Deceased Persons*

> *Dictionary of American Biography.* Considered the best of American biographical dictionaries. Includes articles on over thirteen thousand Americans.
>
> *Dictionary of National Biography.* The most important reference work for British biography.
>
> *Webster's Biographical Dictionary.* Perhaps the most widely used biographical reference work. Includes people from all periods and places.

## (4) Using Electronic Resources

Today's libraries have electronic resources that enable you to find a wide variety of sources. Computer terminals and printers, located throughout the library, enable you to access this material.

### Using electronic resources

You may think that you can find all the information you need on the Internet, but in fact your library subscribes to subscription services that enable you to access more specialized databases than you can access on the Internet. For this reason, you should always begin any research project with a survey of your library's electronic resources.

**Online databases** offer citations of books, articles in journals, magazines, and newspapers, and of reports. Once you have searched the databases and found the right information, you can print out the bibliographic citations and sometimes abstracts (short summaries) or even full text. In some cases, you may be able to download the information onto one of your own disks.

Different libraries offer different databases and make them available in different ways. Many libraries have implemented Web-based systems that make it easy for them to network their databases (and online catalogs) beyond the library's walls. Some libraries may acquire databases on CD-ROM or DVD. Most libraries also subscribe to information service companies, such as DIALOG or Gale, which gives you access to hundreds of databases that would not otherwise be available to you. One of your first tasks should be to discover what your library has to offer. You may find that you can do much of your library research from your home computer or dorm room. Visit your library's Web site or ask a reference librarian for more information.

*General and Specialized Databases* Some databases, called **bibliographic databases,** include references to articles published in magazines and/or scholarly journals and may also be available in print. They provide information about each article but do not usually include the full text of the article itself. Others are **full-text** databases, which include the entire text of articles, online encyclopedias, or other works. These databases are **proprietary,** which means that libraries must subscribe to them in order to make them available to students and faculty. Licensing and copyright agreements generally restrict the use of these databases; they are not available from outside the library to those who are not affiliated with the school.

Date   Volume   Number   Page

**Title: A year of Web pages for every class.** (UCLA policy reviewed)

**Periodical:** The Chronicle of Higher Education, May 15, 1998 v44 n36 pA29.

**Author:** Jeffrey R. Young

**Abstract:** The University of California at Los Angeles debates the use of Web pages for classroom use, unwilling to force instructors to offer online course descriptions and discussions with students. Some administrators and students argue Web pages are not worth the money they cost while others support the "Instructional Enhancement Initiative" which strives to intertwine technology and university life.

**Subjects:** Internet - Usage
Universities and colleges - Innovations

**Features:** photograph;  illustration

**Figure 1** *Database Printout*

Online databases for articles may cover many subjects (*Expanded Academic ASAP* or *LexisNexis Academic Universe,* for example), or they may cover one subject in great detail (*PsycINFO* or *Sociological Abstracts,* for example). The choices available to you may seem overwhelming at first. Assuming that your library offers a variety of databases (some libraries subscribe to hundreds), how do you know which ones will be best for your research topic? One strategy is to begin by searching a general database that includes full-text articles and then move on to a more specialized database that covers your subject in more detail. The specialized databases are more likely to include scholarly and professional journal articles, but they are also less likely to include the full text. They will, however, include abstracts that can tell you a lot about the usefulness of an article. If you are in doubt about which databases would be most useful to you, be sure to ask a librarian for suggestions.

*How to Search Databases* There are two ways to search online databases for information on a topic: by subject headings and by keyword(s). **Subject headings,** sometimes called controlled vocabulary terms, are taken from a list of terms recognized by that database. Sometimes it is easy to choose a subject heading; *global warming* or *greenhouse effect* are obvious. But sometimes these terms are harder to choose. For example, what do you call older people? Are they senior citizens? elderly? aged? How would you know? (Some databases provide a print or online thesaurus to help you pick subject headings.)

The other option is **keyword searching,** which allows you to type in any significant term likely to be found in the title, subject headings, abstract, or (if the full text is available) text of an article. Keyword searching also allows you to link terms using **boolean operators** (AND, OR, NOT). For example, *elderly* AND *abuse* would retrieve articles that mention both elderly people and abuse; *elderly* OR *aged* OR *senior citizens* would retrieve articles that mention any of these terms. Keyword searching is particularly helpful when you need to narrow the focus of your search or to expand it.

Both subject heading and keyword searches are valid ways to find articles on your topic. The most important thing is to be persistent. One good article often leads to another since abstracts and text may suggest other terms you can use. References and footnotes may suggest additional sources as well.

*CD-ROMs and DVDs* Many of the databases available online are also available on CD-ROM or DVD. In some cases, libraries subscribe to a CD-ROM or DVD service or database the same way they do to a printed index or journal and receive updates periodically. In other cases, reference books available in print are also published on CD-ROMs or DVDs—for example, *The Oxford English Dictionary* and *The Encyclopaedia Britannica.* Many libraries offer individual workstations where CD-ROMs or DVDs can be loaded and the information can be viewed and printed out. Increasingly, however, CD-ROMs and DVDs are being phased out in favor of Web-based systems.

```
TI:  Curfews and delinquency in major american cities
AU:  Ruefle, -William; Reynolds, -Kenneth-Mike
SO:  Crime-and-Delinquency.  V.41 July 95 p. 347-63
PY:  1995
AN:  95035204
```
**Figure 2**  *CD-ROM Database Printout*

# 7b  Doing Focused Library Research

Once you have completed your exploratory research and formulated your **research question**, it is time to move to focused research. During **focused research**, you examine the specialized reference works, books, and articles devoted specifically to your topic. You may also need to make use of the special services that many college libraries provide.

See
6c

See
6e

If your library has a Web site (and most libraries do), you may find it provides access to more than the library catalog or online databases. In fact, most library Web sites are gateways to an incredible amount of information, including research guides on a wide variety of topics, electronic journals and newspapers to which the library subscribes, and links to recommended Internet resources. Many library Web sites also include online forms that you can use to ask a question electronically, and some even include an online chat service that enables you to access a librarian from your home or residence hall.

Some examples of library Web sites you can visit are listed below, but don't forget to also check your own library's Web site or ask about available resources at the Reference Desk. You may be surprised to discover how "wired" your library has become.

**http://kirsznermandell.heinle.com**

**Web resources for focused
library research**

General Reference Resources (Carnegie-Mellon U.)
    http://eserver.org/reference/
How to Find Articles (U. of Toronto)
    http://library.scar.utoronto.ca/Bladen_Library/
    Research101/findart.htm

*continued on the following page*

135

*continued from the previous page*

Finding Books (U. of Dayton Libraries—some restrictions)
  http://www.udayton.edu/~library/daynet
Internet Public Library—Newspapers
  http://aristotle.ipl.org/cgi-bin/reading/news.out.pl
Internet Public Library—Magazines
  http://aristotle.ipl.org/reading/serials/
Primary vs. Secondary Sources (U. of Toronto)
  http://library.scar.utoronto.ca/Bladen_Library/
  Research101/primary.htm
Library Catalogs—Terminology
  http://www.nucat.library.nwu.edu
Library Catalogs—Dewey Decimal System
  http://www.oclc.org/fp/

## (1) Consulting Specialized Reference Works

During your exploratory research, you used general reference works to help you narrow your topic and formulate your research question. Now, you can access specialized works to find facts, examples, statistics, definitions, and quotations. The following reference works—many of which are available in electronic as well as in print versions—are most useful for focused research.

### Specialized reference works

*Unabridged Dictionaries* **Unabridged dictionaries**, such as the *Oxford English Dictionary*, are comprehensive works that give detailed information about words.

*Special Dictionaries* These dictionaries focus on such topics as usage, synonyms, slang and idioms, etymologies, and foreign terms; some focus on specific disciplines such as accounting or law.

*Yearbooks and Almanacs* A **yearbook** is an annual publication that updates factual and statistical information already published in a reference source. An **almanac** provides lists, charts, and statistics about a wide variety of subjects.

*World Almanac.* Includes statistics about government, population, sports, and many other subjects. Published annually since 1868.

*Information Please Almanac.* Includes information unavailable in the *World Almanac.* Published annually since 1947.

*Facts on File.* Covering 1940 to the present, this work offers digests of important news stories from metropolitan newspapers.

*Editorials on File.* Reprints important editorials from American and Canadian newspapers.

*Statistical Abstract of the United States.* Summarizes the statistics gathered by the U.S. government. Published annually.

*Atlases* An **atlas** contains maps and charts as well as historical, cultural, political, and economic information.

National Geographic Society. *National Geographic Atlas of the World.* The most up-to-date atlas available.

*Rand McNally Cosmopolitan World Atlas.* A modern and extremely legible medium-sized atlas.

*We the People: An Atlas of America's Ethnic Diversity.* Presents information about specific ethnic groups. Maps show immigration routes and settlement patterns.

*Quotation Books* A **quotation book** contains numerous quotations on a wide variety of subjects. Such quotations can be useful for your paper's introductory and concluding paragraphs.

*Bartlett's Familiar Quotations.* Quotations are arranged chronologically by author.

*The Home Book of Quotations.* Quotations are arranged by subject. An author index and a keyword index are also included.

## (2) Consulting Books

The online catalog gives you the information you need—specifically, the call numbers—for locating specific titles. A **call number** is like a book's address in the library: it tells you exactly where to find the book you are looking for.

AUTHOR: Smith, Richard J.
TITLE: Navigating the Internet / Richard J. Smith, Mark Gibbs
EDITION: 1st ed.
CALL NUMBER: 796.060735
PUBLISHED: Carmel, IN: Sams Publishing, c1993
DESCRIPTION: xxiii, 500p.: ill.; 23cm.
NOTES: "Includes the Internet gazetteer: a complete directory to over 600 locations, groups and other Internet resources dealing with subjects from A to Z"--Cover.
Includes index.
SUBJECTS: Internet (computer network)
OTHER AUTHORS: Gibbs, Mark
ISBN: 0-67230-362-0
OCLC Number: 28642785

**Figure 3** *Online Catalog Entry for a Book*

## ✓checklist Tracking down a missing source

| Problem | Possible Solution |
|---|---|
| ✓ Book has been checked out of library. | Consult person at circulation desk. |
| ✓ Book is not in library's collection. | Check other nearby libraries. Ask instructor if he or she owns a copy. Arrange for interlibrary loan (if time permits). |
| ✓ Journal is not in library's collection/article is ripped out of journal. | Arrange for interlibrary loan (if time permits). Check to see whether article is available in a full-text database. Ask librarian whether article has been reprinted as part of a collection. |

## (3) Consulting Articles

A **periodical** is a newspaper, magazine, scholarly journal, or other publication published at regular intervals (weekly, monthly, or quarterly). Articles in scholarly journals can be the best, most reliable sources you can find on a subject; they provide current information and are written by experts on the topic. Because these journals focus on a particular subject area, they can provide in-depth analysis.

**Periodical indexes** are databases that list articles from a selected group of magazines, newspapers, or scholarly journals. These databases may be available in your library in bound volumes, on microfilm or microfiche, and on CD-ROM or DVD; however, many libraries offer them online. These databases are updated frequently and provide the most current information available.

## Databases for specific disciplines

Choosing the right periodical index for your research is important. Each database, whether print or electronic, has a different focus and indexes different magazines or journals. Some cover many subjects or disciplines; others cover one subject or discipline in great detail. Some include only fairly recent articles, whereas others go back many years. Some focus on news-reporting sources and popular magazines, and others only include articles from scholarly and professional journals.

Using a database that is not appropriate for your topic leads to wasted time and frustration. For example, searching a database that focuses on the humanities will not help you much if you are looking for information on a business topic such as *corporate crime*.

Here is a list of databases commonly found in academic libraries. (Be sure to check your library's Web site or ask a librarian about those available to you.) You may find that you can use more than one index to find information on your topic. Thanks to campus networks and the World Wide Web, many of the databases will be accessible to you from your residence hall or home computer. If you need to search a print index, however, you will still need to visit the library.

| *Category* | *Description* |
|---|---|
| Social Science Index | Political science, psychology, sociology, history, sports |
| Humanities Index | Music, literature, film, arts |
| General Science Index | Science, nursing, medicine, health |
| Business Index | Business |
| Biology and Agricultural Index | Agriculture, ecology, forestry |

## ? Frequently used online databases

| General Indexes | Description |
| --- | --- |
| Ebscohost | Database system for thousands of periodical articles on many subjects |
| Expanded Academic ASAP | A largely full-text database covering all subjects in thousands of magazines and scholarly journals |
| FirstSearch | Full-text articles from many popular and scholarly periodicals |
| LexisNexis Academic | Includes full-text articles from national, international, and local newspapers. Also in cludes large legal and business sections. |
| Readers' Guide to Periodical Literature | Provides indexing to popular periodicals. |

| Specialized Indexes | Description |
| --- | --- |
| Dow Jones Interactive | Full text of articles from U.S. newspapers and trade journals |
| ERIC | Largest database of education-related journal articles and reports in the world |
| General BusinessFile ASAP | A full-text database covering business topics |
| PubMed (MEDLINE) | Covers articles in medical journals. Some may be available in full text. |
| PsycINFO | Covers psychology and related fields |
| Sociological Abstracts | Covers the social sciences |

**Note:** Not all libraries provide access to these indexes from outside the library.

## (4) Using Special Library Services

As you do focused research, consult a librarian if you plan to use any of the following special services.

### Special library services

- **Interlibrary Loans** Your library may be part of a library system that allows loans of books from one location to another. Check with your librarian.
- **Special Collections** Your library may house special collections of books, manuscripts, or documents.
- **Government Documents** A large university library may have a separate government documents area with its own catalog or index. The *Monthly Catalog of U.S. Government Publications* may be located either there or among the indexes in the reference area.
- **Vertical Files** The vertical files include pamphlets from a variety of organizations and interest groups, newspaper clippings, and other material collected by librarians.

## 7c  Evaluating Library Sources

Whenever you find information in the library (print or electronic), take the time to **evaluate** it—to critically assess its usefulness and its reliability. To determine the usefulness of a library source, ask yourself the following questions.

1. ***Does the Source Treat Your Topic in Enough Detail?*** To be useful, your source should treat your topic in detail. Skim a book's table of contents and index for references to your topic. To be of any real help, a book should include a section or chapter on your topic, not simply a footnote or brief reference. For articles, either read the abstract or skim the entire article for key facts, looking closely at section headings, information set in boldface type, and topic sentences. An article

should have your topic as its central subject or at least one of its main concerns.

2. *Is the Source Current?* The date of publication tells you whether the information in a book or article is up to date. A source's currency is particularly important for scientific and technological subjects. But even in the humanities, new discoveries and new ways of thinking lead scholars to reevaluate and modify their ideas. Be sure to check with your instructor to see if he or she prefers sources that have been published after a particular date.

3. *Is the Source Respected?* A contemporary review of a source can help you make this assessment. *Book Review Digest,* available in the reference section of your library, lists popular books that have been reviewed in at least three newspapers or magazines and includes excerpts from representative reviews. Book reviews are also available from the *New York Times Book Review*'s Web site, <http://www.nytimes.com/books>, which includes the text of book reviews that the newspaper has published since 1997.

4. *Is the Source Reliable?* Is a piece of writing largely fact or unsubstantiated opinion? Does the author support his or her conclusions? Does the author include documentation? Is the supporting information balanced? Is the author objective, or does he or she have a particular agenda to advance? Is the author associated with a special-interest group that may affect his or her view of the issue? Compare a few statements with a fairly neutral source—a textbook or an encyclopedia, for instance— to see whether an author seems to be slanting facts.

In general, **scholarly publications**—books and journals aimed at an audience of expert readers—are more respected and reliable than **popular publications**—books, magazines, and newspapers aimed at an audience of general readers. Assuming they are current and written by reputable authors, however, articles from some popular publications may be appropriate for your research. Remember, though, that many popular publications do not adhere to the same rigorous standards as scholarly publications do. For example, although some popular periodicals (such as *Atlantic Monthly* and *Harper's*) generally contain articles that are reliable and carefully researched, other periodicals may not. In addition, although scholarly books and articles go through a long process of peer review before they are published, popular publications often do not. For these reasons, before you use information from popular sources such as *Newsweek* or *Sports Illustrated,* check with your instructor.

The following box summarizes the differences between scholarly and popular publications.

## Scholarly and popular publications

| *Scholarly Publications* | *Popular Publications* |
| --- | --- |
| Scholarly publications report the results of research. | Popular publications entertain and inform. |
| Scholarly publications are frequently published by a university press or have some connection with a university or academic organization. | Popular publications are published by commercial presses. |
| Scholarly publications are **refereed**; that is, an editorial board or group of expert reviewers determines what will be published. | Popular publications are usually not refereed. |
| Scholarly publications are usually written by someone who is a recognized authority in the field about which he or she is writing. | Popular publications may be written by experts in a particular field, but more often they are written by freelance or staff writers. |
| Scholarly publications are written for a scholarly audience, so they often use technical vocabulary and include challenging content. | Popular publications are written for general readers, so they usually use an accessible vocabulary and do not deal with challenging content. |
| Scholarly publications nearly always contain extensive documentation as well as a bibliography of works consulted. | Popular publications rarely cite sources or use documentation. |
| Scholarly publications are published primarily because they make a contribution to a particular field of study. | Popular publications are published primarily to make a profit. |

?

# 7d   Doing Research Outside the Library

## (1) Conducting an Interview

**Interviews** often give you material that you cannot get by any other means—for instance, biographical information, a firsthand account of an event, or the opinions of an expert.

---

http://kirsznermandell.heinle.com

### Conducting an e-mail interview

Using e-mail to conduct an interview can save you a great deal of time. Before you send your questions, make sure the person is willing to cooperate. If the person agrees, send a short list of specific questions. After you have received the answers, send a response thanking the person for his or her cooperation.

---

The kinds of questions you ask in an interview depend on the information you want. **Open-ended questions**—questions designed to elicit general information—allow a respondent great flexibility in answering: *"Do you think students today are motivated? Why or why not?"* **Closed-ended questions**—questions intended to elicit specific information—enable you to zero in on a particular detail about a subject: *"How much money did the government's cost-cutting programs actually save?"*

---

### ✓checklist  Conducting an interview

✓ Always make an appointment.
✓ Prepare a list of specific questions tailored to the subject matter and the time limit of your interview.
✓ Do background reading about your topic. (Do not ask for information that you can easily find elsewhere.)
✓ Have a pen and paper with you. If you want to record the interview, get your subject's permission in advance.
✓ Allow the person you are interviewing to complete an answer before you ask another question.
✓ Take notes, but continue to pay attention as you do so.
✓ Pay attention to the reactions of your interview subject.

✓ Be willing to depart from your prepared list of questions to ask follow-up questions.
✓ At the end of the interview, thank your subject for his or her time and cooperation.
✓ Send a brief note of thanks.

## (2) Conducting a Survey

If you are examining a contemporary social, psychological, or economic issue—the level of satisfaction on your college campus, for instance—a **survey** of attitudes or opinions could be indispensable. Begin by identifying the group of people you will poll. This group can be a **convenient sample**—for example, people in your chemistry lecture—or a **random sample**—names chosen from a telephone directory, for instance. When you choose a sample, your goal is to designate a population that is *representative*. You must also have enough respondents to convince readers that your sample is *significant*. If you poll ten people in your French class about an issue of college policy, and your university has ten thousand students, you cannot expect your readers to be convinced by your results.

You should also be sure your questions are worded clearly and designed to elicit the information you wish to get. For example, short-answer or multiple-choice questions elicit specific responses that can be easily quantified. Paragraph-length responses, however, can be difficult to quantify. Also, be sure that you do not ask so many questions that respondents lose interest and stop answering. Finally, be careful not to ask biased or leading questions.

If your population is your fellow students, you can slip questionnaires under their doors in the residence hall, or you can distribute them in class, if your instructor permits. If your questionnaire is brief, allow respondents a specific amount of time, and collect the forms yourself. If filling out forms on the spot will be time consuming, request that responses be returned to you or placed in a box set up in a central location. (Questions and responses can also be exchanged by e-mail.)

Determining exactly what your results tell you is challenging and sometimes unpredictable. For example, even though only 20 percent of your respondents may be fraternity members, the fact that nearly all fraternity members favor restrictions on hazing would be an unexpected and significant finding.

> **✓checklist** Conducting a survey
> ✓ Determine what you want to know.
> ✓ Select your sample.
> ✓ Design your questions.
> ✓ Distribute the questionnaires.
> ✓ Collect the questionnaires.
> ✓ Analyze your responses.
> ✓ Decide how to use the results in your paper.

# Chapter 8

# Using and Evaluating Internet Sources

## 8a   Understanding the Internet

The **Internet** is a vast system of networks that links millions of computers. Because of its size and diversity, the Internet allows people from all over the world to communicate quickly and easily.

Furthermore, because it is inexpensive to publish text, pictures, and sound online (via the Internet), businesses, government agencies, libraries, and universities are able to make available vast amounts of information: years' worth of newspaper articles, hundreds of thousands of pages of scientific or technical papers, government reports, images of all the paintings in a museum, virtual tours of historically significant buildings or sites—even an entire library of literature.

As you might imagine, the various components of the Internet have revolutionized the way scholars and students conduct research. However, as one scientist put it, the Internet is "like a vast library with all the books strewn on the floor." This chapter will help you understand the various components of the Internet and how to use the Internet for your research.

---

### INFORMATION AVAILABLE ON THE INTERNET

- Breaking news from a variety of news outlets
- Pictures and streaming video as well as live television and radio broadcasts
- Pending legislation, stock market quotes, research study findings, and other current information
- Information disseminated by individuals, institutions, and corporations that is not available in print
- Online editions of newspapers, magazines, and books
- Online editions of scholarly journals

*continued on the following page*

*continued from the previous page*

- Online reference sources, such as encyclopedias, specialized dictionaries, almanacs, and fact books
- Library catalogs and periodical indexes that can help you locate print sources

## 8b Using the World Wide Web for Research

When most people refer to the Internet, they actually mean the **World Wide Web,** which is just a part of the Internet. (See 8c for other components of the Internet that you can use in your research.) The Web relies on **hypertext links,** keywords highlighted in blue (and often underlined). By clicking your mouse on these links, you can move easily from one part of a document to another or from one Web site to another. The Web has become a powerful tool that can give you access to a great deal of print information as well as graphics, sound, animation, film clips, and even live video.

The Web enables you to connect to a vast variety of documents. For example, you can call up a **home page** or **Web page** (an individual document), or a **Web site** (a collection of Web pages). Government agencies, businesses, universities, libraries, newspapers and magazines, journals, and public interest groups, as well as individuals, all operate their own Web sites. Each of these sites contains hypertext links that can take you to other relevant sites. By using these links, you can follow your interests and move from one document to another.

To carry out a Web search, you need a **Web browser,** a tool that enables you to find information on the Web. Two of the most popular browsers—*Netscape Navigator* and *Microsoft Internet Explorer*—display the full range of text, photos, sound, and video available in Web documents. Most new computers come with one of these browsers already installed.

Before you can access the Web, you have to be **online,** connected to an Internet service provider (**ISP**). Most colleges and universities provide Internet access to students free of charge. Once you are online, you use your browser to connect to a **search engine,** a program that helps you retrieve information by searching the documents available on the Internet.

There are three ways to use search engines to find the information you want: *entering an electronic address, using subject guides,* and *doing a keyword search.*

# Using the World Wide Web for Research

## (1) Entering an Electronic Address

The most basic way to access information on the Web is to go directly to a specific electronic address, called a **URL** (uniform resource locator). Search engines and Web browsers display a dialog box that enables you to enter the URL of a particular Web site. (You may also type the URL directly into the "location" text field just below your browser's window.) Once you type in a URL and click on search (or hit *enter* or the return key), you will be connected to the Web site you want. Make sure to type the URL exactly as it appears— without adding spaces or adding or deleting punctuation marks. Remember that omitting just a single letter or punctuation mark will send you to the wrong site—or to no site at all.

Location field

**Figure 1** *Netscape Navigator Home Page*

### What to do if you cannot connect

If you cannot connect to the Web site that you want, do not give up. There are several strategies that you can use to help you connect.

*continued on the following page*

*continued from the previous page*

- Wait a short period of time, and try again. If a Web site is extremely busy, it may block users.
- Make sure that you have typed in the URL correctly. Adding just a space or omitting a slash will change the URL.
- If the URL is very long, delete a section of the URL—from slash to slash—and try again.
- Try using just the base URL—the part that ends with *.com* or *.gov*. If this abbreviated URL does not take you where you want to go, you have an incorrect address.
- If you are following a link from one document to another and cannot connect, type the URL of the link into the location field of your search engine and try again.

## (2) Using Subject Guides

You can also use subject guides to locate information. Some search engines, such as Yahoo!, About.com, and Look Smart, contain a **subject guide**—a list of general categories (*The Arts, Business, Entertainment, Society,* and so on) from which you can choose. Each of these categories will lead you to a more specific list of categories and subcategories until, eventually, you get to the topic you want. For example, clicking on *Society* would lead you to *Activism* and then to *Animal Rights* and eventually to an article concerning cruelty to animals on factory farms. Although using subject guides is a time-consuming strategy for finding specific information, it can be an excellent tool for **exploratory research,** when you want to find or narrow a topic.

See 7a

## (3) Doing a Keyword Search

Finally, you can locate information by doing a **keyword search.** You do this by entering a word or words into your search engine's search field. The search engine will identify any site in its database on which the keyword (or words) you have typed appear. (These sites are called **hits.**) If, for example, you simply type *Civil War* (say, in hope of finding information on Fort Sumter during the Civil War), the search engine will generate an enormous list of hits—well over a million. This list will likely include, along with sites that might be relevant to your research, the Civil War Reenactors home page as well as sites that focus on Civil War music.

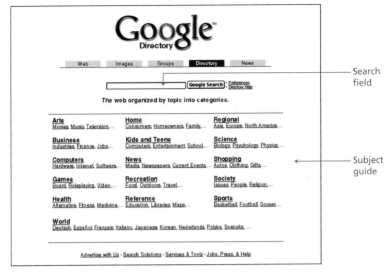

**Figure 2** *Google Subject Directory Page*

Because searching this way is inefficient and time consuming, you need to *focus* your search, just as you do when you use your library's online catalog. You narrow your search by using **search operators,** words and symbols that tell a search engine how to interpret your keywords. One way to focus your search is to put quotation marks around your search term (type *"Fort Sumter"* rather than *Fort Sumter*). This will direct the search engine to locate only documents containing this phrase.

Another way to focus your search is to carry out a **Boolean search,** combining keywords with AND, OR, NOT (typed in all capital letters), or a plus or minus sign to eliminate irrelevant hits from your search. (To do this type of search, you may have to select a search engine's *advanced search* option.) For example, to find Web pages that focus on the battle of Fort Sumter in the Civil War, type *Civil War* AND *Fort Sumter.* If you do, your search will yield only items that contain *both* terms. (If you typed in *Civil War* OR *Fort Sumter,* your search will yield items that contain *either* term.) Some search engines allow you to search using three or more keywords—*Civil War* AND *Fort Sumter* NOT *national monument,* for example. In this case, your search would yield items that contained both the terms *Civil War* and *Fort Sumter,* but *not* the term *national monument.* By limiting your search in this way, you

**151**

would just get items that discussed Fort Sumter and the Civil War and eliminate items that discussed Fort Sumter's current use as a national monument. Focusing your search in this way enables you to avoid irrelevant Web pages.

http://kirsznermandell.heinle.com

### Using search operators

**""** Use quotation marks to search for a specific phrase: *"Baltimore Economy"*

**AND** Use *and* to search for sites that contain both words: *Baltimore* and *Economy*

**OR** Use *or* to search for sites that contain either word: *Baltimore* or *Economy*

**NOT** Use *not* to exclude the word that comes after the *not: Baltimore* and *Economy* not *Agriculture*

**+ (plus sign)** Use a plus sign to include the word that comes after it: *Baltimore + Economy*

**− (minus sign)** Use a minus sign to exclude the word that comes after it: *Baltimore + Economy − Agriculture*

## ? (4) Finding the Right Search Engine

Some search engines are more user-friendly than others; some allow for more sophisticated searching functions; some are updated more frequently; and some are more comprehensive than others. As you try out a number of search engines, you will probably settle on a favorite that you will turn to first whenever you need to find information.

### POPULAR SEARCH ENGINES

*AltaVista* (www.altavista.com): Good, precise engine for focused searches. Fast and easy to use.

*Ask Jeeves* (www.askjeeves.com): Good beginner's site. Allows you to narrow your search by asking questions, such as *Are dogs smarter than pigs?*

*Excite* (www.excite.com): Good for general topics. Because it searches over 250 million Web sites, you often get more information than you need.

*Google* (www.google.com): One of the best search engines available. Accesses a large database that includes both text and graphics. It is easy to navigate, and searches usually yield a high percentage of useful hits.

*Hotbot* (www.hotbot.com): Excellent, fast search engine for locating specific information. Good search options allow you to fine-tune your searches.

*Infoseek* (www.infoseek.com): Enables you to access information in a directory of reviewed sites, news stories, and Usenet groups.

*Lycos* (www.lycos.com): Enables you to search for specific media (graphics, for example). A somewhat small index of Web pages.

*Magellan* (www.magellan.excite.com): Enables you to search sites that have been evaluated for content.

*Northern Light* (www.northernlight.com): Searches Web pages but also lists pay-for-view articles not always listed by other search engines. Arranges results under subject headings.

*WebCrawler* (www.webcrawler.com): Good for beginners. Easy to use.

*Yahoo* (www.yahoo.com): Good for exploratory research. Enables you to search using either subject headings or keywords. Searches its indexes as well as the Web.

Because even the best search engines search only a fraction of what is on the Web, if you use only one search engine, you will most likely miss much valuable information. It is therefore a good idea to repeat each search with several different search engines or to use one of the **metasearch** or **metacrawler** engines that enable you to use several search engines simultaneously.

http://kirsznermandell.heinle.com

**Metasearch engines**
Dogpile (www.dogpile.com)
GoHip (www.gohip.com)
Metacrawler (www.metacrawler.com)

In addition to the popular, general-purpose search engines and metasites, there are also numerous search engines devoted entirely to specific subject areas, such as literature, business, sports, and women's issues. Hundreds of specialized search engines are indexed at Allsearchengines.com (www.allsearchengines.com).

---

http://kirsznermandell.heinle.com

### Specialized search engines

Voice of the Shuttle (humanities search engine)
http://humanitas.ucsb.edu/

Pilot-Search.com (literary search engine)
http://www.Pilot-Search.com/

FedWorld (U.S. government database and report search engine)
http://www.fedworld.gov/

HealthFinder (health, nutrition, and diseases information for consumers)
http://www.healthfinder.org/default.htm

The Internet Movie Database (search engine and database for film facts, reviews, and so on)
http://www.imdb.com

Newsbot (news search engine)
http://www.newsbot.com/

SportQuest (sports search engine)
http://www.sportquest.com/

FindLaw (legal search engine)
http://www.findlaw.com/

Bizbot (business search engine)
http://www.bizbot.net/

---

**Note:** Search Engine Watch at <http://searchenginewatch.com> maintains an extensive, comprehensive, and up-to-date list of the latest search engines. Not only does this site list search engines by category, but it also reviews them.

## ✓checklist Tips for effective searching

✓ *Choose the Right Search Engine* No one all-purpose search site exists. Make sure you review the tips for choosing a search engine on pages 152–153.

✓ *Choose Your Keywords Carefully* A search engine is only as good as the keywords you use.

✓ *Narrow Your Search* Use quotation marks and Boolean search operators to make your searches more productive. Review the box on page 152 before you use any search engine.

✓ *Check Your Spelling* If your search does not yield the results you expect, check to make sure you have spelled your search terms correctly. Even a one-letter mistake can confuse a search engine and cause it to retrieve the wrong information—or no information at all.

✓ *Include Enough Terms* If you are looking for information on housing, for example, search for several different variations of your keyword: *housing, houses, house buyer, buying houses, residential real estate,* and so on. Some search engines, like Infoseek, automatically search plurals; others do not. Some, like AltaVista, automatically search variants of your keyword; others require you to think of the variants by yourself.

✓ *Consult the Help Screen* Most search engines have a *help* screen. If you have trouble with your search, do not hesitate to consult it. A little time here can save you a lot of time later.

✓ *Use More Than One Search Engine* Because different search engines index different sites, try several when you are looking for results. If one does not yield results after a few tries, switch to another. Also, do not forget to do a metasearch with a search engine like Metacrawler.

✓ *Add Useful Sites to Your Bookmarks or Favorites List* Whenever you find a particularly useful Web site, **bookmark** it by selecting this option on the menu bar of your browser (with some browsers, such as *Internet Explorer,* this option is called *Favorites*). If you add a site to your bookmark list, you can return to the site whenever you want to by opening the bookmark menu and selecting it.

## 8c Using Other Internet Tools

In addition to the World Wide Web, the Internet contains a number of other components that you can use to help you gather information for your research.

## (1) Using E-Mail

E-mail can be very useful to you as you do research. You can exchange ideas with classmates, ask questions of your instructors, and even conduct long-distance interviews. You can follow e-mail links in Web documents, and you can also transfer word-processing documents or other files (as e-mail attachments) from one computer to another.

## (2) Using Listservs

**Listservs** (sometimes called **discussion lists**), electronic mailing lists to which you must subscribe, enable you to communicate with groups of people interested in particular topics. (Many schools and even individual courses have listservs.) Individuals in a listserv send e-mails to a main e-mail address, and these messages are routed to all members in the group. Some listserv subscribers may be experts who can answer your queries. Keep in mind, however, that you must evaluate any information you get from a listserv before you use it in your research (**see 8c**).

## (3) Using Newsgroups

Like listservs, **newsgroups** are discussion groups. Unlike listserv messages, which are sent to you as e-mail, newsgroup messages are collected on the **Usenet** system, a global collection of news servers, where anyone can access them. In a sense, newsgroups function as gigantic bulletin boards where users post messages that others can read and respond to. Thus, newsgroups can provide specific information as well as suggestions about where to look for further information. Just as you would with a listserv, evaluate information you get from a newsgroup before you use it (**see 8c**).

## (4) Using Gopher, FTP, and Telnet

At one time, Internet users needed special software to access gopher, telnet, and FTP. Now they can be accessed with most programs that access the Web.

**Gopher** is a tool that organizes textual information into hierarchical menus. Gopher provides access to information about business, medicine, and engineering as well as access to archived newsgroups and electronic books and magazines.

**FTP** (file transfer protocol) enables you to transfer documents at high speed from one computer on the Internet to another. With FTP, you can get the full text of books and articles as well as pictures. The most common use for FTP is in downloading updates from computer software manufacturers.

**Telnet** is a program that enables you to make a connection via telephone to another computer on the Internet. With telnet you can download anything from another host computer.

## (5) Using MUDS, MOOS, IRCS, and Instant Messaging

With e-mails and listservs, there is a delay between the time a message is sent and the time it is received. **MUDS, MOOS, IRCS,** and **instant messaging** enable you to send and receive messages in real time. Communication is **synchronous;** that is, messages are sent and received as they are typed. Synchronous communication programs are being used more and more in college settings—for class discussions, online workshops, and collaborative projects.

### ✓checklist  Observing netiquette

**Netiquette** refers to the guidelines that responsible users of the Internet should follow. When you use the Internet, especially e-mail and synchronous communication, keep the following guidelines in mind.

✓ **Don't Shout** All-uppercase letters indicate that a person is SHOUTING. Not only is this immature, but it is also distracting and irritating.
✓ **Watch Your Tone** Make sure you send the message you actually intend to convey. What may sound humorous to you may seem sarcastic or impolite to someone else.
✓ **Be Careful What You Write** Remember, anything you put in writing will be instantly sent to the address or addresses you have designated. Once you hit *Send*, it is often too late to call back your message. For this reason, treat an e-mail message or a posting as you would a written letter. Take the time to proofread and to consider carefully what you have written.
✓ **Respect the Privacy of Others** Do not forward or post a message that you have received unless you have permission from the sender to do so.

*continued on the following page*

*continued from the previous page*

✓ **Do Not Flame** When you **flame,** you send an insulting electronic message. At best, this response is immature; at worst, it is
disrespectful.
✓ **Make Sure You Use the Correct Electronic Address** Be certain
that your message goes to the right person. Nothing is more em-
barrassing than sending a communication to the wrong address.
✓ **Use Your Computer Facility Ethically and Responsibly** Do not
use computers in public labs for personal communications or
for entertainment. Not only is this a misuse of the facility, but it
also ties up equipment that others may be waiting to use.

# ? 8d   Evaluating Internet Sources

Using the Web for your research has many advantages: it is easy,
convenient, and can yield a great deal of information, some of
which you can get nowhere else. Even with these advantages, using
the Web as a research tool has some significant limitations.

## LIMITATIONS OF THE WEB AS A RESEARCH TOOL

- A Web search can yield more information than you can
reasonably handle or properly evaluate.
- Because it is so convenient, Web research can cause you to
ignore the resources in your college library. Many important
and useful publications are available only in print and on
library databases, not on the Web.
- A Web document may be unstable. Unlike print sources,
Web documents can be altered at any time. For this reason,
you cannot be sure the information you see on a Web site
will be there when you try to access it at a later date. (MLA
recommends that you keep copies of all Web documents you
use in your research.)
- Anyone can publish on the Web, so Web sites can vary
greatly in reliability.
- Authorship and affiliation can sometimes be difficult or
impossible to determine.

Because of these limitations, it is extremely important that you carefully evaluate the content of any Web site for *accuracy, credibility, objectivity, currency, coverage* or *scope,* and *stability.*

**Accuracy** *Accuracy* refers to the reliability of the material itself, accompanied by proper documentation. Keep in mind that factual error—especially errors in facts that are central to the main point of the source—should cause you to question the reliability of the material you are reading.

- Is the text free of basic grammatical and mechanical errors?
- Does the site contain factual errors?
- Does the site provide a list of references?
- Are links available to other references?
- Is the author named or anonymous?
- Can information be verified with print or other resources?

**Credibility** *Credibility* refers to the credentials of the person or organization responsible for the site. Web sites operated by well-known institutions (the Smithsonian or the Library of Congress, for example) have built-in credibility. Those operated by individuals (private Web pages, for example) are often less reliable.

- Does the site list an author?
- Is the author a recognized authority in his or her field?
- Is the site **refereed**? That is, does an editorial board or a group of experts determine what material appears on the Web site?
- Does the organization sponsoring the Web site exist apart from its Web presence?
- Can you determine how long the Web site has existed?

---

**✓checklist** **Evaluating an anonymous or questionable Web source** **?**

When a Web source is anonymous (or has an author whose name is not familiar to you), you have to take special measures to assess its credibility.

✓ *Post a query:* If you subscribe to a relevant newsgroup or a listserv, ask others in the group what they know about the source and its author.

*continued on the following page*

*continued from the previous page*

✓ **Follow the links:** Follow the hypertext links in a document to other documents. If the links take you to legitimate sources, you know the author is aware of these sources of information.

✓ **Do a keyword search:** Do a search using the name of the sponsoring organization or the article as keywords. Other documents (or citations in other works) may identify the author.

✓ **Look at the URL:** The last part of a Web site's URL can tell you whether the site is sponsored by a commercial entity (*.com*), a nonprofit organization (*.org*), an educational institution (*.edu*), the military (*.mil*), or a governmental agency (*.gov*). Knowing this information can tell you whether an organization is trying to sell you something (.com) or just providing information (*.edu* or *.org*).

**Objectivity** *Objectivity* refers to the degree of bias that a Web site exhibits: an objective site is relatively free of bias. Some Web sites make no secret of their biases. They openly advocate a particular point of view or action, or they are clearly trying to sell something. Other Web sites may hide their biases. For example, a Web site may present itself as a source of factual information when it is actually advocating a political point of view.

• Does advertising appear in the text?
• Does a business, a political organization, or a special-interest group sponsor the site?
• Are links provided to sites with a political agenda?
• Does the site express a particular viewpoint?
• Does the site contain links to other sites that express a particular viewpoint?

**Currency** *Currency* refers to how up to date the Web site is. The easiest way to assess a site's currency is to determine when it was last updated. Keep in mind, however, that even if the date on the site is current, the information that the site contains may not be.

• Does the site clearly identify the date it was created?
• Is the most recent update displayed?
• Are all the links to other sites still functioning?
• Is the actual information on the page up to date?

**Coverage or Scope** *Coverage* or *scope* refers to the comprehensiveness of the information on a Web site. More is not necessarily better, but some sites may be scanty or incomplete. Others may provide information that is no more than common knowledge. Still others may present discussions that may not be suitable for college-level research.

- Does the site provide in-depth coverage?
- Does the site provide information that is not available elsewhere?
- Does the site identify a target audience? Does the target audience suggest the site is appropriate for your research needs?

**Stability** *Stability* refers to whether or not the site is being maintained. A stable site will be around when you want to access it again. Web sites that are here today and gone tomorrow make it difficult for readers to check your sources or for you to obtain updated information.

- Has the site been active for a long period of time?
- Is the site updated regularly?
- Is the site maintained by a well-known, reliable organization—that is, one that is likely to be committed to financing the site?

# 8e Useful Web Sites

The Web sites listed here will be useful as you do Internet research.

**Humanities Web Sites**
- *Art History*
  http://witcombe.sbc.edu/ARTHLinks.com
- *Film*
  http://us.imdb.com
- *History*
  http://www.hyperhistory.com/online_n2/History_n2a.html
- *Literature*
  http://digital.library.upenn.edu/books/
- *Philosophy*
  http://plato.stanford.edu
- *Business*
  http://www.ipl.org/ref/RR/static/bus0000.html

## Social Sciences Web Sites

- *Education*
  http://www.education-world.com/
- *Political Science*
  http://politicalresources.net
- *Psychology*
  http://www.psychcrawler.com
- *Sociology and Social Work*
  http://gwbweb.wustl.edu/websites.html

## Natural Sciences Web Sites

- *Biology*
  http://biodiversity.uno.edu
- *Chemistry*
  http://www.ssc.ntu.edu.sg:8000/chemweb/htmlj/
- *Engineering*
  http://www.eng-sol.com
- *Mathematics*
  http://mathworld.wolfram.com/
- *Physics*
  http://www.physicsweb.org/resources/

## Other Useful Web Sites

- Guide to Internet Research and Resources
  http://www.miracosta.cc.ca.us/home/gfloren/INTNET.HTM
- Information on Evaluating Internet Sources (U. VT)
  http://www.lib.vt.edu/research/libinst/evaluating.html
- Internet Research FAQ
  http://www.purefiction.com/pages/res1.htm
- Internet Tutorials
  http://www.albany.edu/library/internet/
- Internet Research Tips
  http://www.albany.edu/library/internet/checklist.html
- Starting Points for Internet Research (Purdue)
  http://owl.english.purdue.edu/internet/tools/research.html
- General Reference Resources (CMU)
  http://eserver.org/reference/
- Selected Web Resources by Academic Subject (Georgetown U.)
  http://gulib.lausun.georgetown.edu/swr/
- (US) Government Information Locator Service
  http://www.gils.net/

## Useful Web Sites

- Internet Public Library—Serials (Magazines)
  http://www.ipl.org/reading/serials/
  http://www.fedworld.gov
- Internet Public Library—Newspapers
  http://www.ipl.org/reading/news/
- Encyclopaedia Britannica Online
  http://www.Britannica.com
- Citing Electronic Sources (APA and MLA)
  http://www.uvm.edu/~ncrane/estyles/
- The World Fact Book
  http://www.odci.gov/cia/publications/factbook/
- Library of Congress
  http://lcweb.loc.gov
- Research-It!
  http://www.iTools.com/research-it/research-it.html

### Recommended Web sites

Many college libraries keep lists of recommended Web sites that librarians have carefully evaluated. Check with a reference librarian to see if your library maintains such a list.

# Chapter 9

# Integrating Sources and Avoiding Plagiarism

As you move through the research process and consult various sources, you take notes in the form of **paraphrase**, **summary**, or **quotation**. When your work is complete, these notes will be integrated into your research paper.

## 9a Integrating Source Material into Your Writing

Weave paraphrases, summaries, and quotations of source material smoothly into your discussion, adding your own analysis or explanation to increase coherence and to show the relevance of your sources to the points you are making. Remember that in your research paper, you are orchestrating a conversation among different speakers, and your own voice should dominate.

**Integrating source material into your writing**

?

To make sure your sentences do not all sound the same, experiment with different methods of integrating source material into your paper.

- Vary the verbs you use to introduce a source's words or ideas (instead of repeating *says* each time).

| | | |
|---|---|---|
| acknowledges | discloses | implies |
| suggests | observes | notes |
| concludes | believes | comments |
| insists | explains | claims |
| predicts | summarizes | illustrates |
| reports | finds | proposes |
| warns | concurs | speculates |
| admits | affirms | indicates |

- Vary the placement of the **identifying tag** (the phrase that identifies the source), putting it sometimes in the middle or at the end of the quoted material instead of always at the beginning.

    Quotation with Identifying Tag in Middle: "A serious problem confronting Amish society from the viewpoint of the Amish themselves," observes Hostetler, "is the threat of absorption into mass society through the values promoted in the public school system" (193).

    Paraphrase with Identifying Tag at End: The Amish are also concerned about their children's exposure to the public school system's values, notes Hostetler (193).

## (1) Integrating Quotations

Be sure to work quotations smoothly into your sentences. Quotations should never be awkwardly dropped into your paper, leaving the exact relationship between the quoted words and your point unclear. Instead, use a brief introductory remark to provide a context for a quotation, quoting only those words you need to make your point.

Unacceptable: For the Amish, the public school system represents a problem. "A serious problem confronting Amish society from the viewpoint of the Amish themselves is the threat of absorption into mass society through the values promoted in the public school system" (Hostetler 193).

Acceptable: For the Amish, the public school system is a problem because it represents "the threat of absorption into mass society" (Hostetler 193).

### Punctuating identifying tags

Whether or not to use a comma with an identifying tag depends on where you place the tag in the sentence. If the identifying tag immediately precedes a quotation, use a comma. If the identifying tag does not immediately precede a quotation, do not use a comma.

As Hostetler points out, "The Amish are successful in maintaining group identity" (56).

*continued on the following page*

*continued from the previous page*

Hostetler points out that the Amish frequently "use severe sanctions to preserve their values" (56).

Never use a comma after *that*.

Incorrect: Hostetler says that, Amish society is "defined by religion" (76).

Correct: Hostetler says that Amish society is "defined by religion" (76).

*Substitutions or Additions within Quotations* When you make changes or additions to make a quotation fit into your paper, acknowledge your changes by enclosing them in brackets (not parentheses).

Original Quotation: "Immediately after her wedding, she and her husband followed tradition and went to visit almost everyone who attended the wedding" (Hostetler 122).

Quotation Revised to Make Verb Tenses Consistent: Nowhere is the Amish dedication to tradition more obvious than in the events surrounding marriage. Right after the wedding celebration, the Amish bride and groom "visit almost everyone who [has] attended the wedding" (Hostetler 122).

Quotation Revised to Supply an Antecedent for a Pronoun: "Immediately after her wedding, [Sarah] and her husband followed tradition and went to visit almost everyone who attended the wedding" (Hostetler 122).

Quotation Revised to Change an Uppercase to a Lowercase Letter: The strength of the Amish community is illustrated by the fact that "[i]mmediately after her wedding, she and her husband followed tradition and went to visit almost everyone who attended the wedding" (Hostetler 122).

*Omissions within Quotations* When you delete unnecessary or irrelevant words, substitute an **ellipsis** (three spaced periods) for the deleted words.

Original: "Not only have the Amish built and staffed their own elementary and vocational schools, but they have gradually organized on local, state, and national levels to cope with the task of educating their children" (Hostetler 206).

Quotation Revised to Eliminate Unnecessary Words: "Not only have the Amish built and staffed their own elementary and vocational schools, but they have gradually organized . . . to cope with the task of educating their children" (Hostetler 206).

## Omissions within quotations

Be sure you do not misrepresent or distort the meaning of quoted material when you delete words from it. For example, do not say, "the Amish have managed to maintain . . . their culture" when the original quotation is "the Amish have managed to maintain *parts of* their culture."

*Long Quotations* Set off a quotation of more than four typed lines of <u>prose</u> (or more than three lines of <u>poetry</u>) by indenting it one inch (ten spaces) from the margin. Double-space, and do not use quotation marks. If you are quoting a single paragraph, do not indent the first line. If you are quoting more than one paragraph, indent the first line of each complete paragraph (including the first one) an additional one-quarter inch (three spaces). Integrate the quotation into your paper by introducing it with a complete sentence followed by a colon. Follow the quotation with parenthetical documentation placed one space after the end punctuation.

See
32b
1 & 2

According to Hostetler, the Amish were not always hostile to public education:

> The one-room rural elementary school served the Amish community well in a number of ways. As long as it was a public school, it stood midway between the Amish community and the world. Its influence was tolerable, depending upon the degree of influence the Amish were able to bring to the situation. (196)

## ? (2) Integrating Paraphrases and Summaries

Introduce paraphrases and summaries with identifying tags, and end them with appropriate documentation. By doing so, you make certain that readers are able to differentiate your ideas from the ideas of your sources.

**Misleading (Ideas of Source Blend with Ideas of Writer):** Art can be used to uncover many problems that children have at home, in school, or with their friends. For this reason, many therapists use art therapy extensively. Children's views of themselves in society are often reflected by their art style. For example, a cramped, crowded art style using only a portion of the paper shows their limited role (Alschuler 260).

**Revised with Identifying Tag (Ideas of Source Differentiated from Ideas of Writer):** Art can be used to uncover many problems that children have at home, in school, or with their friends. For this reason, many therapists use art therapy extensively. According to William Alschuler in *Art and Self-Image*, children's views of themselves in society are often reflected by their art style. For example, a cramped, crowded art style using only a portion of the paper shows a child's limited role (260).

## (3) Synthesizing Sources

A **synthesis** uses paraphrase, summary, and quotation to combine materials from two or more sources, along with your own ideas, to express an original viewpoint. (In this sense, an entire **research paper** is a synthesis.) You begin synthesizing material by comparing your sources and determining how they are alike and different, where they agree and disagree, and whether they reach the same conclusions. As you identify connections between one source and another or between a source and your own ideas, you develop your own perspective on your subject. It is this viewpoint, summarized in a thesis statement (in the case of an entire paper) or in a topic sentence (in the case of a paragraph), that becomes the focus of your synthesis.

See 10c

As you write your synthesis, present your points one at a time, and use material from your sources to support these points. Make certain you use identifying tags as well as the transitional words and phrases that readers need to follow your discussion. Finally, remember that your distinctive viewpoint, not the ideas of your sources, should be central to your discussion.

Following is a synthesis written by a student as part of a research paper:

> Computers have already changed our lives. They carry out (at incredible speed) many of the everyday tasks that make our way of life possible. For example, computer billing, with all its faults, makes modern business possible, and without computers we would not have access to the telephone services or television reception that we take for granted. But computers are more than fast calculators. According to one computer expert, they are well on their way to learning, creating, and someday even thinking (Raphael 21). Another computer expert, Douglas Hofstadter, agrees, saying that someday a computer will have both "will . . . and consciousness" (423). It seems likely, then, that as a result of the computer, our culture will change profoundly (Turkle 15).

## 9b  Avoiding Plagiarism

**Plagiarism** is presenting another person's ideas or words as if they are your own. The availability of electronic resources like full-text databases and the Internet have made plagiarism, whether intentional or inadvertent, much easier. But it has also made it much easier for instructors to detect it. The penalties for intentional plagiarism are often severe, ranging from a failing grade for your paper to permanent expulsion from school. Colleges and universities take this form of academic dishonesty very seriously, especially when it is deliberate.

To avoid the temptation to plagiarize, start your research paper early, choose a topic that interests you, and understand that the skills you learn now will help you in other courses and beyond your college career. Never cut corners by buying a research paper from a Web site or from another student; never ask another student to write your paper for you or to give you a copy of his or her paper to submit as your own. Do not cut and paste text from a Web site or full-text article into your paper without properly documenting your source. Always give credit whenever you use someone else's words or ideas, even if those words or ideas come from an e-mail message. Never use sources you have not actually read or, even worse, invent sources that do not exist. If you paraphrase, do so correctly by following the examples in this chapter; changing a few words here and there is not enough.

Even noted scholars and historians have been known to make "mistakes" when documenting their sources. But there is a difference between honest mistakes and deliberate cheating. Intentional plagiarism is never tolerated because it compromises the educational experience for everyone.

Unintentional plagiarism—occurring, for example, when a student pastes a quoted passage from a computer file directly into a paper and forgets to use quotation marks and documentation— also carries penalties.

The best way to avoid plagiarism is to take careful notes, to distinguish between your ideas and those of your sources, and to give credit to your sources with **documentation**.

See
Chs.
10–12

## Causes of accidental plagiarism

Students may commit accidental plagiarism for a variety of reasons. Be very careful not to make any of the following mistakes:
- Forgetting to put quotation marks in handwritten notes
- Forgetting to circle or boldface quotation marks
- Recording inaccurate bibliographic information
- Carelessly summarizing or paraphrasing sources
- Indiscriminately cutting and pasting passages from electronic sources into a paper
- Mixing up quoted sources with paraphrases and summaries in notes
- Having so many photocopied or downloaded pages that management of sources becomes almost impossible

In general, you must document words and ideas borrowed from your sources. (This rule applies to both print and electronic sources.) Of course, certain items need not be documented: **common knowledge** (information every reader probably knows), facts available from a variety of reference sources, familiar sayings and well-known quotations, and your own original research (interviews and surveys, for example). Information that is in dispute or that is one person's original contribution, however, must be acknowledged. You need not, for example, document the fact that

John F. Kennedy graduated from Harvard in 1940 or that he was elected president in 1960. You must, however, document a historian's evaluation of Kennedy's performance as president or one researcher's recent assertions about Kennedy's private life.

You can avoid plagiarism by using documentation wherever it is required and by adhering to the guidelines that follow.

## (1) Enclose Borrowed Words in Quotation Marks

Original: Historically, only a handful of families have dominated the fireworks industry in the West. Details such as chemical recipes and mixing procedures were cloaked in secrecy and passed down from one generation to the next. . . . One effect of familial secretiveness is that, until recent decades, basic pyrotechnic research was rarely performed, and even when it was, the results were not generally reported in scientific journals. (Conkling, John A. "Pyrotechnics." *Scientific American* July 1990: 96)

Plagiarism: John A. Conkling points out that until recently, little scientific research was done on the chemical properties of fireworks, and when it was, <u>the results were not generally reported in scientific journals</u> (96).

Even though the student writer does document the source of his information, he uses the source's exact words without placing them in quotation marks.

Correct (Borrowed Words in Quotation Marks): John A. Conkling points out that until recently, little scientific research was done on the chemical properties of fireworks, and when it was, "<u>the results were not generally reported in scientific journals</u>" (96).

Correct (Paraphrase): John A. Conkling points out that <u>the little research conducted on the chemical composition of fireworks was seldom reported in the scientific literature</u> (96).

---

http://kirsznermandell.heinle.com

### Plagiarism and Internet sources

Any time you download text from the <u>Internet</u>, you run the risk of committing unintentional plagiarism. To avoid the possibility of plagiarism, follow these guidelines:

See Ch. 8

*continued on the following page*

*continued from the previous page*

- Download information into individual files so you can keep track of your sources.
- Do not simply cut and paste blocks of downloaded text into your paper; summarize or paraphrase this material first.
- If you record the exact words of your source, enclose them in quotation marks.
- Whether your information is from e-mails, online discussion groups, listservs, or World Wide Web sites, give proper credit by providing appropriate documentation.
- Always document figures, tables, charts, and graphs obtained from the Internet or from any other electronic source.

## (2) Do Not Imitate a Source's Syntax and Phrasing

Original: Let's be clear: this wish for politically correct casting goes only one way, the way designed to redress the injuries of centuries. When Pat Carroll, who is a woman, plays Falstaff, who is not, casting is considered a stroke of brilliance. When Josette Simon, who is black, plays Maggie in *After the Fall,* a part Arthur Miller patterned after Marilyn Monroe and which has traditionally been played not by white women, but by blonde white women, it is hailed as a breakthrough.

But when the pendulum moves the other way, the actors' union balks. (Quindlen, Anna. "Error, Stage Left." *New York Times* 12 Aug. 1990, sec. 1: 21)

Plagiarism: Let us be honest. The desire for politically appropriate casting goes in only one direction, the direction intended to make up for the damage done over hundreds of years. When Pat Carroll, a female, is cast as Falstaff, a male, the decision is a brilliant one. When Josette Simon, a black woman, is cast as Maggie in *After the Fall,* a role that Arthur Miller based on Marilyn Monroe and that has usually been played by a woman who is not only white but also blonde, it is considered a major advance.

But when the shoe is on the other foot, the actors' union resists (Quindlen 21).

Although this student does not use the exact words of her source, she closely imitates the original's syntax and phrasing, simply substituting synonyms for the author's words.

# Avoiding Plagiarism

Correct (Paraphrase; One Distinctive Phrase Placed In Quotation Marks): According to Anna Quindlen, the actors' union supports "politically correct casting" (21) only when it means casting a woman or minority group member in a role created for a male or a Caucasian. Thus, it is acceptable for actress Pat Carroll to play Falstaff or for black actress Josette Simon to play Marilyn Monroe; in fact, casting decisions such as these are praised. But when it comes to casting a Caucasian in a role intended for an African American, Asian, or Hispanic, the union objects (21).

**Note:** Although the parenthetical documentation at the end identifies the passage's source, the quotation requires separate documentation.

## (3) Document Statistics Obtained from a Source

Although many people assume that statistics are common knowledge, they are usually the result of original research and must therefore be documented. Moreover, providing the source of statistics allows readers to assess their reliability.

Correct: According to one study, male drivers between the ages of sixteen and twenty-four accounted for the majority of accidents. Of 303 accidents recorded almost one-half took place before the drivers were legally allowed to drive at eighteen (Schuman et al., 1027).

## (4) Differentiate Your Words and Ideas from Those of the Source

Original: At some colleges and universities traditional survey courses of world and English literature . . . have been scrapped or diluted. At others they are in peril. At still others they will be. What replaces them is sometimes a mere option of electives, sometimes "multicultural" courses introducing material from Third World cultures and thinning out an already thin sampling of Western writings, and sometimes courses geared especially to issues of class, race, and gender. Given the notorious lethargy of academic decision-making, there has probably been more clamor than change; but if there's enough clamor, there will be change (Howe, Irving. "The Value of the Canon." *The New Republic* 2 Feb. 1991: 40–47).

Plagiarism: Debates about expanding the literary canon take place at many colleges and universities across the United States.

At many universities the Western literature survey courses have been edged out by courses that emphasize minority concerns. These courses are "thinning out an already thin sampling of Western writings" in favor of courses geared especially to issues of "class, race, and gender" (Howe 40).

Because the student writer does not differentiate his ideas from those of his source, it appears that only the quotation in the last sentence is borrowed when, in fact, the first sentence also owes a debt to the original. The student should have clearly identified the boundaries of the borrowed material by introducing it with an identifying tag and ending with documentation. (Note that a quotation *always* requires separate documentation.)

Correct: Debates about expanding the literary canon take place at many colleges and universities across the United States. According to critic Irving Howe, at many universities the Western literature survey courses have been edged out by courses that emphasize minority concerns (41). These courses, says Howe, are "thinning out an already thin sampling of Western writings" in favor of "courses geared especially to issues of class, race, and gender" (40).

---

## ✓ checklist) Avoiding plagiarism

✓ **Take careful notes.** Be sure you have recorded information from your sources carefully and accurately.

✓ **In your handwritten notes, put all words borrowed from your sources inside circled quotation marks** and enclose your own comments within brackets. If you are taking notes on a computer, boldface all quotation marks.

✓ **In your paper, differentiate your ideas from those of your sources** by clearly introducing borrowed material with an identifying tag and by following it with documentation.

✓ **Enclose all direct quotations** used in your paper within quotation marks.

✓ **Review all paraphrases and summaries in your paper** to make certain they are in your own words and that any distinctive words and phrases from a source are quoted.

✓ **Document all quoted material and all paraphrases and summaries** of your sources.

✓ **Document all facts** that are open to dispute or are not common knowledge.
✓ **Document all opinions, conclusions, figures, tables, statistics, graphs, and charts** taken from a source.
✓ **Never submit the work of another person as your own.** Do not buy a paper from an online paper mill or use a paper given to you by a friend. In addition, do not include in your paper passages that have been written by a friend, relative, or writing tutor.

# PART 4

# Documenting Sources: MLA Style

**10 MLA Documentation Style    182**
   **10a**  Using MLA Style    182
   **10b**  MLA Manuscript Guidelines    205
   **10c**  Sample MLA-Style Research Paper    206

## Works-Cited Format: MLA

*A book by one author*

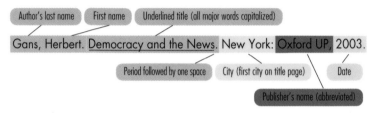

*An article in a scholarly journal with continuous pagination through an annual volume*

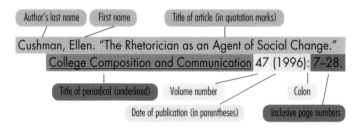

*A home page for a course or a personal home page*

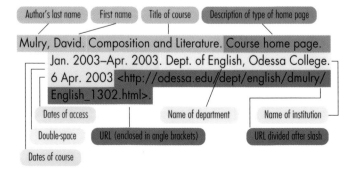

# PART 4

## ? Frequently Asked Questions

**Chapter 10  MLA Documentation Style    182**
- What is MLA style? 182
- How do I list the sources I use in my paper? 187
- How do I document sources I get from the Internet? 195
- How do I type a works-cited list? 206
- What should an MLA paper look like? 210

| **URLs** | *Visit the following sites for answers to more FAQs* |
| --- | --- |

**MLA Style Guide (Capital Comm.-Tech. College, CT)**
*http://webster.commnet.edu/mla.htm*

**MLA Homepage**
*http://www.mla.org/set_stl.htm*

**Dan Kies' Guide to the MLA Style (College of DuPage)**
*http://www.cod.edu/dept/kiesdan/engl_101/mla.htm*

**MLA Style Documentation (U. Wisc.)**
*http://www.wisc.edu/writing/Handbook/DocMLA.html*

**Big Dog Grammar's Quick MLA Guide**
*http://gabiscott.com/bigdog/mla.htm*

**Downloadable MLA Style Guide pdf file (Montana State U.)**
*http://www.lib.montana.edu/instruct/styles/*

**Sample Citations in MLA Style**
*http://perth.uwlax.edu/MurphyLibrary/guides/mla.html*

**Citing Electronic Sources (APA and MLA)**
*http://www.uvm.edu/~ncrane/estyles/*

MLA Documentation Style

 *Directory of MLA Parenthetical References*

1. A work by a single author  (p. 183)
2. A work by two or three authors  (p. 184)
3. A work by more than three authors  (p. 184)
4. A work in multiple volumes  (p. 184)
5. A work without a listed author  (p. 184)
6. A work that is one page long  (p. 184)
7. An indirect source  (p. 184)
8. More than one work  (p. 185)
9. A literary work  (p. 185)
10. An entire work  (p. 186)
11. Two or more authors with the same last name  (p. 186)
12. A government document or a corporate author  (p. 186)
13. An electronic source  (p. 186)

 *Directory of MLA Works-Cited List Entries*

**Entries for Books**

1. A book by one author  (p. 187)
2. A book by two or three authors  (p. 187)
3. A book by more than three authors  (p. 187)
4. Two or more books by the same author  (p. 188)
5. An edited book  (p. 188)
6. A selection in an anthology  (p. 188)
7. More than one essay from the same anthology  (p. 189)
8. A multivolume work  (p. 189)
9. A book in a series  (p. 189)
10. The foreword, preface, or afterword of a book  (p. 189)
11. A short story, play, or poem in an anthology  (p. 189)
12. A short story, play, or poem in a collection of an author's work  (p. 190)
13. A book with a title within its title  (p. 190)
14. A translation  (p. 190)
15. A republished book  (p. 190)
16. A dissertation (published/unpublished)  (p. 190)
17. An article in a reference book (signed/unsigned)  (p. 191)
18. A pamphlet  (p. 191)
19. A government publication  (p. 191)
20. A book by a corporate author  (p. 191)

**Entries for Articles**

21. An article in a scholarly journal with continuous pagination through an annual volume  (p. 192)
22. An article in a scholarly journal with separate pagination in each issue  (p. 192)

23. An article in a weekly magazine (signed/unsigned)   (p. 192)
24. An article in a monthly magazine   (p. 192)
25. An article that does not appear on consecutive pages   (p. 192)
26. An article in a newspaper (signed/unsigned)   (p. 192)
27. An editorial   (p. 193)
28. A letter to the editor   (p. 193)
29. A book review   (p. 193)
30. An article with a title within its title   (p. 193)

**Entries for Other Sources**
31. A lecture   (p. 193)
32. A personal interview   (p. 193)
33. A published interview   (p. 194)
34. A personal letter   (p. 194)
35. A letter published in a collection   (p. 194)
36. A letter in a library's archives   (p. 194)
37. A film   (p. 194)
38. A videotape, DVD, or laser disc   (p. 194)
39. A radio or television program   (p. 194)
40. A recording   (p. 195)
41. A cartoon or comic strip   (p. 195)
42. An advertisement   (p. 195)

**Entries for Electronic Sources (Internet)**
43. A scholarly project or information database on the Internet
    (p. 195)
44. A document within a scholarly project or information data-
    base on the Internet   (p. 196)
45. A home page for a course or a personal home page on the
    Internet   (p. 196)
46. A book on the Internet   (p. 196)
47. An article in a scholarly journal on the Internet   (p. 196)
48. An article in a newspaper on the Internet   (p. 196)
49. An article in a newsletter on the Internet   (p. 196)
50. An article in a magazine on the Internet   (p. 197)
51. A review on the Internet   (p. 197)
52. A letter to the editor on the Internet   (p. 197)
53. An article in an encyclopedia on the Internet   (p. 197)
54. A linked site on the Internet   (p. 197)
55. A painting on the Internet   (p. 197)
56. A photograph on the Internet   (p. 198)
57. A cartoon on the Internet   (p. 198)
58. A map on the Internet   (p. 198)

59. A radio program from an archive on the Internet    (p. 198)
60. An e-mail    (p. 198)
61. An online posting (a newsgroup or online forum)    (p. 198)
62. A synchronous communication (MOO or MUD)    (p. 198)

Entries for Electronic Sources (Subscription Service)
63. A scholarly journal article with separate pagination in each issue from a subscription service    (p. 200)
64. A scholarly journal article with continuous pagination throughout an annual volume from a subscription service    (p. 200)
65. A monthly magazine article from a subscription service    (p. 200)
66. A news service from a subscription service    (p. 200)
67. A news wire from a subscription service    (p. 201)
68. A newspaper article from a subscription service    (p. 201)
69. A pamphlet from a subscription service    (p. 201)
70. A reference book article from a subscription service    (p. 201)
71. A dictionary definition from a subscription service    (p. 201)

Other Electronic Sources
72. A nonperiodical publication on DVD, CD-ROM, or diskette database    (p. 202)
73. A periodical publication on a DVD or CD-ROM database    (p. 202)

# MLA Documentation Style

**Documentation,** the formal acknowledgment of the sources you use in your paper, enables your readers to judge the quality and originality of your work. This chapter explains and illustrates the documentation style recommended by the Modern Language Association (MLA). Chapter 11 discusses the documentation style of the American Psychological Association (APA). Chapter 12 gives an overview of the formats recommended by *The Chicago Manual of Style* (Chicago), the Council of Science Editors (CSE), and organizations in other disciplines.

## 10a   Using MLA Style*

**?** MLA style is required by many teachers of English and other languages as well as by teachers in other humanities disciplines. This method of documentation has three parts: *parenthetical references in the body of the paper* (also known as *in-text citations*), a *works-cited list,* and *content notes.*

### (1) Parenthetical References in the Text

MLA documentation uses **parenthetical references** in the body of the paper keyed to a works-cited list at the end of the paper. A typical parenthetical reference consists of the author's last name and a page number.

The colony's religious and political freedom appealed to many idealists in

Europe (Ripley 132).

To distinguish two or more sources by the same author, include an appropriate shortened title in the parenthetical reference after the author's name.

Penn emphasized his religious motivation (Kelley, William Penn 116).

---

*MLA documentation style follows the guidelines set in the *MLA Handbook for Writers of Research Papers,* 6th ed. New York: MLA, 2003.

If you state the author's name or the title of the work in your discussion, do not include it in the parenthetical reference.

Penn's political motivation is discussed by Joseph J. Kelley in <u>Pennsylvania, The Colonial Years, 1681–1776</u> (44).

### Punctuating with parenthetical references: MLA

*Paraphrases and summaries* Parenthetical references are placed *before* the sentence's end punctuation.

Penn's writings epitomize seventeenth-century religious thought (Dengler and Curtis 72).

*Quotations run in with the text* Parenthetical references are placed *after* the quotation but *before* the end punctuation.

As Ross says, "Penn followed his conscience in all matters" (127).

According to Williams, "Penn's utopian vision was informed by his Quaker beliefs . . ." (72).

*Quotations set off from the text* When you quote more than four lines of **prose** or more than three lines of **poetry**, parenthetical references are placed one space *after* the end punctuation.

According to Arthur Smith, William Penn envisioned a state based on his religious principles:

> Pennsylvania would be a commonwealth in which all individuals would follow God's truth and develop according to God's law. For Penn, this concept of government was self-evident. It would be a mistake to see Pennsylvania as anything but an expression of Penn's religious beliefs. (314)

See 32b1

See 32b2

*Sample MLA Parenthetical References*
*1. A Work by a Single Author*

Fairy tales reflect the emotions and fears of children (Bettelheim 23).

## 2. A Work by Two or Three Authors

The conventions of the ancient Greek theater reflect the culture in which they developed (Watson and McKernie 17).

With the advent of behaviorism, psychology began a new phase of inquiry (Cowen, Barbo, and Crum 31–34).

## 3. A Work by More Than Three Authors

List only the first author, followed by et al. ("and others").

The European powers believed they could change the fundamentals of Muslim existence (Bull et al. 395).

## 4. A Work in Multiple Volumes

If you list more than one volume of a multivolume work in your works-cited list, include the appropriate volume and page number (separated by a colon followed by a space).

The French Revolution had a great influence on William Blake (Raine 1: 52–53).

## 5. A Work without a Listed Author

Use a shortened version of the title in the parenthetical reference, beginning with the word by which it is alphabetized in the works-cited list.

In spite of political unrest, Soviet television remained fairly conservative, ignoring all challenges to the system ("Soviet" 3).

## 6. A Work That Is One Page Long

Do not include a page reference for a one-page article.

Sixty percent of Arab Americans work in white-collar jobs (El-Badru).

## 7. An Indirect Source

If you must use a statement by one author that is quoted in the work of another author, indicate that the material is from an indirect source with the abbreviation qtd. in ("quoted in").

Wagner stated that myth and history stood before him "with opposing claims" (qtd. in Thomas 65).

## 8. More Than One Work

Cite each work as you normally would, separating one from another with a semicolon.

The Brooklyn Bridge has been used as a subject by many American artists

(McCullough 144; Tashjian 58).

**Note:** Long parenthetical references distract readers. Whenever possible, present them as <u>content notes</u>.

See
10a3

## 9. A Literary Work

When citing a work of **prose,** it is often helpful to include more than just the author's name and the page number in the parenthetical citation. Begin with the page number, follow it with a semicolon, and then add any additional information that might be necessary.

In <u>Moby Dick,</u> Melville refers to a whaling expedition funded by Louis XIV of

France (151; ch. 24).

Parenthetical references to **poetry** do not include page numbers. In parenthetical references to long poems, cite division and line numbers, separating them with a period.

In the <u>Aeneid</u>, Virgil describes the ships as cleaving the "green woods

reflected in the calm water" (8.124).

(In this citation, the reference is to book 8, line 124 of the <u>Aeneid.</u>)

When citing short poems, identify the poet and the poem in the text of the paper and use line numbers in the citation.

In "A Song in the Front Yard," Brooks says, "I've stayed in the front yard all

my life / I want a peek at the back" (lines 1–2).

**Note:** When citing lines of a poem, include the word line (or lines) only in the first parenthetical reference; use just numbers in subsequent references.

In citing verse plays, include the act, scene, and line numbers, separated by periods (<u>Macbeth</u> 2.2.14–16). In biblical citations, include an abbreviated title, the chapter, and the verse (Gen. 5.12).

**Note:** Use arabic rather than roman numerals for act and scene numbers of plays.

### 10. An Entire Work

When citing an entire work, include the author's name and the work's title in the text of your paper rather than in a parenthetical reference.

Herbert Gans's The Urban Villagers is a study of an Italian-American

neighborhood in Boston.

### 11. Two or More Authors with the Same Last Name

To distinguish authors with the same last name, include their initials in the parenthetical references.

Recent increases in crime have probably caused thousands of urban

homeowners to install alarms (R. Weishoff, 115). Some of these alarms use

sophisticated sensors that were developed by the army (C. Weishoff, 76).

### 12. A Government Document or a Corporate Author

Cite such works using the organization's name followed by the page number (American Automobile Association 34). You can avoid long parenthetical references by working the organization's name into your paper.

According to the President's Commission for the Study of Ethical Problems in

Medicine and Biomedical and Behavioral Research, the issues relating to

euthanasia are complicated (76).

### 13. An Electronic Source

If a reference to an electronic source includes paragraph numbers rather than page numbers, use the abbreviation par. or pars. followed by the paragraph number or numbers.

The earliest type of movie censorship came in the form of licensing fees, and

in Deer River, Minnesota, "a licensing fee of $200 was deemed not excessive

for a town of 1000" (Ernst, par. 20).

If the electronic source has no page or paragraph numbers, try to cite the work in your discussion rather than in a parenthetical reference.

In her article "Limited Horizons," Lynne Cheney says that schools do best when

students read literature not for what it tells about the workplace, but for its

insights into the human condition.

**Note:** By looking at your works-cited list, readers will be able to determine that the source is electronic and, therefore, not likely to have page numbers.

## (2) Works-Cited List

The **works-cited list,** which appears at the end of your paper, gives publication information for all the research materials you cite. (If your instructor tells you to list all the sources you read, whether you actually cited them or not, give this list the title Works Consulted.) Double-space within and between entries on the list.

*Sample MLA Works-Cited Entries: Books* Book citations include the author's name; book title (underlined); and publication information (place, publisher, date). Capitalize all major words of the title except articles, coordinating conjunctions, prepositions, and the *to* of an infinitive (unless such a word is the first or last word of the title or subtitle). Do not underline the period that follows a book's title.

*1. A Book by One Author*

Use a short form of the publisher's name; *Alfred A. Knopf, Inc.,* for example, is shortened to *Knopf,* and *Oxford University Press* becomes *Oxford UP.*

Bettelheim, Bruno. <u>The Uses of Enchantment: The Meaning and Importance</u>

<u>of Fairy Tales</u>. New York: Knopf, 1976.

When citing an edition other than the first, indicate the edition number that appears on the work's title page.

Gans, Herbert J. <u>The Urban Villagers</u>. 2nd ed. New York: Free, 1982.

*2. A Book by Two or Three Authors*

List the first author last name first. Subsequent authors are listed first name first in the order in which they appear on the title page.

Watson, Jack, and Grant McKernie. <u>A Cultural History of the Theater</u>. New

York: Longman, 1993.

*3. A Book by More Than Three Authors*

List only the first author, followed by et al. ("and others").

Bull, Henry, et al. <u>The Near East</u>. New York: Oxford UP, 1990.

#### 4. Two or More Books by the Same Author

List books by the same author in alphabetical order by title. After the first entry, use three unspaced hyphens followed by a period in place of the author's name.

Thomas, Lewis. <u>The Lives of a Cell: Notes of a Biology Watcher</u>. New York:

Viking, 1974.

- - -. <u>The Medusa and the Snail: More Notes of a Biology Watcher</u>. New York:

Viking, 1979.

If the author is the editor or translator of the second entry, place a comma and the appropriate abbreviation after the hyphens (---, ed.).

#### 5. An Edited Book

An edited book is a work prepared for publication by a person other than the author. If your emphasis is on the *author*'s work, begin your citation with the author's name. After the title, include the abbreviation *Ed.* ("Edited by") followed by the name of the editor or editors.

Bartram, William. <u>The Travels of William Bartram</u>. Ed. Mark Van Doren. New

York: Dover, 1955.

If your emphasis is on the *editor*'s work, begin your citation with the editor's name followed by the abbreviation ed. ("editor") if there is one editor or eds. ("editors") if there is more than one. After the title, give the author's name preceded by the word By.

Van Doren, Mark, ed. <u>The Travels of William Bartram</u>. By William Bartram.

New York: Dover, 1955.

#### 6. A Selection in an Anthology

Even if you cite only one page in your paper, supply inclusive page numbers for the entire essay.

Lloyd, G. E. R. "Science and Mathematics." <u>The Legacy of Greece</u>. Ed. Moses

I. Finley. New York: Oxford UP, 1981. 256–300.

**Note:** Lloyd's initials are separated by a period and one space.

# Using MLA Style

### 7. More Than One Essay from the Same Anthology

List each essay from the same anthology separately, followed by a cross-reference to the entire anthology. Also list complete publication information for the anthology itself.

Bolgar, Robert R. "The Greek Legacy." Finley 429–72.

Finley, Moses I., ed. The Legacy of Greece. New York: Oxford UP, 1981.

Williams, Bernard. "Philosophy." Finley 202–55.

### 8. A Multivolume Work

When all volumes of a multivolume work have the same title, include the number of the volume you are using.

Raine, Kathleen. Blake and Tradition. Vol. 1. Princeton: Princeton UP, 1968.

When you use two or more volumes, cite the entire work.

Raine, Kathleen. Blake and Tradition. 2 vols. Princeton: Princeton UP, 1968.

If the volume you are using has an individual title, however, cite the title without mentioning any other volumes.

Durant, Will, and Ariel Durant. The Age of Napoleon. New York:

Simon, 1975.

### 9. A Book in a Series

If the title page indicates that the book is a part of a series, include the series name, neither underlined nor enclosed in quotation marks, and the series number, followed by a period, before the publication information.

Davis, Bertram H. Thomas Percy. Twayne's English Authors Ser. 313. Boston:

Twayne, 1981.

### 10. The Foreword, Preface, or Afterword of a Book

Taylor, Telford. Preface. Less Than Slaves. By Benjamin B. Ferencz.

Cambridge: Harvard UP, 1979. xiii–xxii.

### 11. A Short Story, Play, or Poem in an Anthology

Chopin, Kate. "The Storm." Literature: Reading, Reacting, Writing. Ed. Laurie G.

Kirszner and Stephen R. Mandell. 5th ed. Boston: Heinle, 2004. 176–79.

Shakespeare, William. <u>Othello, The Moor of Venice</u>. <u>Shakespeare: Six Plays</u>
<u>and the Sonnets</u>. Ed. Thomas Marc Parrott and Edward Hubler. New
York: Scribner's, 1956. 145–91.

## 12. A Short Story, Play, or Poem in a Collection of an Author's Work

Walcott, Derek. "Nearing La Guaira." <u>Selected Poems</u>. New York: Farrar,
1964. 47–48.

## 13. A Book with a Title within Its Title

If the book you are citing contains a title that is normally underlined to indicate italics (a novel, play, or long poem, for example),
do *not* underline the interior title.

Knoll, Robert E., ed. <u>Storm over</u> The Waste Land. Chicago: Scott, 1964.

If the book you are citing contains a title that is normally enclosed within quotation marks, keep the quotation marks.

Herzog, Alan, ed. <u>Twentieth Century Interpretations of "To a Skylark."</u>
Englewood Cliffs: Prentice, 1975.

## 14. A Translation

García Márquez, Gabriel. <u>One Hundred Years of Solitude</u>. Trans. Gregory
Rabassa. New York: Avon, 1991.

## 15. A Republished Book

Include the original publication date after the title of a republished book—for example, a paperback version of a hardcover book.

Wharton, Edith. <u>The House of Mirth</u>. 1905. New York: Scribner's, 1975.

## 16. A Dissertation (Published/Unpublished)

For dissertations published by University Microfilms International (UMI), include the order number.

Peterson, Shawn. <u>Loving Mothers and Lost Daughters: Images of Female</u>
<u>Kinship Relations in Selected Novels of Toni Morrison</u>. Diss. U of
Oregon, 1993. Ann Arbor: UMI, 1994. ATT9322935.

**Note:** University Microfilms, which publishes most of the dissertations in the United States, also publishes in CD-ROM. You will find
the proper format for citing CD-ROMs on page 202.

# Using MLA Style

Use quotation marks for the title of an unpublished dissertation.

Romero, Yolanda Garcia. "The American Frontier Experience in Twentieth-

Century Northwest Texas." Diss. Texas Tech U, 1993.

## 17. An Article in a Reference Book (Signed/Unsigned)

For a signed article, begin with the author's name.

Drabble, Margaret. "Expressionism." The Oxford Companion to English

Literature. 5th ed. New York: Oxford UP, 1985.

When citing familiar encyclopedias, do not include publication information. Enter the title of an unsigned article just as it is listed in the reference book.

"Cubism." The Encyclopedia Americana. 1994 ed.

## 18. A Pamphlet

If no author is listed, enter the underlined title first.

Existing Light Photography. Rochester: Kodak, 1989.

## 19. A Government Publication

If the publication has no listed author, begin with the name of the government, followed by the name of the agency.

United States. Office of Consumer Affairs. 1999 Consumer's Resource

Handbook. Washington: GPO, 1999.

## 20. A Book by a Corporate Author

A book is cited by its corporate author when individual members of the association, commission, or committee that produced it are not identified on the title page.

American Automobile Association. Western Canada and Alaska. Heathrow,

FL: AAA Publishing, 1999.

*Sample MLA Works-Cited Entries: Articles* Article citations include the author's name; the title of the article (in quotation marks); the title of the periodical (underlined); the month (abbreviated except for May, June, and July) and the year; and the pages on which the full article appears, without the abbreviations *p.* or *pp.*

**21. An Article in a Scholarly Journal with Continuous Pagination through an Annual Volume**

For an article in a journal with continuous pagination—for example, one in which an issue ends on page 172 and the next issue begins with page 173—include the volume number, followed by the date of publication (in parentheses). Follow the publication date with a colon, a space, and the inclusive page numbers.

Huntington, John. "Science Fiction and the Future." College English 37

(1975): 340–58.

**22. An Article in a Scholarly Journal with Separate Pagination in Each Issue**

For a journal in which each issue begins with page 1, add a period and the issue number after the volume number.

Sipes, R. G. "War, Sports, and Aggression: An Empirical Test of Two Rival

Theories." American Anthropologist 4.2 (1973): 65–84.

**23. An Article in a Weekly Magazine (Signed/Unsigned)**

For signed articles, start with the author, last name first. In dates, the day precedes the month.

Traub, James. "The Hearts and Minds of City College." New Yorker 7 June

1993: 42–53.

For unsigned articles, start with the title of the article.

"Solzhenitsyn: A Candle in the Wind." Time 23 Mar. 1970: 70.

**24. An Article in a Monthly Magazine**

Roll, Lori. "Careers in Engineering." Working Woman Nov. 1982: 62.

**25. An Article That Does Not Appear on Consecutive Pages**

When, for example, an article begins on page 120 and then skips to page 186, include only the first page number and a plus sign.

Griska, Linda. "Stress and Job Performance." Psychology Today Nov.–Dec.

1995: 120+.

**26. An Article in a Newspaper (Signed/Unsigned)**

Oates, Joyce Carol. "When Characters from the Page Are Made Flesh on the

Screen." New York Times 23 Mar. 1986, late ed.: C1+.

"Soviet Television." <u>Los Angeles Times</u> 13 Dec. 1990, sec. 2: 3+.

**Note:** Omit the article *the* from the title of a newspaper even if the actual title includes the article.

### 27. An Editorial

"Tough Cops, Not Brutal Cops." Editorial. <u>New York Times</u> 5 May 1994, late ed.: A26.

### 28. A Letter to the Editor

Bishop, Jennifer. Letter. <u>Philadelphia Inquirer</u> 10 Dec. 1995: A17.

### 29. A Book Review

Fox-Genovese, Elizabeth. "Big Mess on Campus." Rev. of <u>Illiberal Education: The Politics of Race and Sex on Campus</u>, by Dinesh D'Souza. <u>Washington Post</u> 15 Apr. 1991, ntnl. weekly ed.: 32.

### 30. An Article with a Title within Its Title

If the article you are citing contains a title that is normally enclosed within quotation marks, use single quotation marks for the interior title.

Nash, Robert. "About 'The Emperor of Ice Cream.' " <u>Perspectives</u> 7 (1954): 122–24.

If the article you are citing contains a title that is normally underlined to indicate italics, underline it in your Works Cited entry.

Leicester, H. Marshall, Jr. "The Art of Impersonation: A General Prologue to <u>The Canterbury Tales</u>." <u>PMLA</u> 95 (1980): 213–24.

*Sample MLA Works-Cited Entries: Other Sources*

### 31. A Lecture

Sandman, Peter. "Communicating Scientific Information." Communications Seminar, Dept. of Humanities and Communications. Drexel U, 26 Oct. 1999.

### 32. A Personal Interview

West, Cornel. Personal interview. 28 Dec. 1998.

Tannen, Deborah. Telephone interview. 8 June 1999.

### 33. A Published Interview

Stavros, George. "An Interview with Gwendolyn Brooks." Contemporary Literature 11.1 (Winter 1970): 1–20.

### 34. A Personal Letter

Tan, Amy. Letter to the author. 7 Apr. 1997.

### 35. A Letter Published in a Collection

Joyce, James. "Letter to Louis Gillet." 20 Aug. 1931. James Joyce. By Richard Ellmann. New York: Oxford UP, 1965. 631.

### 36. A Letter in a Library's Archives

Stieglitz, Alfred. Letter to Paul Rosenberg. 5 Sept. 1923. Stieglitz Archive. Yale, New Haven.

### 37. A Film

Include the title of the film (underlined), the distributor, and the date, along with other information of use to readers, such as the names of the performers, the director, and the writer.

Citizen Kane. Dir. Orson Welles. Perf. Welles, Joseph Cotten, Dorothy Comingore, and Agnes Moorehead. RKO, 1941.

If you are focusing on the contribution of a particular person, begin with that person's name.

Wells, Orson, dir. Citizen Kane. Perf. Wells, Joseph Cotton, Dorothy Comingore, and Agnes Moorehead. RKO. 1941.

### 38. A Videotape, DVD, or Laser Disc

Cite a videotape, DVD (digital videodisc), or laser disc like a film, but include the medium before the name of the distributor.

Miller, Arthur. Interview. The Crucible. Dir. William Schiff. Videocassette. The Mosaic Group, 1987.

### 39. A Radio or Television Program

"Prime Suspect 3." Writ. Lynda La Plante. Perf. Helen Mirren. Mystery! PBS. WNET, New York. 28 Apr. 1994.

### 40. A Recording

List the composer, conductor, or performer (whichever you are emphasizing), followed by the title (and, when citing jacket notes, a description of the material), manufacturer, and year of issue.

Boubill, Alain, and Claude-Michel Schönberg. <u>Miss Saigon</u>. Perf. Lea Salonga,

Claire Moore, and Jonathan Pryce. Cond. Martin Koch. Geffen, 1989.

Marley, Bob. "Crisis." Lyrics. <u>Bob Marley and the Wailers</u>. Kava Island

Records, 1978.

### 41. A Cartoon or Comic Strip

Trudeau, Garry. "Doonesbury." Comic strip. <u>Philadelphia Inquirer</u> 19 July

1999: E 13.

### 42. An Advertisement

Microsoft. Advertisement. <u>National Review</u> 28 June 1999: 11.

*Sample MLA Works-Cited Entries: Electronic Sources on the Internet* The documentation style for electronic sources presented here conforms to the most recent guidelines published in the *MLA Handbook for Writers of Research Papers* (6th ed.) and found online at <http://mla.org>. (If your instructor prefers that you use Columbia Online Style for citing electronic sources, see p. 203.)

MLA style recognizes that full source information for electronic sources found on the Internet are not always available. Include in your citation whatever information you can reasonably obtain. MLA recommends that you include *both* the date of the electronic publication (if available) and the date you accessed the source. MLA also requires that you enclose the electronic address (URL) within angle brackets to distinguish the address from the punctuation in the rest of the citation. (If you have to carry a URL over to the next line, divide it after a slash. If it is excessively long, use just the URL of the site's search page, or use the URL of the site's home page, followed by the word path and a colon and then the sequence of links to follow.)

### 43. A Scholarly Project or Information Database on the Internet

<u>Philadelphia Writers Project</u>. Ed. Miriam Kotzen Green. May 1998. Drexel U.

12 June 2001 <http://www.Drexel.edu/letrs/wwp/>.

**44. A Document within a Scholarly Project or Information Database on the Internet**

"D Day: June 7th, 1944." The History Channel Online. 1999. History Channel.

7 June 2002 <http://historychannel.com/thisday/today/997690.html>.

**45. A Home Page for a Course or a Personal Home Page on the Internet**

Multry, David. Composition and Literature. Course home page. Jan.

2003–Apr. 2003. Dept. of English, Odessa College. 6 Apr. 2003

<http://www.odessa.edu/dept/english/dmulryEnglish_1302.html>.

Gainor, Charles. Home page. 22 July 1999

<http://www.chass.utoronto.ca:9094/~char/>.

**46. A Book on the Internet**

Douglass, Frederick. My Bondage and My Freedom. Boston, 1855. 8 June

2000 <gopher://gopher.vt.edu:10024/22/178/3>.

**47. An Article in a Scholarly Journal on the Internet**

When you cite information from an electronic source that has a print version, include the publication information for the printed source, the number of pages or paragraphs (if available), and the date you accessed it.

Dekoven, Marianne. "Utopias Limited: Post-Sixties and Postmodern American

Fiction." Modern Fiction Studies 41.1 (1995): 13 pp. 17 Mar. 1999

<http://muse.jhu.edu/journals/mfs.v041/41.1dwkovwn.html>.

**48. An Article in a Newspaper on the Internet**

Lohr, Steve. "Microsoft Goes to Court." New York Times on the Web 19 Oct.

1998. 29 Apr. 1999 <http://www.nytimes.com/web/docroot/

library.ciber/week/1019business.html>.

**49. An Article in a Newsletter on the Internet**

"Unprecedented Cutbacks in History of Science Funding." AIP Center for His-

tory of Physics 27.2 (Fall 1995). 26 Feb. 1996 <http://www.aip.org/

history/fall95.html>.

**50. An Article in a Magazine on the Internet**

Weiser, Jay. "The Tyranny of Informality." Time 26 Feb. 1996. 1 Mar. 2002

    <http://www.enews.com/magazines.tnr/current/022696.3.html>.

**51. A Review on the Internet**

Ebert, Roger. Rev. of Star Wars: Episode I—The Phantom Menace, dir. George

    Lucas. Chicago Sun-Times Online 8 June 2000. 22 June 2000

    <http://www.suntimes.com/output/ebert1/08show.html>.

**52. A Letter to the Editor on the Internet**

Chen-Cheng, Henry H. Letter. New York Times on the Web 19 July 1999. 19

    July 1999 <http://www.nytimes.com/hr/mo/day/letters/

    ichen-cheng.html>.

**53. An Article in an Encyclopedia on the Internet**

Include the article's title, the title of the database (underlined), the version number, the date of electronic publication, the sponsor, and the date of access as well as the URL.

"Hawthorne, Nathaniel." Encyclopedia Britannica Online. 2002.

    Encyclopaedia Britannica. 16 May 2002 <http://www.search.eb.com/>.

**54. A Linked Site on the Internet**

If you get information from a linked site—that is, if you connect from one site to another—include the title of the document you cite (followed by its date) and the abbreviation Lkd. (followed by the original site from which you accessed your document). Follow this with the date of access and the URL.

Harris, Robert. "Evaluating Information: Tests of Interpreting Quality." 17 Nov.

    1997. Lkd. The Holt Handbook. 28 May 2002 <http://

    holthandbook.heinle.com/6e/student/resources/computer/evalu8.html>.

**55. A Painting on the Internet**

Lange, Dorothea. Looking at Pictures. 1936. Museum of Mod. Art, New York.

    28 June 1999 <http://moma.org/exhibitions/lookingatphotographs/

    lang-fr.html>.

**56. A Photograph on the Internet**

Brady, Mathew. "Ulysses S. Grant 1822–1885." Photograph. Mathew
    Brady's National Portrait Gallery. 2 Oct. 2002 <http://
    www.npg.si.edu/exh/brady/gallery/56gal.html>.

**57. A Cartoon on the Internet**

Stossel, Sage. "Star Wars: The Next Generation." Cartoon. Atlantic Unbound
    2 Oct. 2002. 14 Nov. 2002 <http://www.theatlantic.com/
    unbound/sage/ss990519.htm>.

**58. A Map on the Internet**

"Philadelphia, Pennsylvania." Map. U. S. Gazetteer. US Census Bureau.
    17 July 2000 <http://www.census.gov/cgi-bin/gazetteer>.

**59. A Radio Program Accessed from an Archive on the Internet**

Edwards, Bob. "Country Music's First Family." Morning Edition. 16 July 2002.
    NPR Archives. 2 Oct. 2002 <http://www.npr.org/programs/
    morning/index.html>.

**60. An E-Mail**

Adkins, Camille. E-mail to the author. 28 June 2001.

**61. An Online Posting (Newsgroup or Online Forum)**

Gilford, Mary. "Dog Heroes in Children's Literature." Online posting.
    17 Mar. 1999. 12 Apr. 1999 <news:alt.animals.dogs>.

Schiller, Stephen. "Paper Cost and Publishing Costs." Online posting.
    24 Apr. 1999. 11 May 1999. Book Forum. 17 May 1999
    <www.nytimes.com/webin/webx?13A^41356.ee765e/0>.

**62. A Synchronous Communication (MOO or MUD)**

MOOs (multiuser domain, object oriented) and MUDs (multiuser domain) are Internet programs that enable users to communicate in real time. To cite a communication obtained on a MOO or a
MUD, give the name (or names) of the writer(s), a description of

the event, the date of the event, the forum (LinguaMOO, for example), the date of access, and the URL (starting with *telnet://*).

> Guitar, Gwen. Online discussion of Cathy in Emily Brontë's <u>Wuthering</u>
>
> <u>Heights</u>. 17 Mar. 1999. LinguaMOO. 17 Mar. 1999
>
> <telnet://lingua.utdallas.edu:8888>.

### Internet sources

WARNING: Using information from Internet sources—especially newsgroups and online forums—is risky. Contributors are not necessarily experts, and frequently they are incorrect and misinformed. Unless you can be certain the information you are obtaining from these sources is reliable, do not use it. You can check the reliability of an Internet source by consulting the checklist **Evaluating Internet Sources** or by asking your instructor or reference librarian for guidance.

See 8d

*Sample MLA Works-Cited Entries:*
*Electronic Sources from a Subscription Service*

Subscription information services can be divided into those you subscribe to, such as America Online, and those that your college library subscribes to, such as InfoTrac, LexisNexis, and ProQuest Direct.

If the service you are subscribing to provides a URL, follow the examples in entries 43–53. If the subscription service enables you to use a keyword to access material, provide the keyword (following the date of access) at the end of the entry.

> "Kafka, Franz." <u>Compton's Encyclopedia Online</u>. Vers. 3.0. 2000. America
>
> Online. 8 June 2001. Keyword: Compton's.

If instead of using a keyword, you follow a series of topic labels, list them (separated by semicolons) after the word *Path*.

> "Elizabeth Adams." <u>History Resources</u>. 11 Nov. 2001. America Online. 28 Apr.
>
> 2001. Path: Research; Biography; Women in Science; Biographies.

To cite information from an information service to which your library subscribes, include the underlined name of the database (if known), the name of the service, the library, the date of access, and the URL of the online service's home page.

Luckenbill, Trent. "Environmental Litigation: Down the Endless Corridor."

Environment 8 June 2001: 34–42. ABI/INFORM Global. ProQuest

Direct. Drexel U Lib., Philadelphia, PA. 12 Oct. 2001

<http://www.umi.com/proquest/>.

**63. A Scholarly Journal Article with Separate Pagination in Each Issue from a Subscription Service**

Schaefer, Richard J. "Editing Strategies in Television News Documentaries."

Journal of Communication 47.4 (1997): 69–89. InfoTrac OneFile Plus.

Gale Group Databases. Augusta R. Kolwyck Lib., Chattanooga, TN. 2

Oct. 2002 <http://library.cstcc.cc.tn.us/ref3.shtml>.

**64. A Scholarly Journal Article with Continuous Pagination Throughout an Annual Volume from a Subscription Service**

Hudson, Nicholas. "Samuel Johnson, Urban Culture, and the Geography of

Postfire London." Studies in English Literature 42 (2002): 557–80. Mas-

terFILE Premier. EBSCOhost. Augusta R. Kolwyck Lib., Chattanooga,

TN. 2 Oct. 2002 <http://library.cstcc.cc.tn.us/ref3.shtml>.

**65. A Monthly Magazine Article from a Subscription Service**

Livermore, Beth. "Meteorites on Ice." Astronomy July 1993: 54–8.

Expanded Academic ASAP Plus. Gale Group Databases. Augusta

R. Kolwyck Lib., Chattanooga, TN. 2 Oct. 2002

<http://library.cstcc.cc.tn.us/ref3.shtml>.

Wright, Karen. "The Clot Thickens." Discover Dec. 1999: 40–2. MasterFILE

Premier. EBSCOhost. Augusta R. Kolwyck Lib., Chattanooga, TN. 2

Oct. 2002 <http://library.cstcc.cc.tn.us/ref3.shtml>.

**66. A News Service from a Subscription Service**

Ryan, Desmond. "Some Background on the Battle of Gettysburg." Knight

Ridder/Tribune News Service. 7 Oct. 1993. InfoTrac OneFile Plus.

Gale Group Databases. Augusta R. Kolwyck Lib., Chattanooga, TN. 2 Oct. 2002 <http://infotrac.galegroup.com/menu>.

### 67. A News Wire from a Subscription Service

"General Dwight D. Eisenhower's Official WW II Diaries Discovered." US Newswire 20 Nov. 2001. InfoTrac OneFile Plus. Gale Group Databases. Augusta R. Kolwyck Lib., Chattanooga, TN. 2 Oct. 2002 <http://library.cstcc.cc.tn.us/ref3.shtml>.

### 68. A Newspaper Article from a Subscription Service

Meyer, Greg. "Answering Questions about the West Nile Virus." Dayton Daily News 11 July 2002: Z3–7. LexisNexis Academic. Augusta R. Kolwyck Lib., Chattanooga, TN. 2 Oct. 2002 <http://library.cstcc.cc.tn.us/ref3.shtml>.

### 69. A Pamphlet from a Subscription Service

National Institute of Diabetes and Digestive and Kidney Diseases. Prevent Diabetes Problems: Keep Your Eyes Healthy. Pamphlet. 1 May 2000. Health Reference Center Academic. Gale Group Databases. Augusta R. Kolwyck Lib., Chattanooga, TN. 2 Oct. 2002 <http://library.cstcc.cc.tn.us/ref3.shtml>.

### 70. A Reference Book Article from a Subscription Service

Laird, Judith. "Geoffrey Chaucer." Cyclopedia of World Authors 1997. Magill-OnLiterature. EBSCOhost. Augusta R. Kolwyck Lib., Chattanooga, TN. 2 Oct. 2002 <http://library.cstcc.cc.tn.us/ref3.shtml>.

### 71. A Dictionary Definition from a Subscription Service

"Migraine." Mosby's Medical, Nursing, and Allied Health Dictionary. 1998 ed. Health Reference Center. Gale Group Databases. Augusta R. Kolwyck Lib., Chattanooga, TN. 2 Oct. 2002 <http://library.cstcc.cc.tn.us/ref3.shtml>.

*Other Electronic Sources*

**72. A Nonperiodical Publication on DVD, CD-ROM, or Diskette Database**

Cite a nonperiodical publication on DVD, CD-ROM, or diskette the same way you would cite a book, but also include a description of the medium of publication.

"Windhover." The Oxford English Dictionary. 2nd ed. DVD. Oxford: Oxford

UP, 2001.

"Whitman, Walt." DiskLit: America Authors. CD-ROM. Boston: Hall, 2000.

**73. A Periodical Publication on a DVD or CD-ROM Database**

Zurbach, Kate. "The Linguistic Roots of Three Terms." Linguistic Quarterly 37

(1994): 12–47. InfoTrac: Magazine Index Plus. CD-ROM. Information

Access. Jan. 2001.

## (3) Content Notes

Content notes—multiple bibliographical citations or other material that does not fit smoothly into the text—are indicated by a **superscript** (raised numeral) in the paper. Notes can appear either as footnotes at the bottom of the page or as endnotes on a separate sheet entitled *Notes*, placed after the last page of the paper and before the works-cited list. Content notes are double-spaced within and between entries.

*For Multiple Citations*
*In the Paper*

Many researchers emphasize the necessity of having dying patients share their

experiences.[1]

*In the Note*

[1]Kübler-Ross 27; Stinnette 43; Poston 70; Cohen and Cohen 31–34; Burke

1:91–95.

*For Other Material*
*In the Paper*

The massacre during World War I is an event the survivors could not easily forget.[2]

*In the Note*

²For a firsthand account of these events, see Bedoukian 178–81.

**Columbia Online Style**

Columbia Online Style (COS) was developed to accommodate the wide variety of sources that are available in an electronic environment. For this reason, some instructors prefer their students to use COS style instead of MLA style when they document electronic sources. Remember that the MLA does not recognize COS, so be sure to check with your instructor before you use it.

*Format*

Author's Last Name, First Name. "Title of Document." *Title of Complete*

  *Work* [if applicable]. Version or File Number [if applicable].

  Document date or date of last revision [if different from access date].

  Protocol and address, access path or directories. Access date.

**Note:** Like MLA style, Columbia Online Style requires a double-space within and between entries.

*1. A World Wide Web Site*

Sandy, Adam. "Roller Coaster History." *Coney Island History.* 2001.

  http://www.ultimaterollercoaster.com/coasters/history/

  history-coney.html (12 Nov. 2001).

**Note:** Columbia Online Style uses italics where MLA requires underlining. In addition, angle brackets are not used in COS.

*2. An Online Journal Article*

Dekoven, Marianne. "Utopias Unlimited: Post Sixties and Postmodern

  American Fiction." *Modern Fiction Studies.* 41:1(1995). http://

  muse.jhu.edu/journals/mfs.v041/41.1dwkovwn.html

  (17 Mar. 1999).

*3. An Online Magazine*

Walker, Rob. "Is the Stock Market in Denial?" *Slate* 15 Nov. 2001.

  http://slate.msn.com/?id=2058732 (19 Nov. 2001).

*continued on the following page*

*continued from the previous page*

*4. An Online News Service or Online Newspaper*

McGirk, Tim. "Deep Loyalties, Ancient Hatreds." *Time.com.* 12 Nov.

2001. http://www.time.com/time/magazine/article/

0,9171,1101011119-183964,00.html (19 Nov. 2001).

*5. E-mail, Listservs, and Newsgroups*

Goren, Seth. "Joke of the Week." Personal e-mail (14 Nov. 2001).

Friedlander, Sandy. "Computer Collaboration in the Writing Classroom."

*Alliance for Computers and Writing Listserv.*

acw-l@ unicorn.acs.ttu.edu (17 June 2000).

Provizor, Norman. "Jazz in the 1990s." 2 Mar. 2000. alt.music.jazz.

(5 Mar. 2000).

*6. A Gopher Site*

Douglass, Stephen. "Can Computers Think?" *Journal of Experimental and*

*Artificial Intelligence* (1999). gopher://gopher.liv.ac.uk:80/

00/phil/philos-12-files/searle.harnad (7 Aug. 2000).

*7. An FTP Site*

Johnson, Cassandra. "Cleaning Up Hypertext Links." 3 Dec. 2000.

ftp://ftp.daedalus.com/pub/CCCC95/johnson (14 Oct. 2001).

*8. A Telnet Site*

Rigg, Doreen. "Lesson Plan for Teaching about the Hubble Telescope."

*Space News.* 11 Oct. 2000. telnet://

spacelink.msfc.nasa.gov.guest (2 Dec. 2000).

*9. A Synchronous Communication Site*

Guitar, Gwen. "Update." *DaMOO.* telnet://damoo.csun.edu:7777

(4 Dec. 1996).

**10. An Online Reference Source**

Kevles, D. J. "Human Genome Project." *Columbia Encyclopedia*. 6th ed. NY: Columbia UP, 2001. *America Online*. Reference Desk/ Encyclopedias/Columbia Encyclopedia (17 Nov. 2001).

**11. Electronic Publications and Online Databases**

Cinbac, James. "Wishing Won't Do It: Baby Boomers Save for Retirement." *Business Week* 1 Apr. 2000: 50. *InfoTrac SearchBank*. File #9606273898 (12 Aug. 2000).

**12. Software Programs and Video Games**

*Mac Washer*. Vers. 2.1. St. Louis: Webroot Software, 2000.

*Abuse*. Vers. 3.2. Chicago: Bungie Software Products, 1996.

# 10b  MLA Manuscript Guidelines

Although MLA papers do not usually include abstracts, internal headings, tables, or graphs, this situation is changing. Be sure you know what your instructor expects.

The guidelines in the following checklists are based on the latest version of the *MLA Handbook for Writers of Research Papers*.

## ✓ checklist  Typing your paper

(Use the paper on p. 210 as your model.)

✓ Type your paper with a one-inch margin at the top and bottom and on both sides. Double-space your paper throughout.

✓ Capitalize all important words in your title, but not prepositions, articles, coordinating conjunctions, or the *to* in infinitives (unless they begin or end the title or subtitle). Do not underline your title or enclose it in quotation marks. Never put a period after the title, even if it is a sentence. Double-space between the last line of your title and the first line of the paper.

✓ Indent the first line of every paragraph, as well as the first line of every item on the works-cited list, five spaces (or one-half inch).

*continued on the following page*

*continued from the previous page*

✓ Set a long prose quotation (more than four lines) off from the text by indenting the whole quotation ten spaces (or one inch). If you quote a single paragraph or part of a paragraph, do not indent the first line beyond one inch. If you quote two or more paragraphs, indent the first line of each paragraph an additional quarter inch. (If the first sentence does not begin a paragraph, do not indent it. Indent the first line only in successive paragraphs.)

✓ Number all pages of your paper consecutively—including the first—in the upper right-hand corner, one-half inch from the top, flush right. Type your name followed by a space and the page number on every page.

See 10a

✓ If you use source material in your paper, follow **MLA documentation style**.

---

**?** **✓checklist** **Preparing the MLA works-cited list**

See 10a3

✓ Begin the works-cited list on a new page after the last page of text or **content notes,** numbered as the next page of the paper.

✓ Center the title Works Cited one inch from the top of the page. Double-space between the title and the first entry.

✓ Each entry on the works-cited list has three divisions: author, title, and publication information. Separate divisions with a period and one space.

✓ List entries alphabetically, last name first. Use the author's full name as it appears on the title page. If a source has no listed author, alphabetize it by the first word of the title (not counting the article).

✓ Type the first line of each entry flush with the left-hand margin; indent subsequent lines five spaces (or one-half inch).

✓ Double-space within and between entries.

---

## 10c   Sample MLA-Style Research Paper

The following student paper, "The Great Digital Divide," uses MLA documentation style. It is preceded by a sentence outline and includes a notes page and a works-cited list.

## ✳ MLA Formal Outline

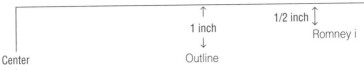

↑
1 inch
↓

1/2 inch ↕
Romney i

Center

Outline

Thesis Statement: Although the Internet has changed our world for the better, it threatens to leave many people behind, creating two distinct classes—those who have access and those who do not.

I. The Internet was created in 1969 under the name ARPANET

    A. ARPANET was designed to serve as America's communication system in case of a nuclear attack.

1 inch
←—→

    B. It was expanded in 1972 into a system of interconnected networks.

    C. In the 1980s, HTML was created to allow information on the Internet to be displayed graphically.

II. Today, many people believe the Internet has ushered in a new age.

    A. Former Vice President Al Gore sees the Internet as an empowering tool.

    B. Gore believes the Internet will bring knowledge and prosperity to the entire world.

III. For many people, however, the benefits of the Internet are not nearly this obvious or far-reaching.

    A. The Internet is still out of reach for many Americans.

        1. The elderly and the physically disabled are less likely than others to use the Internet.

        2. Low-income and minority households are less likely than others to have computers.

## ✳ MLA Formal Outline

Romney ii

B. People without Internet access have difficulties at school, trouble obtaining employment, and fewer opportunities to save money and time as consumers.

C. Two groups that make up much of the "have-not" population are the physically disabled and the elderly.

    1. For the physically disabled, the Internet could be highly beneficial, eliminating physical barriers to sources of entertainment, education, and employment.

    2. Computer programmers often overlook the needs of the physically disabled when designing Web sites.

    3. Although the Web offers the elderly opportunities to converse with family members and access health information, their physical and mental deficits often prevent them from using the Internet.

    4. Content providers and engineers must consider the special needs of the elderly.

IV. Both government and nonprofit organizations are making efforts to bridge the gap between the "haves" and the "have-nots."

A. The federal government has launched programs like Neighborhood Networks to provide Internet access to impoverished communities.

B. Congress is making efforts to decrease the gap between the "haves" and the "have-nots."

C. Nonprofit organizations, such as PBS, are working to raise public awareness.

*MLA Formal Outline*

V.  Despite these efforts, much still needs to be done.

   A. We must examine the content available on the Internet, which often fails to reflect the needs of minorities, the elderly, and those with disabilities.

   B. We must continue to provide training to people unfamiliar with new technology.

   C. We must target the most likely "have-nots."

**?** ✳ *MLA Research Paper Sample Page*

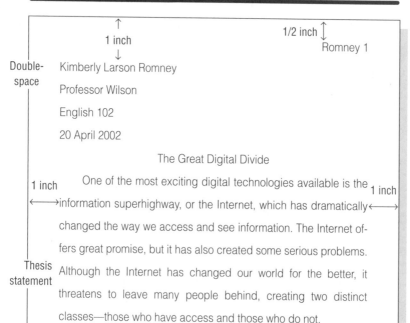

↑
1 inch
↓

1/2 inch ↕
Romney 1

Double-space

Kimberly Larson Romney

Professor Wilson

English 102

20 April 2002

The Great Digital Divide

1 inch →

One of the most exciting digital technologies available is the ← 1 inch → information superhighway, or the Internet, which has dramatically ← →

changed the way we access and see information. The Internet of-

fers great promise, but it has also created some serious problems.

Thesis statement

Although the Internet has changed our world for the better, it

threatens to leave many people behind, creating two distinct

classes—those who have access and those who do not.

Paragraph 2 presents background on history of the Internet, summarizing information from two sources.

The Internet was created in 1969 under the name ARPANET

(ARPA stood for Advanced Research Projects Agency). Funded

by the United States government, ARPA was designed to serve as

America's communication system in case of a nuclear attack. The

first ARPANET system consisted of just four connected computers,

but by 1972, fifty universities and research facilities were linked

(Gibbs and Smith 5). Beginning in 1972, researchers increased

the number of computers that could be on ARPANET, and this new

system was given the name Internet. In the 1980s, a computer lan-

guage called HTML (Hyper Text Markup Language) was created

to allow information on the Internet to be displayed graphically.

This advance gave rise to the World Wide Web, which allowed

## ✳ MLA Research Paper Sample Page

Romney 2

users to access text, graphics, sound, and even video while using hyperlinks to move from one site to another (Wendall).

Today, many people believe the Internet has ushered in a new age, one in which instant communication will bring people closer together and eventually eliminate national boundaries. Former Vice President Al Gore, for example, sees the Internet as a means "to deepen and extend our oldest, and most cherished global values: rising standards of living and literacy, an ever-widening circle of democracy, freedom, and individual empowerment" (par. 4). Gore says that he can see the day when we will "extend our knowledge and our prosperity to our most isolated inner cities, to the barrios, the favelas, the colonias, and our most remote rural villages" (par. 32).

*Parenthetical references cite paragraph numbers because electronic source does not include page numbers*

Despite the optimistic predictions of Gore and others, for many people, the benefits of the Internet are not nearly this obvious or far-reaching. There are many, writes Pippa Norris, who "believe that the digital technologies will reinforce and exacerbate existing disparities" (26). In fact, the Internet remains out of reach for many Americans, creating what the NAACP and others have called a "digital divide" ("NAACP Targets Minority Gap"). Large percentages of the poor, the elderly, and the disabled, as well as members of many minority groups, are excluded from current technological advancements; thus, a gap exists between those who have access to this new technology and those who do not.

*Parenthetical documentation refers to an article accessed from the Internet.*

## MLA Research Paper Sample Page

A recent survey by the US Department of Commerce shows that some significant advances were made between 1998 and 2000 but that inequalities in computer ownership and Internet access continue to exist. The elderly and the physically disabled are two groups that still fall into the "have-not" category. For example, the Internet use rate for individuals 50 years of age and older is only about 30%. Further, people with a disability are half as likely to have access to the Internet as those without a disability: 21.6% compared to 42.1% (United States).

The Department of Commerce report reveals that although all households are more likely to have computers than they were in 1998 (see Fig. 1), people with higher annual household incomes and whites remain more likely to own computers than minorities and people from low-income households. Approximately 70% of households with an income of $75,000 or above have computers, compared to 19% of households earning less than $15,000. The survey also found that only 33% of African American and 34% of Hispanic households have computers, whereas 56% of white households have computers. This disparity exists even at household incomes lower than $15,000 (United States). According to a New York Times article, "at the lowest income levels, the gap is great—a child in a low-income white family is three times as likely to have Internet access as a child in a low-income black family" (Belluck).

Paragraph synthesizes information from a Department of Commerce report and a newspaper article. Because article is only one page long, no page number is needed in the citation.

## ❋ *MLA Research Paper Sample Page*

Romney 4

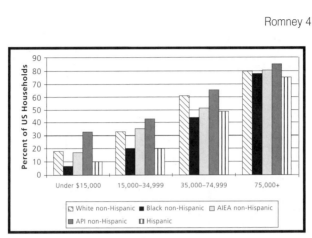

Fig. 1. Percentage of US Households with a Computer by Income by Race/Origin, 1998 and 2000. Source: United States Dept. of Commerce and Natl. Telecommunications and Information Admin., <u>Falling through the Net: Toward Digital Inclusion</u>, Dec. 2000 <http://www.ntia.doc.gov/ntiahome/fttn00/chartl-13.htm#f13>.

Although the Commerce Department report indicates that financial circumstances, age, race, and physical disabilities contribute to the "digital divide," the gap in computer ownership across incomes suggests that other factors may also contribute to the disparity. As Henry Louis Gates, Jr., argues, bridging this gap will "require more than cheap PC's, it will involve content." African Americans are not interested in the Internet, Gates writes, because the content rarely appeals to them. He compares the lack of interest in the Internet with the history of African Americans' relationship with the recording industry: "Blacks began to respond to this

Graph summarizes relevant data.

Source information is typed directly below the figure; this information does *not* appear in the works-cited list.

Summary of newspaper op-ed piece includes two quotations. Because author is mentioned in identifying tag, and because article is only one page long, no parenthetical documentation is needed.

## ✳ MLA Research Paper Sample Page

Romney 5

new medium only when mainstream companies like Columbia Records introduced so-called race records, blues and jazz discs aimed at a nascent African-American market." Gates believes that Web sites that address the needs of African Americans can play the same role that "race records" did for the music industry. Ignoring the problem, he warns, will lead to a form of cyber-segregation that will devastate the African-American community.[1]

Regardless of the causes of the "digital divide," it is clear that those without Internet access are at a disadvantage. They have difficulty at school, trouble obtaining employment, and fewer opportunities to save time and money as consumers. Those to whom the Internet is not available are denied access to special airline discounts, savings on long-distance carriers, and lower prices on computer software. More importantly, they lack access to educational and research materials and to jobs posted on the Web. As the following comment makes clear, with access to only a portion of available goods and services, people who are offline do not have the advantages that people who are online can routinely get:

Their choices will be restricted, and they're going to pay a little bit more for things and they'll have fewer options . . . and it's not going to be one of these things where you see the digital homeless on the street, or sleeping on the steps of City Hall. It's going to be an invisible problem. The people who are digitally dispossessed may not even appreciate that they are dispossessed. (Belluck)

Superscript identifies content note.

Long quotation is typed as a block, without quotation marks, indented ten spaces (or one inch) and double-spaced. Ellipsis indicates that the student has deleted material from the original quotation. Parenthetical documentation follows end punctuation.

1 inch ←→

214

## ✳ *MLA Research Paper Sample Page*

Romney 6

As Belluck observes, the Internet is widening the economic and social divide that already separates people in this country.

Two groups that make up much of the "have-not" population are the physically disabled and the elderly. Both are less likely than others to have access to the Internet and therefore suffer some of the greatest consequences. For the physically disabled, the Internet could be highly beneficial, actually eliminating physical barriers to sources of entertainment, education, and employment. Ironically, however, attitudinal barriers may lead educators, employers, and even family members to dismiss a physically disabled person's ability to use a computer and the Internet. Furthermore, computer programmers often forget to consider the needs of the physically disabled when designing Web sites (Lester). Sadly, those who might gain the most from this technology are overlooked by those who control access.

Similarly, the elderly, who might also benefit greatly from services that the Internet can provide, are often overlooked as potential users of new technology. According to Jennifer O'Neill, speakers at the "Older Adults, Health Information, and the World Wide Web" conference at the National Institutes of Health noted that even if they want to use the Internet, many elderly Americans have difficulty doing so. Although the Web offers the elderly opportunities to converse with family members and access health information, their physical and mental deficits may prevent them from using the Internet: "Seniors often have difficulty navigating

## MLA Research Paper Sample Page

Romney 7

the Web, finding information, and sometimes even remembering the object of their search" (O'Neill). Unless content providers and engineers consider their special needs, the elderly will continue to be "have-nots."

Both public and private sectors recognize the potential danger of the "digital divide" and are taking steps to narrow the gap. For example, the federal government is sponsoring several programs aimed at those groups who are in danger of becoming "have-nots." One such effort is Neighborhood Networks, a program sponsored by the U.S. Department of Housing and Urban Development (HUD) that works to provide computer-training centers to people living in homes that are assisted or insured by HUD ("About Neighborhood Networks").

Exact wording of a piece of key legislation is used to eliminate any possibility of misinterpretation. Each quotation requires its own parenthetical documentation, even though both cite the same source.

Congress, too, is targeting the gap between the "haves" and the "have-nots." In the Telecommunications Act of 1996, the Federal Communications Commission was directed to "set rules requiring telephone and cable television companies to provide universal access to new services like the Internet" (Lohr). Legislators hope this language will encourage regulators to "mandate access and cut-rate service for schools and public libraries" (Lohr).[2]

Nonprofit organizations are also entering the war to close the "digital divide." In an effort to raise public awareness, the Public Broadcasting Corporation (PBS) created a series called Digital Divide to examine race and gender gaps in technology in the classroom and at work. According to "Virtual Diversity," one program in

*MLA Research Paper Sample Page*

Romney 8

this series, both the dynamic of a co-ed classroom and the lack of appealing content make technology seem inaccessible to wome-nand minorities. Only by changing the way classes are conducted and by including content that is interesting to women and minorities can technology and the Internet be made accessible to these populations.

Despite the efforts of government and nonprofit organizations, as well as many businesses, much still needs to be done to ensure that everyone has access to the Internet. First, we must examine the content available on the Internet, which often fails to reflect the needs of minorities, the elderly, and those with disabilities. We must also continue to provide training to people unfamiliar with new technology, and we must ensure that the instructors who are teaching these new technology skills understand the equipment and software they are explaining. Finally, we must target the most likely "have-nots": the poor, minorities, the elderly, the disabled, and girls and young women. Unless we take steps to make the Internet available to all, we will quickly become two separate and unequal societies, one "plugged-in" and privileged and one "unplugged" and marginalized.

> Conclusion recommends solutions for problem of "digital divide." Because the paragraph presents the student's original conclusions, no documentation is needed.

※ *MLA Content Notes Page*

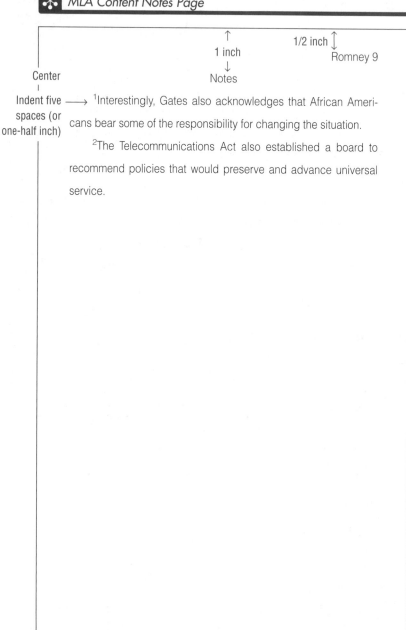

↑
1 inch
↓

1/2 inch ↑
↓
Romney 9

Center

Notes

Indent five
spaces (or
one-half inch) ——→ [1]Interestingly, Gates also acknowledges that African Americans bear some of the responsibility for changing the situation.

[2]The Telecommunications Act also established a board to recommend policies that would preserve and advance universal service.

## ✳ *MLA Works-Cited List*

↑
1/2 inch ↕
1 inch                    Romney 10
↓
Works Cited                    Center

"About Neighborhood Networks." Neighborhood Networks. 3 May → Indent five

2000. 26 June 2000 <http://www.digitaldividenetwork.org>. ← spaces (or one-half inch)

Belluck, Pam. "What Price Will Be Paid by Those Not on the Net?"

New York Times on the Web 22 Sept. 1999. 26 July 2000

<http://www.nytimes.com>.

Gates, Henry Louis, Jr. "One Internet, Two Nations." New York

Times 31 Oct. 1999, late ed.: A25.

Gibbs, Mark, and Richard Smith. Navigating the Internet.

Indianapolis: SAMS, 1993.

Gore, Al. "Building a Global Community." Remarks Prepared for the

15th International ITU Conference. 12 Oct. 1998. 69 pars. 5

July 2000 <http://www.itu.int/Newsarchive/press/PP98/

Documents/Statement_Gore.html>.

Lester, Mary. "The Internet and People with Disabilities." Digital

Divide Network. 2002. 5 Mar. 2002 <http://

www.digitaldividenetwork.org/content/sections/index.cfm>.

Lohr, Steve. "The Great Unplugged Masses Confront the Future."

New York Times on the Web 21 Apr. 1996. 26 July 2000

<http://www.nytimes.com>.

"NAACP Targets Minority Gap in Internet Use, TV Roles."

CNN.com. Cable News Network. 13 Nov. 2000

<http://www.cnn.com/US/9907/13/naacp.gap/>.

As recommended by MLA, the URL for a site's search page may be used instead of an excessively long URL.

If a URL must be broken, divide it after a slash.

## ❋ *MLA Works-Cited List*

Romney 11

Norris, Pippa. <u>Digital Divide: Civic Engagement, Information
Poverty, and the Internet Worldwide</u>. Cambridge University Press: Cambridge, 2001.

O'Neill, Jennifer. "Limited Mobility Doesn't Stop Senior Surfers."
<u>CNN.com</u>. 2001. Cable News Network. 17 Dec. 2001
<http://www.cnn.com/2001/TECH/internet/03/05/
senior.surfers.idg/index.html>.

United States. Dept. of Commerce and Natl. Telecommunications
and Information Admin. <u>Falling through the Net: Toward
Digital Inclusion.</u> Dec. 2000 <http://www.ntia.doc.gov/
ntiahome>.

"Virtual Diversity." <u>Digital Divide</u>. 1 Apr. 2000. 24 June 2000
<http://www.pbs.org/digitaldivide/about.about.htm#series>.

Wendall, Kyla. "Internet History." University of Regina Student
Connection Program. 18 Aug. 1997. 27 June 2000
<http://tdi.uregina.ca/~ursc/internet/history.html>.

# Documenting Sources:
# APA and Other Styles

**11 APA Documentation Style   225**
   **11a** Using APA Style   225
   **11b** APA Manuscript Guidelines   235
   **11c** Sample APA-Style Research Paper   237
**12 Chicago, CSE, and Other Documentation Styles   250**
   **12a** Using Chicago Style   250
   **12b** Chicago-Style Manuscript Guidelines   261
   **12c** Sample Chicago-Style Research Paper (Excerpts)   262
   **12d** Using CSE (formerly CBE) Style   267
   **12e** CSE Manuscript Guidelines   273
   **12f** Sample CSE-Style Research Paper (Excerpts)   274
   **12g** Using Other Documentation Styles   276

## Reference List Format: APA

*A book with one author*

Maslow, A. H. (1974). *Toward a psychology of being.*

Princeton: Van Nostrand.

Author's last name / Initials / Year of publication (in parentheses) / Period / Title italicized (only first word capitalized) / Period

Double space / City / Colon / Publisher (not including terms *Publishers, Co., or Inc.*)

*An article in a scholarly journal with continuous pagination through an annual volume*

Wax, M. (1995). Knowledge, power, and ethics in qualitative social

research. *The American Sociologist, 26,* 22–35.

Author's last name / Initial / Year of publication (in parentheses) / Period / Title of article (only first word capitalized)

Double space / Period / Title of periodical italicized (capitalize all major words) / Volume number italicized / Inclusive page numbers

*An article in an Internet-only journal*

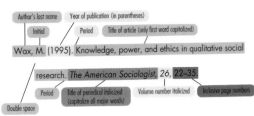

Hornaday, J. & Bunker, C. (2001). The nature of the entrepreneur.

*Personal Psychology, 23,* Article 2353b. Retrieved

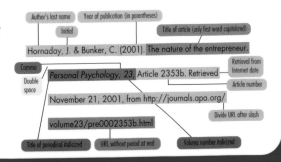

November 21, 2001, from http://journals.apa.org/

volume23/pre0002353b.html

Author's last name / Year of publication (in parentheses) / Initial / Title of article (only first word capitalized)

Comma / Double space / Retrieval from Internet date / Article number / Divide URL after slash / Title of periodical italicized / URL without period at end / Volume number italicized

# PART 5

## ❓ Frequently Asked Questions

**Chapter 11  APA Documentation Style  225**
- When should I use APA documentation ❓  225
- How do I cite a work that has more than two authors ❓  226
- How do I cite an article I found on the Internet ❓  232
- How do I arrange the works in an APA reference list ❓  237
- What should an APA paper look like ❓  237

**Chapter 12  Chicago, CSE, and Other Documentation Styles  250**
- When should I use Chicago-style documentation ❓  250
- What should a Chicago-style paper look like ❓  262
- When should I use CSE documentation ❓  267
- What should a CSE-style paper look like ❓  274
- What other documentation styles are there ❓  276

| **URLs** | *Visit the following sites for answers to more FAQs* |
|---|---|

**American Psychological Association Extension Webpage (WEAPAS)**
*http://www.beadsland.com/weapas/*

**List of APA Style Resources**
*http://www.psychwww.com/resource/apacrib.htm*

**Downloadable APA Style Guide, pdf file (Montana State U.)**
*http://www.lib.montana.edu/instruct/styles/*

**Directory of APA In-Text Citations**

1. A work by a single author (p. 226)
2. A work by two authors (p. 226)
3. A work by three to five authors (p. 226)
4. A work by six or more authors (p. 226)
5. Works by authors with the same last name (p. 227)
6. A work by a corporate author (p. 227)
7. A work with no listed author (p. 227)
8. A personal communication (p. 227)
9. An indirect source (p. 228)
10. A specific part of a source (p. 228)
11. An electronic source (p. 228)
12. Two or more works within the same parenthetical reference (p. 228)
13. A table (p. 229)

**Directory of APA Reference List Entries**

**Entries for Books**

1. A book with one author (p. 229)
2. A book with more than one author (p. 229)
3. An edited book (p. 230)
4. A book with no listed author or editor (p. 230)
5. A work in several volumes (p. 230)
6. A work with a corporate author (p. 230)
7. A government report (p. 230)
8. One selection from an anthology (p. 230)
9. An article in a reference book (p. 230)
10. The foreword, preface, or afterword of a book (p. 231)

**Entries for Articles**

11. An article in a scholarly journal with continuous pagination through an annual volume (p. 231)
12. An article in a scholarly journal with separate pagination in each issue (p. 231)
13. A magazine article (p. 231)
14. A newspaper article (p. 231)
15. A personal letter (p. 232)
16. A letter to the editor (p. 232)
17. A published letter (p. 232)

## Entries for Electronic Sources

18. An Internet article based on a print source (p. 232)
19. An article in an Internet-only journal (p. 232)
20. A document from a university Web site (p. 233)
21. A Web document. (No author identified, no date) (p. 233)
22. An abstract (p. 233)
23. An e-mail (p. 233)
24. A message posted to a newsgroup (p. 233)
25. A daily newspaper (p. 233)
26. A searchable database (p. 234)
27. Computer software (p. 234)

## Entries for Nonprint Sources

28. A television broadcast (p. 234)
29. A television series (p. 234)
30. A motion picture (p. 234)
31. A CD recording (p. 234)
32. An audiocassette recording (p. 234)

# Chapter 11

# APA Documentation Style

## 11a   Using APA Style

APA style* is used extensively in the social sciences. APA documentation has three parts: *in-text citations*, a *reference list*, and optional *content footnotes*. **?**

### (1) In-Text Citations

APA documentation uses short in-text citations in the body of the paper. These citations are keyed to an alphabetical list of references that follows the paper. A typical in-text citation consists of the author's last name (followed by a comma) and the year of publication.

> Many people exhibit symptoms of depression after the death of a pet (Russo, 2000).

If the author's name appears in the introductory phrase, the in-text citation includes just the year of publication.

> According to Russo (2000), many people exhibit symptoms of depression after the death of a pet.

When you are paraphrasing or summarizing a source, you may include the author's name and the date either in the introductory phrase or in parentheses at the end of the paraphrase or summary.

> According to Zinn (1995), this program has had success in training teenage fathers to take financial and emotional responsibility for their offspring.

> This program has had success in training teenage fathers to take financial and emotional responsibility for their offspring (Zinn, 1995).

When quoting directly, include the page number in parentheses after the quotation.

---

*APA documentation style follows the guidelines set in the *Publication Manual of the American Psychological Association*, 5th ed. Washington, DC: APA, 2001.

225

According to Weston (1996), children from one-parent homes read at "a significantly lower level than those from two-parent homes" (p. 58).

Long quotations (forty words or more) are inserted without quotation marks, double-spaced, and indented five to seven spaces (or one-half inch) from the left margin. The citation is placed in parentheses after the final punctuation.

### Sample APA In-Text Citations

### 1. A Work by a Single Author

Many college students suffer from sleep deprivation (Anton, 1999).

### 2. A Work by Two Authors

There is growing concern over the use of psychological testing in elementary schools (Albright & Glennon, 1982).

### 3. A Work by Three to Five Authors

If a work has more than two but fewer than six authors, mention all names in the first reference; in subsequent references in the same paragraph, cite only the first author followed by et al. Add the year when the reference appears in later paragraphs.

*First Reference*

(Sparks, Wilson, & Hewitt, 2001)

*Subsequent References in the Same Paragraph*

(Sparks et al.)

*Reference in Later Paragraphs*

(Sparks et al., 2001)

### 4. A Work by Six or More Authors

When a work has six or more authors, cite the name of the first author followed by et al. and the year in all references.

(Miller et al., 1995).

## Citing works by multiple authors

When referring to multiple authors in your discussion, join the last two names with *and*.

According to Rosen, Wolfe, and Ziff (1988). . . .

In-text citations, however, require an **ampersand.**

(Rosen, Wolfe, & Ziff, 1988).

### 5. Works by Authors with the Same Last Name

If your reference list includes works by two or more primary authors with the same last name, use each author's initials in all in-text citations.

F. Bor (2001) and S. D. Bor (2000) concluded that . . .

### 6. A Work by a Corporate Author

If the name of a corporate author is long, abbreviate it after the first citation.

*First Reference*

(National Institute of Mental Health [NIMH], 2001)

*Subsequent Reference*

(NIMH, 2001)

### 7. A Work with No Listed Author

If a work has no listed author, cite the first two or three words of the title and the year. Use quotation marks around titles of periodical articles and chapters of books; use italics for titles of books, periodicals, brochures, reports, and the like.

("New Immigration," 2000).

### 8. A Personal Communication

Cite letters, memos, telephone conversations, personal interviews, e-mail, messages from electronic bulletin boards, and so on only in the text—*not* in the reference list.

(R. Takaki, personal communication, October 17, 2001).

## 9. An Indirect Source

Cogan and Howe offer very different interpretations of the problem (cited in Swenson, 2000).

## 10. A Specific Part of a Source

Use abbreviations for the words *page* (p.), *chapter* (chap.), and *section* (sec.).

These theories have an interesting history (Lee, 1966, chap. 2).

## 11. An Electronic Source

For an electronic source that does not show page numbers, use the paragraph number preceded by a ¶ symbol or the abbreviation para.

Conversation at the dinner table is an example of a family ritual (Kulp, 2001, ¶ 3).

In the case of an electronic source that does not show either page numbers or paragraph numbers, cite a heading in the source and the number of the paragraph following the heading under which the material is located.

Healthy eating is a never-ending series of free choices (Shapiro, 2001, Introduction section, para. 2).

## 12. Two or More Works within the Same Parenthetical Reference

List works by different authors in alphabetical order, separated by semicolons.

This theory is supported by several studies (Barson & Roth, 1985; Rose, 1987; Tedesco, 1982).

List works by the same author or authors in order of date of publication, with the earliest date first.

This theory is supported by several studies (Weiss & Elliot, 1982, 1984, 1985).

For works by the same author published in the same year, designate the work whose title comes first alphabetically *a*, the one whose title comes next *b*, and so on; repeat the year in each citation.

This theory is supported by several studies (Hossack, 1995a, 1995b).

### 13. A Table

If you use a table from a source, give credit to the author in a note at the bottom of the table. This information is not included in the reference list.

> *Note.* From "Predictors of Employment and Earnings Among JOBS Participants," by P. A. Neenan and D. K. Orthner, 1996, *Social Work Research, 20* (4), p. 233.

## (2) Reference List

The **reference list** gives the publication information for all the sources you cite. It should appear at the end of your paper on a new numbered page entitled References (or Bibliography if you are listing all the works you consulted, whether or not you cited them in your paper).

### Sample APA Reference List Entries: Books

Book citations include the author's name; the year of publication (in parentheses); the book title (italicized); and publication information. Capitalize only the first word of the title and subtitle and any proper nouns. Include additional information necessary for retrieval—edition, report number, or volume number, for example—in parentheses after the title.

### 1. A Book with One Author

Use a short form of the publisher's name. Write out the names of the associations, corporations, and university presses. Include the words *Book* and *Press,* but do not include terms such as *Publishers, Co.,* or *Inc.*

> Maslow, A. H. (1974). *Toward a psychology of being.* Princeton: Van Nostrand.

### 2. A Book with More Than One Author

List up to six authors—by last name and initials. For more than six authors, add et al. after the sixth name.

> Wolfinger, D., Knable, P., Richards, H. L., & Silberger, R. (1990). *The chronically unemployed.* New York: Berman Press.

### 3. An Edited Book

Lewin, K., Lippitt, R., & White, R. K. (Eds.). (1985). *Social learning and imitation*. New York: Basic Books.

### 4. A Book with No Listed Author or Editor

*Writing with a computer* (4th ed.). (2000). Philadelphia: Drexel Press.

### 5. A Work in Several Volumes

Jones, P. R., & Williams, T. C. (Eds.). (1990–1993). *Handbook of therapy* (Vols. 1–2). Princeton: Princeton University Press.

### 6. A Work with a Corporate Author

When the author and the publisher are the same, include the word Author at the end of the citation instead of repeating the publisher's name.

League of Women Voters of the United States. (2001). *Local league handbook*. Washington, DC: Author.

### 7. A Government Report

National Institute of Mental Health. (1987). *Motion pictures and violence: A summary report of research* (DHHS Publication No. ADM 91-22187). Washington, DC: U.S. Government Printing Office.

### 8. One Selection from an Anthology

Give inclusive page numbers preceded by pp. (in parentheses) after the title of the anthology. The title of the selection is not enclosed in quotation marks.

Lorde, A. (1984). Age, race, and class. In P. S. Rothenberg (Ed.), *Racism and sexism: An integrated study* (pp. 352–360). New York: St. Martin's.

**Note:** If you cite two or more selections from the same anthology, give the full citation for the anthology in each entry.

### 9. An Article in a Reference Book

Edwards, P. (Ed.). (1987). Determini229sm. In *The encyclopedia of philosophy* (Vol. 2, pp. 359–373). New York: Macmillan.

## 10. The Foreword, Preface, or Afterword of a Book

> Taylor, T. (1979). Preface. In B. B. Ferencz, *Less than slaves*
> (pp. ii–ix). Cambridge: Harvard University Press.

### Sample APA Reference List Entries: Articles

Article citations include the author's name; the date of publication (in parentheses); the title of the article; the title of the periodical (italicized), the volume number (italicized); the issue number, if any (in parentheses); and the inclusive page numbers. Capitalize only the first word of the article's title and subtitle. Do not underline or italicize the title of the article or enclose it in quotation marks. Give the periodical title in full, and capitalize all words except articles, prepositions, and conjunctions of fewer than four letters. Use p. or pp. when referring to page numbers in newspapers, but omit this abbreviation when referring to page numbers in journals and popular magazines.

## 11. An Article in a Scholarly Journal with Continuous Pagination through an Annual Volume

> Miller, W. (1969). Violent crimes in city gangs. *Journal of Social Issues, 27,* 581–593.

## 12. An Article in a Scholarly Journal with Separate Pagination in Each Issue

> Williams, S., & Cohen, L. R. (1984). Child stress in early learning situations. *American Psychologist, 21*(10), 1–28.

## 13. A Magazine Article

> McCurdy, H. G. (1983, June). Brain mechanisms and intelligence. *Psychology Today, 46,* 61–63.

## 14. A Newspaper Article

If an article appears on nonconsecutive pages, give all page numbers, separated by commas (for example, A1, A14). If the article appears on consecutive pages, indicate the full range of pages (for example, A7–A9).

> James, W. R. (1993, November 16). The uninsured and health care. *Wall Street Journal,* pp. A1, A14.

### 15. A Personal Letter

References to personal letters, like references to all other personal communications, should be included only in the text of the paper, not in the reference list.

### 16. A Letter to the Editor

Williams, P. (2000, July 19). Self-fulfilling stereotypes [Letter to the editor]. *Los Angeles Times,* p. A22.

### 17. A Published Letter

Joyce, J. (1931). Letter to Louis Gillet. In Richard Ellmann, *James Joyce* (p. 631). New York: Oxford University Press.

### Sample APA Reference List Entries: Electronic Sources

APA guidelines for documenting electronic sources focus on Web sources, which often do not contain all the bibliographic information that print sources do. For example, Web sources may not contain page numbers or a place of publication. At a minimum, a Web citation should have a title, a date (the date of publication, update, or retrieval), and an electronic address (URL). If possible, also include the author(s) of a source. When you need to break the URL at the end of a line, break it after a slash or a period (do not add a hyphen). Do not add a period at the end of the URL.

### 18. An Internet Article Based on a Print Source

Winston, E. L. (2000). The role of art therapy in treating chronically depressed patients [Electronic version]. *Journal of Bibliographic Research, 5,* 54–72.

**Note:** If you have seen the article only in electronic format, include the phrase Electronic version in brackets after the title.

### 19. An Article in an Internet-only Journal

If you have reason to believe the article you retrieved is different from the print version, add the date you retrieved it plus the URL.

Hornaday, J., & Bunker, C. (2001). The nature of the entrepreneur. *Personal Psychology, 23,* Article 2353b. Retrieved November 21, 2001, from http://journals.apa.org/volume23/pre002353b.html

### 20. A Document from a University Web Site

Beck, E. (1997, July). *The good, the bad & the ugly: Or, why it's a good idea to evaluate web sources.* Retrieved January 7, 2002, from New Mexico State University Library site: http://lib.nmsu.edu/instruction/evalcrit.html

### 21. A Web Document (No Author Identified, No Date)

The Stratocaster Appreciation Page. (n.d.). Retrieved July 27, 2002, from http://members.tripod.com/~AFH/

**Note:** The abbreviation n.d. stands for "no date."

### 22. An Abstract

Guinot, A., & Peterson, B. R. (1995). *Forgetfulness and partial cognition* (Drexel University Cognitive Research Report No. 21). Abstract retrieved December 4, 2001, from http://www.Drexel.edu/~guinot/deltarule-abstract.html

### 23. An E-mail

As with all other personal communication, references to e-mail sent from one person to another should be included only in the text, not in the reference list.

### 24. A Message Posted to a Newsgroup

List the author's full name—or, if that is not available, the screen name. In brackets after the title, provide information that will help readers access the message.

Shapiro, R. (2001, April 4). Chat rooms and interpersonal communication [Msg 7]. Message posted to news:// sci.psychology.communication

### 25. A Daily Newspaper

Farrell, P. D. (1997, March 23). New high-tech stresses hit traders and investors on the information superhighway. *Wall Street*

*Journal.* Retrieved April 4, 1999, from http://
wall-street.news.com/ forecasts/stress/stress.html

### 26. A Searchable Database

Nowroozi, C. (1992). What you lose when you miss sleep. *Nation's
Business, 80*(9), 73–77. Retrieved April 22, 2001, from Expanded Academic ASAP database.

### 27. Computer Software

Sharp, S. (1995). Career Selection Tests (Version 5.0) [Computer
software]. Chico, CA: Avocation Software.

### Sample APA Reference List Entries: Nonprint Sources
### 28. A Television Broadcast

Murphy J. (Executive Producer). (2002, March 4). *The CBS
evening news* [Television broadcast]. New York: Columbia
Broadcasting Service.

### 29. A Television Series

Sorkin, A., Schlamme, T., & Wells, J. (Executive Producers).
(2002). *The west wing* [Television series]. Los Angeles:
Warner Bros. Television.

### 30. A Motion Picture

Spielberg, S. (Director). (1994). *Schindler's list* [Motion picture].
United States: Universal.

### 31. A CD Recording

Marley, B. (1977). Waiting in vain. On *Exodus* [CD]. New York: Island Records.

### 32. An Audiocassette Recording

Skinner, B. F. (Speaker). (1972). *Skinner on skinnerism.* Holly-
wood, CA: Center for Cassette Studies.

## (3) Content Notes

APA format permits content notes, indicated by **superscripts** (raised numerals) in the text. The notes are listed on a separate numbered page, entitled Footnotes, following the appendixes (or after the reference list if there are no appendixes). Double-space all notes, indenting the first line of each note five to seven spaces (or one-half inch) and beginning subsequent lines flush left. Number the notes with superscripts that correspond to the numbers in your text.

# 11b   APA Manuscript Guidelines

Social science papers include internal headings (for example, Introduction, Methods, Results, Background of Problem, Description of Problem, Solutions, and Conclusion). Each section of a social science paper is a complete unit with a beginning and an end so it can be read separately and still make sense out of context. The body of the paper may discuss charts, graphs, maps, photographs, flowcharts, or tables that appear on separate pages at the end of the paper.

The following guidelines are based on the latest version of the *Publication Manual of the American Psychological Association*.

---

### ✓checklist Typing your paper

(Use the student paper on p. 238 as your model.)

✓ Leave a one-inch margin at the top, bottom, and on both sides. Double-space your paper throughout.

✓ Indent the first line of every paragraph and the first line of every footnote five to seven spaces (or one-half inch) from the left-hand margin. Set off a long quotation of more than forty words in a block format by indenting the entire quotation five to seven spaces (or one-half inch) from the left-hand margin.

✓ Number all pages consecutively. Each page should contain a **page header** (an abbreviated title) and a page number one-half inch from the top and one inch from the right-hand edge of the page. Leave a one-half inch space between the page header and the page number.

✓ Center and type major **headings** with uppercase and lowercase letters. Place minor headings flush left, typed with uppercase and lowercase letters and italicized.

See
44a2

*continued on the following page*

See
44a3

*continued from the previous page*

✓ Format items in a series as a numbered **list**.

✓ Arrange the pages of the paper in the following order:
  - Title page (page 1) includes a page header, running head, title, and byline (your name)
  - Abstract (page 2)
  - Text of paper (beginning on page 3)
  - Reference List (new page)
  - Appendixes (start each on a new page)
  - Footnotes (new page)
  - List of captions for figures (on a separate page)
  - Figures (start each on a new page)
  - Tables (start each on a new page)

✓ Number all tables consecutively, and refer to them by numbers in the text (For example, See Table 4). Tables should be placed on separate pages at the end of the paper. Each table should have a brief explanatory title. Type the word Table along with an arabic numeral flush left above the table (for example, Table 7).

✓ Double-space and type the title of each table (in italics) flush left. Capitalize the first letters of principal words of the title (for example, *Frequency of Negative Responses of Dorm Students to Questions Concerning Alcohol Consumption*).

✓ Number all figures consecutively, and refer to them by numbers in the text (for example, See Figure 1). Figures should be placed on separate pages at the end of the paper. In addition to a number, each figure should have a caption that explains the figure and serves as a title.

✓ Do not include the captions with the figures themselves. Instead, list captions for all the figures together on a separate page. At the top of this page, center the title Figure Captions. Then, for each caption, type the word *Figure* followed by the number (both in italics). Then, type the caption (not italicized). (For example, *Figure 1*. Duration of responses measured in seconds.)

See
11a

✓ If you use source material in your paper, citations should be consistent with **APA documentation style**.

> (✓) **checklist** Preparing the APA reference list
>
> ✓ Begin the reference list on a new page after the last page of text or content notes, numbered as the next page of the paper.
> ✓ Center the title References at the top of the page.
> ✓ List the items on the reference list alphabetically (with author's last name first).
> ✓ Type the first line of each entry at the left-hand margin. Indent subsequent lines five to seven spaces (or one-half inch).
> ✓ Separate the major divisions of each entry with a period and one space.
> ✓ Double-space the reference list within and between entries.

> (✓) **checklist** Arranging works in the APA reference list
>
> ✓ Single-author entries precede multiple-author entries that begin with the same name.
> Field, S. (1987)
> Field, S., & Levitt, M. P. (1984)
> ✓ Entries by the same author or authors are arranged according to date of publication, starting with the earliest date.
> Ruthenberg, H., & Rubin, R. (1985)
> Ruthenberg, H., & Rubin, R. (1987)
> ✓ Entries with the same author or authors and date of publication are arranged alphabetically according to title. Lowercase letters (*a, b, c,* and so on) that indicate the order of publication are placed within parentheses.
> Wolk, E. M. (1996a). Analysis . . .
> Wolk, E. M. (1996b). Hormonal . . .

## 11c    Sample APA-Style Research Paper

The following student paper, "Sleep Deprivation in College Students," uses APA documentation style. It includes a title page, an abstract, a list of references, and two tables.

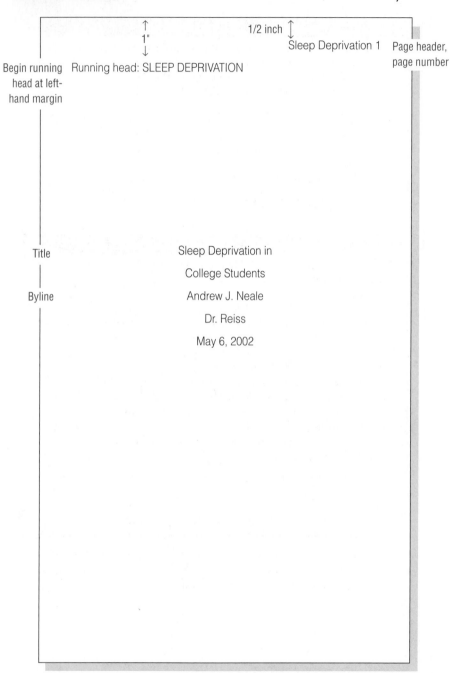

1/2 inch

1"

Sleep Deprivation 1

Page header, page number

Begin running head at left-hand margin

Running head: SLEEP DEPRIVATION

Title

Byline

Sleep Deprivation in

College Students

Andrew J. Neale

Dr. Reiss

May 6, 2002

# Sample APA-Style Research Paper

Page header and number on every page

Center

## Abstract

The present study examined the extent to which sleep deprivation affects college students' scholastic performance. A survey of 50 first-year college students in an introductory biology class was conducted. The survey consisted of five questions regarding the causes and results of sleep deprivation and specifically addressed the students' study methods and the grades they received on the fall midterm. The study's hypothesis was that although students believe that forgoing sleep to study will yield better grades, sleep deprivation actually causes a decrease in scholastic performance. In support of this hypothesis, 70% of the students who received either an A or a B on the fall midterm did not deprive themselves of sleep in order to cram for the test.

Abstract typed as a single paragraph in block format.

239

# APA Documentation Style

Sleep Deprivation 3

Full title (centered)

Sleep Deprivation and College Students

Introduction

For many college students, sleep is a luxury that they feel they cannot afford. Bombarded with tests and assignments and limited by a 24-hour day, students often attempt to make up time by forgoing sleep. Ironically, students may actually impair their scholastic performance by failing to get adequate sleep. According to several psychological and medical studies, sleep deprivation can lead to memory loss and health problems, both of which are more likely to harm a student's academic performance than to help it.

Major heading (centered)

Background

Literature review (¶s 2–6)

Sleep is often overlooked as an essential component of a healthy lifestyle. More than 75% of Americans "wake up regularly to alarms, and almost as many sleep more than an hour or two longer on weekends than on weekdays" (Nowroozi, 1992, p. 74).

Author's name and year of publication placed in parenthetical reference when not mentioned in text. Note that the quotation requires separate documentation and a page number.

Both of these behaviors are results of sleep deprivation, indicating that for most people, sleep is viewed as a luxury rather than a necessity (Nowroozi, 1992). This is particularly true for college students, many of whom are required to memorize a great deal of material before their exams. Students believe that if they read and review immediately before the test—even though this invariably means losing sleep—they will remember more information and thus get better grades. However, this is not true.

In fact, according to Dr. Charles Pollak, head of the sleep-disorder center at Cornell University's New York Hospital in Westchester County, "people who don't get enough sleep can't

Sleep Deprivation 4

think; they can't make appropriate judgments, and they can't maintain long attention spans" (cited in Toufexis, 1990, p. 80). Thus, students who choose studying over sleep might actually be limiting their ability to perform well.

Clearly, sleep deprivation harms, rather than improves, academic performance. A study conducted by professors Mary Carskadon at Brown University in Providence, Rhode Island, and Amy Wolfson at the College of the Holy Cross in Worcester, Massachusetts, showed that high school students who got adequate sleep were more likely to do well in their classes (Carpenter, 2001). According to their study of the correlation between grades and sleep, students who went to bed earlier on both weeknights and weekends earned mainly A's and B's. The students who received D's and F's averaged about 35 minutes less sleep per day than the high achievers (cited in Carpenter, 2001). Apparently, then, sleep is essential to high academic achievement.

Student uses past tense when discussing other researchers' work.

Once students reach college, however, sleep becomes expendable. For example, students believe that if they use the time they would normally sleep to study, they will do better on exams. A recent survey of 144 undergraduate students in introductory psychology classes contradicted this assumption. According to this study, long sleepers, or those individuals who slept 9 or more hours out of a 24-hour day, had significantly higher grade point averages (GPAs) than short sleepers, or individuals who slept less than 7 hours out of a 24-hour day. Thus, contrary to the belief of many college students, more sleep is often a requirement for a high GPA (Kelly, Kelly, & Clanton, 2001).

Many students believe they will be able to remember more material if they do not sleep at all before an exam. They fear that sleeping will interfere with their ability to retain information. A study of the cognitive abilities of 44 college students, however, showed that sleep deprivation actually impaired learning skills (Pilcher & Walters, 1997). College students were either deprived of 24 hours of sleep or allowed to sleep 8 hours before taking the Watson-Glaser Critical Thinking Appraisal, a test that measures critical thinking skills. The participants were then asked to complete two questionnaires about the test, one assessing their effort, concentration, and estimated performance, the other assessing their off-task cognitions. According to the researchers, "sleep-deprived participants performed significantly worse than the nondeprived participants on the cognitive task" (Pilcher & Walters, 1997, p. 123). Surprisingly, "sleep-deprived participants rated their concentration and effort higher than the nondeprived participants did" (Pilcher & Walters, 1997, p. 124). Thus, this study confirms that sleep deprivation actually harms cognitive performance while simultaneously explaining that students nevertheless continue to believe that the less sleep they get, the better they will do.

Student uses past tense when discussing the results of his own survey.

A survey of students in an introductory biology class at the University of Texas demonstrated the effects of sleep deprivation on scholastic performance and supported the hypothesis that despite students' beliefs, forgoing sleep does not lead to better test scores.

**APA Paper 11c**

Sleep Deprivation 6

Methods

To ascertain the causes and results of sleep deprivation, a study of the relationship between sleep and test performance was conducted. A survey of 50 first-year college students in an introductory biology class and their performance on the fall midterm was completed and analyzed.

Each student was asked to complete a survey composed of the following five questions about their sleep patterns and their performance on the fall midterm.

1. Did you deprive yourself of sleep when studying for the fall midterm?

2. Do you regularly deprive yourself of sleep when studying for an exam?

3. What was your grade on the exam?

4. Do you feel your performance was improved or harmed by the amount of sleep you had?

5. Will you deprive yourself of sleep when you study for the final exam?

Indent lists one-half inch. Treat as long block quotation.

To encourage honest responses, the students were not asked to put their names on the survey. Also, to determine whether the students answered question 3 accurately, their responses were compared to the grades the professor gave for the class. The grade distribution on the surveys corresponded to the number of A's, B's, C's, and D's given on the test.

Sleep Deprivation 7

Results

Analysis of the results of the survey indicates a significant dif-

*Tables discussed here are placed at end of paper* ference between the grades of students who were sleep deprived and the grades of those who were not. The results of the survey are presented in Table 1. The results of the survey are shown as percentages of the class in Table 2.

The grades in the class were curved so that out of 50 students, 10 received A's, 20 received B's, 10 received C's, and 10 received D's. For the purposes of this survey, an A or B on the exam indicates that the student performed well. A grade of C or D on the exam is considered a poor grade.

*Statistical findings reported* Of the 50 students in the class, 31 (or 62%) said they deprived themselves of sleep when studying for the fall midterm. Of these students, 17 (or 34%) of the class answered yes to the second question, admitting they regularly deprive themselves of sleep before an exam.

Of the 31 students who said they deprived themselves of sleep when studying for the fall midterm, only 4 earned A's, and the majority of the A's in the class were received by those students who were not sleep-deprived. Even more significant was the fact that of the 4 students who were sleep-deprived and got A's, only one student claimed usually to be sleep-deprived on the day of an exam. Thus, assuming the students who earn A's in a class do well in general, it is possible that sleep deprivation did not help or harm these students' grades. Not surprisingly, of the 4 students who received A's and were sleep-deprived, all of them said they would continue to use sleep deprivation to enable them to study for longer hours.

The majority of those who used sleep deprivation in an effort to obtain a higher grade received B's and C's on the exam. A total of 25 students earned a grade of B on the exam. Of those students, only nine, or 18% of the class, said they were deprived of sleep when they took the test.

Students who said they were sleep deprived when they took the exam received the majority of the poor grades. Ten students got C's on the midterm, and of these 10 students, 100% said they were sleep deprived when they took their test. Of the 10 students (20% of the class) who got D's, 8 said they were sleep deprived. Thus, a significant correlation between poor grades on the exam and sleep deprivation was found.

Conclusions

For many students, sleep is viewed as a luxury rather than a necessity. Particularly during the exam period, students use the hours in which they would normally sleep to study. However, this method does not seem to be effective. The survey discussed here reveals a clear correlation between sleep deprivation and lower exam scores. In fact, the majority of students who performed well on the exam, earning either an A or a B, were not deprived of sleep. Therefore, students who choose studying over sleep should rethink their approach and consider that sleep deprivation may actually lead to impaired academic performance.

Sleep Deprivation 9

References

Carpenter, S. (2001). Sleep deprivation may be undermining teen health. *Monitor on Psychology, 32*(9). Retrieved November 9, 2001, from http://www.apa.org/monitor/oct01/sleepteen.html

Kelly, W. E., Kelly, K. E., & Clanton, R. C. (2001). The relationship between sleep length and grade-point average among college students. *College Student Journal, 35*(1), 84–90.

Nowroozi, C. (1992). What you lose when you miss sleep. *Nation's Business, 80*(9), 73–77. Retrieved April 22, 2001, from Expanded Academic ASAP database.

Pilcher, J. J., & Walters, A. S. (1997). How sleep deprivation affects psychological variables related to college students' cognitive performance. *Journal of American College Health, 46*(3), 121–131.

Toufexis, A. (1990, May 8). Drowsy America: For millions of people caught in the nation's 24-hour whirl, sleep is the last thing on their mind. *Time, 136,* 78–85.

# Sample APA-Style Research Paper

Table 1

*Results of Survey of Students in University of Texas Introduction to Biology Class Examining the Relationship between Sleep Deprivation and Academic Performance*

| Grade Totals | Sleep-Deprived | Not Sleep-Deprived | Usually Sleep-Deprived | Improved | Harmed | Continue Sleep Deprivation? |
|---|---|---|---|---|---|---|
| A = 10 | 4 | 6 | 1 | 4 | 0 | 4 |
| B = 20 | 9 | 11 | 8 | 8 | 1 | 8 |
| C = 10 | 10 | 0 | 6 | 5 | 4 | 7 |
| D = 10 | 8 | 2 | 2 | 1 | 3 | 2 |
| Total | 31 | 19 | 17 | 18 | 8 | 21 |

Table 2

*Results of Survey of Students in University of Texas Introduction to Biology Class Examining the Relationship between Sleep Deprivation and Academic Performance: Results Shown as Percentages of Total Class*

| Grade Totals | Sleep-Deprived | Not Sleep-Deprived | Usually Sleep-Deprived | Improved | Harmed | Continue Sleep Deprivation? |
|---|---|---|---|---|---|---|
| A = 20% | 8% | 12% | 2% | 8% | 0 | 8% |
| B = 40% | 18% | 22% | 16% | 16% | 2% | 16% |
| C = 20% | 20% | 0% | 12% | 10% | 8% | 14% |
| D = 20% | 16% | 4% | 4% | 2% | 6% | 4% |
| Total | 62% | 38% | 34% | 36% | 16% | 42% |

### ◆ *Directory of Chicago-Style Endnotes and Bibliography Entries*

**Entries for Books**

1. A book by one author (p. 251)
2. A book by two or three authors (p. 251)
3. A book by more than three authors (p. 252)
4. An edited book (p. 252)
5. A chapter in a book or an essay in an anthology (p. 252)
6. A multivolume work (p. 253)
7. A book by a corporate author (p. 253)
8. A religious work (p. 253)

**Entries for Articles**

9. An article in a scholarly journal with continuous pagination through an annual volume (p. 254)
10. An article in a scholarly journal with separate pagination in each issue (p. 254)
11. An article in a weekly magazine (signed/unsigned) (p. 254)
12. An article in a monthly magazine (signed/unsigned) (p. 255)
13. An article in a newspaper (signed/unsigned) (p. 255)

**Entries for Other Sources**

14. A government document (p. 256)
15. A personal letter (p. 256)
16. A personal interview (p. 256)
17. A published interview (p. 257)
18. A film or videotape (p. 257)
19. A recording (p. 257)

**Entries for Electronic Sources**

20. A Web site or home page (p. 258)
21. An e-mail message (p. 258)
22. A listserv message (p. 258)
23. An article in an online newspaper (p. 259)
24. An article in an online journal (p. 259)
25. An article in an online magazine (p. 260)

# Chapter 12

# Chicago, CSE, and Other Documentation Styles

## 12a Using Chicago Style

**?** The *Chicago Manual of Style* is used in history and in some social science and humanities disciplines. **Chicago style*** has two parts: *notes at the end of the paper* (**endnotes**) and *a list of bibliographic citations*. (Although Chicago style encourages the use of endnotes, it also allows the use of footnotes at the bottom of the page.)

### (1) Endnotes and Footnotes

The notes format calls for a **superscript** (raised numeral) in the text after source material you have either quoted or referred to. This numeral, placed after all punctuation marks except dashes, corresponds to the numeral that accompanies the note.

*Endnote and Footnote Format: Chicago Style*

*In the Text*

> By November of 1942, the Allies had proof that the Nazis were en-
> gaged in the systematic killing of Jews.[1]

*In the Note*

> 1. David S. Wyman, *The Abandonment of the Jews: America and
> the Holocaust 1941–1945* (New York: Pantheon Books, 1984), 65.

### (2) Bibliography

In addition to the heading *Bibliography*, Chicago style allows *Selected Bibliography, Works Cited, Literature Cited, References,* and *Sources Consulted*.

---

*Chicago style follows the guidelines set in *The Chicago Manual of Style*, 14th ed. Chicago: University of Chicago Press, 1993.

# Using Chicago Style

*Sample Chicago-Style Entries: Books*

Capitalize the first, last, and all major words of titles and subtitles. Although underlining to indicate italics is acceptable, Chicago style recommends the use of italics for titles.

### 1. A Book by One Author

*Endnote*

> 1. Herbert J. Gans, *The Urban Villagers,* 2d ed. (New York: Free Press, 1982), 100.

*Bibliography*

> Gans, Herbert J. *The Urban Villagers.* 2d ed. New York: Free Press, 1982.

### 2. A Book by Two or Three Authors

*Endnote*

*Two Authors*

> 2. Jack Watson and Grant McKerney, *A Cultural History of the Theater* (New York: Longman, 1993), 137.

*Three Authors*

> 2. Nathan Caplan, John K. Whitmore, and Marcella H. Choy, *The Boat People and Achievement in America: A Study of Economic and Educational Success* (Ann Arbor: University of Michigan Press, 1990), 51.

*Bibliography*

*Two Authors*

> Watson, Jack, and Grant McKerney. *A Cultural History of the Theater.* New York: Longman, 1993.

*Three Authors*

> Caplan, Nathan, John K. Whitmore, and Marcella H. Choy. *The Boat People and Achievement in America: A Study of Economic and*

*Educational Success.* Ann Arbor: University of Michigan Press, 1990.

### 3. A Book by More Than Three Authors
**Endnote**

3. Robert E. Spiller et al., eds., *Literary History of the United States* (New York: Macmillan, 1974), 24.

**Bibliography**

Spiller, Robert E., et al., eds. *Literary History of the United States.* New York: Macmillan, 1974.

### 4. An Edited Book
**Endnote**

4. William Bartram, *The Travels of William Bartram,* ed. Mark Van Doren (New York: Dover Press, 1955), 85.

**Bibliography**

Bartram, William. *The Travels of William Bartram.* Edited by Mark Van Doren. New York: Dover Press, 1955.

### 5. A Chapter in a Book or an Essay in an Anthology
**Endnote**

5. Peter Kidson, "Architecture and City Planning," in *The Legacy of Greece,* ed. M. I. Finley (New York: Oxford University Press, 1981), 379.

**Bibliography**

Kidson, Peter. "Architecture and City Planning." In *The Legacy of Greece,* edited by M. I. Finley, 376–400. New York: Oxford University Press, 1981.

### 6. A Multivolume Work

*Endnote*

> 6. Kathleen Raine, *Blake and Tradition* (Princeton: Princeton University Press, 1968), 1:143.

*Bibliography*

> Raine, Kathleen. *Blake and Tradition.* Vol. 1. Princeton: Princeton University Press, 1968.

### 7. A Book by a Corporate Author

If the title page of a publication issued by an organization does not identify a person as the author, the organization is listed as the author, even if its name is repeated in the title, in the series title, or as the publisher.

*Endnote*

> 7. National Geographic Society, *National Parks of the United States,* 3rd ed. (Washington, D.C.: National Geographic Society, 1997), 77.

*Bibliography*

> National Geographic Society. *National Parks of the United States.* 3rd ed. Washington, D.C.: National Geographic Society, 1997.

### 8. A Religious Work

References to religious works such as the Bible are usually confined to the text or notes and not listed in the bibliography. In citing the Bible, include the book (abbreviated), the chapter (followed by a colon), and the verse numbers. Be certain to identify the version. Do not include a page number.

*Endnote*

> 8. Phil. 1:9–11 King James Version.

*Sample Chicago-Style Entries: Articles*

**9. An Article in a Scholarly Journal with Continuous Pagination through an Annual Volume**

*Endnote*

> 9. John Huntington, "Science Fiction and the Future," *College English* 37 (fall 1975): 341.

*Bibliography*

> Huntington, John. "Science Fiction and the Future." *College English* 37 (fall 1975): 340–58.

**10. An Article in a Scholarly Journal with Separate Pagination in Each Issue**

*Endnote*

> 10. R. G. Sipes, "War, Sports, and Aggression: An Empirical Test of Two Rival Theories," *American Anthropologist 4,* no. 2 (1973): 80.

*Bibliography*

> Sipes, R. G. "War, Sports, and Aggression: An Empirical Test of Two Rival Theories." *American Anthropologist 4,* no. 2 (1973): 65–84.

**11. An Article in a Weekly Magazine (signed/unsigned)**

*Endnote*

*Signed*

> 11. Pico Iyer, "A Mum for All Seasons," *Time,* 8 April 2002, 51.

*Unsigned*

> 11. "Burst Bubble," *NewScientist,* 27 July 2002, 24.

*Bibliography*

*Signed*

> Iyer, Pico. "A Mum for All Seasons." *Time,* 8 April 2002, 51.

*Unsigned*

> "Burst Bubble." *NewScientist,* 27 July 2002, 24.

## 12. An Article in a Monthly Magazine (signed/unsigned)

### Endnote

*Signed*

> 12. Tad Suzuki, "Reflecting Light on Photo Realism," *American Artist,* March 2002, 46–51.

*Unsigned*

> 12. "Repowering the U.S. with Clean Energy Development," *BioCycle,* July 2002, 14.

### Bibliography

*Signed*

> Suzuki, Tad. "Reflecting Light on Photo Realism." *American Artist,* March 2002, 46–51.

*Unsigned*

> "Repowering the U.S. with Clean Energy Development." *BioCycle,* July 2002, 14.

## 13. An Article in a Newspaper (signed/unsigned)

### Endnote

*Signed*

> 13. Francis X. Clines, "Civil War Relics Draw Visitors, and Con Artists," *New York Times,* 4 August 2002, sec. A. p. 12, national edition.

*Unsigned*

> 13. "Feds Lead Way in Long-Term Care," *Atlanta Journal-Constitution,* 21 July 2002, sec. E. p. 2.

### Bibliography

*Signed*

> Clines, Francis X. "Civil War Relics Draw Visitors, and Con Artists." *New York Times,* 4 August 2002, sec. A, p. 12, national edition.

*Unsigned*

> "Feds Lead Way in Long-Term Care." *Atlanta Journal-Constitution,* 21 July 2002, sec. E, p. 2.

**Sample Chicago-Style Entries: Other Sources**

*14. A Government Document*
*Endnote*

> 14. Department of Transportation, *The Future of High-Speed Trains in the United States: Special Study, 2001* (Washington, D.C.: GPO, 2002), 203.

*Bibliography*

> U.S. Department of Transportation. *The Future of High-Speed Trains in the United States: Special Study, 2001.* Washington, D.C.: GPO, 2002.

*15. A Personal Letter*
*Endnote*

> 15. Julia Alvarez, letter to the author, 10 April 2002.

*Bibliography*

> Alvarez, Julia. Letter to the author. 10 April 2002.

*16. A Personal Interview*
*Endnote*

> 16. Cornel West, interview by author, tape recording, St. Louis, Mo., 8 June 1994.

*Bibliography*

> West, Cornel. Interview by author. Tape recording. St. Louis, Mo., 8 June 1994.

### 17. A Published Interview
*Endnote*

17. Gwendolyn Brooks, interview by George Stravos, *Contemporary Literature* 11, no. 1 (winter 1970): 12.

*Bibliography*

Brooks, Gwendolyn. Interview by George Stravos. *Contemporary Literature* 11, no. 1 (winter 1970): 1–20.

### 18. A Film or Videotape
*Endnote*

18. *Interview with Arthur Miller,* dir. William Schiff, 17 min., The Mosaic Group, 1987, videocassette.

*Bibliography*

Miller, Arthur. *Interview with Arthur Miller.* Directed by William Schiff. 17 min. The Mosaic Group, 1987. Videocassette.

### 19. A Recording
*Endnote*

19. Bob Marley, "Crisis," on *Bob Marley and the Wailers,* Kava Island Records compact disk 423 095-3.

*Bibliography*

Marley, Bob. "Crisis." On *Bob Marley and the Wailers*. Kava Island Records compact disk 423 095-3.

### Sample Entries: Electronic Sources

*The Chicago Manual of Style,* 14th ed., does not contain guidelines for electronic sources. However, the University of Chicago Press recommends the formats in *Online! A Reference Guide to Using Internet Sources* by Andrew Harnack and Eugene Kleppinger.

Internet citations for electronic sources include the author's name; the title of the document (enclosed in quotation marks); the publication date (or, if no date is available, the abbreviation n.d.); the URL (in angle brackets); and the date of access (in parentheses). The following examples illustrate the formats for endnotes and bibliographic entries:

### 20. A Web Site or Home Page
*Endnote*

> 20. David Perdue, "Dickens's Journalistic Career," *David Perdue's Charles Dickens Page,* 24 September 2002, <http://www.fidnet.com/~dap1955/dickens> (9 October 2002).

*Bibliography*

> Perdue, David. "Dickens's Journalistic Career." *David Perdue's Charles Dickens Page.* 24 September 2002. <http://www.fidnet.com/~dap1955/dickens> (9 October 2002).

### 21. An E-mail Message
Include the author's e-mail address after his or her name.

*Endnote*

> 21. Meg Halverson, <mhalverson@drexel.edu> "Scuba Report," 8 October 2002, personal e-mail (9 October 2002).

*Bibliography*

> Halverson, Meg. <mhalverson@drexel.edu> "Scuba Report." 8 October 2002. Personal e-mail. (9 October 2002).

### 22. A Listserv Message
Include the author's e-mail address after his or her name. Include the listserv address after the date of publication.

*Endnote*

> 22. Dave Shirlaw, <dslaw@aol.com> "Bermuda Wreck," 6 September 2002, <http://lists.asu.edu/archives/sub-arch.html> (9 October 2002).

# Using Chicago Style

*Bibliography*

Shirlaw, Dave. <dslaw@aol.com> "Bermuda Wreck." 6 September 2002. <http://lists.asu.edu/archives/sub-arch.html> (9 October 2002).

### 23. An Article in an Online Newspaper

*Endnote*

23. William J. Broad, "Piece by Piece, the Civil War *Monitor* Is Pulled from the Atlantic's Depths," *New York Times on the Web*, 18 July 2002, <http://query.nytimes.com/search/advanced> (9 October 2002).

*Bibliography*

Broad, William J. "Piece by Piece, the Civil War *Monitor* Is Pulled from the Atlantic's Depths." *New York Times on the Web*. 18 July 2002. <http://query.nytimes.com/search/advanced/> (9 October 2002).

### 24. An Article in an Online Journal

*Endnote*

24. Robert F. Brooks, "Communication as the Foundation of Distance Education," *Kairos: A Journal of Rhetoric, Technology, and Pedagogy 7*, no. 2 (2002), <http://english.ttu.edu/kairos/index.html> (9 October 2002).

*Bibliography*

Brooks, Robert F. "Communication as the Foundation of Distance Education." *Kairos: A Journal of Rhetoric, Technology, and Pedagogy 7*, no. 2 (2002). <http://english.ttu.edu/kairos/index.html> (9 October 2002).

**25. An Article in an Online Magazine**

*Endnote*

> 24. Steven Levy, "I Was a Wi-Fi Freeloader," *Newsweek*, 9 October 2002, <http://www.msnbc.com/news/816606.asp> (9 October 2002).

*Bibliography*

> Levy, Steven. "I Was a Wi-Fi Freeloader." *Newsweek*. 9 October 2002. <http://www.msnbc.com/news/816606.asp> (9 October 2002).

## Subsequent references to the same work

In the first reference to a work, use the full citation; in subsequent references to the same work, list only the author's last name, followed by a comma and a page number.

*First Note on Espinoza*

> 1. J. M. Espinoza, *The First Expedition of Vargas in New Mexico, 1692* (Albuquerque: University of New Mexico Press, 1949), 10–12.

*Subsequent Note*

> 5. Epinoza, 29.

**Note:** *The Chicago Manual of Style* allows the use of the abbreviation *ibid.* ("in the same place") for subsequent references to the same work as long as there are no intervening references. *Ibid.* takes the place of the author's name and the work's title—but not the page number.

*First Note on Espinoza*

> 1. J. M. Espinoza, *The First Expedition of Vargas in New Mexico, 1692* (Albuquerque: University of New Mexico Press, 1949), 10–12.

*Subsequent Note*

2. Ibid., 23.

Keep in mind, however, that the use of Ibid. is giving way to the use of the author's last name and the page number for subsequent references to the same work.

## 12b Chicago-Style Manuscript Guidelines

> **✓checklist Typing your paper**
>
> ✓ On the title page, include the full title of your paper as well as your name. You may also be asked to include the course title, the instructor's name, and the date.
> ✓ Type your paper with a one-inch margin at the top, at the bottom, and on both sides.
> ✓ Double-space your paper throughout.
> ✓ Indent the first line of each paragraph five spaces. Set off a long prose quotation (ten or more typed lines or more than one paragraph) from the text by indenting one-half inch from the left-hand margin. If the quotation is a full paragraph, include the paragraph indentation.
> ✓ Number all pages consecutively in the upper right-hand corner, one-half inch from the top, flush right. Although it is not required, you may include your name before the page number. Although the title page is counted as page 1, it is not numbered. The first full page of the paper will be numbered page 2.
> ✓ Use superscript numbers to indicate in-text citations. Type superscript numbers at the end of cited material (quotations, paraphrases, or summaries). Leave no space between the superscript number and the preceding letter or punctuation mark.
> ✓ If you use source material in your paper, use **Chicago documentation style**.

See
30a

---

## ✓ checklist   Preparing Chicago-style endnotes

✓ Begin the endnotes on a new page after the last page of the paper.
✓ Center the title Notes one inch from the top of the page.
✓ Number the page on which the endnotes appear as the next page of the paper.
✓ Type and number notes in the order in which they appear in the paper, beginning with number 1.
✓ Type the note number on (not above) the line, followed by a period and one space.
✓ Indent the first line of each note three spaces; type subsequent lines flush with the left-hand margin.
✓ Double-space within and between entries.

---

## ✓ checklist   Preparing the Chicago-style bibliography

✓ Type entries on a separate page after the endnotes.
✓ List entries alphabetically according to the author's last name.
✓ Type the first line of each entry flush with the left-hand margin.
✓ Indent subsequent lines three spaces.
✓ Double-space the bibliography within and between entries.

---

## ? 12c   Sample Chicago-Style Research Paper (Excerpts)

The following excerpts are from a history paper that uses Chicago-style documentation.

**CMS Paper 12c**

Gambling on Gambling:

Native Americans and Casinos

By

Angela M. Womack

Title centered and capitalized followed by name

American History 301

Dr. Adkins

December 3, 2003

Course title
Instructor
Date

Page number |
Indent 5 spaces

Gambling on Gambling: Native Americans and Casinos

Foxwoods Resort Casino is the largest gambling establishment in the nation and the third most profitable. With more than 6,400 slot machines, 350 table games, and the "world's largest bingo hall, no one offers more gaming choices."[1] Unlike most internationally recognized casinos, however, Foxwoods is not located in Las Vegas, Nevada, but on the 1,238-acre reservation of the Mashantucket Pequot Indians in Ledyard, Connecticut. Foxwoods is just one example of the many casinos that Native American tribes have begun to operate on their reservation lands. Some Native Americans have referred to the gaming industry as "the new buffalo," their first economic opportunity in over two hundred years.[2] Proponents of this new entrepreneurial effort argue that casinos have helped eliminate many of the problems that have plagued residents of reservations for centuries. Others, however, citing recent legal battles involving Native American casinos and organized crime, contend that casinos only encourage illegal and immoral behavior. Regardless of one's position on this issue, it is clear that casinos have an impact on the lives of Native Americans as individuals and as a group.

Native American tribes began to enter the gaming industry in the late 1970s and early 1980s. As state governments across the country began to use lotteries as a fund-raising tool, many tribes recognized a unique opportunity. Unlike states, which must abide by federal and state laws that limit the amount of prize money they can offer, reservations are only obligated to follow tribal laws.

Superscript numbers refer to endnotes

Double-space

# Sample Chicago-Style Research Paper

3

Recognizing this special status, several tribal governments in Florida and California established bingo games with prizes larger than those offered by the state.[3] When states threatened to close their operations, tribal governments sued them in federal court. In two cases—*Seminole Tribe* v. *Butterworth* (1979) and *California* v. *Cabazon Band* (1987)—the court ruled that tribes may not only engage in gaming, but may operate their institutions free of state control.[4] These decisions allowed for an explosion in Native American gaming activities, and since the early 1990s, Native American tribes have begun to open casinos across the country. According to the National Gaming Commission, in 1997, 183 of the 557 federally registered tribes ran 274 gaming operations.

4

Notes

1. "Gaming at Foxwoods," *Foxwoods Resort and Casino* 12 March 2002, <http://www.foxwoods.com/gaming.html> (18 August 2002).

2. James Popkin, "Gambling with the Mob? Wise Guys Have Set Their Sights on the Booming Indian Casino Business," *U.S. News & World Report,* 15 August 1993, 30.

3. Kathleen McCormick, "In the Clutch of the Casinos," *Planning* 63, no. 6 (1997): 4.

4. McCormick, 5.

Endnotes listed in order in which they appear in paper. Second and subsequent references to sources include only author's last name and page number.

5

Center

Bibliography

Double-
space

Benedict, Jeff. *Without Reservation: The Making of America's Most Powerful Indian Tribe and Foxwoods, the World's Largest Casino.* New York: HarperCollins, 2000.

Article has no listed author; alphabetized according to first significant word of title.

"Bugsy and the Indians: Gambling." *The Economist,* 21 March 1992, A27–A29.

Committee on Indian Affairs. *Indian Gaming: Hearing before the Committee on Indian United States Senate, One Hundred Sixth Congress, Second Session, to Provide Information on the Activities of the National Indian Gaming Commission, July 26, 2000.* Washington D.C.: GPO, 2000.

Entries are listed alphabetically according to the author's last name.

Dale, Mason W. *Indian Gaming: Tribal Sovereignty and American Politics.* Norman: University of Oklahoma Press, 2000.

Dao, James. "Once-Poor Tribe Awaits a Flood of Casino Profits." *New York Times,* 18 July 1993, sec. A, p. 17, national edition.

First line of each entry is flush with left-hand margin; subsequent lines indented 3 spaces.

Eisler, Kim Isaac. *Revenge of the Pequots: How a Small Native American Tribe Created the World's Most Profitable Casino.* New York: Simon & Schuster, 2001.

"Gaming at Foxwoods." *Foxwoods Resort and Casino.* 12 March 2002. <http://www.foxwoods.com/gaming.html> (18 August 2002).

McCormick, Kathleen. "In the Clutch of the Casinos." *Planning* 63, no. 6 (1997): 4–10.

Popkin, James. "Gambling with the Mob? Wise Guys Have Set Their Sights on the Booming Indian Casino Business." *U.S. News & World Report,* August 1993, 30–33.

## ◆ Directory of CSE Reference List Entries

1. A book with one author (p. 269)
2. A book with more than one author (p. 269)
3. An edited book (p. 269)
4. A chapter or other part of a book with a separate title but with the same author (p. 269)
5. A chapter or other part of a book with a different author (p. 270)
6. An article in a journal paginated by issue (p. 270)
7. An article in a journal with continuous pagination (p. 270)
8. A magazine article (signed/unsigned) (p. 270)
9. A newspaper article (signed/unsigned) (p. 271)
10. Religious works (p. 271)
11. Classical literature (p. 271)
12. An audiocassette (p. 271)
13. A videocassette (p. 272)
14. A map (p. 272)
15. An online book (p. 272)
16. An online journal (p. 272)

## 12d   Using CSE (formerly CBE) Style*

**CSE style,** recommended by the Council of Science Editors (CSE) is used in biology, zoology, physiology, anatomy, and genetics. CSE style has two parts—*documentation in the text* and a *reference list.*

### (1) Documentation in the Text

**CSE style** recommends two documentation formats: *citation-sequence format* and *name-year format.*

#### Citation-Sequence Format

The **citation-sequence format** calls for either raised numbers in the text of the paper (the preferred form) or numbers inserted parenthetically in the text of the paper.

One study[1] has demonstrated the effect of low dissolved oxygen.

---

*CSE style follows the guidelines set in the style manual of the Council of Biology Editors: *Scientific Style and Format: The CBE Manual for Authors, Editors, and Publishers,* 6th ed. New York: Cambridge UP, 1994. The Council of Biology Editors has changed its name to the Council of Science Editors.

Chicago, CSE, and Other Documentation Styles

These numbers correspond to a list of references at the end of the paper. When the writer refers to more than one source in a single note, the numbers are separated by a hyphen if they are in sequence ($^{2-3}$) and by a comma if they are not ($^{3,6}$).

### Name-Year Format

The **name-year format** calls for the author's name and the year of publication to be inserted parenthetically in the text. If the author's name is used to introduce the source material, only the date of publication is needed in the parenthetical citation.

> A great deal of heat is often generated during this process (McGinness 1999).

> According to McGinness, a great deal of heat is often generated during this process (1999).

When two or more works are cited in the same parentheses, the sources are arranged chronologically (from earliest to latest) and separated by semicolons.

> Epidemics can be avoided by taking tissue cultures (Domb 1998) and by intervention with antibiotics (Baldwin and Rigby 1984; Martin and others 1992; Cording 1998).

**Note:** The second citation, *Baldwin and Rigby, 1984*, refers to a work by two authors; the third citation, *Martin and others*, refers to a work by three or more authors.

## (2) Reference List

The format of the reference list depends on the documentation format you use. If you use the name-year documentation format, your reference list will resemble the reference list for an **APA** paper. If you use the citation-sequence documentation style, your sources will be listed by number, in the order in which they appear in your text, on a *References* page. This section presents guidelines for assembling the citation-sequence reference list.

See
11a2

# Using CSE (formerly CBE) Style

### Sample CSE Reference List Entries: Books

List the author or authors with last name followed by a space but not a comma; then, list the initial or initials that represent the first and middle names (followed by a period), the title (not underlined, and with only the first word capitalized), the place of publication, the full name of the publisher (followed by a semicolon), the year (followed by a period), and the total number of pages (including back matter, such as the index).

### 1. A Book with One Author

1. Hawking SW. Brief history of time: from the big bang to black holes. New York: Bantam; 1995. 198 p.

**Note:** No period separates the initials that represent the author's first and middle names.

### 2. A Book with More Than One Author

2. Horner JR, Gorman J. Digging dinosaurs. New York: Workman; 1988. 210 p.

### 3. An Edited Book

3. Goldfarb TD, editor. Taking sides: clashing views on controversial environmental issues. 2nd ed. Guilford (CT): Dushkin; 1987, 323 p.

The name of the publisher's state, province, or country can be added within parentheses to clarify the location. The two-letter postal service abbreviation can be used for the state or province.

### 4. A Chapter or Other Part of a Book with a Separate Title but with the Same Author

4. Asimov I. Exploring the earth and cosmos: the growth and future of human knowledge. New York: Crown; 1984. Part III, The horizons of matter; p 245–94.

### 5. A Chapter or Other Part of a Book with a Different Author

5. Gingerich O. Hints for beginning observers. In: Mallas JH, Kreimer E, editors. The Messier album: an observer's handbook. Cambridge: Cambridge Univ Pr; 1978: p 194–5.

### Sample CSE Reference List Entries: Articles

List the author or authors (last name first), the title of the article (not in quotation marks, and with only the first word capitalized), the abbreviated name of the journal (with all major words capitalized, but not italicized or underlined), the year (followed by a semicolon), the volume number (followed by a colon), and inclusive page numbers. No spaces separate the year, the volume, and the page numbers. Month names longer than three letters are abbreviated to their first three letters.

### 6. An Article in a Journal Paginated by Issue

6. Sarmiento JL, Gruber N. Sinks for anthropogenic carbon. Phy Today 2002;55(8):30–6.

### 7. An Article in a Journal with Continuous Pagination

7. Brazil K, Krueger P. Patterns of family adaptation to childhood asthma. J of Pediatric Nursing 2002;17:167–73.

Omit the month (and day for weeklies) and issue number for journals with continuous pagination in volumes.

### 8. A Magazine Article (Signed/Unsigned)

*Signed*

8. Nadis S. Using lasers to detect E.T. Astronomy 2002 Sep:44–9.

*Unsigned*

8. [Anonymous]. Brown dwarf glows with radio waves. Astronomy 2001 Jun:28.

# Using CSE (formerly CBE) Style

## 9. A Newspaper Article (Signed/Unsigned)

*Signed*

> 9. Husted B. Don't wiggle out of untangling computer wires. Atlanta Journal-Constitution 2002 Jul 21;Sect Q1(col 1).

*Unsigned*

> 9. [Anonymous]. Scientists find gene tied to cancer risk. New York Times 2002 Apr 22;Sect A18(col 6).

## 10. Religious Works

*General Reference*

> 10. The Bible. Philippians 1:9–11.

*Specific Reference*

> 10. The new Jerusalem Bible. Garden City (NY): Doubleday; 1985. Luke 15:11–32.p.1715–6.

## 11. Classical Literature

*General Reference*

> 11. The Odyssey. 17:319–32.

*Specific Reference*

> 11. Homer. Odyssey; Book 17:319–332. In: Lombardo S, translator and editor. The essential Homer: selections from the Iliad and the Odyssey. Indianapolis: Hackett; 2000.p. 391–2.

## 12. An Audiocassette

> 12. Bronowski J. Ascent of man [audiocassette]. New York: Jeffrey Norton Pub; 1974. 1 audiocassette: 2-track, 55 min.

### 13. A Videocassette

13. Stoneberger B. Women in science [videocassette]. Clark R, editor. American Society for Microbiology, producer. Madison (WI): Hawkhill; 1998. 1 videocassette: 42 min, sound, color, 1/2-in. Accompanied by: 1 guide.

### 14. A Map

*A Sheet Map*

14. Amazonia: a world resource at risk [ecological map]. Washington: Nat Geographic Soc; 1992. 1 sheet.

*A Map in an Atlas*

14. Central Africa [political map]. In: Hammond citation world atlas. Maplewood (NJ): Hammond; 1996. p 114–5. Color, scale 1:13,800,000.

### 15. An Online Book

15. Bohm D. Causality and chance in modern physics [monograph online]. Philadelphia: Univ of Pennsylvania Pr; 1999. Available from: http://www.netlibrary.com/ ebook_info.asp?product_id=17169 via the INTERNET. Accessed 2002 Aug 17.

### 16. An Online Journal

16. Lasko P. The *Drosophila melanogaster* genome: translation factors and RNA binding proteins. J of Cell biol [serial online] 2000;150(2):F51–6. Available from: http://www.jcb.org/ search.dtl via the INTERNET. Accessed 2002 Aug 15.

# 12e   CSE Manuscript Guidelines

---

## ✓checklist  Typing your paper

✓ Type your name, the course, and the date flush left one inch from the top of the first page.

✓ If required, include an abstract (a 250-word summary of the paper) on a separate page following the title page.

✓ Indent the first line of each paragraph five spaces.

✓ Insert tables and figures in the body of the paper. Number tables and figures in separate sequences (Table 1, Table 2; Figure 1, Figure 2; and so on).

✓ Number pages consecutively in the upper right-hand corner.

✓ If you use source material in your paper, follow **CSE documentation style**.

See
12d

---

## ✓checklist  Preparing the CSE reference list

✓ Begin the reference list on a new page after the last page of the paper, numbered as the next page of the paper.

✓ Center the title References, Literature Cited, or References Cited about one inch from the top of the page.

✓ List the entries in the order in which they appear in the paper, not alphabetically.

✓ Number the entries consecutively; type the note numbers flush left on (not above) the line, followed by a period.

✓ Leave two spaces between the period and the first letter of the entry; align subsequent lines directly beneath the first letter of the author's last name.

✓ Double-space within and between entries.

# ? 12f   Sample CSE-Style Research Paper (Excerpts)

The following excerpts are from a biology research paper that illustrates the citation-sequence format recommended by the *CSE Style Manual*.

---

Maternal Smoking

1

June M. Fahrman

Biology 306

April 17, 2002

Maternal Smoking: Deleterious

Effects on the Fetus

Introduction

The placenta, lifeline between fetus and mother, has been the subject of various studies aimed at determining the mechanisms by which substances in the mother's bloodstream affect the fetus. For example, cigarette smoking is clearly associated with an increased risk in the incidence of low-birthweight infants,[1] due both to prematurity and to intrauterine growth retardation.[2]

Development of the Placenta

At the morula stage of development, less than one week after fertilization, two types of cells can be distinguished. . . .

# Sample CSE-Style Research Paper

## Conclusion

In summary, abundant evidence exists as to the harmful effects maternal smoking may have on the fetus. These effects include low birthweight, low IQ scores, minimal brain dysfunction, shorter stature, prenatal mortality, and premature birth. . . .

## References

1. Rakel RE. Conn's current therapy 1988. Philadelphia: W. B. Saunders;1988. 360 p.

2. Meberg A, Sande H, Foss OP, Stenwig JT. Smoking during pregnancy—effects on the fetus and on thiocyanate levels in mother and baby. Acta. Paediatr Scand 1979;68:547–552.

3. Lehtovirta P, Forss M. The acute effect of smoking on intervillous blood flow of the placenta. Brit Obs Gyn 1978; 85:729–731.

4. Phelan JP. Diminished fetal reactivity with smoking. Amer Obs Gyn 1980;136:230–233.

5. VanDerVelde WJ. Structural changes in the placenta of smoking mothers: a quantitative study. Placenta 1983;4:231–240.

# 12g   Using Other Documentation Styles

**?**   The following style manuals describe documentation formats used in various fields.

### Chemistry

Dodd, Janet S. American Chemical Society. *The ACS Guide: A Manual for Authors and Editors.* 2nd ed. Washington: Amer. Chemical Soc., 1997.

### Geology

United States Geological Survey. *Suggestions to Authors of the Reports of the United States Geological Survey.* 7th ed. Washington: GPO, 1991.

### Government Documents

Garner, Diane L. *The Complete Guide to Citing Government Information Resources: A Manual for Writers and Librarians.* Rev. Ed. Bethesda: Congressional Information Service, 1993.

United States Government Printing Office. *Style Manual.* Washington: GPO, 2000.

### Journalism

Goldstein, Norm, ed. *Associated Press Stylebook and Briefing on Media Law.* 35th ed. New York: Associated Press. 2000.

### Law

*The Bluebook: A Uniform System of Citation.* Comp. Editors of *Columbia Law Review* et al. 16th ed. Cambridge: Harvard Law Rev. Assn., 1996.

## Mathematics

American Mathematical Society. *AMS Author Handbook.* Providence: Amer. Mathematical Soc., 1998.

## Medicine

Iverson, Cheryl. *Manual of Style: A Guide for Authors and Editors.* 9th ed. Chicago: Amer. Medical Assn., 1997.

## Music

Holman, D. Kirn, ed. *Writing about Music: A Style Sheet from the Editors of 19th-Century Music.* Berkeley: U California P, 1988.

## Physics

American Institute of Physics. *AIP Style Manual.* 5th ed. New York: Am. Inst. of Physics, 1995.

## Scientific and Technical Writing

Rubens, Philip, ed. *Science and Technical Writing: A Manual of Style.* 2nd ed. New York: Routledge, 2001.

# PART 6

## Five Common Sentence Errors

**13 Revising Sentence Fragments 281**
    **13a** Attaching the Fragment to an Independent Clause 282
    **13b** Deleting the Subordinating Conjunction or
        Relative Pronoun 283
    **13c** Supplying the Missing Subject or Verb 284

**14 Revising Comma Splices and Fused Sentences 285**
    **14a** Revising with Periods 285
    **14b** Revising with Semicolons 286
    **14c** Revising with Coordinating Conjunctions 287
    **14d** Revising with Subordinating Conjunctions or
        Relative Pronouns 287

**15 Revising Agreement Errors 288**
    **15a** Making Subjects and Verbs Agree 288
    **15b** Making Pronouns and Antecedents Agree 292

**16 Revising Awkward or Confusing Sentences 295**
    **16a** Revising Unwarranted Shifts 295
    **16b** Revising Mixed Constructions 297
    **16c** Revising Faulty Predication 298
    **16d** Revising Incomplete or Illogical Comparisons 299

**17 Revising Misplaced and Dangling Modifiers 300**
    **17a** Revising Misplaced Modifiers 300
    **17b** Revising Intrusive Modifiers 302
    **17c** Revising Dangling Modifiers 302

# PART 6

## ? Frequently Asked Questions

Chapter 13 **Revising Sentence Fragments** **281**
- What exactly is a sentence fragment**?** 281
- How do I turn a fragment into a complete sentence**?** 282
- Are sentence fragments ever acceptable**?** 284

Chapter 14 **Revising Comma Splices and Fused Sentences** **285**
- What are comma splices and fused sentences, and how are they different from run-on sentences**?** 285
- How do I revise a comma splice or a fused sentence**?** 285

Chapter 15 **Revising Agreement Errors** **288**
- What do I do if a phrase like *along with* comes between the subject and the verb**?** 289
- If a subject has two parts, is the verb singular or plural**?** 289
- Do subjects like *anyone* take singular or plural verbs**?** 290
- Can I use *they* and *their* to refer to words like *everyone***?** 294

Chapter 16 **Revising Awkward or Confusing Sentences** **295**
- What is the difference between direct and indirect discourse**?** 297
- How do I correct an incomplete or illogical comparison**?** 299

Chapter 17 **Revising Misplaced and Dangling Modifiers** **300**
- What are misplaced modifiers, and how do I revise them**?** 300
- What are dangling modifiers, and how do I revise them**?** 302

| **URLs** | *Visit the following sites for answers to more FAQs* |
|---|---|

**Run-ons/Comma Splices/Fused Sentences**
   *http://owl.english.purdue.edu/handouts/print/grammar/PDFs/g_sentpr.pdf*

**Agreement**
   *http://andromeda.rutgers.edu/~jlynch/Writing/a.html#agreement*

**Improving Sentence Clarity (Purdue)**
   *http://owl.english.purdue.edu/handouts/general/gl_sentclar.html*

# Chapter 13

# Revising Sentence Fragments

A **sentence fragment** is an incomplete sentence—a clause or a phrase—that is punctuated as though it were a sentence. A sentence may be incomplete for any of the following reasons.

- It lacks a subject.

    Many astrophysicists now believe galaxies are distributed in clusters. <u>And even form supercluster complexes.</u>

- It lacks a verb.

    Every generation has its defining moments. <u>Usually the events with the most news coverage.</u>

- It lacks both a subject and a verb.

    Researchers are engaged in a variety of studies. <u>Suggesting a link between alcoholism and heredity.</u> (*Suggesting* is a **verbal**, which cannot serve as a sentence's main verb.)

- It is a **dependent clause**, a clause that begins with a subordinating conjunction or relative pronoun.

    Bishop Desmond Tutu was awarded the 1984 Nobel Peace Prize. <u>Because he struggled to end apartheid.</u>

    The pH meter and the spectrophotometer are two scientific instruments. <u>That changed the chemistry laboratory dramatically.</u>

## Maintaining sentence boundaries

When readers cannot see where sentences begin and end, they have difficulty understanding what you have written. For instance, in the following sequence, it is impossible to tell to which sentence the fragment belongs.

The course requirements were changed last year. <u>Because a new professor was hired at the very end of the spring semester.</u> I was unable to find out about this change until after preregistration.

**✓ checklist Revising sentence fragments**

To revise a sentence fragment, use one or more of the following strategies.

✓ Attach the fragment to an adjacent independent clause that contains the missing words.

✓ Delete the subordinating conjunction or relative pronoun.

✓ Supply the missing subject or verb (or both).

## 13a Attaching the Fragment to an Independent Clause

Writer's Resource CD-ROM

See B3.2

In most cases, the simplest way to correct a fragment is by attaching it to an adjacent **independent clause** that contains the missing words. The result is a complete sentence.

See B3.1

                                                          for
President Johnson did not seek reelection/ ~~For~~ a number of reasons. (**prepositional phrase** fragment)

See B3.1

                                                        to
Students sometimes take a leave of absence/ ~~To~~ decide on definite career goals. (**verbal phrase** fragment)

                                          , realizing
The pilot changed course/ ~~Realizing~~ the weather was worsening. (verbal phrase fragment)

See 19b3

                                                       , the
Brian was the star forward of the Blue Devils/ ~~The~~ team with the most wins. (**appositive** fragment)

See ESL 47b4

                                                    , such
Fairy tales are full of damsels in distress/ ~~Such~~ as Rapunzel. (appositive fragment)

                                                    and
People with dyslexia have trouble reading/ ~~And~~ may also find it difficult to write. (part of compound predicate)

                                              and
They took only a compass and a canteen/ ~~And~~ some trail mix. (part of compound object)

although
Property taxes rose sharply/ ~~Although~~ city services declined.
(**dependent clause** fragment)

, which
The battery is dead/ ~~Which~~ means the car won't start.
(dependent clause fragment)

**Revising sentence fragments: Lists**

When a fragment takes the form of a list, add a colon to connect the list to the independent clause that introduces it.

See
22a1

Tourists often outnumber residents in four European
cities/: Venice, Florence, Canterbury, and Bath.

## 13b Deleting the Subordinating Conjunction or Relative Pronoun

Writer's
Resource
CD-ROM

When a fragment consists of a dependent clause that is punctuated as though it were a complete sentence, you can correct it by
attaching it to an adjacent independent clause, as illustrated in
**13a.** Alternatively, you can simply delete the subordinating conjunction or relative pronoun.

City
Property taxes rose sharply. ~~Although city~~ services declined.
(subordinating conjunction *although* deleted)

This
The battery is dead. ~~Which~~ means the car won't start. (relative
pronoun *which* replaced by *this*, a word that can serve as the
sentence's subject.)

**Note:** Simply deleting the subordinating conjunction or relative
pronoun is usually the least desirable way to revise a sentence
fragment because it is likely to create two choppy sentences and
obscure the connection between them.

# 13c   Supplying the Missing Subject or Verb

Another way to correct a fragment is to add the missing words (a subject or a verb or both) needed to make it a sentence.

It was divided
In 1948, India became independent. ∧~~Divided~~ into the nations of India and Pakistan. (verbal phrase fragment)

It reminds
A familiar trademark can increase a product's sales. ∧~~Reminding~~ shoppers the product has a long-standing reputation. (verbal phrase fragment)

**?**

### Revising sentence fragments

Sentence fragments are often used in speech and in e-mail as well as in journalism, advertising, and creative writing. In most college writing situations, however, sentence fragments are not acceptable. Do not use them without carefully considering their suitability for your audience and purpose.

# Chapter 14

# Revising Comma Splices and Fused Sentences

A **run-on sentence** is created when two <u>independent clauses</u> are joined without the necessary punctuation or connective word. A run-on sentence is not just a long sentence—in fact, run-ons can be quite short—but a grammatically incorrect construction. *Comma splices* and *fused sentences* are two kinds of run-on sentences.

A **comma splice** is an error that occurs when two independent clauses are joined with just a comma. A **fused sentence** is an error that occurs when two independent clauses are joined with no punctuation.

> Comma Splice: Charles Dickens created the character of Mr. Micawber, he also created Uriah Heep.
>
> Fused Sentence: Charles Dickens created the character of Mr. Micawber he also created Uriah Heep.

---

**✓checklist** Revising comma splices and fused sentences

To revise a comma splice or fused sentence, use one of the following strategies.
✓ Add a period between the clauses.
✓ Add a semicolon between the clauses.
✓ Add an appropriate coordinating conjunction.
✓ Subordinate one clause to the other, creating a complex sentence.

---

## 14a Revising with Periods

You can revise a comma splice or fused sentence by adding a period between the independent clauses, creating two separate sentences. This is a good strategy to use when the clauses are long or when they are not closely related.

In 1894, Frenchman Alfred Dreyfus was falsely convicted of
                    . His
treason/ ~~his~~ struggle for justice pitted the army against the civil

libertarians.

### Comma splices and fused sentences

Using a comma to punctuate an interrupted quotation that consists of two complete sentences creates a comma splice. Instead,
use a period.

                                          . In
"This is a good course," Eric said/ "~~in~~ fact, I wish I'd taken it
sooner."

## 14b   Revising with Semicolons

You can revise a comma splice or fused sentence by adding a
**semicolon** between two closely related clauses that convey parallel
or contrasting information.

See
30a

In pre–World War II western Europe, only a small elite had access
to a university education/ this situation changed dramatically
after the war.

Chippendale chairs have straight legs/ however, Queen Anne
chairs have curved legs.

See
3b2

**Note:** When you use a **transitional word or phrase** (such as *however,*
*therefore,* or *for example*) to connect two independent clauses, the transitional element must be preceded by a semicolon and followed by a
comma. If you link the two clauses with a comma alone, you create a
comma splice. If you omit punctuation entirely, you create a fused
sentence.

## 14c   Revising with Coordinating Conjunctions

You can use a coordinating conjunction (*and, or, but, nor, for, so, yet*) to join two closely related clauses of equal importance into one **compound sentence**. The coordinating conjunction you choose indicates the relationship between the clauses: addition (*and*), contrast (*but, yet*), causality (*for, so*), or a choice of alternatives (*or, nor*). Be sure to add a comma before the coordinating conjunction.

Writer's Resource CD-ROM

See 21a1

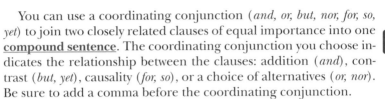

and

Elias Howe invented the sewing machine,ⱼJulia Ward Howe was a poet and social reformer.

## 14d   Revising with Subordinating Conjunctions or Relative Pronouns

When the ideas in two independent clauses are not of equal importance, you can use a subordinating conjunction or relative pronoun to join the clauses into one **complex sentence**, placing the less important idea in the dependent clause.

Writer's Resource CD-ROM

See 21a2

because

Stravinsky's ballet *The Rite of Spring* shocked Parisians in 1913ⱼ its rhythms seemed erotic.

who

Lady Mary Wortley Montagu, ⱼhad suffered from smallpox herself, ~~she~~ helped spread the practice of inoculation.

# Chapter 15

# Revising Agreement Errors

**Agreement** is the correspondence between words in number, gender, and person. Subjects and verbs agree in **number** (singular or plural) and **person** (first, second, or third); pronouns and their antecedents agree in number, person, and gender.

See 16a4

> **ESL Note:** For more information on person, number, and tense, see **47c1**.

## 15a Making Subjects and Verbs Agree

Writer's Resource CD-ROM

See 18b1

See 15a4

Singular subjects take singular verbs, and plural subjects take plural verbs. **Present tense** verbs, except *be* and *have*, add *-s* or *-es* when the subject is third-person singular. (Third-person singular subjects include nouns; the personal pronouns *he, she, it,* and *one;* and many **indefinite pronouns.**)

The <u>president</u> <u>has</u> the power to veto congressional legislation.

<u>She</u> frequently <u>cites</u> statistics to support her points.

In every group <u>somebody</u> <u>emerges</u> as a natural leader.

Present tense verbs do not add *-s* or *-es* when the subject is a plural noun, a first-person or second-person pronoun (*I, we, you*), or a third-person plural pronoun (*they*).

<u>Experts</u> <u>recommend</u> that dieters avoid processed meat.

At this stratum, <u>we</u> <u>see</u> rocks dating back ten million years.

<u>They</u> <u>say</u> that some wealthy people default on their student loans.

In the following special situations, subject-verb agreement can be troublesome.

### (1) Words between Subject and Verb

If a modifying phrase comes between subject and verb, the verb should agree with the subject, not with a word in the modifying phrase.

The <u>sound</u> of the drumbeats <u>builds</u> in intensity in *The Emperor Jones.*

The <u>games</u> won by the intramural team <u>are</u> few and far between.

**Note:** When phrases introduced by *along with, as well as, in addition to, including,* and *together with* come between subject and verb, these phrases do not change the subject's number: Heavy <u>rain</u>, along with high winds, <u>causes</u> hazardous driving conditions.

## (2) Compound Subjects Joined by *And*

Compound subjects joined by *and* usually take plural verbs.

<u>Air bags and antilock brakes</u> <u>are</u> standard on all new models.

There are, however, two exceptions to this rule. First, compound subjects joined by *and* that stand for a single idea or person are treated as a unit and used with singular verbs.

<u>Rhythm and blues</u> <u>is</u> a forerunner of rock and roll.

Second, when *each* or *every* precedes a compound subject joined by *and,* the subject takes a singular verb.

<u>Every desk and file cabinet</u> <u>was</u> searched before the letter was found.

## (3) Compound Subjects Joined by *Or*

Compound subjects joined by *or* or by *either . . . or* or *neither . . . nor* may take singular or plural verbs.

If both subjects are singular, use a singular verb; if both subjects are plural, use a plural verb.

<u>Either radiation or chemotherapy</u> <u>is</u> combined with surgery for effective results. (Both *radiation* and *chemotherapy* are singular, so the verb is singular.)

<u>Either radiation treatments or chemotherapy sessions</u> <u>are</u> combined with surgery for effective results. (Both *treatments* and *sessions* are plural, so the verb is plural.)

If one subject is singular and the other is plural, the verb agrees with the subject that is nearer to it.

Either radiation treatments or chemotherapy is combined with surgery for effective results. (Singular verb agrees with *chemotherapy*.)

Either chemotherapy or radiation treatments are combined with surgery for effective results. (Plural verb agrees with *treatments*.)

## (4) Indefinite Pronoun Subjects

**?**

See ESL 47b3

Some **indefinite pronouns**—*both, many, few, several, others*—are always plural and take plural verbs. Most others—*another, anyone, everyone, one, each, either, neither, anything, everything, something, nothing, nobody,* and *somebody*—are singular and take singular verbs.

Anyone is welcome to apply for the scholarship.

Each of the chapters includes a review exercise.

A few indefinite pronouns—*some, all, any, more, most,* and *none*—can be singular or plural, depending on the noun they refer to.

Some of this trouble is to be expected. (*Some* refers to *trouble*.)

Some of the spectators are restless. (*Some* refers to *spectators*.)

## (5) Collective Noun Subjects

A **collective noun** names a group of persons or things—for instance, *navy, union, association, band*. When it refers to the group as a unit (as it usually does), a collective noun takes a singular verb; when it refers to the individuals or items that make up the group, it takes a plural verb.

To many people, the royal family symbolizes Great Britain. (The family, as a unit, is the symbol.)

The family all eat at different times. (Each member eats separately.)

Phrases that name fixed amounts—*three-quarters, twenty dollars, the majority*—are treated like collective nouns. When the amount denotes a unit, it takes a singular verb; when it denotes parts of the whole, it takes a plural verb.

Three-quarters of his usual salary is not enough to live on.

Three-quarters of the patients improve dramatically after treatment.

## Subject-verb agreement with collective nouns

*The number* is always singular, and *a number* is always plural.

The number of voters <u>has</u> declined.

A number of students <u>have</u> missed preregistration.

## (6) Singular Subjects with Plural Forms

A singular subject takes a singular verb, even if the form of the subject is plural.

<u>Statistics</u> <u>deals</u> with the collection and analysis of data.

When such a word has a plural meaning, however, use a plural verb.

The <u>statistics</u> <u>prove</u> him wrong.

## Subject-verb agreement with foreign plurals

Some nouns retain their Latin plural forms, which do not look like English plural forms. Be particularly careful to use the correct verbs with such words.

| | |
|---|---|
| criterion is | criteria are |
| medium is | media are |
| bacterium is | bacteria are |

## (7) Inverted Subject-Verb Order

Even when <u>word order</u> is inverted and the verb comes before the subject (as it does in questions and in sentences beginning with *there is* or *there are*), the subject and verb must agree.

See ESL
47f

<u>Is</u> <u>either</u> answer correct?

There <u>are</u> currently thirteen circuit <u>courts</u> of appeals in the federal system.

## (8) Linking Verbs

See
20a

A **linking verb** should agree with its subject, not with the subject complement.

The problem was termites.

Termites were the problem.

## (9) Relative Pronouns

See
A2

When you use a **relative pronoun** (*who, which, that,* and so on) to introduce a dependent clause, the verb in that clause agrees with the pronoun's **antecedent,** the word to which the pronoun refers.

The farmer is among the ones who suffer during a grain embargo.

The farmer is the only one who suffers during a grain embargo.

# 15b  Making Pronouns and Antecedents Agree

Writer's
Resource
CD-ROM

Singular pronouns—such as *he, him, she, her, it, me, myself,* and *one-self*—should refer to singular antecedents. Plural pronouns—such as *we, us, they, them,* and *their*—should refer to plural antecedents.

## (1) Compound Antecedents

In most cases, use a plural pronoun to refer to a **compound antecedent** (two or more antecedents connected by *and*).

Mormonism and Christian Science were similar in their beginnings.

However, if a compound antecedent denotes a single unit—one person or thing or idea—use a singular pronoun to refer to the compound antecedent.

In 1904, the husband and father brought his family to America.

Use a singular pronoun when a compound antecedent is preceded by *each* or *every.*

Every programming language and software package has its limitations.

Use a singular pronoun to refer to two or more singular antecedents linked by *or* or *nor.*

Neither Thoreau nor Whitman lived to see his work read widely.

When one part of a compound antecedent is singular and one part is plural, the pronoun agrees in person and number with the antecedent that is nearer to it.

Neither the boy nor his parents had their seatbelts fastened.

## (2) Collective Noun Antecedents

If the meaning of a collective noun antecedent is singular (as it will be in most cases), use a singular pronoun. If the meaning is plural, use a plural pronoun.

The teachers' union announced its plan to strike. (The members act as a unit.)

The team ran on to the field and took their positions. (Each member acts individually.)

## (3) Indefinite Pronoun Antecedents

Most **indefinite pronouns**—*each, either, neither, one, anyone,* and the like—are singular and are used with singular pronouns.

See A2

Neither of the men had his proposal ready by the deadline.

Each of these neighborhoods has its own traditions and values.

**?** **Pronoun-antecedent agreement**

In speech and in informal writing, many people use the plural pronouns *they* or *their* with singular indefinite pronouns that refer to people, such as *someone*, *everyone*, and *nobody*.

Everyone can present their own viewpoint.

In college writing, however, you should not use a plural pronoun with a singular subject. Instead, you can use both masculine and feminine pronouns.

Everyone can present his or her own viewpoint.

Or, you can make the sentence's subject plural.

All participants can present their own viewpoints.

The use of *his* alone to refer to a singular indefinite pronoun (Everyone can present *his* own viewpoint) is considered **sexist language**.

# Chapter 16

# Revising Awkward or Confusing Sentences

The most common causes of awkward or confusing sentences are *unwarranted shifts, mixed constructions, faulty predication,* and *illogical comparisons.*

## 16a  Revising Unwarranted Shifts

### (1) Shifts in Tense

Verb **tense** in a sentence or in a related group of sentences should not shift without good reason—to indicate changes of time, for example.

> See 18b

*The Wizard of Oz* is a classic film that <u>was made</u> in 1939. (acceptable shift from present to past)

Unwarranted shifts in tense can be confusing.

I registered for the advanced philosophy seminar because I wanted a challenge. However, after the first week I ~~start~~ <sup>started</sup> having trouble understanding the reading. (unwarranted shift from past to present)

Jack Kerouac's novel *On the Road* follows a group of friends who ~~drove~~ <sup>drive</sup> across the United States. (unwarranted shift from present to past)

**Note:** The present tense is generally used in <u>writing about literature</u>.

> See 43b

### (2) Shifts in Voice

Unwarranted shifts from active to passive <u>voice</u> (or from passive to active) can be confusing. In the following sentence, for instance,

> See 18d

> See ESL 47c6

the shift from active (*wrote*) to passive (*was written*) makes it unclear who wrote *The Great Gatsby.*

                                                      wrote

F. Scott Fitzgerald wrote *This Side of Paradise,* and later ‸*The Great Gatsby*. ~~was written.~~

---

**closeUP**

### Shifts in voice

    Sometimes a shift from active to passive voice within a sentence may be necessary to give the sentence proper emphasis.

    Even though consumers protested, the sales tax was increased.

Here the shift from active (*protested*) to passive (*was increased*) keeps the focus on consumer groups and the issue they protested. To say *the legislature increased the sales tax* would change the emphasis of the sentence.

---

## (3) Shifts in Mood

 See 18c

    Unnecessary shifts in **mood** also create awkward sentences. The following sentence shifts unnecessarily from the imperative to the indicative mood:

                                        be

Next, heat the mixture in a test tube, and ‸~~you should make~~ sure it does not boil.

## (4) Shifts in Person and Number

**Person** indicates who is speaking (first person—*I, we*), who is spoken to (second person—*you*), and who is spoken about (third person—*he, she, it,* and *they*). Most awkward sentences caused by unwarranted shifts are the result of shifts between second and third person.

                  you

When ~~someone~~ look*s* for a car loan, you compare the interest rates of several banks. (shift from third to second person)

**Number** indicates one (singular—*novel, it*) or more than one (plural—*novels, they, them*). Singular pronouns should refer to singular **antecedents** and plural pronouns to plural antecedents.

See 15b

he or she
If a person does not study regularly, ~~they~~ will have a difficult time passing Spanish.

**ESL Note:** For more on person and number, **see 47c1.**

### (5) Shifts from Direct to Indirect Discourse

**?**

**Direct discourse** reports the exact words of a speaker or writer. It is always enclosed in **quotation marks** and is often accompanied by an identifying tag (*he says, she said*). **Indirect discourse** summarizes the words of a speaker or writer. No quotation marks are used, and the reported words are often introduced with the word *that* or, in the case of questions, with *who, what, why, whether, how,* or *if.*

See 32a

Direct Discourse: My instructor said, "I <u>want</u> your paper by this Friday."

Indirect Discourse: My instructor said <u>that he wanted</u> my paper by this Friday.

Statements and questions that shift between indirect and direct discourse are often confusing.

During the trial, John Brown repeatedly defended his actions and
he was
said that ~~I am~~ not guilty. (shift from indirect to direct discourse)

"Are you                    ?"
My mother asked, ~~was I~~ ever going to get a job. (question is neither indirect nor direct discourse)

**ESL Note:** For information on word order in direct and indirect quotations, **see 47f4.**

## 16b Revising Mixed Constructions

A **mixed construction** is created when a dependent clause, prepositional phrase, or independent clause is incorrectly used as the subject of a sentence.

Because she studies every day, ~~explains why~~ she gets good grades. (dependent clause used as subject)

By calling for information, ~~is the way to~~ *, you can* learn more about the benefits of ROTC. (prepositional phrase used as subject)

*Being*
~~He was~~ late ~~was what~~ made him miss Act 1. (independent clause used as subject)

## 16c   Revising Faulty Predication

**Faulty predication** occurs when a sentence's predicate does not logically complete its subject.

### (1) Incorrect Use of *Be*

Faulty predication is especially common in sentences that contain a **linking verb**—a form of the verb *be*, for example—and a subject complement.

Mounting costs and decreasing revenues ~~were~~ *caused* the downfall of the hospital.

This sentence incorrectly states that mounting costs and decreasing revenues *were* the downfall of the hospital when, in fact, they were the *reasons* for its downfall.

### (2) *Is When* or *Is Where*

Another kind of faulty predication occurs when a sentence that presents a definition contains a construction like *is where* or *is when*.

Taxidermy is ~~where you construct~~ *the construction of* a lifelike representation of an animal from its preserved skin. (In a definition, *is* must be preceded and followed by nouns or noun phrases.)

### (3) *The Reason . . . Is Because*

A similar type of problem occurs when the phrase *the reason is* precedes *because*. In this situation, *because* (which means "for the reason that") is redundant and should be deleted.

that
The reason we drive is ~~because~~ we are afraid to fly.

## 16d Revising Incomplete or Illogical Comparisons

A comparison tells how two things are alike or unlike. When you make a comparison, be sure it is **complete** (that readers can tell which two items are being compared) and **logical** (that it equates two comparable items). **?**

than Nina's
My chemistry course is harder. (What two things are being compared?)

dog's
A pig's intelligence is greater than a ~~dog~~. (illogically compares "a pig's intelligence" to "a dog")

# Chapter 17

# Revising Misplaced and Dangling Modifiers

A **modifier** is a word, phrase, or clause that describes, limits, or qualifies another word or word group in a sentence. A modifier should be placed close to its **headword,** the word or phrase it modifies. **Faulty modification** is the confusing placement of modifiers or the modification of nonexistent words.

Writer's
Resource
CD-ROM

## 17a   Revising Misplaced Modifiers

A **misplaced modifier** is a word or word group whose placement suggests that it modifies one word or phrase when it is intended to modify another.

> Wendy watched the storm, fierce
> ~~Fierce~~ and threatening,̖ ~~Wendy watched the storm,̖~~  (Was Wendy fierce and threatening?)

> The lawyer argued that the defendant, with
> ~~With~~ an IQ of just 52, ~~the lawyer argued that the defendant~~ should not get the death penalty. (Did the lawyer have an IQ of 52?)

### (1) Placing Modifying Words Precisely

**Limiting modifiers** such as *almost, only, even,* and *just* should always immediately precede the words they modify. A different placement will change the meaning of a sentence.

> Nick *just* set up camp at the edge of town. (He did it just now.)

> *Just* Nick set up camp at the edge of town. (He did it alone.)

> Nick set up camp *just* at the edge of town. (His camp was precisely at the edge.)

When a limiting modifier is placed so it is not clear whether it modifies a word before it or one after it, it is called a **squinting modifier.**

⑦ ⌒⌒⌒ ⌒⌒⌒ ⑦
The life that everyone thought would fulfill her <u>totally</u> bored her.

To correct a squinting modifier, place the modifier so it clearly modifies its headword.

The life that everyone thought would <u>totally</u> fulfill her bored her. (She was expected to be totally fulfilled.)

The life that everyone thought would fulfill her bored her <u>totally</u>. (She was totally bored.)

## (2) Relocating Misplaced Phrases

When you revise, relocate misplaced verbal phrases, placing them directly before or directly after the words or word groups they modify.

Roller-skating along the shore,
∧Jane watched the boats.~~roller-skating along the shore~~/ (Can boats rollerskate?)

Place prepositional phrase modifiers immediately after the words they modify.

Created by a famous artist,
∧*Venus de Milo* is a statue ~~created by a famous artist~~ with no arms. (Did the artist have no arms?)

## (3) Relocating Misplaced Dependent Clauses

Dependent clauses that serve as modifiers must be clearly related to their headwords. An adjective clause usually appears immediately after the words it modifies.

, which will benefit everyone,
This diet program∧ will limit the consumption of possible carcinogens/∧~~which will benefit everyone~~/ (Will carcinogens benefit everyone?)

An adverb clause can appear in various positions, but its relationship to its headword must be clear and logical.

After they had a glass of wine, the
∧~~The~~ parents checked to see that the children were sleeping;∧ ~~after they had a glass of wine~~/ (Did the children drink the wine?)

**301**

# 17b  Revising Intrusive Modifiers

An **intrusive modifier** interrupts a sentence, making it difficult to understand.

Revise when a long modifying phrase comes between an auxiliary verb and a main verb.

> Without
> ~~She had, without~~ giving it a second thought or considering the
>                        she had
> consequences, ^planned to reenlist.

Revise when modifiers awkwardly interrupt an infinitive—that is, when modifiers come between the word *to* and the base form of the verb.

> defeat his opponent
> He hoped to ^quickly and easily, ~~defeat his opponent~~/

# 17c  Revising Dangling Modifiers

A **dangling modifier** is a word or phrase that cannot logically modify any word or word group in the sentence.

> Dangling: Using this drug, many undesirable side effects are experienced. (Who is using this drug?)

One way to correct this dangling modifier is to create a new subject by adding a word or word group that *using this drug* can logically modify.

> Revised: Using this drug, patients experience many undesirable side effects.

Another way to correct the dangling modifier is to *create a dependent clause.*

> Revised: Many undesirable side effects are experienced when this drug is used.

## Revising Dangling Modifiers

These two options for correcting dangling modifiers are illustrated below.

### (1) Creating a New Subject

                                      the technician lifted
Using a pair of forceps, ∧the skin of the rat's abdomen.~~was lifted.~~
(Modifier cannot logically modify *skin*.)

                                      Meg found
With fifty more pages to read, ∧*War and Peace* ~~was~~ absorbing.
(Modifier cannot logically modify *War and Peace*.)

### Dangling modifiers and the passive voice

Most sentences that include dangling modifiers do not include a headword because they are in the passive voice. Changing the **passive voice** to **active voice** corrects the dangling modifier by changing the subject of the sentence's main clause to a word that the dangling modifier can logically modify.

See
18d

See ESL
47c6

### (2) Creating a Dependent Clause

Before                                      was implemented,
∧~~To implement~~ a plus/minus grading system, ∧all students were polled. (Modifier cannot logically modify *students*.)

Because the magazine had been on
∧~~On~~ the newsstands only an hour, its sales surprised everyone.
(Modifier cannot logically modify *sales*.)

# PART 7

## Sentence Grammar

**18 Using Verbs Correctly: Form, Tense, Mood, and Voice   307**
**18a** Using Verbs Correctly   307
**18b** Understanding Tense   310
**18c** Understanding Mood   314
**18d** Understanding Voice   316

**19 Using Pronouns Correctly   317**
**19a** Understanding Pronoun Case   317
**19b** Determining Pronoun Case in Special Situations   318
**19c** Revising Pronoun Reference Errors   320

**20 Using Adjectives and Adverbs Correctly   322**
**20a** Using Adjectives   322
**20b** Using Adverbs   323
**20c** Using Comparative and Superlative Forms   323
**20d** Avoiding Illogical Comparatives and Superlatives   325
**20e** Avoiding Double Negatives   326

# PART 7

## ? Frequently Asked Questions

**Chapter 18 Using Verbs Correctly: Form, Tense, Mood, and Voice   307**
- What is an irregular verb**?**   307
- What is the difference between *lie* and *lay***?**   310
- Which is correct, "I wish I were" or "I wish I was"**?**   315
- What is the passive voice**?**   316
- Is active voice always better than passive voice**?**   316

**Chapter 19 Using Pronouns Correctly   317**
- Is *I* always more appropriate than *me***?**   318
- How do I know whether to use *who* or *whom***?**   318
- What is an antecedent**?**   320
- When should I use *who, which,* and *that***?**   321

**Chapter 20 Using Adjectives and Adverbs Correctly   322**
- What is the difference between an adjective and an adverb**?**   322
- How do I know when to use *more* and when to use an -*er* ending**?**   324
- How do I know when to use *most* and when to use an -*est* ending**?**   324
- What's wrong with *most unique***?**   325
- Why is a double negative wrong**?**   326

---

**URLs**   *Visit the following sites for answers to more FAQs*

**Verb Tense (U. Ottawa)**
*http://www.uottawa.ca/academic/arts/writcent/hypergrammar/usetense.html*

**Verb Tense Consistency (Emory U.)**
*http://www.emory.edu/ENGLISH/WC/verbconsist.html*

**Using Pronouns Clearly**
*http://owl.english.purdue.edu/handouts/grammar/g_pronuse.html*

**Pronoun Types and Common Mistakes (Emory U.)**
*http://www.emory.edu/ENGLISH/WC/pronounref.html*

**Adjectives**
*http://www.ccc.commnet.edu/grammar/adjectives.htm*

**Adverbs**
*http://www.ccc.commnet.edu/grammar/adverbs.htm*

# Chapter 18

# Using Verbs Correctly: Form, Tense, Mood, and Voice

## 18a   Using Verbs Correctly

Writer's
Resource
CD-ROM

Every verb has four **principal parts:** a **base form** (the form of the verb used with *I, we, you,* and *they* in the present tense),[*] a **present participle** (the *-ing* form of the verb), a **past tense form,** and a **past participle.**

### (1) Regular Verbs

A **regular verb** forms both its past tense and its past participle by adding *-d* or *-ed* to the base form of the verb.

---

**PRINCIPAL PARTS OF REGULAR VERBS**

| Base Form | Past Tense Form | Past Participle |
|---|---|---|
| smile | smiled | smiled |
| talk | talked | talked |
| jump | jumped | jumped |

---

### (2) Irregular Verbs

**Irregular verbs** do not follow the pattern just discussed. The chart that follows lists the principal parts of the most frequently used irregular verbs. (When in doubt about the form of a verb, look up the base form in the dictionary. If the dictionary lists only the base form, then the verb is regular.)

---

[*]Note: The verb *be* is so irregular that it is the one exception to this definition; its base form is *be.*

## FREQUENTLY USED IRREGULAR VERBS

| Base Form | Past Tense Form | Past Participle |
|-----------|-----------------|-----------------|
| arise | arose | arisen |
| awake | awoke, awaked | awoke, awaked |
| be | was/were | been |
| beat | beat | beaten |
| begin | began | begun |
| bend | bent | bent |
| bet | bet, betted | bet |
| bite | bit | bitten |
| blow | blew | blown |
| break | broke | broken |
| bring | brought | brought |
| build | built | built |
| burst | burst | burst |
| buy | bought | bought |
| catch | caught | caught |
| choose | chose | chosen |
| cling | clung | clung |
| come | came | come |
| cost | cost | cost |
| deal | dealt | dealt |
| dig | dug | dug |
| dive | dived, dove | dived |
| do | did | done |
| drag | dragged | dragged |
| draw | drew | drawn |
| drink | drank | drunk |
| drive | drove | driven |
| eat | ate | eaten |
| fall | fell | fallen |
| fight | fought | fought |
| find | found | found |
| fly | flew | flown |
| forget | forgot | forgotten, forgot |
| freeze | froze | frozen |
| get | got | gotten |
| give | gave | given |
| go | went | gone |
| grow | grew | grown |
| hang (execute) | hanged | hanged |
| hang (suspend) | hung | hung |
| have | had | had |

| Base Form | Past Tense Form | Past Participle |
|---|---|---|
| hear | heard | heard |
| keep | kept | kept |
| know | knew | known |
| lay | laid | laid |
| lead | led | led |
| lend | lent | lent |
| let | let | let |
| lie (recline) | lay | lain |
| lie (tell an untruth) | lied | lied |
| make | made | made |
| prove | proved | proved, proven |
| read | read | read |
| ride | rode | ridden |
| ring | rang | rung |
| rise | rose | risen |
| run | ran | run |
| say | said | said |
| see | saw | seen |
| set (place) | set | set |
| shake | shook | shaken |
| shrink | shrank, shrunk | shrunk, shrunken |
| sing | sang | sung |
| sink | sank | sunk |
| sit | sat | sat |
| sneak | sneaked | sneaked |
| speak | spoke | spoken |
| speed | sped, speeded | sped, speeded |
| spin | spun | spun |
| spring | sprang | sprung |
| stand | stood | stood |
| steal | stole | stolen |
| strike | struck | struck, stricken |
| swear | swore | sworn |
| swim | swam | swum |
| swing | swung | swung |
| take | took | taken |
| teach | taught | taught |
| throw | threw | thrown |
| wake | woke, waked | waked, woken |
| wear | wore | worn |
| wring | wrung | wrung |
| write | wrote | written |

### Troublesome irregular verbs: Lie/lay and sit/set

**?**

*Lie* means "to recline" and does not take an object ("He likes to *lie* on the floor"); *lay* means "to place" or "to put" and does take an object ("He wants to *lay* a rug on the floor").

| Base Form | Past Tense Form | Past Participle |
|-----------|-----------------|-----------------|
| lie       | lay             | lain            |
| lay       | laid            | laid            |

*Sit* means "to assume a seated position" and does not take an object ("She wants to *sit* on the table"); *set* means "to place" or "to put" and usually takes an object ("She wants to *set* a vase on the table").

| Base Form | Past Tense Form | Past Participle |
|-----------|-----------------|-----------------|
| sit       | sat             | sat             |
| set       | set             | set             |

## 18b   Understanding Tense

Writer's
Resource
CD-ROM

See ESL
47c3

<u>Tense</u> is the form a verb takes to indicate when an action occurred or when a condition existed.

---

### ENGLISH VERB TENSES

**Simple Tenses**
Present (I *finish,* she or he *finishes*)
Past (I *finished*)
Future (I *will finish*)

**Perfect Tenses**
Present perfect (I *have finished,* she or he *has finished*)
Past perfect (I *had finished*)
Future perfect (I *will have finished*)

**Progressive Tenses**
Present progressive (I *am finishing,* she or he *is finishing*)
Past progressive (I *was finishing*)
Future progressive (I *will be finishing*)
Present perfect progressive (I *have been finishing*)
Past perfect progressive (I *had been finishing*)
Future perfect progressive (I *will have been finishing*)

## (1) Using the Simple Tenses

The **simple tenses** include *present, past,* and *future.*

The **present tense** usually indicates an action that is taking place at the time it is expressed in speech or writing or an action that occurs regularly.

I <u>see</u> your point. (an action taking place when it is expressed)

We <u>wear</u> wool in the winter. (an action that occurs regularly)

### Special uses of the present tense

The present tense has four special uses.

To Indicate Future Time: The grades <u>arrive</u> next Thursday.
To State a Generally Held Belief: Studying <u>pays</u> off.
To State a Scientific Truth: An object at rest <u>tends</u> to stay at rest.
To Discuss a Literary Work: *Family Installments* <u>tells</u> the story of a Puerto Rican family.

The **past tense** indicates that an action has already taken place.

John Glenn <u>orbited</u> the earth three times on February 20, 1962. (an action completed in the past)

As a young man, Mark Twain <u>traveled</u> through the Southwest. (an action that occurred once or many times in the past but did not extend into the present)

The **future tense** indicates that an action will or is likely to take place.

Halley's Comet <u>will reappear</u> in 2061. (a future action that will definitely occur)

The land boom in Nevada <u>will</u> probably <u>continue</u>. (a future action that is likely to occur)

## (2) Using the Perfect Tenses

The <u>perfect tenses</u> designate actions that were or will be completed before other actions or conditions. The perfect tenses are

See ESL 47c3

formed with the appropriate tense form of the auxiliary verb *have* plus the past participle.

The **present perfect** tense can indicate two types of continuing action beginning in the past.

Dr. Kim <u>has finished</u> studying the effects of BHA on rats. (an action that began in the past and is finished at the present time)

My mother <u>has invested</u> her money wisely. (an action that began in the past and extends into the present)

The **past perfect** tense indicates an action occurring before a certain time in the past.

By 1946, engineers <u>had built</u> the first electronic digital computer.

The **future perfect** tense indicates that an action will be finished by a certain future time.

By Tuesday, the transit authority <u>will have run</u> out of money.

## (3) Using the Progressive Tenses

The <u>progressive tenses</u> express continuing action. They are formed with the appropriate tense of the verb *be* plus the present participle.

The **present progressive** tense indicates that something is happening at the time it is expressed in speech or writing.

The volcano <u>is erupting</u>, and lava <u>is flowing</u> toward the town.

The **past progressive** tense indicates two kinds of past action.

Roderick Usher's actions <u>were becoming</u> increasingly bizarre. (a continuing action in the past)

The French revolutionary Marat was stabbed to death while he <u>was bathing</u>. (an action occurring at the same time in the past as another action)

The **future progressive** tense indicates a continuing action in the future.

The treasury secretary <u>will be</u> carefully <u>monitoring</u> the money supply.

The **present perfect progressive** tense indicates action continuing from the past into the present and possibly into the future.

Rescuers <u>have been working</u> around the clock.

The **past perfect progressive** tense indicates that a past action went on until another one occurred.

Before President Kennedy was assassinated, he <u>had been working</u> on civil rights legislation.

The **future perfect progressive** tense indicates that an action will continue until a certain future time.

By eleven o'clock we <u>will have been driving</u> for seven hours.

## (4) Using Verb Tenses in a Sentence

You use different tenses in a sentence to indicate that actions are taking place at different times. By choosing tenses that accurately express these times, you make it easier for readers to follow the sequence of actions.

The debate <u>was</u> not impressive, but the election <u>will determine</u> the winner.

When a **verb** appears in a dependent clause, its tense depends on the tense of the main verb in the independent clause. When the main verb is in the past tense, the verb in the dependent clause is usually in the past or past perfect tense. When the main verb is in the past perfect tense, the verb in the dependent clause is usually in the past tense. (When the main verb in the independent clause is in any tense except the past or past perfect, the verb in the dependent clause may be in any tense needed for meaning.)

| Main Verb | Verb in Dependent Clause |
|---|---|
| George Hepplewhite <u>was</u> (past) an English cabinetmaker | who <u>designed</u> (past) distinctive chair backs. |
| The battle <u>had ended</u> (past perfect) | by the time reinforcements <u>arrived</u>. (past) |

When an **infinitive** appears in a verbal phrase, the tense it expresses depends on the tense of the sentence's main verb. The *present infinitive* (the *to* form of the verb) indicates an action happening at the same time as or later than the main verb. The *perfect infinitive* (*to have* plus the past participle) indicates action happening earlier than the main verb.

| Main Verb | Infinitive |
|---|---|
| I <u>went</u> | <u>to see</u> the Rangers play last week. (The going and seeing occurred at the same time.) |
| I <u>want</u> | <u>to see</u> the Rangers play tomorrow. (Wanting occurs in the present, and seeing will occur in the future.) |
| I would <u>like</u> | <u>to have seen</u> the Rangers play. (Liking occurs in the present, and seeing would have occurred in the past.) |

When a **participle** appears in a verbal phrase, its tense depends on the tense of the sentence's main verb. The *present participle* indicates action happening at the same time as the action of the main verb. The *past participle* or the *present perfect participle* indicates action occurring before the action of the main verb.

| Participle | Main Verb |
|---|---|
| <u>Addressing</u> the 1896 Democratic Convention, | William Jennings Bryan <u>delivered</u> his Cross of Gold speech. (The addressing and the delivery occurred at the same time.) |
| <u>Having written</u> her term paper, | Camille <u>studied</u> for her history final. (The writing occurred before the studying.) |

## 18c Understanding Mood

**Mood** is the form a verb takes to indicate whether a writer is making a statement, asking a question, giving a command, or expressing a wish or a contrary-to-fact statement. The three moods in English are the *indicative*, the *imperative*, and the *subjunctive*.

The **indicative** mood expresses an opinion, states a fact, or asks a question: Jackie Robinson <u>had</u> a great impact on professional baseball.

The **imperative** mood is used in commands and direct requests. Usually the imperative includes only the base form of the verb without a subject: <u>Use</u> a dictionary.

The **subjunctive** mood causes the greatest difficulty for writers.

## (1) Forming the Subjunctive Mood

The **present subjunctive** uses the base form of the verb, regardless of the subject. The **past subjunctive** has the same form as the past tense of the verb. (The auxiliary verb *be*, however, takes the form *were* regardless of the number or person of the subject.)

Dr. Gorman suggested that I <u>study</u> the Cambrian Period. (present subjunctive)

I wish I <u>were</u> going to Europe. (past subjunctive)

## (2) Using the Subjunctive Mood

Use the present subjunctive in *that* clauses after words such as *ask, suggest, require, recommend,* and *demand.*

The report recommended that juveniles <u>be</u> given mandatory counseling.

Captain Ahab insisted that his crew <u>hunt</u> the white whale.

Use the past subjunctive in **conditional statements** (statements beginning with *if* that are contrary to fact, including statements that express a wish). **?**

If John <u>were</u> here, he could see Marsha. (John is not here.)

The father acted as if he <u>were</u> having the baby. (The father couldn't be having the baby.)

I wish I <u>were</u> more organized. (expresses a wish)

### Conditional statements

If an *if* clause expresses a condition that is possible, use the indicative mood, not the subjunctive.

If a peace treaty <u>is</u> signed, the world will be safer. (A peace treaty is possible.)

# 18d Understanding Voice

Writer's
Resource
CD-ROM

See ESL
47c6

Voice is the form that a verb takes to indicate whether its subject acts or is acted upon. When the subject of a verb does something—that is, acts—the verb is in the **active voice.** When the subject of a verb receives the action—that is, is acted upon—the verb is in the **passive voice.**

Active Voice:  Hart Crane <u>wrote</u> *The Bridge.*

Passive Voice:  *The Bridge* <u>was written</u> by Hart Crane.

### Voice

See
22e

Because the active voice emphasizes the doer of an action, it is usually briefer, clearer, and more <u>emphatic</u> than the passive voice. Some situations, however, may require use of the passive voice. For example, you should use passive constructions when the actor is unknown or unimportant or when the reciept of an action should logically receive the emphasis.

DDT <u>was found</u> in soil samples. (Passive voice emphasizes finding DDT; who found it is not important.)

Grits <u>are eaten</u> throughout the South. (Passive voice emphasizes that grits are eaten, not those who eat them.)

Still, whenever possible, you should use active voice in your college writing.

Chapter **19**

# Using Pronouns Correctly

## 19a Understanding Pronoun Case

Writer's Resource CD-ROM

Pronouns change **case** to indicate their function in a sentence. English has three cases: *subjective, objective,* and *possessive.*

| PRONOUN CASE FORMS | | | | | | | |
|---|---|---|---|---|---|---|---|
| **Subjective** | | | | | | | |
| I | he, she | it | we | you | they | who | whoever |
| **Objective** | | | | | | | |
| me | him, her | it | us | you | them | whom | whomever |
| **Possessive** | | | | | | | |
| my, mine | his, her hers | its | our ours | your yours | their theirs | whose | |

### (1) Subjective Case

A pronoun takes the **subjective case** in the following situations.

Subject of a Verb: <u>I</u> bought a new mountain bike.
Subject Complement: It was <u>he</u> for whom the men were looking.

### (2) Objective Case

A pronoun takes the **objective case** in these situations.

Direct Object: Our sociology instructor asked Adam and <u>me</u> to work on the project.
Indirect Object: The plumber's bill gave <u>him</u> quite a shock.
Object of a Preposition: Between <u>us</u> we own ten shares of stock.

317

**?** **Pronoun case in compound constructions**

*I* is not necessarily more appropriate than *me.* In compound constructions like the following, *me* is correct.

Just between you <u>and</u> me [not *I*], I think the results are inconclusive. (*Me* is the object of the preposition *between.*)

### (3) Possessive Case

A pronoun takes the **possessive case** when it indicates ownership (*our* car, *your* book). The possessive case is also used before a

See
A3

**gerund**.

Napoleon approved of <u>their</u> [not *them*] ruling Naples. (*Ruling* is a gerund.)

## 19b  Determining Pronoun Case in Special Situations

Writer's
Resource
CD-ROM

### (1) Comparisons with *Than* or *As*

When a comparison ends with a pronoun, the pronoun's function in the sentence dictates your choice of pronoun case. If the pronoun functions as a subject, use the subjective case; if it functions as an object, use the objective case. You can determine the function of the pronoun by completing the comparison.

Darcy likes John more than <u>I</u>. (*I* is the subject: more than I like John)

Darcy likes John more than <u>me</u>. (*Me* is the object: more than she likes me)

### (2) *Who* and *Whom*

**?** The case of the pronouns *who* and *whom* depends on their function *within their own clause.* When a pronoun serves as the subject of its clause, use *who* or *whoever;* when it functions as an object, use *whom* or *whomever.*

The Salvation Army gives food and shelter to <u>whoever</u> is in need. (*Whoever* is the subject of the dependent clause *whoever is in need.*)

I wonder <u>whom</u> jazz musician Miles Davis influenced. (*Whom* is the object of *influenced* in the dependent clause *whom jazz musician Miles Davis influenced.*)

**Pronoun case in questions**

To determine whether to use subjective case (*who*) or objective case (*whom*) in a question, use a personal pronoun to answer the question. If the personal pronoun is the subject, use *who*; if the personal pronoun is the object, use *whom*.

<u>Who</u> wrote *The Age of Innocence*? <u>She</u> wrote it. (subject)

<u>Whom</u> do you support for mayor? I support <u>her</u>. (object)

## (3) Appositives

An <u>appositive</u> is a noun or noun phrase that identifies or renames an adjacent noun or pronoun. The case of a pronoun in an appositive depends on the function of the word the appositive identifies.

See ESL 47b4

We heard two Motown recording artists, Smokey Robinson and <u>him</u>. (*Artists* is the object of the verb *heard*, so the pronoun in the appositive *Smokey Robinson and him* takes the objective case.)

Two Motown recording artists, Smokey Robinson and <u>he</u>, recorded for Motown Records. (*Artists* is the subject of the sentence, so the pronoun in the appositive *Smokey Robinson and he* takes the subjective case.)

## (4) *We* and *Us* before a Noun

When a first-person plural pronoun directly precedes a noun, the case of the pronoun depends on the way the noun functions in the sentence.

<u>We</u> women must stick together. (*Women* is the subject of the sentence, so the pronoun *we* must be in the subjective case.)

Teachers make learning easy for <u>us</u> students. (*Students* is the object of the preposition *for*, so the pronoun *us* must be in the objective case.)

## 19c Revising Pronoun Reference Errors

Writer's
Resource
CD-ROM

See ESL
47b1

An **antecedent** is the word or word group to which a pronoun refers. The connection between a pronoun and its antecedent should always be clear. If the pronoun reference is not clear, you will need to revise the sentence.

### (1) Ambiguous Antecedent

Sometimes a pronoun—for example, *this, that, which,* or *it*—could refer to more than one antecedent in the sentence. In such cases, substitute a noun for the pronoun to eliminate the ambiguity.

The accountant took out his calculator and completed the tax
                the calculator
return. Then, he put ~~it~~ into his briefcase.

Sometimes a pronoun does not seem to refer to any specific antecedent. In such cases, supply a noun to clarify the reference.

Some one-celled organisms contain chlorophyll yet are considered
           paradox
animals. This illustrates the difficulty of classifying single-celled

organisms.

### (2) Remote Antecedent

The farther a pronoun is from its antecedent, the more difficult it is for readers to make a connection between them. If a pronoun's antecedent is far away from it, replace the pronoun with a noun.

During the mid-1800s, many Czechs began to immigrate to

America. By 1860, about 23,000 Czechs had left their country;
                         America's
by 1900, 13,000 Czech immigrants were coming to ~~its~~ shores

each year.

### (3) Nonexistent Antecedent

Sometimes a pronoun refers to a nonexistent antecedent. In such cases, replace the pronoun with a noun.

Our township has decided to build a computer lab in the
elementary school because ~~they~~ ^teachers feel that fourth graders should
begin using computers.

### Pronoun reference

Expressions such as "*It* says in the paper" and "*They* said on the
news" refer to unidentified antecedents and are not acceptable in
college writing. Substitute the appropriate noun for the unclear
pronoun: "The *article* in the paper says. . . ." and "In his commentary, *Ted Koppel* observes. . . ."

## (4) *Who, Which, and That*

In general, *who* refers to people or to animals that have names.
*Which* and *that* refer to things or to unnamed animals. When referring to an antecedent, be sure to choose the appropriate pronoun
(*who, which,* or *that*).

David Henry Hwang, <u>who</u> wrote the Tony Award–winning play
*M. Butterfly*, also wrote *Family Devotions* and *FOB*.

The spotted owl, <u>which</u> lives in old growth forests, is in danger
of extinction.

Houses <u>that</u> are built today are usually more energy efficient
than those built twenty years ago.

Never use *that* to refer to a person.

The man ^who ~~that~~ holds the world record for eating hot dogs is my
neighbor.

# Chapter 20

# Using Adjectives and Adverbs Correctly

**?** **Adjectives** modify nouns and pronouns. **Adverbs** modify verbs, adjectives, or other adverbs—or entire phrases, clauses, or sentences.

The *function* of a word, not its form, determines whether it is an adjective or an adverb. Although many adverbs (such as *immediately* and *hopelessly*) end in *-ly*, others (such as *almost* and *very*) do not. Moreover, some words that end in *-ly* (such as *lively*) are adjectives.

> **ESL Note:** For information on correct placement of adjectives and adverbs in a sentence, **see 47d1.** For information on correct order of adjectives in a series, **see 47d2.**

## 20a   Using Adjectives

Writer's
Resource
CD-ROM

See
B2

Be sure to use an adjective, not an adverb, as a subject complement. A **subject complement** is a word that follows a linking verb and modifies the sentence's subject, not its verb. A **linking verb** does not show physical or emotional action. *Seem, appear, believe, become, grow, turn, remain, prove, look, sound, smell, taste, feel,* and the forms of the verb *be* are or can be used as linking verbs.

Michelle seemed <u>brave</u>. (*Seemed* shows no action and is therefore a linking verb. Because *brave* is a subject complement that modifies the noun *Michelle,* it takes the adjective form.)

Michelle smiled <u>bravely</u>. (*Smiled* shows action, so it is not a linking verb. *Bravely* modifies *smiled,* so it takes the adverb form.)

**Note:** Sometimes the same verb can function as either a linking verb or an action verb.

He looked <u>hungry</u>. (*Hungry* modifies the subject.)

He looked <u>hungrily</u> at the sandwich. (*Hungrily* modifies the verb.)

## 20b   Using Adverbs

Be sure to use an adverb, not an adjective, to modify verbs, adjectives, or other adverbs—or entire phrases, clauses, or sentences.

Most students did <del>great</del> on the midterm. [very well]

My parents dress a lot more conservative than my friends do. [ly]

### Using adjectives and adverbs

In informal speech, adjective forms such as *good, bad, sure, real, slow, quick,* and *loud* are often used to modify verbs, adjectives, and adverbs. Avoid these informal modifiers in college writing.

The program ran <del>real good</del> the first time we tried it, but the new system performed <del>bad</del>. [really well] [badly]

## 20c   Using Comparative and  Superlative Forms

Most adjectives and adverbs have **comparative** and **superlative** forms that can be used with nouns to indicate <u>degree</u>.

Writer's
Resource
CD-ROM

See ESL
47d3

### COMPARATIVE AND SUPERLATIVE FORMS

| Form | Function | Example |
|------|----------|---------|
| Positive | Describes a quality; indicates no comparisons | big |
| Comparative | Indicates comparisons between *two* qualities (greater or lesser) | bigger |
| Superlative | Indicates comparisons among *three or more* qualities (greatest or least) | biggest |

NOTE: Some adverbs, particularly those indicating time, place, and degree (*almost, very, here, yesterday, immediately*), do not have comparative or superlative forms.

## (1) Comparative Forms

**?**

To form the comparative, all one-syllable adjectives and many two- syllable adjectives (particularly those that end in *-y, -ly, -le, -er,* and *-ow*) add *-er:* slow<u>er</u>, funni<u>er</u>. (Note that a final *y* becomes *i* before *-er* is added.)

Other two-syllable adjectives and all long adjectives form the comparative with *more:* <u>more</u> famous, <u>more</u> incredible.

Adverbs ending in *-ly* also form the comparative with *more:* <u>more</u> slowly. Other adverbs use the *-er* ending to form the comparative: soon<u>er</u>.

All adjectives and adverbs indicate a lesser degree with *less:* <u>less</u> lovely, <u>less</u> slowly.

## (2) Superlative Forms

**?**

Adjectives that form the comparative with *-er* add *-est* to form the superlative: nic<u>est</u>, funni<u>est</u>. Adjectives that indicate the comparative with *more* use *most* to indicate the superlative: <u>most</u> famous, <u>most</u> challenging.

The majority of adverbs use *most* to indicate the superlative: <u>most</u> quickly. Others use the *-est* ending: soon<u>est</u>.

All adjectives and adverbs use *least* to indicate the least degree: <u>least</u> interesting, <u>least</u> willingly.

### Using comparatives and superlatives

- Never use both *more* and *-er* to form the comparative or both *most* and *-est* to form the superlative.

  Nothing could have been ~~more~~ easier.

  Jack is the ~~most~~ meanest person in town.

- Never use the superlative when comparing only two things.

  Stacy is the ~~oldest~~ older of the two sisters.

- Never use the comparative when comparing more than two things.

  We chose the ~~earlier~~ earliest of the four appointments.

### (3) Irregular Comparatives and Superlatives

Some adjectives and adverbs have irregular comparative and superlative forms. Instead of adding a word or an ending to the positive form, they use different words to indicate the comparative and the superlative.

#### IRREGULAR COMPARATIVES AND SUPERLATIVES

| | Positive | Comparative | Superlative |
|---|---|---|---|
| **Adjectives:** | good | better | best |
| | bad | worse | worst |
| | a little | less | least |
| | many, some, much | more | most |
| **Adverbs:** | well | better | best |
| | badly | worse | worst |

## 20d Avoiding Illogical Comparatives and Superlatives

Many adjectives and adverbs can logically exist only in the positive degree. For example, words like *perfect, unique, excellent, impossible, parallel, empty,* and *dead* cannot have comparative or superlative forms.

an
I read ~~the most~~ excellent story.

The vase in her collection was ~~very~~ unique.

These words can, however, be modified by words that suggest approaching the absolute state—*nearly* or *almost,* for example.

He revised until his draft was <u>almost perfect.</u>

# ? 20e    Avoiding Double Negatives

Be careful not to create a <u>double negative</u> by using a negative modifier (such as *never, no,* or *not*) with another negative word, such as *nearly, hardly, none,* or *nothing.* Remember that many contractions include the negative *not.*

Old dogs cannot learn ~~no~~ new tricks.

This instructor doesn't give ~~no~~ partial credit.

# PART 8

## Sentence Style

**21  Writing Varied Sentences    329**
- **21a**  Using Compound, Complex, and Compound-Complex Sentences   329
- **21b**  Varying Sentence Length   331
- **21c**  Breaking Up Strings of Compound Sentences   332
- **21d**  Varying Sentence Types   333
- **21e**  Varying Sentence Openings   334
- **21f**  Varying Standard Word Order   334

**22  Writing Emphatic Sentences    336**
- **22a**  Conveying Emphasis through Word Order   336
- **22b**  Conveying Emphasis through Sentence Structure   338
- **22c**  Conveying Emphasis through Parallelism and Balance   338
- **22d**  Conveying Emphasis through Repetition   339
- **22e**  Conveying Emphasis through Active Voice   339

**23  Writing Concise Sentences    341**
- **23a**  Eliminating Wordiness   341
- **23b**  Eliminating Unnecessary Repetition   343
- **23c**  Tightening Rambling Sentences   344

**24  Using Parallelism    346**
- **24a**  Using Parallelism Effectively   346
- **24b**  Revising Faulty Parallelism   347

# PART 8

## ? Frequently Asked Questions

**Chapter 21** **Writing Varied Sentences** **329**
- How do I combine choppy sentences to make my writing "flow"**?** 331
- What do I do if I have a whole string of compound sentences**?** 332
- What should I do if every sentence starts with *I* or another subject**?** 334

**Chapter 22** **Writing Emphatic Sentences** **336**
- Is it OK to start a sentence with *there is* or *there are*? 336
- Is repeating words and phrases ever a good idea**?** 339
- When can I use passive voice**?** 340

**Chapter 23** **Writing Concise Sentences** **341**
- How can I tell which words I really need and which can be cut**?** 341
- How do I edit a long, rambling sentence**?** 344

**Chapter 24** **Using Parallelism** **346**
- What is parallelism**?** 346
- How can I use parallelism to improve my writing**?** 347
- How can I correct faulty parallelism**?** 347

| **URLs** | *Visit the following sites for answers to more FAQs* |
| --- | --- |

**Elementary Rules of Composition from Strunk's Elements of Style**
*http://www.bartleby.com/141/strunk5.html*

**Sentence Craft (L. Behrens, UCSB)**
*http://www.writing.ucsb.edu/faculty/behrens/index.html*

**Writing Concise Sentences**
*http://www.ccc.commnet.edu/grammar/concise.htm*

**Eliminating "Word Clutter"**
*http://www.rscc.cc.tn.us/OWL/Clutter.html*

**Parallel Structure (Bellevue [WA] C.C.)**
*http://www.bcc.ctc.edu/writinglab/Parallel.html*

# Chapter 21

# Writing Varied Sentences

Varying the way you construct your sentences can help make your writing lively and interesting. This strategy can also help you emphasize the most important ideas in your sentences.

## 21a Using Compound, Complex, and Compound-Complex Sentences

Writer's
Resource
CD-ROM

Paragraphs that mix simple, compound, and complex sentences are more varied—and therefore more interesting—than those that do not.

### (1) Compound Sentences

A **compound sentence** is created when two or more independent clauses are joined with *coordinating conjunctions, transitional words and phrases, correlative conjunctions, semicolons,* or *colons.*

Coordinating Conjunctions
The pianist made some mistakes, <u>but</u> the concert was a success.

**Note:** Use a comma before a coordinating conjunction—*and, or, nor, but, for, so,* and *yet*—that joins two independent clauses.

See
29a

Transitional Words and Phrases
Aerobic exercise can help lower blood pressure; <u>however</u>, those with high blood pressure should still limit salt intake.

The saxophone does not belong to the brass family; <u>in fact</u>, it is a member of the woodwind family.

**Note:** Use a semicolon—not a comma—before a transitional word or phrase that joins two independent clauses. Frequently used <u>**transitional words and phrases**</u> include conjunctive adverbs like *consequently, finally, still,* and *thus* as well as expressions like *for example, in fact,* and *for instance.*

See
3b2

Correlative Conjunctions
Diana <u>not only</u> passed the exam, <u>but</u> she <u>also</u> received the highest grade in the class.

<u>Either</u> he left his coat in his locker, <u>or</u> he left it on the bus.

Semicolons
Alaska is the largest state; Rhode Island is the smallest.

Colons
He got his orders: he was to leave for France on Sunday.

## (2) Complex Sentences

A **complex sentence** consists of one independent clause and at least one dependent clause. A **subordinating conjunction** or **relative pronoun** links the independent and dependent clauses and indicates the relationship between them.

      (dependent clause)        (independent clause)
[After the town was evacuated], [the hurricane began].

      (independent clause)        (dependent clause)
[Officials watched the storm], [which threatened to destroy the town].

Sometimes a dependent clause may be embedded within an independent clause.

              (dependent clause)
Town officials, [who were very concerned], watched the storm.

| FREQUENTLY USED SUBORDINATING CONJUNCTIONS | | |
|---|---|---|
| after | before | until |
| although | if | when |
| as | once | whenever |
| as if | since | where |
| as though | that | wherever |
| because | unless | while |
| **RELATIVE PRONOUNS** | | |
| that | whatever | who (whose, whom) |
| what | which | whoever (whomever) |

### (3) Compound-Complex Sentences

A **compound-complex sentence** consists of two or more independent clauses and at least one dependent clause.

(dependent clause)
[When small foreign imports began dominating the U.S.
(independent clause)
automobile industry], [consumers were very responsive],but
(independent clause)
[American autoworkers were dismayed].

## 21b Varying Sentence Length

### (1) Combining Choppy Simple Sentences

Strings of short simple sentences can be tedious—and sometimes hard to follow, as the following paragraph illustrates.

John Peter Zenger was a newspaper editor. He waged and won an important battle for freedom of the press in America. He criticized the policies of the British governor. He was charged with criminal libel as a result. Zenger's lawyers were disbarred by the governor. Andrew Hamilton defended him. Hamilton convinced the jury that Zenger's criticisms were true. Therefore, the statements were not libelous.

You can revise choppy sentences like these by using *coordination, subordination,* or *embedding* to combine them with adjacent sentences.

**Coordination** pairs similar elements—words, phrases, or clauses—giving equal weight to each.

John Peter Zenger was a newspaper editor. He waged and won an important battle for freedom of the press in America. <u>He criticized the policies of the British governor, and he was charged with criminal libel as a result.</u> Zenger's lawyers were disbarred by the governor. Andrew Hamilton defended him. Hamilton convinced the jury that Zenger's criticisms were true. Therefore, the statements were not libelous.

Two choppy sentences linked with *and,* creating compound sentence

**Subordination** places the more important idea in an independent clause and the less important idea in a dependent clause.

<u>John Peter Zenger was a newspaper editor who waged and won an important battle for freedom of the press in America.</u> He criticized the policies of the British governor, and he was

Complex sentence

331

Complex
sentence
charged with criminal libel as a result. <u>When Zenger's lawyers</u> <u>were disbarred by the governor, Andrew Hamilton defended</u> <u>him.</u> Hamilton convinced the jury that Zenger's criticisms were true. Therefore, the statements were not libelous.

**Embedding** is the working of additional words and phrases into sentences.

The sentence
*Hamilton*
*convinced the*
*jury . . .*
becomes the
phrase
*convincing*
*the jury*
John Peter Zenger was a newspaper editor who waged and won an important battle for freedom of the press in America. He criticized the policies of the British governor, and he was charged with criminal libel as a result. <u>When Zenger's lawyers</u> <u>were disbarred by the governor, Andrew Hamilton defended</u> <u>him, convincing the jury that Zenger's criticisms were true.</u> Therefore, the statements were not libelous.

This final revision of the original string of choppy sentences uses coordination, subordination, and embedding to vary sentence length, retaining the final short simple sentence for emphasis.

### (2) Following a Long Sentence with a Short One

Another way to add interest with sentences of varying lengths is to follow one or more long sentences with a short one. This shifting of gears also places emphasis on the short sentence.

Over the years, vitamin boosters say, a misconception has grown that as long as there are no signs or symptoms of say, scurvy, then we have all of the vitamin C we need. Although we know how much of a particular vitamin or mineral will prevent clinical disease, we have practically no information on how much is necessary for peak health. <u>In short, we know how sick is sick, but</u> <u>we don't know how well is well.</u>

(*Philadelphia Magazine*)

## 21c Breaking Up Strings of Compound Sentences

**?**  An unbroken series of compound sentences can be dull. Moreover, when you connect clauses only with coordinating conjunctions, you do not indicate exactly how ideas are related or which is most important.

All Compound Sentences: A volcano that is erupting is considered *active*, <u>but</u> one that may erupt is designated *dormant*, <u>and</u>

one that has not erupted for a long time is called *extinct.* Most active volcanoes are located in "The Ring of Fire," a belt that circles the Pacific Ocean, <u>and</u> they can be extremely destructive. Italy's Vesuvius erupted in AD 79, <u>and</u> it destroyed the town of Pompeii. In 1883, Krakatau, located between the Indonesian islands of Java and Sumatra, erupted, <u>and</u> it caused a tidal wave, <u>and</u> more than 36,000 people were killed. Martinique's Mont Pelée erupted in 1902, and its lava <u>and</u> ash killed 30,000 people, and this completely wiped out the town of St. Pierre.

Varied Sentences: A volcano that is erupting is considered *active.* [**simple sentence**] One that may erupt is designated *dormant,* and one that has not erupted for a long time is called *extinct.* [**compound sentence**] Most active volcanoes are located in "The Ring of Fire," a belt that circles the Pacific Ocean. [**simple sentence with modifier**] Active volcanoes can be extremely destructive. [**simple sentence**] Erupting in AD 79, Italy's Vesuvius destroyed the town of Pompeii. [**simple sentence with modifier**] When Krakatau, located between the Indonesian islands of Java and Sumatra, erupted in 1883, it caused a tidal wave that killed 36,000 people. [**compound-complex sentence with modifier**] The eruption of Martinique's Mont Pelée in 1902 produced lava and ash that killed 30,000 people, completely wiping out the town of St. Pierre. [**complex sentence with modifier**]

## 21d   Varying Sentence Types

Another way to achieve sentence variety is to mix <u>declarative</u> sentences (statements) with occasional <u>imperative</u> sentences (commands or requests) and **rhetorical questions** (questions that readers are not expected to answer).

See
B4.2

Local television newscasts seem to be delivering less and less news. Although we tune in to be updated on local, national, and world events, only about 30 percent of most newscasts is devoted to news. The remaining time is spent on feature stories, advertising, weather, sports, and casual conversation between anchors. Given this focus on "soft" material, what options do those of us wishing to find out what happened in the world have? [**rhetorical question**] Critics of local television have a few suggestions. First, write to your local station's management voicing your concern; then, try to get others to sign a petition. [**imperatives**] If changes are not made, you can turn off your television and read the newspaper.

Other options for varying sentence types include mixing simple, compound, and complex sentences **(see 21a);** mixing cumulative and periodic sentences **(see 22b);** and using balanced sentences where appropriate **(see 22c).**

## 21e  Varying Sentence Openings

Rather than beginning every sentence with the subject, try beginning with modifying *words, phrases,* or *clauses.*

### Words
<u>Proud</u> and <u>relieved</u>, they watched their daughter receive her diploma. (adjectives)

<u>Hungrily,</u> he devoured his lunch. (adverb)

### Phrases
<u>For better or worse,</u> credit cards are now widely available to college students. (prepositional phrase)

<u>Located on the west coast of Great Britain</u>, Wales is part of the United Kingdom. (participial phrase)

<u>His interest widening</u>, Picasso designed ballet sets and illustrated books. (absolute phrase)

### Clauses
<u>After Woodrow Wilson was incapacitated by a stroke</u>, his wife unofficially performed many presidential duties. (adverb clause)

## 21f  Varying Standard Word Order

### (1) Inverting Word Order
You can vary standard subject-verb-object (or subject-verb-complement) word order by placing the complement or direct object *before* the verb instead of in its conventional position or by placing the verb *before* the subject instead of after it.

(object)   (verb)
↓          ↓
A cheery smile he had for everyone.
↑
(subject)

(complement)
↓
Hardest hit were the coastal areas.
    ↑        ↑
  (verb)  (subject)

Inverting word order draws attention to the word or word group that appears in an unexpected place—but overuse of inverted word order can be distracting, so use it in moderation.

## (2) Separating Subject from Verb

You can also vary conventional word order by placing words or phrases between the subject and verb—but be sure the word group is not so long that it obscures the connection between subject and verb or creates an **agreement** error.

See 15a1

  (subject)                                         (verb)
Many <u>states</u>, hoping to reduce needless fatalities, <u>require</u> that children ride in government-approved child safety seats.

**ESL Note:** For more on word order, including information on correct word order in questions, **see 47f.**

# Chapter 22

# Writing Emphatic Sentences

In speaking, we emphasize certain ideas and deemphasize others with intonation and gesture; in writing, we convey emphasis through the selection and arrangement of words.

## 22a Conveying Emphasis through Word Order

Readers tend to focus on the *beginning* and *end* of a sentence, expecting to find key information there.

### (1) Beginning with Important Ideas

Placing key ideas at the beginning of a sentence stresses their importance. The unedited version of the following sentence places emphasis on the study, not on those who conducted it or those who participated in it. Editing focuses attention on the researcher, not on the study.

~~In a landmark study of alcoholism~~, Dr. George Vaillant of Harvard ⁁ *, in a landmark study of alcoholism,* followed two hundred Harvard graduates and four hundred inner-city, working-class men from the Boston area.

**?** (close**UP**)

#### Writing emphatic sentences

Placing an empty phrase like *there is* or *there are* at the beginning of a sentence generally weakens the sentence.

MIT places
~~There is~~ heavy emphasis ~~placed~~ on the development of computational skills. ~~at MIT.~~

## (2) Ending with Important Ideas

Placing key elements at the end of a sentence is another way to convey their importance.

*Using a Colon or a Dash* A colon or a dash can add emphasis by isolating an important word or phrase at the end of a sentence.

Beth had always dreamed of owning one special car: a 1953 Corvette.

The elderly need a good deal of special attention—and they deserve that attention.

### Placing transitional expressions

When they are placed at the end of a sentence, conjunctive adverbs or other transitional expressions lose their power to indicate the relationship between ideas. Place <u>transitional words and phrases</u> earlier in the sentence, where they can serve this purpose and also add emphasis.

See
3b2

however,
Smokers do have rights;∧they should not try to impose their habit on others∧, however.

*Using Climactic Word Order* **Climactic word order,** the arrangement of a series of items from the least to the most important, places emphasis on the last item in the series.

Binge drinking can lead to vandalism, car accidents, and even death. (*Death* is the most serious consequence.)

## (3) Experimenting with Word Order

In English sentences, the most common order is subject-verb-object (or subject-verb-complement). When you depart from this expected word order, you call attention to the word, phrase, or clause you have relocated.

More modest and less inventive than Turner's paintings are John Constable's landscapes.

See
21f1
Here the writer calls special attention to the modifying phrase *more modest and less inventive than Turner's paintings* by **inverting word order**, placing the complement and the verb before the subject.

## 22b Conveying Emphasis through Sentence Structure

### (1) Using Cumulative Sentences

A **cumulative sentence** begins with an independent clause, followed by additional words, phrases, or clauses that expand or develop it.

> She holds me in strong arms, arms that have chopped cotton, dismembered trees, scattered corn for chickens, cradled infants, shaken the daylights out of half-grown upstart teenagers.
> (Rebecca Hill, *Blue Rise*)

Because it presents its main idea first, a cumulative sentence tends to be clear and straightforward. (Most English sentences are cumulative.)

### (2) Using Periodic Sentences

A **periodic sentence** moves from supporting details, expressed in modifying phrases and dependent clauses, to the sentence's key idea, which is placed in the independent clause.

> Unlike World Wars I and II, which ended decisively with the unconditional surrender of U.S. enemies, the war in Vietnam did not end when American troops withdrew.

**Note:** In some periodic sentences, the modifying phrase or dependent clause comes between subject and predicate.

> Columbus, after several discouraging and unsuccessful voyages, finally reached America.

## 22c Conveying Emphasis through Parallelism and Balance

See
24a
By reinforcing the correspondence between grammatical elements, **parallelism** helps writers convey information clearly, quickly, and emphatically.

We seek an individual <u>who is</u> a self-starter, <u>who owns</u> a late-model automobile, and <u>who is</u> willing to work evenings. (classified advertisement)

<u>Do not pass</u> go; <u>do not collect</u> $200. (instructions)

The Faust legend is central <u>in Benét's *The Devil and Daniel Webster,*</u> in Goethe's *Faust,* and <u>in Marlowe's *Dr. Faustus.*</u> (exam answer)

A **balanced sentence** is neatly divided between two parallel structures—for example, two independent clauses in a compound sentence. The symmetrical structure of a balanced sentence highlights correspondences or contrasts between clauses.

In the 1950s, the electronic miracle was the television; in the 1980s, the electronic miracle was the computer.

Alive, the elephant was worth at least a hundred pounds; dead, he would only be worth the value of his tusks, five pounds, possibly.
(George Orwell, "Shooting an Elephant")

## 22d   Conveying Emphasis through Repetition

<u>Unnecessary repetition</u> makes sentences dull and monotonous as well as wordy.

See 23b

He had a good arm and <u>also</u> could field well, and he was ~~also~~ a fast runner.

Effective repetition, however, can place emphasis on key words or ideas.

**?**

They decided to begin again: <u>to begin</u> hoping, <u>to begin</u> trying to change, <u>to begin</u> working toward a goal.

During those years when I was just learning to speak, my mother and father addressed me only <u>in Spanish</u>; <u>in Spanish</u> I learned to reply.
(Richard Rodriguez, *Aria: A Memoir of a Bilingual Childhood*)

## 22e   Conveying Emphasis through Active Voice

See 18d

<u>Active voice</u> verbs are generally more emphatic—and more concise—than <u>passive voice</u> verbs.

See ESL 47c6

# Writing Emphatic Sentences

**Passive:** The prediction that oil prices will rise is being made by economists.

**Active:** Economists are predicting that oil prices will rise.

The passive voice tends to focus your readers' attention on the action or on its receiver rather than on who is performing it. The receiver of the action is the subject of a passive sentence, so the actor fades into the background (*by economists*) or is omitted (*the prediction . . . is being made*).

**?**   Sometimes, of course, you want to stress the action rather than the actor. If so, it makes sense to use the passive voice. You also use the passive voice when the identity of the person performing the action is irrelevant or unknown: *The course was canceled.* For this reason, the passive voice is frequently used in scientific and technical writing: *The beaker was filled with a saline solution.*

# Chapter 23

# Writing Concise Sentences

A sentence is not concise simply because it is short; a concise sentence contains only the words necessary to make its point.

## 23a  Eliminating Wordiness

A good way to find out which words are essential in a sentence is to underline the key words. Then, look carefully at the remaining words so you can see which are unnecessary and eliminate <u>wordiness</u> by deleting them.

See ESL 47g

It seems to me that it does not make sense to allow any <u>bail</u> to be <u>granted</u> to <u>anyone</u> who has ever been <u>convicted</u> of a <u>violent crime</u>.

The underlining shows you immediately that none of the words in the long introductory phrase are essential. The following revision includes just the words necessary to convey the key ideas:

Bail should not be granted to anyone who has ever been convicted of a violent crime.

Whenever possible, delete nonessential words—*deadwood, utility words,* and *circumlocution*—from your writing.

### (1) Eliminating Deadwood

**Deadwood** is a term used for unnecessary phrases that simply take up space and add nothing to meaning.

Many
∧~~There were many~~ factors ~~that~~ influenced his decision to become a priest.

The two plots are ~~both~~ similar in ~~the way~~ that they trace the characters' increasing rage.

Shoppers ~~who are~~ looking for bargains often go to outlets.

They played ^an exhausting^ a racquetball game ~~that was exhausting~~.

^This^ ~~In this~~ article ~~it~~ discusses lead poisoning.

The only truly tragic character in *Hamlet* ^is^ ~~would have to be~~ Ophelia.

Deadwood also includes unnecessary statements of opinion, such as *I believe, I feel,* and *it seems to me.*

^The^ ~~In my opinion, the~~ characters seem undeveloped.

^This^ ~~As far as I'm concerned, this~~ course looks interesting.

## (2) Eliminating Utility Words

**Utility words** contribute nothing to a sentence. Utility words include nouns with imprecise meanings (*factor, situation, type, aspect,* and so on); adjectives so general that they are almost meaningless (*good, bad, important*); and common adverbs denoting degree (*basically, actually, quite, very, definitely*). Often you can just delete the utility word; if you cannot, replace it with a more precise word.

^Registration^ ~~The registration situation~~ was disorganized.

The scholarship ~~basically~~ offered Fran ^an^ ~~a good~~ opportunity to study Spanish.

It was ~~actually~~ a worthwhile book, but I didn't ~~completely~~ finish it.

## (3) Avoiding Circumlocution

Taking a roundabout way to say something (using ten words when five will do) is called **circumlocution.** Instead of complicated constructions, use concise, specific words and phrases that come right to the point.

^The^ ~~It is not unlikely that the~~ trend toward lower consumer spending will ^probably^ continue.

Joel was in the army ^~~during the same time that~~ I was in college.
(while)

## Revising wordy phrases

A wordy phrase can almost always be replaced by a more concise, more direct term.

| Wordy | Concise |
|---|---|
| at the present time | now |
| at this point in time | now |
| for the purpose of | for |
| due to the fact that | because |
| on account of the fact that | because |
| until such time as | until |
| in the event that | if |
| by means of | by |
| in the vicinity of | near |
| have the ability to | be able to |

## 23b  Eliminating Unnecessary Repetition

Repetition can make your writing more **emphatic**, but unnecessary repetition and **redundant** word groups (repeated words or phrases that say the same thing) can obscure your meaning. Correct unnecessary repetition by using one of the following strategies.

See 22d

### (1) Deleting Redundancy

People's clothing ~~attire~~ can reveal a good deal about their personalities.

### (2) Substituting a Pronoun

Fictional detective Miss Marple has solved many crimes. *The Murder at the Vicarage* was one of ^~~Miss Marple's~~ most challenging cases.
(her)

### (3) Creating an Appositive

Red Barber, ~~was~~ a sportscaster/, ~~He~~ was known for his colorful expressions.

### (4) Creating a Compound

John F. Kennedy was the youngest man ever elected president/
and
∧~~He was~~ also the first Catholic to hold this office.

### (5) Creating a Complex Sentence

which
Americans value freedom of speech/∧ ~~Freedom of speech~~ is guaranteed by the First Amendment.

## 23c  Tightening Rambling Sentences

**?** The combination of nonessential words, unnecessary repetition, and complicated syntax creates **rambling sentences.** Revising rambling sentences frequently requires extensive editing.

### (1) Eliminating Excessive Coordination

When you string a series of clauses together with coordinating conjunctions, you create a rambling, unfocused compound sentence. To revise such sentences, first identify the main idea or ideas, and then subordinate the supporting details.

Wordy: Benjamin Franklin was the son of a candlemaker, but he later apprenticed as a printer, and this experience led to his buying *The Pennsylvania Gazette,* and he managed this periodical with great success.

Concise: Benjamin Franklin, the son of a candlemaker, later apprenticed as a printer, an experience that led to his buying *The Pennsylvania Gazette,* which he managed with great success.

## (2) Eliminating Adjective Clauses

A series of **adjective clauses** is also likely to produce a rambling sentence. To revise, substitute concise modifying words or phrases for adjective clauses.

See
B3.2

Wordy: *Moby Dick,* which is a novel about a white whale, was written by Herman Melville, who was friendly with Nathaniel Hawthorne, who urged him to revise the first draft.

Concise: *Moby Dick,* a novel about a white whale, was written by Herman Melville, who revised the first draft at the urging of his friend Nathaniel Hawthorne.

## (3) Eliminating Passive Constructions

Excessive use of the **passive voice** can create rambling sentences. Correct this problem by changing passive to active voice.

See
18d

Wordy: "Buy American" rallies are being organized by concerned Americans who hope that jobs can be saved by such gatherings.

Concise: Concerned Americans are organizing "Buy American" rallies, hoping that such gatherings can save jobs.

## (4) Eliminating Wordy Prepositional Phrases

When you revise, substitute adjectives or adverbs for wordy **prepositional phrases**.

See
B3.1

        dangerous               exciting
The trip was ~~one of danger~~ but also ~~one of excitement.~~

        confidently             authoritatively
He spoke ~~in a confident manner~~ and ~~with a lot of authority.~~

## (5) Eliminating Wordy Noun Constructions

Substitute strong verbs for wordy **noun phrases**.

See
B3.1

        decided
We have ~~made the decision~~ to postpone the meeting until ~~the~~

                         appear
~~appearance of~~ all the board members.

**345**

# Chapter 24

# Using Parallelism

**Parallelism**—the use of matching words, phrases, clauses, or sentence structures to express equivalent ideas—adds unity, balance, and force to your writing. Effective parallelism can help you write clearer sentences, but **faulty parallelism** can create awkward sentences that obscure your meaning and confuse readers.

See 24b

Writer's Resource CD-ROM

## 24a   Using Parallelism Effectively

**?**

Parallelism highlights the correspondence between *items in a series, paired items,* and elements in *lists* and *outlines.*

### (1) With Items in a Series

<u>Eat</u>, <u>drink</u>, and <u>be</u> merry.

<u>Baby food consumption</u>, <u>toy production</u>, and <u>marijuana use</u> are likely to decline as the U.S. population ages.

Three factors influenced his decision to seek new employment: <u>his desire to relocate</u>, <u>his need for greater responsibility</u>, and <u>his dissatisfaction with his current job</u>.

**Note:** For information on punctuating items in a series, **see 29b and 30b.**

### (2) With Paired Items

The thank-you note was <u>short</u> but <u>sweet</u>.

<u>Roosevelt represented the United States</u>, and <u>Churchill represented Great Britain</u>.

<u>Ask not what your country can do for you</u>; <u>ask what you can do for your country</u>.

(John F. Kennedy, inaugural address)

Paired elements linked by **correlative conjunctions** (such as *not only/but also, both/and, either/or, neither/nor,* and *whether/or*) should be parallel.

The design team paid close attention not only <u>to color</u> but also <u>to texture</u>.

Either <u>repeat physics</u> or <u>take calculus</u>.

Parallelism also highlights the contrast between paired elements linked by *than* or *as.*

Richard Wright and James Baldwin chose <u>to live in Paris</u> rather than <u>to remain in the United States</u>.

Success is as much <u>a matter of hard work</u> as <u>a matter of luck</u>.

### (3) In Lists and Outlines

Elements in a list should be parallel.

The Irish potato famine had four major causes:
1. The establishment of the landlord-tenant system
2. The failure of the potato crop
3. The reluctance of England to offer adequate financial assistance
4. The passage of the Corn Laws

Elements in an **<u>outline</u>** should also be parallel.

See
1c6

## 24b  Revising Faulty Parallelism

Writer's
Resource
CD-ROM

**Faulty parallelism** occurs when elements that have the same function in a sentence are not presented in parallel terms.

Many people in developing countries suffer because the countries lack sufficient housing to accommodate them, sufficient <u>sufficient</u> <u>to serve them.</u> food to feed them, and ∧their health-care facilities ∧are inadequate.

To correct faulty parallelism, match nouns with nouns, verbs with verbs, and phrases or clauses with similarly constructed phrases or clauses.

Popular exercises for men and women include yoga, weight lifting
~~lifters~~, and jogging.
∧

having
I look forward to hearing from you and to ~~have~~ an opportunity
∧
to tell you more about myself.

**Repeating key words**

Although the use of similar grammatical structures may sometimes be enough to convey parallelism, sentences are often clearer if certain key words (for example, prepositions that introduce items in a series) are also parallel. In the following sentence, repeating the preposition *by* makes it clear that *not* applies only to the first phrase.

Computerization has helped industry by not allowing labor
by
costs to skyrocket, increasing the speed of production, and
∧
by
∧
improving efficiency.

# PART 9

# Using Words Effectively

**25 Choosing Words   351**
   **25a**  Choosing an Appropriate Level of Diction   351
   **25b**  Choosing the Right Word   353
   **25c**  Avoiding Inappropriate Language   354
   **25d**  Using Figures of Speech   356
   **25e**  Avoiding Biased Language   356

**26 Using a Dictionary   359**
**27 A Glossary of Usage   363**

# PART 9

## ? Frequently Asked Questions

**Chapter 25 Choosing Words 351**
- How formal should I be in my college writing? 352
- How do I know whether I am using exactly the right word? 353
- What is a cliché? 355
- What is sexist language and how can I avoid it? 357

**Chapter 26 Using a Dictionary 359**
- What kind of dictionary should I use? 359
- Should I use a thesaurus? 360
- Is an electronic dictionary better than a print dictionary? 361

**Chapter 27 A Glossary of Usage 363**
- Is *criteria* singular or plural? 365
- Which is correct, *everyday* or *every day*? 366
- What is the difference between *imply* and *infer*? 367

**URLs** *Visit the following sites for answers to more FAQs*

**Roget's Thesaurus**
*http://www.thesaurus.com/*

**dictionary.com's list of online dictionaries**
*http://www.dictionary.com*

**Cliché Finder**
*http://www.westegg.com/cliche/*

**Webster's Dictionary Online**
*http://www.m-w.com*

**Dictionaries in 230 Languages**
*http://www.yourdictionary.com*

**Words of Expressions Commonly Misused
(Strunk's *Elements of Style*)**
*http://www.bartleby.com/141/strunk3.html*

**A Word a Day (wordsmith.org): new word defined,
with examples, each day.**
*http://www.wordsmith.org/words/today.html*

**Paul Brians' Common Errors in English (Usage)**
*http://www.wsu.edu/~brians/errors/errors.html*

# Chapter 25

# Choosing Words

## 25a Choosing an Appropriate Level of Diction

**Diction,** which comes from the Latin word for *say,* means the choice and use of words. Different audiences and situations call for different levels of diction.

### (1) Formal Diction

**Formal diction** is grammatically correct and uses words familiar to an educated audience. A writer who uses formal diction often maintains emotional distance from the audience by using the impersonal *one* rather than the more personal *I* and *you.* In addition, the tone of the writing—as determined by word choice, sentence structure, and choice of subject—is dignified and objective.

> We learn to perceive in the sense that we learn to respond to things in particular ways because of the contingencies of which they are a part. We may perceive the sun, for example, simply because it is an extremely powerful stimulus, but it has been a permanent part of the environment of the species throughout its evolution, and more specific behavior with respect to it could have been selected by contingencies of survival (as it has been in many other species).
>
> (B.F. Skinner, *Beyond Freedom and Dignity*)

### (2) Informal Diction

**Informal diction** is the language that people use in conversation. You should use informal diction in your college writing only to imitate speech or dialect or to give a paper a conversational tone.

*Colloquial Diction* **Colloquial diction** is the language of everyday speech. Contractions—*isn't, I'm*—are typical colloquialisms, as are **clipped forms**—*phone* for *telephone, TV* for *television, dorm* for *dormitory.* Other colloquialisms include placeholders like *kind of* and utility words like *nice* for *acceptable, funny* for *odd,* and *great* for almost anything. Colloquial English also includes verb forms like *get across* for *communicate, come up with* for *find,* and *check out* for *investigate.*

*Slang* **Slang** is a vivid and forceful use of language that packs a rhetorical punch. For this reason, it calls attention to itself. It is often restricted to a single group of people—urban teenagers, rock musicians, or computer users, for example. Slang words are constantly changing. Words like *uptight, groovy,* and *hippie* emerged in the 1960s. During the 1970s, technology, music, politics, and feminism influenced slang, giving us words like *hacker, disco, stonewalling,* and *macho.* The 1980s contributed expressions like *sound bite, yuppie,* and *chocoholic;* slang in the 1990s included expressions such as *wonk, hip-hop, downsize,* and *flame.*

*Regionalisms* **Regionalisms** are words, expressions, and idiomatic forms that are used in particular geographical areas but may not be understood by a general audience. In eastern Tennessee, for example, a paper bag is a *poke,* and empty soda bottles are *dope bottles.* In Lancaster, Pennsylvania, which has a large Amish population, it is not unusual to hear an elderly person saying *darest* for *dare not* or *daresome* for *adventurous.* And New Yorkers stand *on line* for a movie, whereas people in most other parts of the country stand *in line.*

*Nonstandard Diction* **Nonstandard diction** refers to words and expressions not generally considered a part of standard English—words like *ain't, nohow, anywheres, nowheres, hisself,* and *theirselves.*

No absolute rules distinguish standard from nonstandard usage. In fact, some linguists reject the idea of nonstandard usage altogether, arguing that this designation serves only to relegate both the language and those who use it to second-class status.

## ? (3) College Writing

The level of diction appropriate for college writing depends on your assignment and your audience. A personal-experience essay calls for a somewhat informal style, but a research paper, an exam, or a report calls for more formal vocabulary and a more objective tone. In general, most college writing falls somewhere between formal and informal English, using a conversational tone but maintaining grammatical correctness and using a specialized vocabulary when the situation requires it. (This level of diction is used in this book.)

> **Note:** Keep in mind that colloquial expressions are almost always inappropriate in your college writing, as are slang, regionalisms, and other nonstandard usages.

## 25b  Choosing the Right Word

Choosing the right word to use in a particular context is very important. If you use the wrong word—or even *almost* the right one—you run the risk of misrepresenting your ideas.

### (1) Denotation and Connotation

A word's **denotation** is its explicit dictionary meaning, what it stands for without any emotional associations. A word's **connotations** are the emotional, social, and political associations it has in addition to its denotative meaning.

| Word | Denotation | Connotation |
|------|-----------|-------------|
| politician | someone who holds a political office | opportunist; wheeler-dealer |

Selecting a word with the appropriate connotation can be a challenge. For example, the word *skinny* has negative connotations, whereas *thin* is neutral, and *slender* is positive. And *mentally ill, insane, neurotic, crazy, psychopathic,* and *emotionally disturbed* have different emotional, social, and political connotations that affect the way people respond. If you use terms without considering their connotations, you run the risk of undercutting your credibility, to say nothing of confusing and possibly angering your readers.

### (2) Euphemisms

A **euphemism** is a polite term used in place of a blunt or harsh term that describes a subject society considers offensive or unpleasant. College writing is no place for euphemisms. Say what you mean—*pregnant,* not *expecting; died,* not *passed away;* and *strike,* not *work stoppage.*

### (3) Specific and General Words

**Specific** words refer to particular persons, items, or events; **general** words denote an entire class or group. *Queen Elizabeth II,* for example, is more specific than *monarch; jeans* is more specific than *clothing;* and *SUV* is more specific than *vehicle.* You can use general words to characterize entire classes of items, but you must use specific words to clarify such generalizations.

353

### (4) Abstract and Concrete Words

**Abstract** words—*beauty, truth, justice,* and so on—refer to ideas, qualities, or conditions that cannot be perceived by the senses. **Concrete** words name things that readers can see, hear, taste, smell, or touch. As with general and specific words, whether a word is abstract or concrete is relative. The more concrete your words and phrases, the more vivid the image you evoke in the reader.

#### Using Concrete Words

See
23a2

Take particular care to avoid abstract terms such as *nice, great,* and *terrific* that say nothing and could be used in almost any sentence. These <u>utility words</u> convey only enthusiasm, not precise meanings. Replace them with more specific words.

a complex and suspensefully plotted mystery.
The book was ̭ ~~good~~

## 25c  Avoiding Inappropriate Language

### (1) Jargon

**Jargon,** the specialized or technical vocabulary of a trade, profession, or academic discipline, is useful for communicating in the field in which it was developed. Outside that field, however, it is often confusing.

Original: The patient had an acute myocardial infarction.

Translation: The patient had a heart attack.

When you write for a general audience, avoid jargon. Remember, always use a vocabulary that is appropriate for your audience and purpose.

### (2) Neologisms

**Neologisms** are newly coined words that are not part of standard English. New situations call for new words, and frequently such words become a part of the language—*e-mail, voice mail, carjack,* and *outsource,* for example. Others, however, are never fully accepted. If you are not sure whether to use a term, look it up in a current college **dictionary**. If it is not there, you probably should not use it.

See Ch 26

### (3) Pretentious Diction

Good writing is usually clear and direct, not pompous or flowery. Revise to eliminate **pretentious diction,** inappropriately elevated and wordy language.

As I fell ~~into slumber~~, I ~~cogitated~~ about my day ~~ambling~~ through ~~the splendor of~~ the Appalachian Mountains.

asleep    thought    hiking

---

## close**UP**

### Pretentious diction

Pretentious diction is formal diction used in an inappropriate situation. In this context, it is always out of place. For every word that is pretentious, you should try to find a clear and direct alternative.

| *Pretentious* | *Clear* |
|---|---|
| ascertain | discover |
| commence | start |
| implement | carry out |
| minuscule | small |
| reside | live |
| terminate | end |
| utilize | use |

---

### (4) Clichés

**Clichés** are trite expressions that have lost their impact because they have been so overused. Familiar sayings like "last but not least," "better late than never," and "what goes around comes around," for example, do little to enhance your writing.

The purpose of college writing is always to convey information clearly; clichés do just the opposite. Take the time to think of fresh expressions.

## 25d   Using Figures of Speech

Writers often use **figures of speech** (such as *similes* and *metaphors*) to go beyond the literal meanings of words, thereby achieving special effects and adding interest and variety to their writing. Although you should not overuse figures of speech, do not be afraid to use them when you think they will help you communicate your ideas to your readers.

### Commonly used figures of speech

A **simile** is a comparison between two unlike items on the basis of a shared quality. Similes are introduced by *like* or *as*.

Like travelers with exotic destinations on their minds, the graduates were remarkably forceful.
(Maya Angelou, *I Know Why the Caged Bird Sings*)

A **metaphor** also compares two dissimilar things, but instead of saying that one thing is *like* another, it *equates* them.

Perhaps it is easy for those who have never felt the stinging darts of segregation to say, "Wait."
(Martin Luther King, Jr., "Letter from Birmingham Jail")

An **analogy** explains an unfamiliar concept or thing by comparing it to a more familiar one.

According to Robert Frost, writing free verse is like playing tennis without a net.

**Personification** gives an idea or inanimate object human attributes, feelings, or powers. We use personification every day in expressions such as *The engine died* or *The wind roared.*

## 25e   Avoiding Biased Language

### (1) Offensive Labels

When referring to a racial, ethnic, or religious group, use words with neutral connotations or words that the group itself uses in *formal* speech or writing.

Also, avoid potentially offensive labels relating to age (*brat, codger*), social class or geography (*beaner, redneck, hillbilly*), occupation (*shrink, shyster*), marital status (*old maid*), physical ability, or sexual orientation.

## (2) Sexist Language     **?**

Sexist language entails much more than the use of derogatory words such as *hunk, chick,* and *bimbo*. Assuming that some professions are exclusive to one gender—for instance, that *nurse* denotes only women and that *doctor* denotes only men—is also sexist. So is the use of job titles such as *postman* for *letter carrier, fireman* for *firefighter,* and *stewardess* for *flight attendant.*

Sexist language also occurs when a writer fails to apply the same terminology to both men and women. For example, refer to two scientists with PhDs not as Dr. Sagan and Mrs. Yallow, but as Dr. Sagan and Dr. Yallow. Refer to two writers as James and Wharton, or Henry James and Edith Wharton, not James and Mrs. Wharton.

In your writing, always use *women*—not *girls, gals,* or *ladies*—when referring to adult females. Use *Ms.* as the form of address when a woman's marital status is unknown or irrelevant. (If the woman you are addressing refers to herself as *Mrs.* or *Miss,* however, use the form of address she prefers.) Finally, avoid using the generic *he* or *him* when your subject could be either male or female. Use the third-person plural or the phrase *he* or *she* (not *he/she*).

> **Sexist:** Before boarding, each passenger should make certain that <u>he</u> has <u>his</u> ticket.
>
> **Revised:** Before boarding, <u>passengers</u> should make certain that <u>they</u> have <u>their</u> tickets.
>
> **Revised:** Before boarding, each <u>passenger</u> should make certain that <u>he or she</u> has a ticket.

Remember, however, not to overuse *his* or *her* or *he* or *she* constructions, which can make your writing repetitious and wordy.

**Avoiding sexist language**

When trying to avoid sexist use of *he* and *him* in your writing, be careful not to use *they* or *their* to refer to a singular antecedent.

*continued on the following page*

*continued from the previous page*

Drivers
~~Any driver~~ caught speeding should have their driving
privileges suspended.

---

**✓checklist Eliminating sexist language**

| ✓ Sexist Usage | ✓ Possible Revisions |
|---|---|
| Mankind | People, human beings |
| Man's accomplishments | Human accomplishments |
| Man-made | Synthetic |
| Female engineer (lawyer, accountant, etc.), male model | Engineer, (lawyer, accountant, etc.), model |
| Policeman/woman | Police officer |
| Salesman/woman/girl | Salesperson/representative |
| Businessman/woman | Businessperson, executive |
| <u>Everyone</u> should complete <u>his</u> application by Tuesday. | <u>Everyone</u> should complete <u>his or her</u> application by Tuesday. <u>All students</u> should complete <u>their</u> applications by Tuesday. |

# Chapter 26

# Using a Dictionary

Every writer should own a dictionary. The most widely used type of dictionary is a one-volume **desk dictionary** or **college dictionary.** To fit a lot of information into a small space, dictionaries use a system of symbols, abbreviations, and typefaces. Each dictionary uses a slightly different system, so consult the preface of your dictionary to determine how its system operates. This chapter describes one typical system.

A labeled entry from *The American Heritage College Dictionary* appears below.

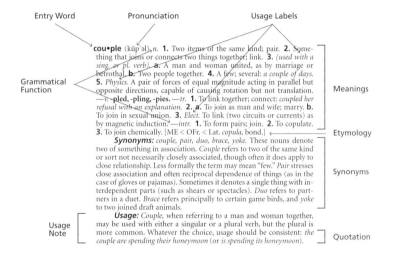

*Entry Word, Pronunciation Guide, and Part-of-Speech Label* The **entry word,** which appears in boldface at the beginning of the entry, gives the spelling of a word and indicates how the word is divided into syllables.

col • or *n.* Also chiefly British col • our

The **pronunciation guide** appears in parentheses or between slashes after the main entry. Dictionaries use symbols to represent sounds, and an explanation of these symbols usually appears at the bottom of each page or across the bottom of facing pages throughout the alphabetical listing.

Abbreviations called **part-of-speech labels** indicate parts of speech and grammatical forms.

**See 18a**

If a verb is <u>regular</u>, the entry provides only the base form of the verb. If a verb is <u>irregular</u>, the part-of-speech label indicates the irregular principal parts of the verb.

> **with • draw** . . . *v.* -drew, -drawn, -drawing

In addition, the label indicates whether a verb is transitive (*tr.*), intransitive (*intr.*), or both.

Part-of-speech labels also indicate the plural form of irregular nouns. (When the plural form is regular, it is not shown.)

> **child** . . . *n. pl.* chil · dren

**See 20c**

Finally, part-of-speech labels indicate the <u>comparative</u> and <u>superlative</u> forms of both regular and irregular adjectives and adverbs.

*Etymology* The **etymology** of a word—its history, its evolution over the years—appears in brackets either before or after the list of meanings.

*Meanings* Some dictionaries give the most common meaning first and then list less common ones. Other begin with the oldest meaning and move to the most current ones. Check the preface of your dictionary to find out how its entries are arranged.

*Synonyms and Antonyms* A dictionary entry often lists synonyms (and occasionally antonyms) in addition to definitions. **Synonyms** are words that have similar meanings, such as *well* and *healthy*. **Antonyms** are words that have opposite meanings, such as *courage* and *cowardice*.

**Using a thesaurus**

**?** When you consult a print or online **thesaurus,** a list of synonyms and antonyms, remember that no two words have exactly the same meanings. Use synonyms carefully, checking your dictionary to make sure the connotation of the synonym is very close to that of the original word.

*Idioms* Dictionary entries often show how certain words are used in set expressions called **idioms.** The meaning of such phrases cannot always be determined from the words alone. For example, what are we to make of the expressions "catch a cold" and "take a walk"?

Dictionaries also indicate the idiomatic use of <u>prepositions</u>. For example, we do not say that we *abide with* a decision; we say *abide by.*

See ESL
47e3

*Usage Labels* Dictionaries use **usage labels** to indicate in what contexts words are acceptable. Among these labels are *nonstandard* (in wide use but not considered standard usage); *informal/colloquial* (part of the language of conversation and acceptable in informal writing); *slang* (appropriate only in extremely informal situations); *dialect/regional* (limited to a certain geographical region); *obsolete* (no longer in use); *archaic/rare* (once common but now seldom used); and *poetic* (common only in poetry).

http://kirsznermandell.heinle.com

**Electronic dictionaries**

**?**

Electronic dictionaries include the same amount of information that one-volume desk dictionaries have. Electronic dictionaries come in two forms—CD-ROM and online. Typically, you have to download a CD-ROM dictionary onto your hard drive before you can use it with your word processing program. To use an online dictionary, you have to log on to a Web site such as <http://www.m-w.com/dictionary.htm>.

# Chapter 27

# A Glossary of Usage

This glossary of usage lists words and phrases that writers often find troublesome.

**ESL Note:** For a list of commonly confused words that present particular challenges for ESL writers, **see 47h.**

***a, an*** Use *a* before words that begin with consonants and words with initial vowels that sound like consonants: *a* person, *a* historical document, *a* one-horse carriage, *a* uniform. Use *an* before words that begin with vowels and words that begin with a silent *h: an* artist, *an* honest person.

***accept, except*** *Accept* is a verb that means "to receive"; *except* as a preposition or conjunction means "other than" and as a verb means "to leave out": The auditors will *accept* all your claims *except* the last two. Some businesses are *excepted* from the regulation.

***advice, advise*** *Advice* is a noun meaning "opinion or information offered"; *advise* is a verb that means "to offer advice to": The broker *advised* her client to take his attorney's *advice.*

***affect, effect*** *Affect* is a verb meaning "to influence"; *effect* can be a verb or a noun—as a verb it means "to bring about," and as a noun it means "result": We know how the drug *affects* patients immediately, but little is known of its long-term *effects*. The arbitrator tried to *effect* a settlement between the parties.

***all ready, already*** *All ready* means "completely prepared"; *already* means "by or before this or that time": I was *all ready* to help, but it was *already* too late.

***all right, alright*** Although the use of *alright* is increasing, current usage calls for *all right.*

***allusion, illusion*** An *allusion* is a reference or hint; an *illusion* is something that is not what it seems: The poem makes an *allusion* to the Pandora myth. The shadows created an optical *illusion.*

***a lot*** *A lot* is always two words.

***among, between*** *Among* refers to groups of more than two things; *between* refers to just two things: The three parties agreed *among* themselves to settle the case. There will be a brief intermission *between* the two acts. (Note that *amongst* is British, not American, usage.)

**amount, number** *Amount* refers to a quantity that cannot be counted; *number* refers to things that can be counted: Even a small *amount* of caffeine can be harmful. Seeing their commander fall, a large *number* of troops ran to his aid.

**an, a** See **a, an.**

**and/or** In business or technical writing, use *and/or* when either or both of the items it connects can apply. In college writing, however, avoid the use of *and/or.*

**as . . . as . . .** In such constructions, *as* signals a comparison; therefore, you must always use the second *as:* John Steinbeck's *East of Eden* is *as* long *as* his *The Grapes of Wrath.*

**as, like** *As* can be used as a conjunction (to introduce a complete clause) or as a preposition; *like* should be used as a preposition only: In *The Scarlet Letter,* Hawthorne uses imagery *as* (not *like*) he does in his other works. After classes, Fred works *as* a manager of a fast-food restaurant. Writers *like* Carl Sandburg appear once in a generation.

**at, to** Many people use the prepositions *at* and *to* after *where* in conversation: *Where* are your working *at? Where* are you going *to?* This usage is redundant and should not appear in college writing.

**awhile, a while** *Awhile* is an adverb; *a while,* which consists of an article and a noun, is used as the object of a preposition: Before we continue, we will rest *awhile.* (modifies the verb *rest*); Before we continue, we will rest for *a while.* (object of the preposition *for*)

**bad, badly** *Bad* is an adjective, and *badly* is an adverb: The school board decided that *Huckleberry Finn* was a *bad* book. American automobile makers did not do *badly* this year. After verbs that refer to any of the senses or after any other linking verb, use the adjective form: He looked *bad.* He felt *bad.* It seemed *bad.*

**being as, being that** These awkward phrases add unnecessary words and weaken your writing. Use *because* instead.

**beside, besides** *Beside* is a preposition meaning "next to"; *besides* can be either a preposition meaning "except" or "other than" or an adverb meaning "as well": *Beside* the tower was a wall that ran the length of the city. *Besides* its industrial uses, laser technology has many other applications. Edison invented not only the lightbulb but the phonograph *besides.*

*between, among* See **among, between.**

*bring, take* *Bring* means "to transport from a farther place to a nearer place"; *take* means "to carry or convey from a nearer place to a farther one": *Bring* me a souvenir from your trip. *Take* this message to the general and wait for a reply.

*can, may* *Can* denotes ability, and *may* indicates permission: If you *can* play, you *may* use my piano.

*capital, capitol* *Capital* refers to a city that is an official seat of government; *capitol* refers to a building in which a legislature meets: Washington, DC, is the *capital* of the United States. When we were there, we visited the *Capitol* building.

*center around* This imprecise phrase is acceptable in speech and informal writing but not in college writing. Use *center on* instead.

*cite, site* *Cite* is a verb meaning "to quote as an authority or example"; *site* is a noun meaning "a place or setting": Jeff *cited* five sources in his research paper. The builder cleared the *site* for the new bank.

*climactic, climatic* *Climactic* means "of or related to a climax"; *climatic* means "of or related to climate": The *climactic* moment of the movie occurred unexpectedly. If scientists are correct, the *climatic* conditions of Earth are changing.

*coarse, course* *Coarse* is an adjective meaning "inferior" or "having a rough, uneven texture"; *course* is a noun meaning "a route or path," "an area on which a sport is played," or "a unit of study": *Coarse* sandpaper is used to smooth the surface. The *course* of true love never runs smoothly. Last semester I had to drop a *course*.

*complement, compliment* *Complement* means "to complete or add to"; *compliment* means "to give praise": A double-blind study would *complement* their preliminary research. My instructor *complimented* me on my improvement.

*conscious, conscience* *Conscious* is an adjective meaning "having one's mental faculties awake"; *conscience* is a noun that means the moral sense of right and wrong: The patient will remain *conscious* during the procedure. His *conscience* would not allow him to lie.

*continual, continuous* *Continual* means "recurring at intervals"; *continuous* refers to an action that occurs without interruption: A pulsar is a star that emits a *continual* stream of electromagnetic radiation. (It emits radiation at regular intervals.) A small battery allows the watch to run *continuously* for five years. (It runs without stopping.)

*could of, should of, would of* The contractions *could've*, *should've*, and *would've* are often misspelled as the nonstandard constructions *could of, should of,* and *would of.* Use *could have, should have,* and *would have* in college writing.

*council, counsel* A *council* is "a body of people who serve in a legislative or advisory capacity"; *counsel* means "to offer advice or guidance": The city *council* argued about the proposed ban on smoking. The judge *counseled* the couple to settle their differences.

*couple of* *Couple* means "a pair," but *couple of* is often used colloquially to mean "several" or "a few." In your college writing, specify "four points" or "two examples" rather than using "a couple of."

*criterion, criteria* *Criteria*, from the Greek, is the plural of *criterion,* meaning "standard for judgment": Of all the *criteria* for hiring graduating seniors, class rank is the most important *criterion.* **?**

*data* *Data* is the plural of the Latin *datum,* meaning "fact." In everyday speech and writing, *data* is often used as the singular as well as the plural form. In college writing, use *data* only for the plural: The *data* discussed in this section *are* summarized in Appendix A.

*different from, different than* *Different than* is widely used in American speech. In college writing, use *different from.*

*discreet, discrete* *Discreet* means "careful or prudent"; *discrete* means "separate or individually distinct": Because Madame Bovary was not *discreet,* her reputation suffered. Atoms can be broken into hundreds of *discrete* particles.

*disinterested, uninterested* *Disinterested* means "objective" or "capable of making an impartial judgment"; *uninterested* means "indifferent or unconcerned": The American judicial system depends on *disinterested* jurors. Finding no treasure, Hernando de Soto was *uninterested* in going farther.

*don't, doesn't* *Don't* is the contraction of *do not; doesn't* is the contraction of *does not.* Do not confuse the two: My dog *doesn't* (not *don't*) like to walk in the rain.

*effect, affect* See **affect, effect.**

*e.g.* *E.g.* is an abbreviation for the Latin *exempli gratia,* meaning "for example" or "for instance." In college writing, do not use *e.g.* Instead, use its English equivalent.

*emigrate from, immigrate to* To *emigrate* is "to leave one's country and settle in another"; to *immigrate* is "to come to another country and reside there." The noun forms of these words are *emigrant* and *immigrant:* My great-grandfather *emigrated from* Warsaw along with many other *emigrants* from Poland. Many people *immigrate* to the United States for economic reasons, but such *immigrants* still face great challenges.

**eminent, imminent** *Eminent* is an adjective meaning "standing above others" or "prominent"; *imminent* means "about to occur": Oliver Wendell Holmes, Jr., was an *eminent* jurist. In ancient times, a comet signaled *imminent* disaster.

**enthused** *Enthused,* a colloquial form of *enthusiastic,* should not be used in college writing.

**etc.** *Etc.,* the abbreviation of *et cetera,* means "and the rest." Do not use it in your college writing. Instead, say "and so on"—or, better yet, specify exactly what *etc.* stands for.

**everyday, every day** *Everyday* is an adjective that means "ordinary" or "commonplace"; *every day* means "occurring daily": In the Gettysburg Address, Lincoln used *everyday* language. She exercises almost *every day.*

**everyone, every one** *Everyone* is an indefinite pronoun meaning "every person"; *every one* means "every individual or thing in a particular group": *Everyone* seems happier in the spring. *Every one* of the packages had been opened.

**except, accept** See **accept, except.**

**explicit, implicit** *Explicit* means "expressed or stated directly"; *implicit* means "implied" or "expressed or stated indirectly": The director *explicitly* warned the actors to be on time for rehearsals. Her *implicit* message was that lateness would not be tolerated.

**farther, further** *Farther* designates distance; *further* designates degree: I have traveled *farther* from home than any of my relatives. Critics charge that welfare subsidies encourage *further* dependence.

**fewer, less** Use *fewer* with nouns that can be counted: *fewer* books, *fewer* people, *fewer* dollars. Use *less* with quantities that cannot be counted: *less* pain, *less* power, *less* enthusiasm.

**firstly (secondly, thirdly, . . .)** Archaic forms meaning "in the first . . . second . . . third place." Use *first, second, third.*

**further, farther** See **farther, further.**

**good, well** *Good* is an adjective, never an adverb: She is a *good* swimmer. *Well* can function as an adverb or as an adjective. As an adverb, it means "in a good manner": She swam *well* (not *good*) in the meet. *Well* is used as an adjective with verbs that denote a state of being or feeling. Here *well* can mean "in good health": I feel *well*.

**got to** *Got to* is not acceptable in college writing. To indicate obligation, use *have to, has to,* or *must.*

**hanged, hung** Both *hanged* and *hung* are past participles of *hang. Hanged* is used to refer to executions; *hung* is used to mean "suspended": Billy Budd was *hanged* for killing the master-at-arms. The stockings were *hung* by the chimney with care.

**he, she** Traditionally *he* has been used in the generic sense to refer to both males and females. To acknowledge the equality of the sexes, however, avoid the generic *he.* Use plural pronouns whenever possible. **See 25e.2.**

**hopefully** The adverb *hopefully,* meaning "in a hopeful manner," should modify a verb, an adjective, or another adverb. Do not use *hopefully* as a sentence modifier meaning "it is hoped." Rather than "*Hopefully,* scientists will soon discover a cure for AIDS," write "*I hope* scientists will soon discover a cure for AIDS."

**i.e.** *I.e.* is an abbreviation for the Latin *id est,* meaning "that is." In college writing, do not use *i.e.* Instead, use its English equivalent.

**if, whether** When asking indirect questions or expressing doubt, use *whether:* He asked *whether* (not *if*) the flight would be delayed. The flight attendant was not sure *whether* (not *if*) it would be delayed.

*illusion, allusion* See **allusion, illusion.**

*immigrate to, emigrate from* See **emigrate from, immigrate to.**

*implicit, explicit* See **explicit, implicit.**

**imply, infer** *Imply* means "to hint" or "to suggest"; *infer* means "to conclude from": Mark Antony *implied* that the conspirators had murdered Caesar. The crowd *inferred* his meaning and called for justice.

*infer, imply* See **imply, infer.**

**inside of, outside of** *Of* is unnecessary when *inside* and *outside* are used as prepositions. *Inside of* is colloquial in references to time: He waited *inside* (not *inside of*) the coffee shop. He could run a mile in *under* (not *inside of*) eight minutes.

**irregardless, regardless** *Irregardless* is a nonstandard version of *regardless.* Use *regardless* instead.

**is when, is where** These constructions are faulty when they appear in definitions: A playoff *is* (not *is when*) an additional game played to establish the winner of a tie.

**its, it's** *Its* is a possessive pronoun; *it's* is a contraction of *it is: It's* no secret that the bank is out to protect *its* assets.

**kind of, sort of** *Kind of* and *sort of* to mean "rather" or "somewhat" are colloquial and should not appear in college writing: It is well known that Napoleon was *rather* (not *kind of*) short.

**lay, lie** See **lie, lay.**

**leave, let** *Leave* means "to go away from" or "to let remain"; *let* means "to allow" or "to permit": *Let* (not *leave*) me give you a hand.

**less, fewer** See **fewer, less.**

**let, leave** See **leave, let.**

**lie, lay** *Lie* is an intransitive verb (one that does not take an object) meaning "to recline." Its principal forms are *lie, lay, lain, lying:* Each afternoon she would *lie* in the sun and listen to the surf. *As I Lay Dying* is a novel by William Faulkner. By 1871, Troy had *lain* undisturbed for two thousand years. The painting shows a nude *lying* on a couch. *Lay* is a transitive verb (one that takes an object) meaning "to put" or "to place." Its principal forms are *lay, laid, laid, laying:* The Federalist Papers *lay* the foundation for American conservatism. In October 1781, the British *laid* down their arms and surrendered. He had *laid* his money on the counter before leaving. We watched the stonemasons *laying* a wall.

**like, as** See **as, like.**

**loose, lose** *Loose* is an adjective meaning "not rigidly fastened or securely attached"; *lose* is a verb meaning "to misplace": The marble facing of the building became *loose* and fell to the sidewalk. After only two drinks, most people *lose* their ability to judge distance.

**lots, lots of, a lot of** These words are colloquial substitutes for *many, much,* or *a great deal of.* Avoid their use in college writing: The students had many (not *lots of* or *a lot of*) options for essay topics.

**man** Like the generic pronoun *he, man* has been used in English to denote members of both sexes. This usage is being replaced by *human beings, people,* or similar terms that do not specify gender. See **25e.2.**

**may, can** See **can, may.**

**may be, maybe** *May be* is a verb phrase; *maybe* is an adverb meaning "perhaps": She *may be* the smartest student in the class. *Maybe* her experience has given her an advantage.

**media, medium** *Medium*, meaning a "means of conveying or broadcasting something," is singular; *media* is the plural form and requires a plural verb: The *media* have distorted the issue.

**might have, might of** *Might of* is a nonstandard spelling of the contraction of *might have* (*might've*). Use *might have* in college writing.

**number, amount** See **amount, number.**

**OK, O.K., okay** All three spellings are acceptable, but this term should be avoided in college writing. Replace it with a more specific word or words: The lecture was *adequate* (not *okay*), if uninspiring.

**outside of, inside of** See **inside of, outside of.**

**passed, past** *Passed* is the past tense of the verb *pass; past* means "belonging to a former time" or "no longer current": The car must have been going eighty miles per hour when it *passed* us. In the envelope was a bill marked *past* due.

**percent, percentage** *Percent* indicates a part of a hundred when a specific number is referred to: "*10 percent* of his salary." *Percentage* is used when no specific number is referred to: "a *percentage* of next year's receipts." In technical and business writing, it is permissible to use the % sign after percentages you are comparing. Write out the word *percent* in college writing.

**phenomenon, phenomena** A *phenomenon* is a single observable fact or event. It can also refer to a rare or significant occurrence. *Phenomena* is the plural form and requires a plural verb: Many supposedly paranormal *phenomena* are easily explained.

**plus** As a preposition, *plus* means "in addition to." Avoid using *plus* as a substitute for *and:* Include the principal, *plus* the interest, in your calculations. Your quote was too high; moreover (not *plus*), it was inaccurate.

**precede, proceed** *Precede* means "to go or come before"; *proceed* means "to go forward in an orderly way": Robert Frost's *North of Boston* was *preceded* by an earlier volume. In 1532, Francisco Pizarro landed at Tumbes and *proceeded* south.

**principal, principle** As a noun, *principal* means "a sum of money (minus interest) invested or lent" or "a person in the leading position"; as an adjective, it means "most important"; a *principle* is a noun meaning a rule of conduct or a basic truth: He wanted to reduce the *principal* of the loan. The *principal* of the high school is a talented administrator. Women are the *principal* wage earners in many American households. The Constitution embodies certain fundamental *principles.*

**quote, quotation** *Quote* is a verb. *Quotation* is a noun. In college writing, do not use *quote* as a shortened form of *quotation:* Scholars attribute these *quotations* (not *quotes*) to Shakespeare.

**raise, rise** *Raise* is a transitive verb, and *rise* is an intransitive verb—that is, *raise* takes an object, and *rise* does not: My grandparents *raised* a large family. The sun will *rise* at 6:12 this morning.

**real, really** *Real* means "genuine" or "authentic"; *really* means "actually." In your college writing, do not use *real* as an adjective meaning "very."

**reason is that, reason is because** *Reason* should be used with *that* and not with *because,* which is redundant: The *reason* he left *is that* (not *is because*) you insulted him.

**regardless, irregardless** See **irregardless, regardless.**

**respectably, respectfully, respectively** *Respectably* means "worthy of respect"; *respectfully* means "giving honor or deference"; *respectively* means "in the order given": He skated quite *respectably* at his first Olympics. The seminar taught us to treat others *respectfully.* The first- and second-place winners were Tai and Kim, *respectively.*

**rise, raise** See **raise, rise.**

**set, sit** *Set* means "to put down" or "to lay." Its principal forms are *set* and *setting:* After rocking the baby to sleep, he *set* her down carefully in her crib. After *setting* her down, he took a nap. *Sit* means "to assume a sitting position." Its principal forms are *sit, sat,* and *sitting:* Many children *sit* in front of the television five to six hours a day. The dog *sat* by the fire. We were *sitting* in the airport when the flight was canceled.

**shall, will** *Will* has all but replaced *shall* to express all future action.

**should of** See **could of, should of, would of.**

**since** Do not use *since* for *because* if there is any chance of confusion. In the sentence "*Since* President Nixon traveled to China, trade between China and the United States has increased," *since* could mean either "from the time that" or "because." To be clear, use *because.*

**sit, set** See **set, sit.**

*so* Avoid using *so* alone as a vague intensifier meaning "very" or "extremely." Follow *so* with *that* and a clause that describes the result: She was *so* pleased with their work *that* she took them out to lunch.

*sometime, sometimes, some time* *Sometime* means "at some time in the future"; *sometimes* means "now and then"; *some time* means "a period of time": The president will address Congress *sometime* next week. All automobiles, no matter how reliable, *sometimes* need repairs. It has been *some time* since I read that book.

*sort of, kind of* See **kind of, sort of.**

*stationary, stationery* *Stationary* means "staying in one place"; *stationery* means "materials for writing" or "letter paper": The communications satellite appears to be *stationary* in the sky. The secretaries supply departmental offices with *stationery.*

*supposed to, used to* *Supposed to* and *used to* are often misspelled. Both verbs require the final *d* to indicate past tense.

*take, bring* See **bring, take.**

*than, then* *Than* is a conjunction used to indicate a comparison; *then* is an adverb indicating time: The new shopping center is bigger *than* the old one. He did his research; *then,* he wrote a report.

*that, which, who* Use *that* or *which* when referring to a thing; use *who* when referring to a person: It was a speech *that* inspired many. The movie, *which* was a huge success, failed to impress her. Anyone *who* (not *that*) takes the course will benefit.

*their, there, they're* *Their* is a possessive pronoun; *there* indicates place and is also used in the expressions *there is* and *there are; they're* is a contraction of *they are:* Watson and Crick did *their* DNA work at Cambridge University. I love Los Angeles, but I wouldn't want to live *there. There* is nothing we can do to resurrect an extinct species. When *they're* well treated, rabbits make excellent pets.

*themselves; theirselves, theirself* *Theirselves* and *theirself* are nonstandard variants of *themselves.*

*then, than* See **than, then.**

*till, until, 'til* *Till* and *until* have the same meaning, and both are acceptable. *Until* is preferred in college writing. *'Til,* a contraction of *until,* should be avoided.

*to, at* See **at, to.**

**to, too, two** *To* is a preposition that indicates direction; *too* is an adverb that means "also" or "more than is needed"; *two* expresses the number 2: Last year we flew from New York *to* California. "Tippecanoe and Tyler, *too*" was William Henry Harrison's campaign slogan. The plot was *too* complicated for the average reader. Just north of *Two* Rivers, Wisconsin, is a petrified forest.

**try to, try and** *Try and* is the colloquial equivalent of the more formal *try to:* He decided to *try to* (not *try and*) do better. In college writing, use *try to.*

**-type** Deleting this empty suffix eliminates clutter and clarifies meaning: Found in the wreckage was an *incendiary* (not *incendiary-type*) device.

**uninterested, disinterested** See **disinterested, uninterested.**

**unique** Because *unique* means "the only one," not "remarkable" or "unusual," never use constructions like "the most unique" or "very unique."

**until** See **till, until, 'til.**

**used to** See **supposed to, used to.**

**utilize** In most cases, replace *utilize* with *use* (*utilize* often sounds pretentious).

**wait for, wait on** To *wait for* means "to defer action until something occurs." To *wait on* means "to act as a waiter": I am *waiting for* (not *on*) dinner.

**weather, whether** *Weather* is a noun meaning "the state of the atmosphere"; *whether* is a conjunction used to introduce an alternative: The *weather* outside is frightful, but the fire inside is delightful. It is doubtful *whether* we will be able to ski tomorrow.

**well, good** See **good, well.**

**were, we're** *Were* is a verb; *we're* is the contraction of *we are:* The Trojans *were* asleep when the Greeks attacked. We must act now if *we're* going to succeed.

**whether, if** See **if, whether.**

**which, who, that** See **that, which, who.**

**who, whom** When a pronoun serves as the subject of its clause, use *who* or *whoever;* when it functions in a clause as an object, use *whom* or *whomever:* Sarah, *who* is studying ancient civilizations, would like to visit Greece. Sarah, *whom* I met in France, wants me to travel to Greece with her. To determine which to use at the beginning of a question, use a personal pronoun to answer the question: *Who* tried to call me? *He* called. (subject); *Whom* do you want for the job? I want *her.* (object)

***who's, whose*** *Who's* means "who is"; *whose* indicates possession: *Who's* going to take calculus? The writer *whose* book was in the window was autographing copies.

***will, shall*** See **shall, will.**

***would of*** See **could of, should of, would of.**

***your, you're*** *Your* indicates possession, and *you're* is the contraction of *you are:* You can improve *your* stamina by jogging two miles a day. *You're* certain to be the winner.

# Understanding Punctuation

**28 Using End Punctuation   379**
   **28a**  Using Periods   379
   **28b**  Using Question Marks   381
   **28c**  Using Exclamation Points   381

**29 Using Commas   382**
   **29a**  Setting Off Independent Clauses   382
   **29b**  Setting Off Items in a Series   382
   **29c**  Setting Off Introductory Elements   384
   **29d**  Setting Off Nonessential Material   385
   **29e**  Using Commas in Other Conventional Contexts   388
   **29f**  Using Commas to Prevent Misreading   389
   **29g**  Editing Misused Commas   389

**30 Using Semicolons   392**
   **30a**  Separating Independent Clauses   392
   **30b**  Separating Items in a Series   392
   **30c**  Editing Misused Semicolons   393

**31 Using Apostrophes   394**
   **31a**  Forming the Possessive Case   394
   **31b**  Indicating Omissions in Contractions   396
   **31c**  Forming Plurals   397

**32 Using Quotation Marks   398**
   **32a**  Setting Off Quoted Speech or Writing   398
   **32b**  Setting Off Long Prose Passages and Poetry   400
   **32c**  Setting Off Titles   401
   **32d**  Setting Off Words Used in Special Ways   402
   **32e**  Using Quotation Marks with Other Punctuation   402
   **32f**  Editing Misused Quotation Marks   403

**33 Using Other Punctuation Marks   405**
   **33a**  Using Colons   405
   **33b**  Using Dashes   406
   **33c**  Using Parentheses   407
   **33d**  Using Brackets   408
   **33e**  Using Slashes   409
   **33f**  Using Ellipses   409

# PART 10

## ? Frequently Asked Questions

**Chapter 28  Using End Punctuation    379**
- Do abbreviations always include periods?    380
- How are periods used in electronic addresses?    380

**Chapter 29  Using Commas    382**
- Do I need a comma before the *and* that comes between the last two items in a series?    382
- How do I use commas with *that* and *which*?    386
- How do I use commas with *however* and *for example*?    387
- Should I always use a comma before *and* and *but*?    390

**Chapter 30  Using Semicolons    392**
- When do I use a semicolon?    392
- Do I introduce a list with a semicolon or a colon?    393

**Chapter 31  Using Apostrophes    394**
- How do I form the possessive if a singular noun ends in *-s*?    394
- How do I form the possessive if a plural noun ends in *-s*?    394
- What is the difference between *its* and *it's*?    396

**Chapter 32  Using Quotations Marks    398**
- When do I use quotation marks with titles?    401
- Does punctuation go inside or outside quotation marks?    402
- What if a quotation is inside another quotation?    403

**Chapter 33  Using Other Punctuation Marks    405**
- When do I use a colon to introduce a quotation?    406
- When should I use parentheses?    407
- How do I show that I have deleted words from a quotation?    409

---

**URLs**    *Visit the following sites for answers to more FAQs*

**Punctuation Guide (Purdue)**
*http://owl.english.purdue.edu/handouts/grammar/#punctuation*
**Almost Everything You Need to Know about Commas**
*http://uark.edu/campus-resources/qwrtcntr/resources/handouts/commas.html*
**Using Semicolons (U. Richmond)**
*http://writing.richmond.edu/writing/wweb/semicolon.html*
**Apostrophe (U. of Arkansas)**
*http://uark.edu/campus-resources/qwrtcntr/resources/handouts/apostro.html*
**Quotation Marks**
*http://owl.english.purdue.edu/handouts/grammar/g-quote.html*

(Further explanations and examples are located in the sections listed in parentheses after each example.)

### SEPARATING INDEPENDENT CLAUSES

**With a Comma and a Coordinating Conjunction**

The House approved the bill, but the Senate rejected it. **(29a)**

**With a Semicolon**

Paul Revere's *The Boston Massacre* is traditional American protest art; Edward Hicks's paintings are socially conscious art with a religious strain. **(30a)**

**With a Semicolon and a Transitional Word or Phrase**

Thomas Jefferson brought two hundred vanilla beans and a recipe for vanilla ice cream back from France; thus, he gave America its all-time favorite ice-cream flavor. **(30a)**

**With a Colon**

A *U.S. News & World Report* survey has revealed a surprising fact: Americans spend more time at malls than anywhere else except at home and at work. **(33a2)**

### SEPARATING ITEMS IN A SERIES

**With Commas**

*Chipmunk, raccoon,* and *Mugwump* are Native American words. **(29b)**

**With Semicolons**

As ballooning became established, a series of firsts ensued: The first balloonist in the United States was 13-year-old Edward Warren, 1784; the first woman aeronaut was a Madame Thible who, depending on your source, either recited poetry or sang as she lifted off; the first airmail letter, written by Ben Franklin's grandson, was carried by balloon; and the first bird's-eye photograph of Paris was taken from a balloon. (Elaine B. Steiner, *Games*) **(30b)**

*continued on the following page*

*continued from the previous page*

## SETTING OFF EXAMPLES, EXPLANATIONS, OR SUMMARIES

**With a Colon**
She had one dream: to play professional basketball. (**33a2**)

**With a Dash**
"Study hard," "Respect your elders," "Don't talk with your mouth full"—Sharon had often heard her parents say these things. (**33b2**)

## SETTING OFF NONESSENTIAL MATERIAL

**With a Single Comma**
His fear increasing, he waited to enter the haunted house. (**29d3**)

**With a Pair of Commas**
Mark McGwire, not Sammy Sosa, was the first to break Roger Maris's home run record. (**29d3**)

**With Dashes**
Neither of the boys—both nine-year-olds—had any history of violence. (**33b1**)

**With Parentheses**
In some European countries (notably Sweden and France), high-quality day care is offered at little or no cost to parents. (**33c1**)

# Chapter 28

# Using End Punctuation

## 28a   Using Periods

Writer's
Resource
CD-ROM

### (1) Ending a Sentence

Use a period to signal the end of a statement, a mild command or polite request, or an indirect question.

Something is rotten in Denmark. (statement)

Be sure to have the oil checked before you start out. (mild command)

When the bell rings, please exit in an orderly fashion. (polite request)

They wondered whether the water was safe to drink. (indirect question)

### (2) Marking an Abbreviation

Use periods in most abbreviations.

Mr. Spock        Aug.        Dr. Dolittle
9 p.m.           etc.        1600 Pennsylvania Ave.

If an abbreviation ends the sentence, do not add another period:

He promised to be there at 6 a.m.

However, add a question mark if the sentence is a question:

Did he arrive at 6 p.m.?

If the abbreviation falls *within* a sentence, use normal punctuation after the period.

He promised to be there at 6 p.m. but he forgot.

## Abbreviations without periods

Abbreviations composed of all capital letters do not usually require periods unless they stand for initials of people's names (E.B. White).

MD      RN      BC

Familiar abbreviations of names of corporations or government agencies and abbreviations of scientific and technical terms do not require periods.

CD-ROM     NYU     DNA     EPA     HBO

**Acronyms**—new words formed from the initial letters or first few letters of a series of words—do not include periods.

modem     op-ed     scuba     radar
OSHA     AIDS     NAFTA     CAT scan

**Clipped forms** (commonly accepted shortened forms of words, such as *gym, dorm, math,* and *fax*) do not use periods.

**Postal abbreviations** do not include periods

TX     CA     MS     PA     FL     NY

## (3) Marking Divisions in Dramatic, Poetic, and Biblical References

Periods separate act, scene, and line numbers in plays; book and line numbers in long poems; and chapter and verse numbers in biblical references. (Do not space between the periods and the elements they separate.)

Dramatic Reference: *Hamlet* 2.2.1–5

Poetic Reference: *Paradise Lost* 7.163–67

Biblical Reference: *Judges* 4.14

## (4) Marking Divisions in Electronic Addresses

Periods, along with other punctuation marks (such as slashes and colons), are also used in electronic addresses (URLs).

http://kirsznermandell.heinle.com

**Note:** When you type a URL, do not end it with a period or add spaces after periods within the address.

# 28b   Using Question Marks

Writer's
Resource
CD-ROM

### (1) Marking the End of a Direct Question

Use a question mark to signal the end of a direct question.

Who was that masked man **?** (direct question)

"Is this a silver bullet **?**" they asked. (declarative sentence opening with a direct question)

### (2) Marking Questionable Dates and Numbers

Use a question mark in parentheses to indicate that a date or number is uncertain.

Aristophanes, the Greek playwright, was born in 448**(?)** BC and died in 380**(?)** BC.

### (3) Editing Misused Question Marks

Use a period, not a question mark, with an indirect question.

The personnel officer asked whether he knew how to type̶?̶.

Do not use a question mark to convey sarcasm. Instead, suggest your attitude through your choice or words.

not very

I refused his‸ generous ̶(̶?̶)̶ offer.

# 28c   Using Exclamation Points

Writer's
Resource
CD-ROM

Use an exclamation point to signal the end of an emotional or emphatic statement, an emphatic interjection, or a forceful command.

Remember the *Maine***!**

"No! Don't leave**!**" he cried.

---

**close∪P**

**Using exclamation points**

Except for recording dialogue, exclamation points are almost never appropriate in college writing. Even in informal writing, use exclamation points sparingly.

# Chapter 29

# Using Commas

## 29a  Setting Off Independent Clauses

Writer's
Resource
CD-ROM

See
A7

Use a comma when you form a compound sentence by linking two independent clauses with a **coordinating conjunction** or a pair of **correlative conjunctions**.

The House approved the bill, <u>but</u> the Senate rejected it.

<u>Either</u> the hard drive is full, <u>or</u> the modem is too slow.

**Note:** You may omit the comma if two clauses connected by a coordinating conjunction are very short: Love it or leave it.

See
Ch. 30

### Using commas

Use a **semicolon**—not a comma—to separate two independent clauses linked by a coordinating conjunction when at least one of the clauses already contains a comma or when the clauses are especially complex.

## 29b  Setting Off Items in a Series

Writer's
Resource
CD-ROM

Use commas between items in a series of three or more **coordinate elements** (words, phrases, or clauses joined by a coordinating conjunction).

*Chipmunk*, *raccoon*, and *Mugwump* are Native American words.

You may pay <u>by check</u>, <u>with a credit card</u>, or <u>in cash</u>.
<u>Brazilians speak Portuguese</u>, <u>Colombians speak Spanish</u>, and <u>Haitians speak French and Creole</u>.

**?**

**Note:** To avoid ambiguity, always use a comma before the coordinating conjunction that separates the last two items in a series.

The party was made special by the company, the light from the hundreds of twinkling candles⁄and the enormous piñata.

Do not use a comma to introduce or to close a series.

Three important criteria are⁄fat content, salt content, and taste.

The provinces Quebec, Ontario, and Alberta⁄are in Canada.

**Note:** If a phrase or clause in a **series** already contains commas, separate the items with semicolons.

See
30b

Use a comma between items in a series of two or more **coordinate adjectives**—adjectives that modify the same word or word group—unless they are joined by a conjunction.

She brushed her <u>long</u> <u>shining</u> hair.

The baby was <u>tired</u> and <u>cranky</u> and <u>wet</u>. (no comma required)

> **✓checklist Punctuating adjectives in a series**
>
> ✓ If you can reverse the order of the adjectives or insert *and* between the adjectives without changing the meaning, the adjectives are coordinate, and you should use a comma.
>
> She brushed her <u>long</u> <u>shining</u> hair.
>
> She brushed her <u>shining</u> <u>long</u> hair.
>
> She brushed her <u>long</u> [and] <u>shining</u> hair.
>
> ✓ If you cannot reverse the order of the adjectives or insert *and*, the adjectives are not coordinate, and you should not use a comma.
>
> <u>Ten red</u> balloons fell from the ceiling.
>
> <u>Red ten</u> balloons fell from the ceiling.
>
> <u>Ten</u> [and] <u>red</u> balloons fell from the ceiling.
>
> NOTE: Numbers—such as *ten*—are not coordinate with other adjectives.

**ESL Note:** For more information on the correct order of **adjectives in a series**, see **47d2**.

## 29c   Setting Off Introductory Elements

### (1) Dependent Clauses

An introductory dependent clause is generally set off from the rest of the sentence by a comma.

Although the CIA used to call undercover agents *penetration agents*, they now routinely refer to them as *moles*.

If the dependent clause is short and designates time, you may omit the comma—provided the sentence will be clear without it.

When I exercise I drink plenty of water.

**Note:** Do not use a comma to set off a dependent clause at the *end* of a sentence.

### (2) Verbal and Prepositional Phrases

Introductory verbal and prepositional phrases are usually set off by commas.

Thinking this might be his last chance, Scott struggled toward the South Pole. (participial phrase)

To write well, one must read a lot. (infinitive phrase)

During the Depression, movie attendance rose. (prepositional phrase)

If the introductory phrase is short and no ambiguity is possible, you may omit the comma.

After the exam I took a four-hour nap.

**Using commas**

Verbal phrases that serve as subjects are *not* set off by commas.

Laughing out loud can release tension. (gerund phrase)

To know him is to love him. (infinitive phrase)

### (3) Transitional Words and Phrases

When a __transitional word or phrase__ begins a sentence, it is usually set off with a comma.

See 3b2

<u>However</u>, any plan that is enacted must be fair.

<u>In other words</u>, we cannot act hastily.

## 29d   Setting Off Nonessential Material

Writer's
Resource
CD-ROM

Use commas to set off nonessential material whether it appears at the beginning, in the middle, or at the end of a sentence.

### (1) Nonrestrictive Modifiers

Use commas to set off **nonrestrictive modifiers,** which supply information that is not essential to the meaning of the word or word group they modify. (Do *not* use commas to set off **restrictive modifiers,** which supply information essential to the meaning of the word or word group they modify.)

Nonrestrictive (commas required): Actors, <u>who have inflated egos</u>, are often insecure. (*All* actors—not just those with inflated egos—are insecure.)

Restrictive (no commas): Actors <u>who have inflated egos</u> are often insecure. (Only those actors with inflated egos—not all actors—are insecure.)

In the following examples, commas set off only nonrestrictive modifiers—those that supply nonessential information—never restrictive modifiers, which supply essential information.

*Adjective Clauses*

Restrictive:  Speaking in public is something <u>that most people fear.</u>
Nonrestrictive:  He ran for the bus, <u>which was late as usual.</u>

*Prepositional Phrases*

Restrictive:  The man <u>with the gun</u> demanded their money.
Nonrestrictive:  The clerk, <u>with a nod,</u> dismissed me.

*Verbal Phrases*

Restrictive: The candidates <u>running for mayor</u> have agreed to a debate.

Nonrestrictive: The marathoner, <u>running his fastest,</u> beat his previous record.

*Appositives*

Restrictive: The film <u>*Citizen Kane*</u> made Orson Welles famous.

Nonrestrictive: *Citizen Kane,* <u>Orson Welles's first film,</u> made him famous.

---

### ✓checklist  Restrictive and nonrestrictive modifiers

To determine whether a modifier is restrictive or nonrestrictive, ask these questions:

✓ Is the modifier essential to the meaning of the noun it modifies (*The man <u>with the gun</u>,* not just any man)? If so, it is restrictive and does not take commas.

✓ Is the modifier introduced by *that* (*something <u>that most people fear</u>*)? If so, it is restrictive. *That* cannot introduce a nonrestrictive clause.

✓ Can you delete the relative pronoun without causing ambiguity or confusion (*something <u>[that] most people fear</u>*)? If so, the clause is restrictive.

✓ Is the appositive more specific than the noun that precedes it (*the film <u>Citizen Kane</u>*)? If so, it is restrictive.

---

### ⌐close**UP**

**?**  **Using commas with *that* and *which***

*That* introduces only restrictive clauses.

I bought a used car <u>that</u> cost $2,000.

*Which* introduces both restrictive and nonrestrictive clauses.

Restrictive: I bought a used car <u>which</u> cost $2,000.

Nonrestrictive: The used car I bought, <u>which</u> cost $2,000, broke down after a week.

Many writers, however, prefer to use *which* only to introduce nonrestrictive clauses.

## (2) Transitional Words and Phrases

See 3b2

<u>Transitional words and phrases</u>—which include conjunctive adverbs like *however, therefore, thus,* and *nevertheless* as well as expressions like *for example* and *on the other hand*—qualify, clarify, and make connections. However, they are not essential to meaning. For this reason, they are always set off by commas when they interrupt or come at the end of a clause (as well as when they begin a sentence).

The Outward Bound program, <u>for example,</u> is extremely safe.

Other programs are not so safe, <u>however.</u>

### Transitional words and phrases

When a transitional word or phrase joins two independent clauses, it must be preceded by a semicolon and followed by a comma.

Laughter is the best medicine; <u>of course,</u> penicillin also comes in handy sometimes.

## (3) Contradictory Phrases and Absolute Phrases

A phrase that expresses contradiction is usually set off by commas.

This medicine is taken after meals, <u>never on an empty stomach.</u>

Mark McGwire, <u>not Sammy Sosa,</u> was the first to break Roger Maris's home run record.

An **absolute phrase,** which usually consists of a noun plus a participle, is always set off by commas from the sentence it modifies.

<u>His fear increasing,</u> he waited to enter the haunted house.

Many soldiers were lost in Southeast Asia, <u>their bodies never recovered.</u>

## (4) Miscellaneous Nonessential Elements

Other nonessential elements usually set off by commas include tag questions, names in direct address, mild interjections, and *yes* and *no.*

This is your first day on the job, isn't it?

I wonder, Mr. Honeywell, whether Mr. Albright deserves a raise.

Well, it's about time.

Yes, we have no bananas.

Writer's
Resource
CD-ROM

# 29e Using Commas in Other Conventional Contexts

## (1) With Direct Quotations

In most cases, use commas to set off a direct quotation from the **identifying tag** (*he said, she answered,* and so on).

Emerson said, "I greet you at the beginning of a great career."

"I greet you at the beginning of a great career," Emerson said.

"I greet you," Emerson said, "at the beginning of a great career."

When the identifying tag comes between two complete sentences, however, the tag is introduced by a comma but followed by a period.

"Winning isn't everything," Vince Lombardi said. "It's the only thing."

If the first sentence of an interrupted quotation ends with a question mark or exclamation point, do not use commas.

"Should we hold the front page?" she asked. "It's a slow news day."

"Hold the front page!" he cried. "There's breaking news!"

## (2) With Titles or Degrees Following a Name

Hamlet, Prince of Denmark, is Shakespeare's most famous character.

Michael Crichton, MD, wrote *Jurassic Park.*

### (3) In Addresses and Dates

When a date or address falls within a sentence, a comma follows the last element. No comma separates the street number from the street or the state name from the zip code.

Her address is 600 West End Avenue, New York, NY 10024.

On August 30, 1983, the space shuttle *Challenger* was launched.

**Note:** When only the month and year are given, no commas are used (August 1983).

## 29f Using Commas to Prevent Misreading

In some cases, you must use a comma to avoid ambiguity. For example, consider the following sentence:

Those who can, sprint the final lap.

Without the comma, *can* appears to be an auxiliary verb ("Those who can sprint. . . ."), and the sentence seems incomplete. The comma tells readers to pause, thereby preventing confusion.

Also use a comma to acknowledge the omission of a repeated word, usually a verb, and to separate words repeated consecutively.

Pam carried the box; Tim, the suitcase.

Everything bad that could have happened, happened.

## 29g Editing Misused Commas

Writer's
Resource
CD-ROM

Do not use commas in the following situations.

### (1) To Set Off Restrictive Modifiers

Commas are used to set off **nonrestrictive modifiers** only. Do not use commas to set off restrictive elements.

See
29d1

The film, *Malcolm X*, was directed by Spike Lee.

They planned a picnic, in the park.

## (2) Between Inseparable Grammatical Constructions

Do not place a comma between grammatical elements that cannot be logically separated: a subject and its predicate, a verb and its complement or direct object, a preposition and its object, or an adjective and the word or phrase it modifies.

A woman with dark red hair, opened the door. (comma incorrectly placed between subject and predicate)

Louis Braille developed, an alphabet of raised dots for the blind. (comma incorrectly placed between verb and object)

They relaxed somewhat during, the last part of the obstacle course. (comma incorrectly placed between preposition and object)

Wind-dispersed weeds include the well-known and plentiful, dandelions, milkweed, and thistle. (comma incorrectly placed between adjective and words it modifies)

## (3) Between a Verb and an Indirect Quotation or Indirect Question

Do not use commas between verbs and indirect quotations or indirect questions.

General Douglas MacArthur vowed, that he would return. (comma incorrectly placed between verb and indirect quotation)

The landlord asked, if we would sign a two-year lease. (comma incorrectly placed between verb and indirect question)

## (4) In Compounds That Are Not Composed of Independent Clauses

Do not use commas before coordinating conjuctions like *and* and *but* when they join two elements of a compound subject, predicate, object, or complement.

During the 1400s plagues, and pestilence were common. (compound subject)

Many women thirty-five and older are returning to college, and tend to be good students. (compound predicate)

Mattel has marketed a lab coat̷and an astronaut suit for its Barbie doll. (compound object)

People buy bottled water because it is pure, and fashionable. (compound complement)

## (5) Before a Dependent Clause at the End of a Sentence

A comma is not generally used before a dependent clause that falls at the end of a sentence.

Jane Addams founded Hull House̷because she wanted to help Chicago's poor.

# Chapter 30

# Using Semicolons

**?** The semicolon is used only between items of equal grammatical rank: two independent clauses, two phrases, and so on.

Writer's
Resource
CD-ROM

## 30a Separating Independent Clauses

Use a semicolon between closely related independent clauses that convey parallel or contrasting information but are not joined by a coordinating conjunction.

> Paul Revere's *The Boston Massacre* is traditional American protest art; Edward Hicks's paintings are socially conscious art with a religious strain.

See
Ch. 14

### Using semicolons

Using only a comma or no punctuation at all between independent clauses creates a <u>comma splice</u> or <u>fused sentence</u>.

Use a semicolon before a transitional word or phrase that joins two independent clauses (the transitional element is followed by a comma).

> Thomas Jefferson brought two hundred vanilla beans and a recipe for vanilla ice cream back from France; <u>thus</u>, he gave America its all-time favorite ice cream flavor.

Writer's
Resource
CD-ROM

## 30b Separating Items in a Series

Use semicolons between items in a series when one or more of these items include commas.

As ballooning became established, a series of firsts ensued: The first balloonist in the United States was 13-year-old Edward Warren, 1784; the first woman aeronaut was a Madame Thible who, depending on your source, either recited poetry or sang as she lifted off; the first airmail letter, written by Ben Franklin's grandson, was carried by balloon; and the first bird's-eye photograph of Paris was taken by a balloon.

(Elaine B. Steiner, *Games*)

Laramie, Wyoming; Wyoming, Delaware; and Delaware, Ohio, were three of the places they visited.

## 30c Editing Misused Semicolons

Do not use semicolons in the following situations.

Writer's
Resource
CD-ROM

### (1) Between a Phrase and a Clause

Use a comma, not a semicolon, between a phrase and a clause.

Increasing rapidly, computer crime poses a challenge for government, financial, and military agencies.

### (2) Between a Dependent and an Independent Clause

Use a comma, not a semicolon, between a dependent and an independent clause.

Because drugs can now suppress the body's immune reaction, fewer organ transplants are rejected.

### (3) To Introduce a List

Use a colon, not a semicolon, to introduce a list.

Despite the presence of CNN and Fox News, the evening news remains a battleground for the four major television networks: CBS, NBC, ABC, and Fox.

**?**

See
33a1

### (4) To Introduce a Quotation

Do not use a semicolon to introduce a quotation.

Marie Antoinette may not have said, "Let them eat cake."

393

# Chapter 31

# Using Apostrophes

Use an apostrophe to form the possessive case, to indicate omissions in contractions, and to form certain plurals.

## 31a Forming the Possessive Case

Writer's
Resource
CD-ROM

The possessive case indicates ownership. In English, the possessive case of nouns and indefinite pronouns is indicated either with a phrase that includes the word *of* (the hands *of* the clock) or with an apostrophe and, in most cases, an *s* (the clock's hands).

### (1) Singular Nouns and Indefinite Pronouns

To form the possessive case of singular nouns and indefinite pronouns, add *'s*.

"The Monk's Tale" is one of Chaucer's *Canterbury Tales*.

When we would arrive was anyone's guess.

### ? (2) Singular Nouns Ending in *-s*

To form the possessive case of singular nouns that end in *-s*, add *'s* in most cases.

Reading Henry James's *The Ambassadors* was not Maris's idea of fun.

**Note:** With some singular nouns that end in *-s*, pronouncing the possessive ending as a separate syllable can sound awkward. In such cases, it is acceptable to use just an apostrophe: Crispus Attucks' death, Aristophanes' *Lysistrata*.

### ? (3) Plural nouns

To form the possessive case of regular plural nouns (those that end in *-s* or *-es*), add only an apostrophe.

Laid-off employees received two weeks' severance pay and three months' medical benefits.

## Forming the Possessive Case

The Lopezes' three children are triplets.

To form the possessive case of nouns that have irregular plurals, add *'s*.

*The Children's Hour* is a play by Lillian Hellman.

### (4) Compound Nouns or Groups of Words

To form the possessive case of compound words or of groups of words, add *'s* to the last word.

the secretary of state's resignation        someone else's responsibility

### (5) Two or More Items

To indicate individual ownership of two or more items, add *'s* to each item.

Ernest Hemingway's and Gertrude Stein's writing styles have some similarities.

To indicate joint ownership, add *'s* only to the last item.

We studied Lewis and Clark's expedition.

### Apostrophes with plural nouns and personal pronouns

- Do not use apostrophes with plural nouns that are not possessive.

  The Thompson's are out.

  Down vest's are warm.

  The Philadelphia Seventy-Sixer's have had good years and bad.

- Do not use apostrophes to form the possessive case of personal pronouns.

  This ticket must be your's or her's.

  The next turn is their's.

  The doll had lost it's right eye.

  The next great moment in history is our's.

*continued on the following page*

*continued from the previous page*

See
31b1

**?**

Note: Be careful not to confuse <u>contractions</u> (which always include apostrophes) with the possessive forms of personal pronouns (which never include apostrophes).

| **Contraction** | **Possessive Form** |
|---|---|
| <u>Who's</u> on first? | <u>Whose</u> book is this? |
| <u>They're</u> playing our song. | <u>Their</u> team is winning. |
| <u>It's</u> raining. | <u>Its</u> paws were muddy. |
| <u>You're</u> a real pal. | <u>Your</u> résumé is very impressive. |

Writer's
Resource
CD-ROM

# 31b  Indicating Omissions in Contractions

### (1) Omitted Letters

Apostrophes replace omitted letters in contractions that combine a pronoun and a verb (*he + will = he'll*) or the elements of a verb phrase (*do + not = don't*).

---

**FREQUENTLY USED CONTRACTIONS**

| | |
|---|---|
| it's (it is) | let's (let us) |
| we've (we have) | isn't (is not) |
| who's (who is, who has) | you'd (you would) |
| they're (they are) | wouldn't (would not) |
| we'll (we will) | don't (do not) |
| I'm (I am) | won't (will not) |

NOTE: Contractions are generally not used in college writing.

---

### (2) Omitted Numbers

In informal writing, an apostrophe may also be used to represent the century in a year: Class of '03, the '60s. In college writing, however, write out the number in full: 2003, 1960s.

# 31c   Forming Plurals

In a few special situations, add *'s* to form plurals.

> ## FORMING PLURALS WITH APOSTROPHES
>
> **Plurals of Letters**
> The Italian language has no *f*'s or *k*'s.
>
> **Plurals of Words Referred to as Words**
> The supervisor would accept no *if*'s, *and*'s, or *but*'s.
>
> Note: <u>Elements spoken of as themselves</u> (letters, numerals, or words) are set in italic type; the plural ending, however, is not.

See
36c

# Chapter 32

# Using Quotation Marks

Use quotation marks to set off brief passages of quoted speech or writing, to set off titles, and to set off words used in special ways. Do not use quotation marks when quoting long passages of prose or poetry.

## 32a   Setting Off Quoted Speech or Writing

When you quote a word, phrase, or brief passage of someone's speech or writing, enclose the quoted material in a pair of quotation marks.

> Gloria Steinem observed, "We are becoming the men we once hoped to marry."

> Galsworthy describes Aunt Juley as "prostrated by the blow" (329). (Note that in this example from a student paper, the end punctuation follows the parenthetical documentation.)

### Using quotation marks with dialogue

When you record **dialogue** (conversation between two or more people), enclose the quoted words in quotation marks. Begin a new paragraph each time a new speaker is introduced.

When you are quoting several paragraphs of dialogue by one speaker, begin each new paragraph with quotation marks. However, use closing quotation marks only at the end of the *entire quoted passage,* not at the end of each paragraph.

Special rules govern the punctuation of a quotation when it is used with an **identifying tag,** a phrase (such as *he said*) that identifies the speaker or writer. Punctuation guidelines for various situations involving identifying tags are outlined below.

## Setting Off Quoted Speech or Writing

### (1) Identifying Tag in the Middle of a Quoted Passage

Use a pair of commas to set off an identifying tag that interrupts a quoted passage.

"In the future," pop artist Andy Warhol once said, "everyone will be world famous for fifteen minutes."

If the identifying tag follows a completed sentence but the quoted passage continues, use a period after the tag, and begin the new sentence with a capital letter and quotation marks.

"Be careful," Erin warned. "Reptiles can be tricky."

### (2) Identifying Tag at the Beginning of a Quoted Passage

Use a comma after an identifying tag that introduces quoted speech or writing.

The Raven repeated, "Nevermore."

Use a **colon** instead of a comma before a quotation if the identifying tag is a complete sentence.

See 33a3

She gave her final answer: "No."

### (3) Identifying Tag at the End of a Quoted Passage

Use a comma to set off a quotation from an identifying tag that follows it.

"Be careful out there," the sergeant warned.

If the quotation ends with a question mark or an exclamation point, use that punctuation mark instead of the comma. In this situation, the tag begins with a lowercase letter even though it follows end punctuation.

"Is Ankara the capital of Turkey ?" she asked.

"Oh, boy !" he cried.

**Note:** Commas and periods are always placed *inside* quotation marks. For information on placement of other punctuation marks with quotation marks, **see 32e.**

# 32b Setting Off Long Prose Passages and Poetry

Writer's
Resource
CD-ROM

## (1) Long Prose Passages

Do not enclose a **long prose passage** (a passage of more than four lines) in quotation marks. Instead, set it off by indenting the entire passage one inch (or ten spaces) from the left-hand margin. Double-space above and below the quoted passage, and double-space between lines within it. Introduce the passage with a colon.

The following portrait of Aunt Juley illustrates several of the devices Galsworthy uses throughout <u>The Forsyte Saga,</u> such as a journalistic detachment that is almost cruel in its scrutiny, a subtle sense of the grotesque, and an ironic stance:

> Aunt Juley stayed in her room, prostrated by the blow. Her face, discoloured by tears, was divided into compartments by the little ridges of pouting flesh which had swollen with emotion. . . . At fixed intervals she went to her drawer, and took from beneath the lavender bags a fresh pocket-handkerchief. Her warm heart could not bear the thought that Ann was lying there so cold. (329)

Many similar portraits of characters appear throughout the novel.

### Quoting long prose passages

When you quote a long prose passage that is a single paragraph, do not indent the first line. When quoting two or more paragraphs, however, indent the first line of each paragraph (including the first) *three* additional spaces. If the first sentence of the quoted passage does not begin a paragraph in the source, do not indent it—but do indent the first line of each subsequent paragraph. If the passage you are quoting includes material set in quotation marks, keep the quotation marks.

**Note:** With long prose passages, parenthetical documentation is placed one space *after* the end punctuation. (With short prose passages, parenthetical documentation goes *before* the end punctuation.)

## (2) Poetry

Treat one line of poetry like a short prose passage: enclose it in quotation marks, and run it into the text. If you quote two or three lines of poetry, separate the lines with **slashes,** and run the quotation into the text. (Leave one space before and one space after the slash.)

> Alexander Pope writes, "True Ease in Writing comes from Art, not Chance, / As those move easiest who have learned to dance."

If you quote more than three lines of poetry, set them off like a **long prose passage**. (For special emphasis, you may set off fewer lines in this manner.) Be sure to reproduce punctuation, spelling, capitalization, and indentation of the quoted lines *exactly* as they appear in the poem.

See 32b1

> Wilfred Owen, a poet who was killed in action in World War I, expressed the
> horrors of war with vivid imagery:
>
>> Bent double, like old beggars under sacks.
>>
>> Knock-kneed, coughing like hags, we cursed through sludge.
>>
>> Till on the haunting flares we turned our backs
>>
>> And towards our distant rest began to trudge. (1–4)

## 32c  Setting Off Titles

<u>Titles</u> of short works and titles of parts of long works are enclosed in quotation marks. Other titles are italicized.

See 36a

**Note:** MLA style recommends underlining to indicate italics.

### TITLES REQUIRING QUOTATION MARKS

**Articles in Magazines, Newspapers, and Professional Journals**
"Why Johnny Can't Write" (*Newsweek*)
**Essays, Short Stories, Short Poems, and Songs**
"Fenimore Cooper's Literary Offenses"
"Flying Home"

*continued on the following page*

*continued from the previous page*

"The Road Not Taken"
"The Star-Spangled Banner"

**Chapters or Sections of Books**

"Miss Sharp Begins to Make Friends" (Chapter 10 of *Vanity Fair*)

**Episodes of Radio or Television Series**

"Lucy Goes to the Hospital" (*I Love Lucy*)

## 32d Setting Off Words Used in Special Ways

Enclose a word used in a special or unusual way in quotation marks. (If you use *so-called* before the word, do not use quotation marks as well.)

It was clear that adults approved of children who were "readers," but it was not at all clear why this was so.
(Annie Dillard, *New York Times Magazine*)

Also enclose a **coinage**—an invented word—in quotation marks.

After the twins were born, the minivan became a "babymobile."

## 32e Using Quotation Marks with Other Punctuation

**Writer's Resource CD-ROM**

Place quotation marks *after* the comma or period at the end of a quotation.

Many, like the poet Robert Frost, think about "the road not taken," but not many have taken "the one less traveled by."

Place quotation marks *before* a semicolon or colon at the end of a quotation.

Students who do not pass the test receive "certificates of completion"; those who pass are awarded diplomas.

Taxpayers were pleased with the first of the candidate's promised "sweeping new reforms": a balanced budget.

If a question mark, exclamation point, or dash is part of the quotation, place the quotation marks *after* the punctuation.

"Who's there?" she demanded.

"Stop!" he cried.

"Should we leave now, or—" Vicki paused, unable to continue.

If a question mark, exclamation point, or dash is *not* part of the quotation, place the quotation marks *before* the punctuation.

Did you finish reading "The Black Cat"?

Whatever you do, don't yell "Uncle"!

The first story—Updike's "A & P"—provoked discussion.

**Quotations within quotations**

Use *single* quotation marks to enclose a quotation within a quotation.

> Claire noted, "Liberace always said, 'I cried all the way to the bank.' "

Also use single quotation marks within a quotation to indicate a title that would normally be enclosed in double quotation marks.

> I think what she said was, "Play it, Sam. Play 'As Time Goes By.' "

Use double quotation marks around quotations or titles within a <u>long prose passage</u>.

See
32b1

## 32f   Editing Misused Quotation Marks

Writer's
Resource
CD-ROM

Do not use quotation marks in the following situations.

### (1) To Set Off Indirect Quotations

Quotation marks should not be used to set off **indirect quotations** (someone else's written or spoken words that are not quoted exactly).

Freud wondered ~~"~~what women wanted.~~"~~

## (2) To Set Off Slang or Technical Terms

Do not use quotation marks to set off slang or technical terms. (Note that slang is not appropriate in college writing.)

Dawn is "into" running.

"Biofeedback" is sometimes used to treat migraines.

### Titles of your own papers

Do not use quotation marks (or italics) to set off the title of your own paper.

# Chapter 33

# Using Other Punctuation Marks

## 33a Using Colons

Writer's
Resource
CD-ROM

The **colon** is a strong punctuation mark that points readers ahead to the rest of the sentence. When a colon introduces a list or series, explanatory material, or a quotation, it must be preceded by a complete sentence.

### (1) Introducing Lists or Series

Use colons to set off lists or series, including those introduced by phrases like *the following* or *as follows.*

Waiting tables requires three skills: memory, speed, and balance.

### (2) Introducing Explanatory Material

Use colons to introduce material that explains, exemplifies, or summarizes. Frequently this material is presented in the form of an **appositive,** a word group that identifies or renames an adjacent noun or pronoun.

Diego Rivera painted a controversial mural: the one commissioned for Rockefeller Center in the 1930s.

She had one dream: to play professional basketball.

Sometimes a colon separates two independent clauses, the second illustrating or clarifying the first.

A *U.S. News & World Report* survey has revealed a surprising fact: Americans spend more time at shopping malls than anywhere else except at home and at work.

### Using colons

When a complete sentence follows a colon, the sentence may begin with either a capital or a lowercase letter. However, if the sentence is a quotation, the first word is always capitalized (unless it was not capitalized in the source).

### **(3) Introducing Quotations**

See
32b1

When you quote a <u>long prose passage</u>, always introduce it with a colon. Also use a colon before a short quotation when it is introduced by a complete independent clause.

With dignity, Bartleby repeated the words again: "I prefer not to."

---

#### OTHER CONVENTIONAL USES OF COLONS

**To Separate Titles from Subtitles**

*Family Installments: Memories of Growing Up Hispanic*

**To Separate Minutes from Hours**

6:15 a.m.

See
32b1

**After Salutations in <u>Business Letters</u>**

Dear Dr. Evans:

**To separate place of publication from name of publisher in a <u>works-cited list</u>**

See
10a2

Boston: Heinle, 2003.

---

### **(4) Editing Misused Colons**

Do not use colons after expressions such as *namely, for example, such as,* or *that is.*

The Eye Institute treats patients with a wide variety of conditions, such as: myopia, glaucoma, and cataracts.

Do not place colons between verbs and their objects or complements or between prepositions and their objects.

James Michener wrote: *Hawaii, Centennial, Space,* and *Poland.*

Hitler's armies marched through: the Netherlands, Belgium, and France.

##  33b   Using Dashes

Writer's
Resource
CD-ROM

### **(1) Setting Off Nonessential Material**

See
29d

Like commas, **dashes** can set off <u>nonessential material</u>, but unlike commas, dashes tend to call attention to the material they set off. Indicate a dash with two unspaced hyphens (which most word processing programs will convert to a dash).

For emphasis, you may use dashes to set off explanations, qualifications, examples, definitions, and appositives.

> Neither of the boys━both nine-year-olds━had any history of violence.

> Too many parents learn the dangers of swimming pools the hard way━after their toddler has drowned.

### (2) Introducing a Summary

Use a dash to introduce a statement that summarizes a list or series before it.

> "Study hard," "Respect your elders," "Don't talk with your mouth full"━Sharon had often heard her parents say these things.

### (3) Indicating an Interruption

In dialogue, a dash may indicate a hesitation or an unfinished thought.

> "I think━no, I know━this is the worst day of my life," Julie sighed.

### (4) Editing Overused Dashes

Because too many dashes can make a passage seem disorganized and out of control, do not overuse them.

> Registration was a nightmare. ~~most~~ Most of the courses I wanted to take—geology and conversational Spanish, for instance—met at inconvenient times━or were closed by the time I tried to sign up for them.

## 33c   Using Parentheses

### (1) Setting Off Nonessential Material

Use parentheses to enclose material that is relatively unimportant in a sentence—for example, material that expands, clarifies, illustrates, or supplements.

Writer's
Resource
CD-ROM

In some European countries (notably Sweden and France), high-quality day care is offered at little or no cost to parents.

When a complete sentence set off by parentheses falls within another sentence, it should not begin with a capital letter or end with a period.

The area is so cold (temperatures average in the low twenties) that it is virtually uninhabitable.

If the parenthetical sentence does *not* fall within another sentence, however, it must begin with a capital letter and end with appropriate punctuation.

The region is very cold. (Temperatures average in the low twenties.)

### (2) Using Parentheses in Other Situations

Use parentheses around letters and numbers that identify points on a list, dates, cross-references, and documentation.

All reports must include the following components: (1) an opening summary, (2) a background statement, and (3) a list of conclusions.

Russia defeated Sweden in the Great Northern War (1700–1721).

Other scholars also make this point (see p. 54).

One critic has called the novel "puerile" (Arvin 72).

**Note:** When one set of parentheses falls within another, use brackets in place of the inner set.

Writer's
Resource
CD-ROM

# 33d Using Brackets

### (1) Setting Off Comments within Quotations

Brackets within quotations tell readers that the enclosed words are yours and not those of your source. You can bracket an explanation, a clarification, a correction, or an opinion.

"Even at Princeton he [F. Scott Fitzgerald] felt like an outsider."

If a quotation contains an error, indicate that the error is not yours by following the error with the Latin word *sic* ("thus") in brackets.

"The octopuss [sic] is a cephalopod mollusk with eight arms."

**Using brackets to edit quotations**

Use brackets to indicate changes that you make in order to fit a quotation smoothly into your sentence.

See 9a1

### (2) Using Brackets in Place of Parentheses within Parentheses

Use brackets to indicate parentheses that fall within parentheses.

In her study of American education ( *The Troubled Crusade* [ New York: Basic, 1963 ] ), Diane Ravitch addresses issues like educational reforms and campus unrest.

## 33e  Using Slashes

Writer's Resource CD-ROM

### (1) Separating One Option from Another

The either/or fallacy is a common error in logic.

Writer/director M. Night Shyamalan spoke at the film festival.

Notice that in this case there is no space before or after the slash.

### (2) Separating Lines of Poetry Run into the Text

The poet James Schevill writes, "I study my defects / And learn how to perfect them."

In this case, leave one space before and one space after the slash.

## 33f  Using Ellipses

Writer's Resource CD-ROM

### (1) Indicating an Omission in Quoted Prose

Use an **ellipsis**—three *spaced* periods—to indicate you have omitted words from a prose quotation. (If you are not following MLA style, do not use brackets.) When deleting material from a

409

quotation, be very careful not to change the meaning of the original passage.

> Original: "When I was a young man, being anxious to distinguish myself, I was perpetually starting new propositions." (Samuel Johnson)
>
> With Omission: "When I was a young man, ... I was perpetually starting new propositions."

Note that when you delete words immediately after an internal punctuation mark (such as the comma in the above example), you retain the punctuation before the ellipsis.

When you delete material *at the end of a sentence,* place the sentence's period or other end punctuation before the ellipsis.

> According to humorist Dave Barry, "from outer space Europe appears to be shaped like a large ketchup stain. ..."

> Note: Never begin a quoted passage with an ellipsis.

### Deletion from Middle of One Sentence to End of Another
According to Donald Hall, "Everywhere one meets the idea that reading is an activity desirable in itself. ... People surround the idea of reading with piety and do not take into account the purpose of reading."

### Deletion from Middle of One Sentence to Middle of Another
"When I was a young man, ... I found that generally what was new was false." (Samuel Johnson)

An ellipsis in the middle of a quoted passage can indicate the omission of a word, a sentence or two, or even a whole paragraph or more.

> Note: If a quoted passage already contains ellipses, MLA recommends that you enclose your own ellipses in brackets to distinguish them from those that appear in the original quotation.

**Using ellipses**

If a quotation ending with an ellipsis is followed by parenthetical documentation, the final punctuation *follows* the documentation.
As Jarman argues, "Compromise was impossible ..." (161).

## (2) Indicating an Omission in Quoted Poetry

Use an ellipsis when you omit a word or phrase from a line of poetry. When you omit one or more lines of poetry, use a complete line of spaced periods.

Original:

Stitch! Stitch! Stitch!

In poverty, hunger, and dirt,

And still with a voice of dolorous pitch,

Would that its tone could reach the Rich,

She sang this "Song of the Shirt!"

(Thomas Hood)

With Omission:

Stitch! Stitch! Stitch!

In poverty, hunger, and dirt,

. . . . . . . . . . . . . . . . . . . . . . .

She sang this "Song of the Shirt!"

# PART 11

# Understanding Spelling
# and Mechanics

**34 Spelling    415**
    **34a**  Understanding Spelling and Pronunciation    415
    **34b**  Learning Spelling Rules    417

**35 Capitalization    421**
    **35a**  Capitalizing the First Word of a Sentence    421
    **35b**  Capitalizing Proper Nouns    421
    **35c**  Capitalizing Important Words in Titles    424
    **35d**  Capitalizing the Pronoun *I*, the Interjection *O*, and Other Single Letters in Special Constructions    424
    **35e**  Editing Misused Capitals    424

**36 Italics    426**
    **36a**  Setting Off Titles and Names    426
    **36b**  Setting Off Foreign Words and Phrases    427
    **36c**  Setting Off Elements Spoken of as Themselves and Terms Being Defined    427
    **36d**  Using Italics for Emphasis    428

**37 Hyphens    429**
    **37a**  Breaking a Word at the End of a Line    429
    **37b**  Dividing Compound Words    429

**38 Abbreviations    432**
    **38a**  Abbreviating Titles    432
    **38b**  Abbreviating Organization Names and Technical Terms    432
    **38c**  Abbreviating Dates, Times of Day, Temperatures, and Numbers    433
    **38d**  Editing Misused Abbreviations    433

**39 Numbers    436**
    **39a**  Spelled-Out Numbers versus Numerals    436
    **39b**  Conventional Uses of Numerals    437

# PART 11

## ? Frequently Asked Questions

### Chapter 34 Spelling 415
- Why is English spelling so hard? 415
- Do I still need to proofread if I run a spell check? 417
- Are there any spelling rules I can memorize? 417
- How do I find the correct spelling of a word if I don't know how to spell it? 420

### Chapter 35 Capitalization 421
- Is the first word of a line of poetry always capitalized? 421
- Are *east* and *west* capitalized? 422
- Are *black* and *white* capitalized when they refer to race? 423
- Which words in titles are not capitalized? 424
- Are the names of seasons capitalized? 425

### Chapter 36 Italics 426
- What kinds of titles are italicized? 426

### Chapter 37 Hyphens 429
- Should I use a hyphen to divide a URL at the end of a line? 429
- Where do I put the hyphen when I have to divide a compound noun? 429

### Chapter 38 Abbreviations 432
- Is it OK to use abbreviations for technical terms? 432
- Are abbreviations like *e.g.* and *etc.* acceptable in college writing? 434

### Chapter 39 Numbers 436
- When do I spell out a number, and when do I use a numeral? 436

> **URLs** *Visit the following sites for answers to more FAQs*
>
> **Spelling Test and Tips**
> *http://www.sentex.net/~mmcadams/spelling.html*
> **Steve Tripp's Capitalization Page + Exercises**
> *http://www.u-aizu.ac.jp/~tripp/cap.html*
> **Using Hyphens**
> *http://owl.english.purdue.edu/handouts/grammar/g_hyphen.html*
> **Abbreviations and Acronyms (U. Colorado)**
> *http://www.colorado.edu/Publications/styleguide/abbrev.html*
> **Steve Tripp's "Numbers in Formal English"**
> *http://www.u-aizu.ac.jp/~tripp/numbers.html*

# Chapter 34

# Spelling

Most people can spell even difficult words "almost" correctly; usually only a letter or two are wrong. For this reason, memorizing a few rules and their exceptions and learning the correct spelling of the most commonly misspelled words can make a big difference.

## 34a Understanding Spelling and Pronunciation

Because pronunciation in English often provides few clues to spelling, you must memorize the spellings of many words and use a dictionary or spell checker regularly.    **?**

### (1) Vowels in Unstressed Positions

Many unstressed vowels sound exactly alike. For instance, it is hard to tell from pronunciation alone that the *i* in *terrible* is not an *a*. In addition, the unstressed vowels *a*, *e*, and *i* are impossible to distinguish in the suffixes *-able* and *-ible*, *-ance* and *-ence*, and *-ant* and *-ent*.

| | | |
|---|---|---|
| comfort<u>able</u> | brilli<u>ance</u> | serv<u>ant</u> |
| compat<u>ible</u> | excell<u>ence</u> | independ<u>ent</u> |

### (2) Silent Letters

Some English words contain silent letters, such as the *b* in *climb* and the *t* in *mortgage*.

| | | |
|---|---|---|
| ais<u>l</u>e | depo<u>t</u> | <u>p</u>neumonia |
| clim<u>b</u> | k<u>n</u>ig<u>h</u>t | sil<u>h</u>ouette |
| condem<u>n</u> | mor<u>t</u>gage | sovereign |

## (3) Words That Are Often Pronounced Carelessly

Most of us pronounce words rather carelessly in everyday speech. Consequently, when spelling, we may leave out, add, or transpose letters.

| | | |
|---|---|---|
| candidate | library | recognize |
| environment | lightning | specific |
| February | nuclear | supposed to |
| government | perform | surprise |
| hundred | quantity | used to |

## (4) American and British Spellings

Some words are spelled one way in the United States and another way in Great Britain and the Commonwealth nations.

| American | British |
|---|---|
| color | colour |
| defense | defence |
| judgment | judgement |
| theater | theatre |
| toward | towards |
| traveled | travelled |

## (5) Homophones

**Homophones** are words—such as *accept* and *except*—that are pronounced alike but spelled differently.

| | |
|---|---|
| accept | to receive |
| except | other than |
| affect | to have an influence on (*verb*) |
| effect | result (*noun*); to cause (*verb*) |
| its | possessive of *it* |
| it's | contraction of *it is* |
| principal | most important (*adjective*); head of a school (*noun*) |
| principle | a basic truth; rule of conduct |

For a full list of these and other homophones, along with their meanings and sentences illustrating their use, **see Chapter 27,** "A Glossary of Usage."

**ESL Note:** For a list of commonly confused words that present challenges for ESL writers, **see 47h.**

## Spelling: one word or two?

Some words may be written as one word or two, depending on meaning.

*any way vs. anyway*
The early pioneers made the trip west *any way* they could.
It began to rain, but the game continued *anyway*.

*every day vs. everyday*
*Every day* brings new opportunities.
John thought of his birthday as an *everyday* event.

Other words are frequently misspelled because people are not sure whether they are one word or two.

| One Word | Two Words |
|----------|-----------|
| already | a lot |
| cannot | all right |
| classroom | even though |
| overweight | no one |

Consult a dictionary if you have any doubts about whether a word is written as one word or two.

http://kirsznermandell.heinle.com

**Running a spell check**
If you use a spell checker, remember that spell checkers will not identify a word that is spelled correctly but used incorrectly—*then* for *than* or *its* for *it's*, for example—or a typo that creates another word, such as *form* for *from*. For this reason, you need to proofread your papers even after you run a spell check.

# 34b Learning Spelling Rules

Writer's Resource CD-ROM

Memorizing a few reliable rules can help you overcome problems caused by the general inconsistency between pronunciation and spelling.

# Spelling

## (1) The *ie/ei* Combinations

Use *i* before *e* except after *c* or when pronounced *ay*, as in *neighbor.*

*I* BEFORE *E:* belief, chief, niece, friend
*EI* AFTER *C:* ceiling, deceit, receive
*EI* PRONOUNCED *AY:* weigh, freight, eight

**Exceptions:** *either, neither, foreign, leisure, weird,* and *seize.* In addition, if the *ie* combination is not pronounced as a unit, the rule does not apply: *atheist, science.*

## (2) Doubling Final Consonants

The only words that double their consonants before a suffix that begins with a vowel (*-ed* or *-ing*) are those that pass the following three tests:

1. They have one syllable or are stressed on the last syllable.
2. They contain only one vowel in the last syllable.
3. They end in a single consonant.

The word *tap* satisfies all three conditions: it has only one syllable, it contains only one vowel (*a*), and it ends in a single consonant (*p*). Therefore, the final consonant doubles before a suffix beginning with a vowel (*tapped, tapping*). The word *relent* meets only two of the three conditions: it is stressed on the last syllable, and it has one vowel in the last syllable, but it does not end in a single consonant. Therefore, its final consonant is not doubled (*relented, relenting*).

## (3) Silent *e* before a Suffix

When a suffix that begins with a consonant is added to a word ending in a silent *e*, the *e* is generally kept: *hope/hopeful; lame/lamely; bore/boredom.* **Exceptions:** *argument, truly, ninth, judgment,* and *acknowledgment.*

When a suffix that begins with a vowel is added to a word ending in a silent *e*, the *e* is generally dropped: *hope/hoping; trace/traced; grieve/grievance; love/lovable.* **Exceptions:** *changeable, noticeable,* and *courageous.*

## (4) *Y* before a Suffix

When a word ends in a consonant plus *y*, the *y* generally changes to an *i* when a suffix is added (beauty + ful = beautiful). The *y* is kept, however, when the suffix *-ing* is added (tally + ing = tallying) and in some one-syllable words (dry + ness = dryness).

When a word ends in a vowel plus *y*, the *y* is kept (joy + ful = joyful; employ + er = employer). **Exception:** day + ly = daily.

## (5) *Seed* Endings

Endings with the sound *seed* are nearly always spelled *cede*, as in *precede, intercede, concede,* and so on. The only exceptions are *supersede, exceed, proceed,* and *succeed.*

## (6) *-Able, -Ible*

If the root of a word is itself a word, the suffix *-able* is most commonly used. If the root of a word is not a word, the suffix *-ible* is most often used.

|              |              |
|--------------|--------------|
| *comfort*able | *compat*ible |
| *agree*able   | *incred*ible |
| *dry*able     | *plaus*ible  |

## (7) Plurals

Most nouns form plurals by adding *s: savage/savages, tortilla/tortillas, boat/boats.* There are, however, a number of exceptions.

***Words Ending in -f or -fe*** Some words ending in *-f* or *-fe* form plurals by changing the *f* to *v* and adding *es* or *s: life/lives, self/selves.* Others add just *s: belief/beliefs, safe/safes.* Words ending in *-ff* take *s* to form plurals: *tariff/tariffs.*

***Words Ending in -y*** Most words that end in a consonant followed by *y* form plurals by changing the *y* to *i* and adding *es: baby/babies.* **Exceptions:** proper nouns such as *Kennedys* (never *Kennedies*).

Words that end in a vowel followed by a *y* form plurals by adding *s: monkey/monkeys.*

*Words Ending in -o*   Words that end in a vowel followed by *o* form the plural by adding *s: radio/radios, stereo/stereos, zoo/zoos.* Most words that end in a consonant followed by *o* add *es* to form the plural: *tomato/tomatoes, hero/heroes.* **Exceptions:** *silo/silos, piano/pianos, memo/memos, soprano/sopranos.*

*Words Ending in -s, -ss, -sh, -ch, -x, and -z*   These words form plurals by adding *es: Jones/Joneses, mass/masses, rash/rashes, lunch/lunches, box/boxes, buzz/buzzes.* **Exceptions:** Some one-syllable words that end in -s or -z double their final consonants when forming plurals: *quiz/quizzes.*

*Compound Nouns*   **Compound nouns**—nouns formed from two or more words—usually form the plural with the last word in the compound construction: *welfare state/welfare states; snowball/snowballs.* However, where the first element of the compound noun is more important than the others, form the plural with the first element: *sister-in-law/sisters-in-law, attorney general/attorneys general, hole in one/holes in one.*

*Foreign Plurals*   Some words, especially those borrowed from Latin or Greek, keep their foreign plurals.

| Singular | Plural |
|---|---|
| basis | bases |
| criterion | criteria |
| datum | data |
| larva | larvae |
| medium | media |
| memorandum | memoranda |
| stimulus | stimuli |

**?**

http://kirsznermandell.heinle.com

**Spelling an unfamiliar word**

Most spell checkers have a "guess" function that enables you to check the spelling of a word you think you might have misspelled. You highlight the word in question, and the computer will generate a list of possible words.

# Chapter 35

# Capitalization

## 35a  Capitalizing the First Word of a Sentence

Writer's
Resource
CD-ROM

Capitalize the first word of a sentence, including a sentence of quoted speech or writing.

As Shakespeare wrote, "Who steals my purse steals trash."

Do not capitalize a sentence set off within another sentence by dashes or parentheses.

Finding the store closed—it was a holiday—they went home.

The candidates are Frank Lester and Jane Lester (they are not related).

Capitalization is optional when a complete sentence is introduced by a <u>colon</u>.

See
33a2

### close **UP**

**Using capital letters in poetry**     **?**

Remember that the first word of a line of poetry is generally capitalized. If the poet uses a lowercase letter to begin a line, however, follow that style when you quote the line.

## 35b  Capitalizing Proper Nouns

Writer's
Resource
CD-ROM

**Proper nouns**—the names of specific persons, places, or things—are capitalized, and so are adjectives formed from proper nouns.

### (1) Specific People's Names

Eleanor Roosevelt        Medgar Evers

Capitalize a title when it precedes a person's name (Senator Barbara Boxer) or is used instead of the name (Dad). Do not capitalize titles that *follow* names (Barbara Boxer, the senator from California) or those that refer to the general position, not the particular person who holds it (a stay-at-home dad).

You may, however, capitalize titles that indicate very high-ranking positions even when they are used alone or when they follow a name: the Pope; George W. Bush, President of the United States. Never capitalize a title denoting a family relationship when it follows an article or a possessive pronoun (an uncle, his mom).

Capitalize titles or abbreviations of academic degrees even when they follow a name: Dr. Benjamin Spock, Benjamin Spock, MD.

### (2) Names of Particular Structures, Special Events, Monuments, and So On

| | |
|---|---|
| the *Titanic* | the World Series |
| the Brooklyn Bridge | Mount Rushmore |

### (3) Places and Geographical Regions

| | |
|---|---|
| Saturn | the Straits of Magellan |
| Budapest | the Western Hemisphere |

**?** Capitalize *north, east, south,* and *west* when they denote particular geographical regions, but not when they designate directions.

There are more tornadoes in Kansas than in the East. (*East* refers to a specific region.)

Turn west at Broad Street and continue north to Market. (*West* and *north* refer to directions, not specific regions.)

### (4) Days of the Week, Months, and Holidays

| | |
|---|---|
| Saturday | Rosh Hashanah |
| January | Cinco de Mayo |

### (5) Historical Periods and Events, Documents, and Names of Legal Cases

| | |
|---|---|
| the Reformation | the Treaty of Versailles |
| the Battle of Gettysburg | *Brown v. Board of Education* |

### (6) Philosophic, Literary, and Artistic Movements

| | |
|---|---|
| Naturalism | Neoclassicism |
| Romanticism | Expressionism |

422

## (7) Races, Ethnic Groups, Nationalities, and Languages

African American      Korean
Latino/Latina         Dutch

**Note:** When the words *black* and *white* refer to races, they have traditionally not been capitalized. Current usage is divided on whether to capitalize *black*.

## (8) Religions and Their Followers; Sacred Books and Figures

Jews      the Talmud      Buddha
Islam     God             the Scriptures

## (9) Specific Organizations

the New York Yankees      the American Bar Association
the Democratic Party      the Anti-Defamation League

## (10) Businesses, Government Agencies, and Other Institutions

Congress                                Lincoln High School
the Environmental Protection Agency     the University of Maryland

## (11) Brand Names and Words Formed from Them

Coke      Astroturf      Rollerblades      Post-it

**Note:** Brand names that over long use have become synonymous with the product—for example, *nylon* and *aspirin*—are no longer capitalized. (Consult a dictionary to determine whether or not to capitalize a familiar brand name.)

## (12) Specific Academic Courses and Departments

Sociology 201      English Department

**Note:** Do not capitalize a general subject area (sociology, zoology) unless it is the name of a language (French).

## (13) Adjectives Formed from Proper Nouns

Keynesian economics      Elizabethan era
Freudian slip            Shakespearean sonnet

When words derived from proper nouns have lost their specialized meanings, do not capitalize them: *china bowl, french fries.*

## 35c Capitalizing Important Words in Titles

**?** In general, capitalize all words in titles with the exception of articles (*a, an,* and *the*), prepositions, coordinating conjunctions, and the *to* in infinitives. If an article, preposition, or coordinating conjunction is the *first* or *last* word in the title, however, do capitalize it.

The Declaration of Independence          *A Man and a Woman*
*Across the River and into the Trees*          *What Friends Are For*

## 35d Capitalizing the Pronoun *I*, the Interjection *O*, and Other Single Letters in Special Constructions

Always capitalize the pronoun *I*, even if it is part of a contraction (*I'm, I'll, I've*).
Always capitalize the interjection *O.*

Give us peace in our time, O Lord.

However, capitalize the interjection *oh* only when it begins a sentence.
Many other single letters are capitalized in certain usages. Check your dictionary to determine whether to use a capital letter.

an A in history          vitamin B
D day          C major

Writer's
Resource
CD-ROM

## 35e Editing Misused Capitals

Do not use capital letters for emphasis or as an attention-getting device. If you are not certain whether a word should be capitalized, consult your dictionary.

## (1) Seasons ?

Do not capitalize the names of the seasons—summer, fall, winter, spring—unless they are strongly personified, as in *Old Man Winter.*

## (2) Centuries and Loosely Defined Historical Periods

Do not capitalize the names of centuries or of general historical periods.

seventeenth-century poetry    the automobile age

Do, however, capitalize names of specific historical, anthropological, and geological periods.

the Renaissance    Iron Age    Paleozoic Era

## (3) Diseases and Other Medical Terms

Do not capitalize names of diseases or medical tests or conditions unless a proper noun is part of the name or unless the disease is an <u>acronym</u>.

See 28a2

| | | |
|---|---|---|
| smallpox | Apgar test | AIDS |
| Reye's syndrome | mumps | SIDS |

# Chapter 36

# Italics

Writer's Resource CD-ROM
See 32c

## 36a  Setting Off Titles and Names

Use italics for the categories of titles and names listed in the box below. All other titles are set off with **quotation marks**.

**?**  **TITLES AND NAMES SET IN ITALICS**

> **Books:** *David Copperfield, The Bluest Eye*
>
> **Newspapers:** the *Washington Post,* the *Philadelphia Inquirer*
>
> (According to MLA style, introductory articles are not italicized in titles of newspapers.)
>
> **Magazines and Journals:** *Rolling Stone, Scientific American*
>
> **Online Magazines and Journals:** *salon.com, theonion.com*
>
> **Web Sites or Home Pages:** *urbanlegends.com, movie-mistakes.com*
>
> **Pamphlets:** *Common Sense*
>
> **Films:** *Casablanca, Citizen Kane*
>
> **Television programs:** *60 Minutes, The Bachelor, Fear Factor*
>
> **Radio programs:** *All Things Considered, A Prairie Home Companion*
>
> **Long poems:** *John Brown's Body, The Faerie Queen*
>
> **Plays:** *Macbeth, A Raisin in the Sun*
>
> **Long musical works:** *Rigoletto, Eroica*
>
> **Software programs:** *Word, PowerPoint*
>
> **Paintings and sculpture:** *Guernica, Pietà*
>
> **Ships:** *Lusitania,* U.S.S. *Saratoga*
>
> (S.S. and U.S.S. are not italicized.)
>
> **Trains:** *City of New Orleans, The Orient Express*
>
> **Aircraft:** *The Hindenburg, Enola Gay*
>
> (Only particular aircraft, not makes or types such as Piper Cub or Boeing 757, are italicized.)
>
> **Spacecraft:** *Challenger, Enterprise*

**Sacred books and well-known documents**

Names of sacred books, such as the Bible and the Koran, and well-known documents, such as the Constitution and the Declaration of Independence, are neither italicized nor placed within quotation marks.

## 36b  Setting Off Foreign Words and Phrases

Writer's
Resource
CD-ROM

Italics are often used to set off foreign words and phrases that have not become part of the English language.

*"C'est la vie,"* Madeleine said when she saw the long line for the concert.

*Spirochaeta plicatilis* is a corkscrew-like bacterium.

If you are not sure whether a foreign word has been assimilated into English, consult a dictionary.

## 36c  Setting Off Elements Spoken of as Themselves and Terms Being Defined

Use italics to set off letters, numerals, and words that refer to the letters, numerals, and words themselves.

Is that a *p* or a *g*?

I forget the exact address, but I know it has a *3* in it.

Does *through* rhyme with *cough*?

Also use italics to set off words and phrases that you go on to define.

A *closet drama* is a play meant to be read, not performed.

**Note:** When you quote a dictionary definition, put the words you are defining in italics and the definition itself in quotation marks.

To *infer* means "to draw a conclusion"; to *imply* means "to suggest."

427

# 36d  Using Italics for Emphasis

Writer's
Resource
CD-ROM

Italics can occasionally be used for emphasis.

Initially, poetry might be defined as a kind of language that says *more* and says it *more intensely* than does ordinary language.
(Lawrence Perrine, *Sound and Sense*)

However, overuse of italics is distracting. Instead of italicizing, try to indicate emphasis with word choice and sentence structure

**Using italics**

MLA style recommends that you underline to indicate italics. However, you may italicize if your instructor prefers.

# Chapter 37

# Hyphens

**Hyphens** have two conventional uses: to break a word at the end of a line and to link words in certain compounds.

## 37a Breaking a Word at the End of a Line

A computer never breaks a word at the end of a line; if the full word will not fit, it is brought down to the next line. Sometimes, however, you will want to break a word with a hyphen—for example, to fill in space at the end of a line. When you break a word at the end of a line, divide it only between syllables, consulting a dictionary if necessary. Never divide a word at the end of a page, and never hyphenate one-syllable words. In addition, never leave a single letter at the end of a line or carry only one or two letters to the next line.

If you divide a **compound word** at the end of a line, put the hyphen between the elements of the compound (*snow-mobile*, not *snowmo-bile*).

See 37b

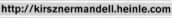

**http://kirsznermandell.heinle.com**

**Dividing electronic addresses (URLs)**

Do not insert a hyphen to divide an electronic address (URL) at the end of a line. (Readers might think the hyphen is part of the address.) MLA style requires that you break the URL at a slash. If this is not possible, break it in a logical place—after a period, for example—or avoid the problem entirely by moving the entire URL to the next line.

## 37b Dividing Compound Words

A **compound word** is composed of two or more words. Some familiar compound words are always hyphenated: *no-hitter, helter-skelter.* Other compounds are always written as one word: *fireplace, peacetime.*

Finally, some compounds are always written as two separate words: *labor relations, bunk bed.* Your dictionary can tell you whether a particular compound requires a hyphen.

Hyphens are generally used in the following compounds.

## (1) In Compound Adjectives

A **compound adjective** is a series of two or more words functioning together as an adjective. When a compound adjective *precedes* the noun it modifies, use hyphens to join its elements.

The research team tried to use <u>nineteenth-century</u> technology to design a <u>space-age</u> project.

When a compound adjective *follows* the noun it modifies, do not use hyphens to join its elements.

The three <u>government-operated</u> programs were run smoothly, but the one that was not <u>government operated</u> was short of funds.

**Note:** A compound adjective formed with an adverb ending in *-ly* is not hyphenated even when it precedes the noun.

Many <u>upwardly mobile</u> families are on tight budgets.

Use **suspended hyphens**—hyphens followed by a space or by appropriate punctuation and a space—in a series of compounds that modify the same word.

Graduates of <u>two-</u> and <u>four-year</u> colleges were eligible for the grants.

The exam called for <u>sentence-</u>, <u>paragraph-</u>, and <u>essay-length</u> answers.

## (2) With Certain Prefixes or Suffixes

Use a hyphen between a prefix and a proper noun or proper adjective.

mid-July   pre-Columbian

Use a hyphen to connect the prefixes *all-, ex-, half-, quarter-, quasi-,* and *self-* and the suffix *-elect* to a noun.

ex-senator   self-centered
quarter-moon  president-elect

**Note:** The words *selfhood, selfish,* and *selfless* do not include hyphens because in these cases, *self* is the root, not a prefix.

## (3) In Compound Numerals and Fractions

Hyphenate compounds that represent numbers below one hundred, even if they are part of a larger number.

the twenty-first century        three hundred sixty-five days

Also hyphenate the written form of a fraction when it modifies a noun.

a two-thirds share of the business

## (4) For Clarity

Hyphenate to prevent readers from misreading one word for another.

In order to reform criminals, we must re-form our ideas about prisons.

Hyphenate to avoid certain hard-to-read combinations, such as two *i*'s (*semi-illiterate*) or more than two of the same consonant (*shell-less*).

Hyphenate in most cases between a capital initial and a word when the two combine to form a compound: *A-frame, T-shirt.*

## (5) In Coined Compounds

A **coined compound,** one that uses a new combination of words as a unit, requires hyphens.

He looked up with a who-do-you-think-you-are expression.

# Chapter 38

# Abbreviations

Generally speaking, **abbreviations** are not appropriate in college writing except in tables, charts, and works-cited lists. Some abbreviations are acceptable in scientific, technical, or business writing, or only in a particular discipline. If you have questions about the appropriateness of a particular abbreviation, check the style manual of the field for which you are writing.

## 38a   Abbreviating Titles

Titles before and after proper names are usually abbreviated.

| | |
|---|---|
| Mr. Homer Simpson | Rep. Chaka Fattah |
| Henry Kissinger, PhD | Dr. Martin Luther King, Jr. |

Do not, however, use an abbreviated title without a name.

   doctor
The ~~Dr.~~ diagnosed hepatitis.

## 38b   Abbreviating Organization Names and Technical Terms

See 28a2

You may refer to well-known businesses and government, social, and civic organizations by capitalized initials. These **abbreviations** fall into two categories: those in which the initials are pronounced as separate units (MTV) and **acronyms,** in which the initials are pronounced as words (NATO).

You may also use accepted abbreviations for complex technical terms that are not well known, but be sure to spell out the full term the first time you mention it, followed by the abbreviation in parentheses.

Citrus farmers have been using ethylene dibromide (EDB), a chemical pesticide, for more than twenty years. Now, however, EDB has contaminated water supplies.

## 38c Abbreviating Dates, Times of Day, Temperatures, and Numbers

Writer's
Resource
CD-ROM

Dates, times of day, temperatures, and numbers are often abbreviated.

50 BC (BC follows the date)      AD 432 (AD precedes the date)
3:03 p.m.                        180° F (Fahrenheit)

Always capitalize BC and AD. (The alternatives BCE, for "before the Common Era," and CE, for "Common Era," are also capitalized.) The abbreviations a.m. and p.m. are used only when they are accompanied by numbers.

morning.
I'll see you in the ~~a.m.~~

Avoid the abbreviation *no.* except in technical writing, and then use it only before a specific number: *The unidentified substance was labeled no. 52.*

---

**close UP**

### Abbreviations in MLA documentation

See
10a

MLA documentation style requires abbreviations of publishers' company names—for example, *Columbia UP* for *Columbia University Press*—in the works-cited list. Do not, however, use such abbreviations in the body of your paper. MLA style also permits the use of abbreviations that designate parts of written works (*ch. 3, sec. 7*)—but only in the works-cited list and parenthetical documentation. These abbreviations should be spelled out in the text of your paper.

---

## 38d Editing Misused Abbreviations

Writer's
Resource
CD-ROM

In college writing, abbreviations are not used in the following cases.

### (1) Names of Days, Months, or Holidays

Do not abbreviate days of the week, months, or holidays.

Saturday, December          Christmas
On ~~Sat., Dec.~~ 23, I started my ~~Xmas~~ shopping.

## (2) Names of Streets and Places

In general, do not abbreviate names of streets and places.

Drive    New York City.
He lives on Riverside ~~Dr.~~ in ~~NYC~~

**Exceptions:** The abbreviation *US* is often acceptable (*US Coast Guard*), as is *DC* in *Washington, DC.* Also permissible are *Mt.* before the name of a mountain (*Mt. Etna*) and *St.* in a place name (*St. Albans*).

## (3) Names of Academic Subjects

Do not abbreviate names of academic subjects.

Psychology         literature
~~Psych.~~ and English ~~lit.~~ are required courses.

## (4) Names of Businesses

Write company names exactly as the firms themselves write them, including the distinction between the ampersand (&) and the word *and: Western Union Telegraph Company, Charles Schwab & Co., Inc.* Abbreviations for *company, corporation,* and the like are used only along with a company name.

corporation              company
The ~~corp.~~ merged with a ~~co.~~ in Ohio.

## (5) Latin Expressions

Abbreviations of the common Latin phrases *i.e.* ("that is"), *e.g.* ("for example"), and *etc.* ("and so forth") are not appropriate in college writing.

for example,
Other musicians (~~e.g.~~ Bruce Springsteen) have also been influenced by Bob Dylan.

and other poems.
Poe wrote "The Raven," "Annabel Lee," ~~etc.~~

## (6) Units of Measurement

In technical writing, some units of measurement are abbreviated when preceded by a numeral.

The hurricane had winds of 35 mph.

One new Honda gets over 50 mpg.

MLA style, however, requires that you write out units of measurement and spell out words such as *inches, feet, years, miles, pints, quarts,* and *gallons.*

## (7) Symbols

The symbols %, =, +, and # are acceptable in technical and scientific writing but not in nontechnical college writing. The symbol $ is acceptable before specific numbers ($15,000) but not as a substitute for the words *money* or *dollars.*

# Chapter 39

# Numbers

Convention determines when to use a **numeral** (22) and when to spell out a number (twenty-two). Numerals are commonly used in scientific and technical writing and in journalism, but they are used less often in the humanities.

**Note:** The guidelines in this chapter are based on the *MLA Handbook for Writers of Research Papers*, 6th ed. (2003). APA style, however, requires that all numbers below ten be spelled out if they do not represent specific measurements and that numbers ten and above be expressed in numerals.

Writer's
Resource
CD-ROM

## 39a   Spelled-Out Numbers versus Numerals

Unless a number falls into one of the categories listed in **39b**, spell it out if you can do so *in one or two words*.

The Hawaiian alphabet has only <u>twelve</u> letters.

Class size stabilized at <u>twenty-eight</u> students.

The subsidies are expected to total about <u>two</u> million dollars.

Numbers *more than two words* long are expressed in figures.

The dietitian prepared <u>125</u> sample menus.

The developer of the community purchased <u>300,000</u> doorknobs, <u>153,000</u> faucets, and <u>4,000</u> manhole covers.

**Note:** Numerals and spelled-out numbers should generally not be mixed in the same passage. For consistency, then, the number 4,000 in the preceding example is expressed in figures even though it could be written in just two words.

Never begin a sentence with a numeral. If necessary, reword the sentence.

**Faulty:**  250 students are currently enrolled in World History 106.

**Revised:**  Current enrollment in World History 106 is 250 students.

# 39b   Conventional Uses of Numerals

Writer's
Resource
CD-ROM

## (1) Addresses

111 Fifth Avenue, New York, NY 10003

## (2) Dates

January 15, 1929        1914–1919

## (3) Exact Times

9:16        10 a.m. (or 10:00 a.m.)

**Exceptions:** Spell out times of day when they are used with *o'clock: eleven o'clock,* not *11 o'clock.* Also spell out times expressed as round numbers: *They were in bed by ten.*

## (4) Exact Sums of Money

$25.11        $6,752.00

**Note:** You may spell out a round sum of money if you use sums infrequently in your paper, provided you can do so in two or three words.

five dollars        two thousand dollars

## (5) Divisions of Written Works

Use arabic (not roman) numerals for chapter and volume numbers; acts, scenes, and lines of plays; chapters and verses of the Bible; and line numbers of long poems.

## (6) Measurements before an Abbreviation or Symbol

12″        55 mph
32°        15 cc

## (7) Percentages, Decimals, and Fractions

80%        3.14        6¾

**Note:** You may spell out a percentage *(eighty percent)* if you use percentages infrequently in your paper, provided the percentage can be expressed in two or three words.

## (8) Ratios, Scores, and Statistics

Children preferred Fun Flakes over Graino by a ratio of 20 to 1.

The Orioles defeated the Phillies 6 to 0.

The median age of the voters was 42; the mean age was 40.

## (9) Identification Numbers

Route 66          Track 8          Channel 12

# PART 12

## College Survival Skills

**40 Ten Habits of Successful Students 441**
40a Learn to Manage Your Time Effectively 441
40b Put Studying First 442
40c Be Sure You Understand School and Course Requirements 443
40d Be an Active Learner in the Classroom 444
40e Be an Active Learner Outside the Classroom 444
40f Take Advantage of College Services 445
40g Use the Library 445
40h Use Technology 446
40i Make Contacts—and Use Them 446
40j Be a Lifelong Learner 447

**41 Developing Active Reading Skills 449**
41a Previewing 449
41b Highlighting 450
41c Annotating 450

**42 Writing Essay Exams 452**
42a Planning an Essay Exam Answer 452
42b Developing a Thesis and a List of Points 454
42c Writing and Revising an Essay Exam Answer 455
42d Sample Essay Exam Answer 456

**43 Writing about Literature 460**
43a Reading Literature 460
43b Writing about Literature 462
43c Sample Student Paper (without Sources) 464
43d Sample Student Paper (with Sources) 468

**44 Designing Documents and Web Sites 475**
44a Understanding Document Design 475
44b Designing a Web Site 485

**45 Writing for the Workplace 491**
45a Writing Business Letters 491
45b Writing Letters of Application 493
45c Designing Print Résumés 495
45d Designing Scannable Résumés 498
45e Writing Memos 500
45f Writing E-Mail 502

**46 Making Oral Presentations 504**
46a Getting Started 504
46b Planning Your Speech 505
46c Preparing Your Notes 506
46d Preparing Visual Aids 507
46e Rehearsing Your Speech 510
46f Delivering Your Speech 510

# PART 12

## ? Frequently Asked Questions

**Chapter 40  Ten Habits of Successful Students  441**
- What strategies can I use to help me manage my time?  441
- What is the best way to study?  442
- What college services can help me?  445

**Chapter 41  Developing Active Reading Skills  449**
- What kinds of highlighting symbols should I use?  450
- How do I take marginal notes?  450

**Chapter 42  Writing Essay Exams  452**
- How do I organize an essay exam answer?  454
- What should I look for when I reread my answer?  455
- What does an effective essay exam answer look like?  456

**Chapter 43  Writing about Literature  460**
- Do I put a title in quotation marks or underline it?  464
- What does a paper about literature look like?  466

**Chapter 44  Designing Documents and Web Sites  475**
- What is document design?  475
- Should I use headings in my paper?  477
- Should I use numbers or bullets when I make a list?  479
- What kind of visuals should I use in my paper?  480

**Chapter 45  Writing for the Workplace  491**
- How do I write a letter to apply for a job?  494
- What should a résumé look like?  496–497
- Should I post my résumé on a Web site?  498

**Chapter 46  Making Oral Presentations  504**
- What kind of notes should I use?  506
- Should I use visual aids?  507

**URLs**  *Visit the following sites for answers to more FAQs*

**The Reading Comprehension Page (Muskingum College)**
*http://muskingum.edu/~cal/database/reading.html#Strategies*
**Tips on Essay Exams (UNC)**
*http://www.unc.edu/depts/wcweb/handouts/essay-exams.html*
**Writing about Literature (The Citadel)**
*http://www.citadel.edu/citadel/otherserv/wctr/writinglit.html*
**A Beginner's Guide to HTML**
*http://www.ncsa.uiuc.edu/General/Internet/WWW/*
*HTMLPrimerAll.html*
**Cover Letter and Résumé Workshops (Purdue)**
*http://owl.english.purdue.edu/workshops/hypertext/coverletter/*
*index.html*

# Chapter 40

# Ten Habits of Successful Students

As you have probably already observed, the students who are most successful in school are not always the ones who enter with the best grades. In fact, successful students have *learned* to be successful: they have developed specific strategies for success, and they apply those strategies to their education. If you take the time, you too can learn the habits of successful students and apply them to your own college education—and, later on, to your career.

1. Successful students manage their time.
2. Successful students put studying first.
3. Successful students understand what is required of them.
4. Successful students are active learners in the classroom.
5. Successful students are active learners outside the classroom.
6. Successful students use college services.
7. Successful students use the library.
8. Successful students use technology.
9. Successful students make contacts.
10. Successful students are lifelong learners.

## 40a   Learn to Manage Your Time Effectively

One of the most difficult things about college is the demands it makes on your time. It is hard, especially at first, to balance studying, course work, family life, friendships, and a job. But if you do not take control of your schedule, it will take control of you; if you do not learn to manage your time, you will always be struggling to catch up.

Fortunately, there are two tools you can use to help you manage your time: a personal organizer and a calendar. Of course, simply buying an organizer and a calendar will not solve your time-management problems—you have to *use* them. Moreover, you have to use them effectively and regularly.

**?**

First of all, carry your organizer with you at all times, and post your calendar in a prominent place (perhaps above your desk or next to your phone). Then, remember to record *in both places* not only school-related deadlines, appointments, and reminders (every assignment due date, study group meeting, conference appointment, and exam) but also outside responsibilities like work hours and dental appointments. Record items as soon as you learn of them; if you do not write something down immediately, you are likely to forget it. (If you make an entry in your organizer while you are in class, be sure to copy it onto your calendar when you get back from school.)

You can also use your organizer to help you plan a study schedule. You do this by blocking out times to study or to complete assignment-related tasks—such as an Internet search for a research paper—in addition to appointments and deadlines. (It is a good idea to make these entries in pencil so you can adjust your schedule as new responsibilities arise.) If you have a schedule, you will be less likely to procrastinate—and therefore less likely to become overwhelmed.

The bottom line is this: your college years can be a very stressful time, but although some degree of stress is inevitable, it can be kept in check. If you are an organized person, you will be better able to handle the pressures of a college workload.

## 40b  Put Studying First

To be a successful student, you need to understand that studying is something you do *regularly*, not just right before an exam. You also need to know that studying does not mean memorizing facts; it means reading, rereading, and discussing ideas until you understand them.

To make studying a regular part of your day, set up a study space that includes everything you need (supplies, good light, a comfortable chair) and does not include anything you do not need (clutter, distractions). Then, set up a tentative study schedule. Try to designate at least two hours each day to complete assignments due right away, to work on those due later on, and to reread class notes. Then, when you have exams and papers to do, you can adjust your schedule accordingly.

Successful students often form study groups, and this is a strategy you should use whenever you can—particularly in a course you find challenging. A study group of four or five students who meet regularly (not just the night before an exam) can make studying more focused and effective as well as more enjoyable and less stressful. By discussing concepts with your classmates, you can try out your ideas and get feedback, clarify complex concepts, and formulate questions for your instructor.

## 40c Be Sure You Understand School and Course Requirements

To succeed in school, you need to know what is expected of you—and, if you are not sure, to ask.

When you first arrived at school, you probably received a variety of orientation materials—a student handbook, library handouts, and so on—that set forth the rules and policies of your school. Read these documents carefully (if you have not already done so), and be sure you understand what they ask of you. If you do not, ask your peer counselor or your adviser for clarification.

You also need to understand the specific requirements of each course you take. Education is a series of contracts between you and your instructors, and each course syllabus explains the terms of a particular contract. In a syllabus, you learn each instructor's policies about attendance and lateness, assignments and deadlines, plagiarism, and classroom etiquette. In addition, a syllabus may explain penalties for late assignments or missed quizzes, tell how much each assignment is worth, or note additional requirements, such as fieldwork or group projects. Requirements vary significantly from course to course, so read each syllabus very carefully—and also pay close attention to any supplementary handouts your instructors distribute.

As the semester progresses, your instructors will give you additional information about their expectations. For example, before an exam you will be told what material will be covered, how much time you will have to complete the test, and whether you will be expected to write an essay or fill in an answer sheet that will be graded electronically. When a paper is assigned, you may be given specific information not only about its content, length, and due date but also about its format (font size, line spacing, and margin width, for example). If your instructor does not give you this information, it is your responsibility to find out what is expected of you.

## 40d   Be an Active Learner in the Classroom

Education is not about sitting passively in class and waiting for information and ideas to be given to you. It is up to you to be an active participant in your own education.

First, take as many small classes as you can. These classes give you the opportunity to interact with other students and with your instructor. If a large course has recitation sections, be sure to attend these regularly, even if they are not required. Also be sure to take as many classes as possible that require writing. Good writing skills are essential to your success as a student, and you need all the practice you can get.

Take responsibility for your education by attending class regularly and arriving on time. Listen attentively, and take careful, complete notes. (Try to review these notes later with other students to make sure you have not missed anything important.) Do your homework on time, and keep up with the reading. When you read an assignment, apply the techniques of **active reading**, interacting with the text instead of just seeing what is on the page. If you have time, read beyond the assignment, looking on the Internet and in books, magazines, and newspapers for related information that interests you.

See
Ch. 41

As important as it is to listen and take notes in class, it is just as important (particularly in small classes and recitations) to participate in class discussions: to ask and answer questions, volunteer opinions, and give helpful feedback to other students. By participating in such discussions, you learn more about the subject matter being discussed, and you also learn to listen to other points of view, to test your ideas, and to respect the ideas of others.

## 40e   Be an Active Learner Outside the Classroom

Taking an active role in your education is also important outside the classroom. Do not be afraid to approach your instructors; take advantage of their office hours, and keep in touch with them by e-mail. Get to know your major adviser well, and be sure he or she knows who you are and where your academic interests lie. Make appointments, ask questions, explore possible solutions to problems: this is how you learn.

Participate in the life of your school. Read your school newspaper, check the Web site regularly, join clubs, and apply for internships. This participation in life outside the classroom can help you develop new interests and friendships as well as enhance your education.

Finally, participate in the life of your community. Take service learning courses, if they are offered at your school, or volunteer at a local school or social agency. As successful students know, education is more than just attending classes.

## 40f Take Advantage of College Services ?

Colleges and universities offer students a wide variety of support services. Most students will need help of one kind or another at some point during their college careers; if help is available, it makes sense to use it.

For example, if you are struggling with a particular course, you can go to the tutoring service offered by your school's academic support center or by an individual department. Often, the tutors are students who have done well in the course, and their perspective will be very helpful. If you need help with writing or revising a paper, you can make an appointment with the writing lab, where tutors will give you advice (but will *not* rewrite or edit your paper for you). If you are having trouble deciding on what courses to take or what to major in, see your academic adviser. If you are having trouble adjusting to college life, your peer counselor or (if you live in a dorm) your resident adviser may be able to help you. If not, or if you have a personal or family problem you would rather not discuss with another student, make an appointment at your school's counseling center, where you can get advice from professionals who understand student problems.

Many other services are available at your school's computer center, job placement service, financial aid office, and elsewhere. Your academic adviser or instructors can tell you where to find the help you need, but it is up to you to make the appointment.

## 40g Use the Library

As more and more material becomes available on the Internet, you may begin to think of your college library as outdated or even obsolete. But learning to use the library is an important part of your education.

445

The library has a lot to offer. First, the library can provide a quiet place to study—something you may need if you have a large family or noisy roommates. The library also contains materials that cannot be found online—rare books, special collections, audiovisual materials—as well as electronic databases that contain material you will not find on the Internet. (At some schools, you will be able to access the library's electronic databases on your home computer; at others, you will not.)

Finally, the library is the place where you have access to the experience and expert knowledge of your school's reference librarians. These professionals can answer questions, guide your research, and point you to sources that you might never have found on your own.

# 40h   Use Technology

As technology has become more and more important in the world, technological competence has become essential to success in college.

Naturally, it makes sense to develop good word-processing skills and to be comfortable with the Internet. You should also know how to send and receive e-mail from your university account as well as how to attach files to your e-mail. Beyond the basics, learn  how to manage the files you download, how to **evaluate Internet sources**, and how to use the electronic resources of your library. You might also find it helpful to know how to scan documents, (images as well as text) and how to paste these files into your documents. If you do not have these skills, you need to find someone (in the library or in the computer lab) who can help you get them.

Finally, you need to know not only how to use technology to enhance a project—for example, how to use PowerPoint for an **oral presentation**—but also *when* to use technology (and when  not to).

See
8d

See
Ch. 46

# 40i   Make Contacts—and Use Them

One of the most important things you can do for yourself, both for the short term and for the long term, is to make contacts while you are in school and to use them both during college and after you graduate.

446

Your first contacts are your fellow students. Be sure you have the names, phone numbers, and e-mail addresses of at least two students in each of your classes. These contacts will be useful to you if you miss class, if you need help understanding your notes, or if you want to find someone to study with.

You should also build relationships with students with whom you participate in college activities, such as the college newspaper or the tutoring center. These people are likely to share your goals and interests, and so you may want to get feedback from them as you move on to choose a major, consider further education, and make career choices.

Finally, develop relationships with your instructors, particularly those in your major area of study. One of the things cited most often in studies of successful students is the importance of **mentors,** experienced individuals whose advice you trust. Long after you leave college, you will find these contacts useful. Keep in touch; it will pay off.

## 40j   Be a Lifelong Learner

Your education should not stop when you graduate from college, and this is something you should be aware of from the first day you set foot on campus. To be a successful student, you need to see yourself as a lifelong learner.

Get in the habit of reading newspapers; know what is happening in the world outside school. Talk to people outside the college community, so you remember there are issues that have nothing to do with courses and grades. Never miss an opportunity to learn: try to get in the habit of attending plays and concerts sponsored by your school or community and lectures offered at your local library or bookstore.

And think about your future, the life you will lead after college. Think about who you want to be and what you have to do to get there. This is what successful students do.

> **✓checklist** Becoming a successful student
>
> ✓ Do you have a personal organizer? a calendar? Do you use them regularly?
> ✓ Have you set up a comfortable study space?
> ✓ Have you made a study schedule?
>
> *continued on the following page*

Ten Habits of Successful Students

*continued from the previous page*

✓ Have you joined a study group?

✓ Have you read your course syllabi and orientation materials carefully?

✓ Are you attending classes regularly and keeping up with your assignments?

✓ Do you take advantage of your instructors' office hours?

✓ Do you participate in class?

✓ Do you participate in college life?

✓ Do you know where to get help if you need it?

✓ Do you know how to use your college library? Do you use it?

✓ Are you satisfied with your level of technological expertise? Do you know where to get additional instruction?

✓ Are you trying to make contacts and find mentors?

✓ Do you see yourself as a lifelong learner?

# Chapter 41

# Developing Active Reading Skills

Knowing how to read effectively is an important skill, one that every college student should master. When you read, your goal should be not just to understand the literal meanings of the words on the page, but also to understand what those words suggest. And, if you are reading a book or article that takes a position on a subject or an issue, you will also have to assess the writer's credibility and <u>evaluate</u> the soundness of his or her ideas. In such cases,  you will need to be open to new ideas and willing to question what you read and how you react.

Central to developing effective reading skills is learning the techniques of active reading. **Active reading** means reading with pen in hand, physically marking the text to help you distinguish important points from not-so-important ones. In the process, you identify parallels and to connect causes with effects and generalizations with specific examples.

## 41a  Previewing

The first time you approach a book or article, **preview** it—that is, skim it to get a sense of the writer's subject and emphasis.

When you preview a *book*, begin by looking at its table of contents, especially at the sections that pertain to your topic. A quick glance at the index will reveal the kind and amount of coverage the book gives to subjects that may be important to you. As you leaf through the chapters, look at pictures, graphs, or tables, reading the captions that accompany them.

When you preview a *magazine article* (in print or online), scan the introductory and concluding paragraphs for summaries of the author's main points. (Journal articles in the sciences and social sciences often begin with summaries called **abstracts.**) Thesis statements, topic sentences, repeated key terms, transitional words and phrases, and transitional paragraphs can also help you to identify the points a writer is making. In addition, look for the visual cues—such as headings and lists—that writers use to emphasize ideas.

# 41b   Highlighting

When you have finished previewing a work, **highlight** it to identify the writer's key points and their relationships to one another. As you highlight, use symbols and underlining to identify important ideas. (If you are working with a print source, photocopy the pages; if you use an online source, print it out.) Be sure to use symbols that you will be able to understand when you reread your material later on.

> ### ✓checklist   Using highlighting symbols
>
> ✓ Underline important information.
> ✓ Box or circle key words and phrases.
> ✓ Put a question mark next to confusing passages, unclear points, or words you have to look up.
> ✓ Draw lines or arrows to identify connections between ideas.
> ✓ Number points that appear in sequence.
> ✓ Draw a vertical line in the margin to set off an important section of text.
> ✓ Star especially important ideas.

# 41c   Annotating

After you have read through a reading selection once, start to read more critically. At this stage, you should **annotate** the pages, recording your reactions to what you read. This process of recording notes in the margins or between the lines will help you understand the writer's ideas and your own reactions to those ideas.

Some of your responses may be relatively straightforward. For example, you may define new words, identify unfamiliar references, or jot down brief summaries. Other responses may be more personal. For example, you may identify a parallel between your own experience and one described in the reading selection, or you may record your opinion of the writer's position. Still other annotations may require you to think critically, identifying points that confirm (or dispute) your own ideas, questioning the appropriateness or accuracy of the writer's support, uncovering the writer's biases or faulty reasoning, or even questioning (or challenging) the writer's conclusion.

The following passage illustrates a student's annotations of a section of an article (note that it also includes her highlighting).

We can see every problem with the schools clearly except one: the fact that our decision to abandon the schools has helped create all the other problems. One small example: In the early 1980s, Massachusetts passed one of those tax cap measures, called Proposition 2½, which has turned out to be a force for genuine evil in the public schools. Would Proposition 2½ have passed had the middle class still had a stake in the schools? I wonder. I also wonder whether 20 years from now, in the next round of breast-beating memoirs, the exodus of the white middle class from the public schools will finally be seen for what it was. Individually, every parent's rationale made impeccable sense—"I can't deprive my children of a decent education"—but collectively, it was a deeply destructive act.

*Is this "one small example" enough to support his point?*

*Also—exodus from city to suburbs*

*(Do all parents have same motives?)*

The main reason the white middle class fled, of course, is race, or more precisely, the complicated admixture of race and class and good intentions gone awry. The fundamental good intention— which even today strikes one as both moral and right—was to integrate the public classroom, and in so doing, to equalize the resources available to all school children. In Boston, this was done through enforced busing. In Washington, it was done through a series of judicial edicts that attempted to spread the good teachers and resources throughout the system. In other big city districts, judges weren't involved; school committees, seeing the handwriting on the wall, tried to do it themselves.

*Reasonable assumption?*

*Why does he assume intent was "good" & "moral"? Is he right?*

However moral the intent, the result almost always was the same. The white middle class left. The historic parental vigilance I mentioned earlier had had a lot to do with creating the two-tiered system—one in which schools attended by the kids of the white middle class had better teachers, better equipment, better everything than those attended by the kids of the poor. This did not happen because the white middle-class parents were racists, necessarily; it happened because they knew how to manipulate the system and were willing to do so on behalf of their kids. Their neighborhood schools became little havens of decent education, and they didn't much care what happened in the other public schools.

*Where did they go? (Our neighborhood schools = mostly minority now)*

*How does he know they weren't?*

*Interesting point—but is it true?*

(From Joseph Nocera, "How the Middle Class Has Helped Ruin the Public Schools," *Washington Monthly*, February 1989; reprinted in the *Utne Reader*, September/October 1990)

# Chapter 42

# Writing Essay Exams

To prepare to write an essay exam, you must do more than memorize facts; you must synthesize information and arrange ideas into clear, well-organized paragraphs and essays.

## 42a   Planning an Essay Exam Answer

Because you are under pressure during an exam and tend to write quickly, you may be tempted to skip the planning and revision stages of the writing process. But if you write in a frenzy and hand in your exam without a second glance, you are likely to produce a disorganized or even incoherent answer. With careful planning and editing, you can write an answer that demonstrates your understanding of the material.

### (1) Review Your Material

Be sure you know beforehand the scope and format of the exam. How much of your text and class notes will be covered—the entire semester's work or only the material covered since the last test? Will you have to answer every question, or will you be able to choose among alternatives? Will the exam be composed entirely of fill-in, multiple-choice, or true/false questions, or will it call for sentence-, paragraph-, or essay-length answers? Will the exam test your ability to recall specific facts, or will it require you to demonstrate your understanding of the course material by drawing conclusions?

Exams challenge you to recall and express in writing what you already know—what you have read, what you have heard in class, what you have reviewed in your notes. Before you even take any exam, then, you must study: reread your text and class notes, highlight key points, and perhaps outline particularly important sections of your notes. When you prepare for a short-answer exam, you may memorize facts without analyzing their relationship to one another or their relationship to a body of knowledge as a whole: the definition of *pointillism,* the date of Queen Victoria's death, the formula for a quadratic equation, three reasons for the fall of Rome, two examples of conditioned reflexes, four features of a feudal economy, six steps in the process of synthesizing vitamin C. When you prepare for an essay exam, however, you must do more than remember bits of information; you must also make connections among ideas.

When you are sure you know what to expect, see if you can anticipate the essay questions your instructor might ask. Try out likely questions on classmates, and see whether you can do some collaborative brainstorming to outline answers to possible questions. If you have time, you might even practice answering one or two of these questions in writing.

## (2) Consider Your Audience and Purpose

The primary audience for any exam is the instructor who prepared it. As you read the questions, then, think about what your instructor has emphasized in class. Keep in mind that your purpose is to demonstrate that you understand the material, not to make clever remarks or to introduce irrelevant information. Also, make every effort to use the vocabulary of the specific academic discipline and to follow any discipline-specific stylistic conventions that your instructor has discussed.

## (3) Read through the Entire Exam

Before you begin to write, read the entire exam carefully to determine your priorities and your strategy. First, be sure that your copy of the test is complete and that you understand exactly what each question requires. If you need clarification, ask your instructor or proctor for help. Then, plan carefully, deciding how much time you should devote to answering each question. Often, the point value of each question or the number of questions on the exam determines how much time you should spend on each answer. If an essay question is worth fifty out of one hundred points, for example, you will probably have to spend at least half (and perhaps more) of your time planning, writing, and proofreading your answer.

Next, decide where to start. Responding first to short answers (or to questions whose answers you are sure of) is usually a good strategy. This tactic ensures that you will not become bogged down in a question that baffles you, left with too little time to write a strong answer to a question that you understand well. Moreover, starting with the questions that you are sure of can help build your confidence.

### (4) Read Each Question Carefully

To write an effective answer, you need to understand the question. As you read any essay question, you may find it helpful to underline key words and important terms.

Sociology: <u>Distinguish</u> among <u>Social Darwinism</u>, <u>instinct theory</u>, and <u>sociobiology</u>, giving <u>examples</u> of each.

Music: <u>Explain how</u> Milton <u>Babbitt</u> used the <u>computer</u> to expand <u>Schoenberg's twelve-tone</u> method.

Philosophy: <u>Define existentialism</u> and <u>identify three</u> influential existentialist <u>works</u>, explaining <u>why</u> they are important.

Look carefully at the wording of each question. If the question calls for a *comparison and contrast* of *two* styles of management, a *description* or *analysis* of *one* style, no matter how comprehensive, will not be acceptable. If the question asks for causes *and* effects, a discussion of causes alone will not do.

**Key words in exam questions**

- Explain
- Compare
- Contrast
- Trace
- Evaluate
- Discuss

- Clarify
- Relate
- Justify
- Analyze
- Summarize
- Describe

- Classify
- Identify
- Illustrate
- Define
- Support
- Interpret

### (5) Brainstorm to Find Ideas

See
1b5

Once you understand the question, begin **brainstorming**, quickly jotting down all the relevant ideas you can remember. Then, determine which points are most useful, and delete less promising ones. A quick review of the exam question and your supporting ideas should lead you to a workable thesis for your essay answer.

## ? 42b   Developing a Thesis and a List of Points

See
1c3

Often you can rephrase the exam question as a **thesis statement**. For example, the American history exam question "Give a detailed summary of the effects of the Great Depression on the United

States, briefly discussing the major causes of the economic collapse" suggests the following thesis statement.

The Great Depression, caused by the American government's economic policies, had major political, economic, and social effects on the United States.

Because time is limited, you will probably not have time to construct a formal outline; instead, make a quick list of your major points in the order in which you plan to discuss them. (Use the inside cover of your exam book.) Check this list against the exam question to make certain it covers everything the question calls for—and *only* what the question calls for.

## 42c Writing and Revising an Essay Exam Answer

Do not waste your valuable time trying to create an elaborate or unusual introduction. A simple statement of your thesis is usually all you need; this approach is economical, and it reminds you to address the question directly. Follow your outline point by point, using clear topic sentences and transitions to indicate your progression and to help your reader see that you are answering the question in full. Such signals, along with **parallel** sentence structure and repeated key words, make your answer easy to follow. Your conclusion should be a clear, simple restatement of the thesis or a brief summary of your essay's main points.

See 24a

Essay answers should be complete and detailed, but they should not contain irrelevant material. Every unnecessary fact or opinion increases your chance of error, so be careful not to repeat yourself or to volunteer unrequested information, and do not express your own feelings or opinions unless they are specifically called for. In addition, be sure to support all your general statements with specific examples.

Finally, leave enough time to reread and revise what you have written. Have you left out words or written illegibly? Is your thesis statement clearly worded? Does your essay support your thesis statement and answer the question? Are your facts correct, and are your ideas presented in a logical order? If a sentence—or even a whole paragraph—seems irrelevant, cross it out. If you suddenly remember something you want to add, insert a few additional words with a caret ($_\wedge$). Insert a longer addition at the end of your answer, boxed and labeled so your instructor will know where it belongs. (Do not waste time recopying entire passages unless what you have written is illegible.) Finally, check sentence structure, word choice, spelling, and punctuation. If you have additional time, reread your answer again. It generally pays to use all the time provided.

# 42d Sample Essay Exam Answer

In the following one-hour essay answer, notice how the student restates the question in her thesis statement and keeps the question in focus by repeating key words like *cause, effect, result, response,* and *impact.*

? ✳ *Effective Essay Exam Answer*

Question: Give a detailed summary of the effects of the Great Depression on the United States, briefly discussing the major causes of the economic collapse.

Introduction— thesis statement rephrases exam question

The Great Depression, caused by the American government's economic policies, had major political, economic, and social effects on the United States.

The Depression was precipitated by the stock market crash of October 1929, but its actual causes were more subtle: they lay in

Policies leading to Depression

(¶ 2 summarizes causes)

the US government's economic policies. First, personal income was not well distributed. Although production rose during the 1920s, the farmers and other workers got too little of the profits; instead, a disproportionate amount of income went to the richest 5 percent of the population. The tax policies at this time made inequalities in income even worse. A good deal of income also went into development of new manufacturing plants. This expansion stimulated the economy but encouraged the production of more goods than consumers could purchase. Finally, during the economic boom of the 1920s, the government did not attempt to limit speculation or impose regulations on the securities market; it also

# Sample Essay Exam Answer

did little to help build up farmers' buying power. Even after the crash began, the government made mistakes: instead of trying to counter the country's deflationary economy, the government focused on keeping the budget balanced and making sure the United States adhered to the gold standard.

The Depression, devastating to millions of individuals, had a tremendous impact on the nation as a whole. Its political, economic, and social consequences were great. *(Transition from causes to effects)*

Between October 1929 and Roosevelt's inauguration on March 4, 1932, the economic situation grew worse. Businesses were going bankrupt, banks were failing, and stock prices were falling. Farm prices fell drastically, and hungry farmers were forced to burn their corn to heat their homes. There was massive unemployment, with millions of workers jobless and humiliated, losing skills and self-respect. President Hoover's Reconstruction Finance Corporation made loans available to banks, railroads, and businesses, but Hoover felt state and local funds (not the federal government) should finance public works programs and relief. Confidence in the president declined as the country's economic situation worsened. *(Early effects (¶s 4–8 summarize important results in chronological order)*

One result of the Depression was the election of Franklin Delano Roosevelt. By the time of his inauguration, most American banks had closed, thirteen million workers were unemployed, and millions of farmers were threatened by foreclosure. Roosevelt's response was immediate: two days after he took office, he closed all banks and took steps to support the stronger ones with loans and to prevent the weaker ones from reopening. During the first hundred days of his administration, he kept Congress in special session. Under his leadership, Congress enacted emergency measures designed to provide "Relief, Recovery, and Reform." *(Additional effects: Roosevelt's emergency measures)*

**457**

# Writing Essay Exams

Additional effects: Roosevelt's reform measures

In response to the problems caused by the Depression, Roosevelt set up agencies to reform some of the conditions that had helped to cause the Depression in the first place. The Tennessee Valley Authority, created in May 1933, was one of these. Its purposes were to control floods by building new dams and improving old ones and to provide cheap, plentiful electricity. The TVA improved the standard of living of area farmers and drove down the price of power all over the country. The Agricultural Adjustment Administration, created the same month as the TVA, provided for taxes on basic commodities, with the tax revenues used to subsidize farmers to produce less. This reform measure caused prices to rise.

Additional effects: NIRA, other laws, etc.

Another response to the problems of the Depression was the National Industrial Recovery Act. This act established the National Recovery Administration, an agency that set minimum wages and maximum hours for workers and set limits on production and prices. Other laws passed by Congress between 1935 and 1940 strengthened federal regulation of power, interstate commerce, and air traffic. Roosevelt also changed the federal tax structure to redistribute income.

Additional effects: Social Security, WPA, etc.

One of the most important results of the Depression was the Social Security Act of 1935, which established unemployment insurance and provided financial aid for the blind and disabled and for dependent children and their mothers. The Works Progress Administration (WPA) gave jobs to over two million workers, who built public buildings, roads, streets, bridges, and sewers. The WPA also employed artists, musicians, actors, and writers. The Public Works Administration (PWA) cleared slums and created public housing. In the National Labor Relations Act (1935), workers

458

received a guarantee of government protection for their unions against unfair labor practices by management.

As a result of the economic collapse known as the Great De- Conclusion
pression, Americans saw their government take responsibility for
providing immediate relief, for helping the economy recover, and
for taking steps to ensure that the situation would not be repeated.
The economic, political, and social effects of the laws passed during the 1930s is still with us, helping to keep our government and
our economy stable.

Notice that in her answer the student does not include any irrelevant material: she does not, for example, describe the conditions
of people's lives in detail, blame anyone in particular, discuss the
president's friends and enemies, or consider parallel events in
other countries. She covers only what the question asks for. Notice,
too, how topic sentences ("One result of the Depression . . ."; "In
response to the problems caused by the Depression . . ."; "One of
the most important results of the Depression . . .") keep the primary purpose of the discussion in focus and guide her instructor
through the essay.

## Writing in-class essays

Many of the strategies that can help you to write strong responses to essay exams can also help you plan, write, and revise
other kinds of in-class essays.

If you are asked to write an in-class essay, follow the steps outlined in this chapter, and be sure you understand exactly what you
are being asked to do and how much time you have in which to do
it. Keep in mind, however, that in-class essays, unlike essay exams,
may be evaluated as much on their style and structure as on their
content. This means, for example, that they should have fully developed introductory and concluding paragraphs.

# Chapter 43

# Writing about Literature

Learning to read, respond to, and write about literature are important skills that can serve you while you are a college student, as well as later, in your life beyond the classroom.

## 43a  Reading Literature

When you read a literary work you plan to write about, use the same critical thinking skills and <u>active reading</u> strategies you apply to other works you read: preview the work and highlight it to identify key ideas and cues to meaning; then annotate it carefully.

As you read and take notes, focus on the special concerns of literary analysis, considering elements like a short story's plot, a poem's rhyme or meter, or a play's staging. Look for *patterns,* related groups of words, images, or ideas that run through a work. Look for *anomalies,* unusual forms, unique uses of language, unexpected actions by characters, or original treatments of topics. Finally, look for *connections,* links with other literary works, with historical events, or with biographical information.

### Reading literature

When you read a work of literature, keep in mind that you do not read to discover the one correct meaning the writer has hidden between the lines of the work. The "meaning" of a literary work is created by the interaction between a text and its readers. Do not assume, however, that a work can mean whatever you want it to mean; ultimately, your interpretation must be consistent with the stylistic signals, thematic suggestions, and patterns of imagery in the text.

## ✓ checklist Reading literature

**Reading Fiction**

✓ **Plot** What happens in the story? What conflicts can you identify? Are they resolved? How are the events arranged? Why are they arranged in this way?

✓ **Character** Who is the protagonist? The antagonist? What roles do minor characters play? What are each character's most striking traits? Does the protagonist grow and change during the story? Are the characters portrayed sympathetically? How do characters interact with one another?

✓ **Setting** Where and when is the story set? How does the setting influence the plot? How does it affect the characters?

✓ **Point of View** Is the story told by an anonymous third-person narrator or by a character who uses first-person (*I* or *we*) point of view? Is the first-person narrator trustworthy? Is the narrator a participant in the action or just a witness to the story's events? How would a different point of view change the story?

✓ **Style, Tone, and Language** Is the level of diction formal? Informal? Is the style straightforward or complex? Is the tone intimate or distant? What kind of imagery and figures of speech are used?

✓ **Theme** What central theme or themes does the story explore?

**Reading Poetry**

✓ **Voice** Who is the poem's speaker? What is the speaker's attitude toward the poem's subject? How would you characterize the speaker's tone?

✓ **Word Choice and Word Order** What words seem important? Why? What does each word say? What does it suggest? Are any words repeated? Why? Is the poem's diction formal or informal? Is the arrangement of words conventional or unconventional?

✓ **Imagery** What images are used in the poem? To what senses (sight, sound, smell, taste, or touch) do they appeal? Is one central image important? Is there a pattern of related images?

✓ **Figures of Speech** Does the poet use simile? Metaphor? Personification? What do these figures of speech contribute to the poem?

✓ **Sound** Does the poem include rhyme? Where? Does it have regular meter (that is, a regular pattern of stressed and unstressed syllables)? Does the poem include repeated consonant or vowel sounds? What do these elements contribute to the poem?

✓ **Form** Is the poem written in open form (with no definite pattern of line length, rhyme, or meter) or in closed form (conforming to a pattern)? Why do you think this kind of form is used?

*continued on the following page*

continued from the previous page

✓ **Theme** What central theme or themes does the poem explore?

**Reading Drama**

✓ **Plot** What happens in the play? What conflicts are developed? How are they resolved? Are there any subplots? What events, if any, occur offstage?

✓ **Character** Who are the major characters? The minor characters? What relationships exist among them? What are their most distinctive traits? What do we learn about characters from their words and actions? From the play's stage directions? From what other characters tell us? Does the main character change or grow during the course of the play?

✓ **Staging** When and where is the play set? How do the scenery, props, costumes, lighting, and music work together to establish this setting? What else do these elements contribute to the play?

✓ **Theme** What central theme or themes does the play explore?

## 43b  Writing about Literature

See 1b5

When you have finished your reading and annotating, <u>brainstorm</u> to discover a topic to write about; then, organize your material. As you arrange related material into categories, you will begin to see a structure for your paper. At this point, you are ready to start drafting your essay.

When you write about literature, your goal is to make a point and support it with appropriate references to the work under discussion or to related works or secondary sources. As you write, you observe the conventions of literary criticism, which has its own specialized vocabulary and formats. You also respond to certain discipline-specific assignments. For instance, you may be asked to **analyze** a work, to take it apart and consider one or more of its elements—perhaps the plot or characters in a story or the use of language in a poem. Or, you may be asked to **interpret** a work, to try to discover its possible meanings. Finally, you may be called on to **evaluate** a work, to judge its strengths and weaknesses.

More specifically, you may be asked to trace the critical or popular reception to a work, to compare two works by a single writer (or by two different writers), or to consider the relationship between a work of literature and a literary movement or historical period.

# Writing about Literature

You may be asked to analyze a character's motives or the relationship between two characters or to comment on a story's setting or tone. Whatever the case, understanding exactly what you are expected to do will make your writing task easier.

---

## ✓ checklist  Writing about literature

✓ Use present-tense verbs when discussing works of literature: "The character of Mrs. Mallard's husband is not developed. . . ."

✓ Use past-tense verbs only when discussing historical events ("Owen's poem conveys the destructiveness of World War I, which at the time the poem *was* written *was* considered to be. . . ."); when presenting historical or biographical data ("Her first novel, *published* in 1811 when Austen *was* thirty-six, . . ."); or when identifying events that occurred prior to the time of the story's main action ("Miss Emily is a recluse; since her father *died* she has lived alone except for a servant.").

✓ Support all points with specific, concrete examples from the work you are discussing, briefly summarizing key events, quoting dialogue or description, describing characters or setting, or paraphrasing ideas.

✓ Combine paraphrase, summary, and quotation with your own interpretations, weaving quotations smoothly into your paper **(see 6f, 9a).**

✓ Be careful to acknowledge all sources, including the work or works under discussion. Check to see you have introduced the words or ideas of others with a reference to the source and followed borrowed material with appropriate parenthetical documentation. Also, be sure you have quoted accurately and enclosed the words of others in quotation marks.

✓ Use parenthetical documentation **(see 10a1)** and include a works-cited list **(see 10a2)** in accordance with MLA documentation style.

✓ When citing a part of a short story or novel, supply the page number (168). For a poem, give the line numbers, including the word lines in the first parenthetical reference (lines 2–4). For a classic verse play, include act, scene, and line numbers (1.4.29–31). For other plays, supply act and/or scene numbers. (When quoting more than four lines of prose or more than three lines of poetry, follow the guidelines outlined in **32b.**)

✓ Avoid subjective expressions like *I feel, I believe, it seems to me,* and *in my opinion*. These weaken your paper by suggesting its ideas are "only" your opinion and have no validity in themselves.

*continued on the following page*

*continued from the previous page*

✓ Avoid unnecessary plot summary. Your goal is to draw a conclusion about one or more works and to support that conclusion with pertinent details. If a plot development supports a point you wish to make, a *brief* summary is acceptable. But plot summary is no substitute for analysis.

✓ Use literary terms accurately. For example, be careful not to confuse *narrator* or *speaker* with *writer* (feelings or opinions expressed by a narrator or character do not necessarily represent those of the writer). You should not say, "In the poem's last stanza, *Frost expresses* his indecision" when you mean the poem's *speaker* is indecisive.

**?** ✓ Underline titles of novels and plays to indicate italics **(see 36a);** enclose titles of short stories and poems within quotation marks **(see 32c).**

## 43c   Sample Student Paper (without Sources)

Daniel Johanssen, a student in an introductory literature course, wrote an essay about Delmore Schwartz's 1959 poem "The True-Blue American," which follows. Daniel's essay appears on pages 466–468. (Note that because all students in the class selected poems from the same text, Daniel's instructor did not require a works-cited page.)

### The True-Blue American

Jeremiah Dickson was a true-blue American,

For he was a little boy who understood America, for he felt that he must

Think about *everything;* because that's *all* there is to think about,

Knowing immediately the intimacy of truth and comedy,

5 Knowing intuitively how a sense of humor was a necessity

For one and for all who live in America. Thus, natively, and

Naturally when on an April Sunday in an ice cream parlor Jeremiah

Was requested to choose between a chocolate sundae and a banana split

He answered unhesitatingly, having no need to think of it

10 Being a true-blue American, determined to continue as he began:

Rejecting the either-or of Kierkegaard,[1] and many another European;

Refusing to accept alternatives, refusing to believe the choice of between;

Rejecting selection; denying dilemma; electing absolute affirmation:

knowing

15    in his breast

The infinite and the gold

Of the endless frontier, the deathless West.

"Both: I will have them both!" declared this true-blue American

In Cambridge, Massachusetts, on an April Sunday, instructed

20    By the great department stores, by the Five-and-Ten,

Taught by Christmas, by the circus, by the vulgarity and grandeur of

Niagara Falls and the Grand Canyon,

Tutored by the grandeur, vulgarity, and infinite appetite gratified and

Shining in the darkness, of the light

25 On Saturdays at the double bills of the moon pictures,

The consummation of the advertisements of the imagination of the light

Which is as it was—the infinite belief in infinite hope—

of Columbus, Barnum, Edison, and Jeremiah Dickson.

---

[1]Søren Kierkegaard (1813–1855)—Danish philosopher who greatly influenced twentieth-century existentialism. *Either-Or* (1841) is one of his best-known works.

Johanssen 1

Daniel Johanssen

Professor Stang

English 1001

8 April 2003

Paper title is centered

Irony in "The True-Blue American"

Title of poem is in quotation marks

The poem "The True-Blue American" by Delmore Schwartz is not as simple and direct as its title suggests. In fact, the title is extremely ironic. At first, the poem seems patriotic, but actually the flag-waving strengthens the speaker's criticism. Even though the

Thesis statement

poem seems to support and celebrate America, it is actually a bitter critique of the negative aspects of American culture.

According to the speaker, the primary problem with America is that its citizens falsely believe themselves to be authorities on everything. The following lines introduce the theme of the "know-it-

Slash separates lines of poetry

all" American: "For he was a little boy who understood America, for he felt that he must / Think about everything; because that's all there is to think about" (lines 2–3). This theme is developed later in

Parenthetical documentation indicates line numbers

a series of parallel phrases that seem to celebrate the value of immediate intuitive knowledge and a refusal to accept or to believe anything other than what is American (4–6).

Americans are ambitious and determined, but these qualities are not seen in the poem as virtues. According to the speaker, Americans reject sophisticated "European" concepts like doubt and choices and alternatives and instead insist on "absolute affirmation" (13)—simple solutions to complex problems. This unwillingness to compromise translates into stubbornness and

Johanssen 2

materialistic greed. This tendency is illustrated by the boy's asking

for <u>both</u> a chocolate sundae <u>and</u> a banana split at the ice cream

parlor—not "either-or" (11). Americans are characterized as pio-

neers who want it all, who will stop at nothing to achieve "The infi-

nite and the gold / Of the endless frontier, the deathless West"

(16–17). For the speaker, the pioneers and their "endless frontier"

are not noble or self-sacrificing; they are like greedy little boys at

an ice cream parlor.

According to the speaker, the greed and materialism of Amer-

ica began as grandeur but ultimately became mere vulgarity. Simi-

larly, the "true-blue American" is not born a vulgar parody of

grandeur; he learns it from his true-blue fellows:

> instructed
> By the great department stores, by the Five-
> and-Ten,
> Taught by Christmas, by the circus, by the vulgarity
> and grandeur of
> Niagara Falls and the Grand Canyon,
> Tutored by the grandeur, vulgarity, and infinite
> appetite gratified. . . . (19–23)

More than 3 lines of poetry are set off from text. Quotation is indented 10 spaces (or 1″) from left margin; no quotation marks are used.

Among the "tutors" the speaker lists are such American institutions

as department stores and national monuments. Within these insti-

tutions, grandeur and vulgarity coexist; in a sense, they are one

and the same.

The speaker's negativity climaxes in the phrase "Shining in the

darkness, of the light" (24). This paradoxical statement suggests the negative truths hidden beneath America's glamorous surface. All the grand and illustrious things of which Americans are so proud are personified by Jeremiah Dickson, the spoiled brat in the ice cream parlor.

**Conclusion reinforces thesis**

Like America, Jeremiah has unlimited potential. He has native intuition, curiosity, courage, and a pioneer spirit. Unfortunately, however, both America and Jeremiah Dickson are limited by their willingness to be led by others, by their greed and impatience, and by their preference for quick, easy, unambiguous answers rather than careful philosophical analysis. Regardless of his—and America's—potential, Jeremiah Dickson is doomed to be hypnotized and seduced by glittering superficialities, light without substance, and to settle for the "double bills of the moon pictures" (25) rather than the enduring truths of a philosopher like Kierkegaard.

## 43d  Sample Student Paper (with Sources)

Cathy Thomason, a student in an introductory literature course, wrote an essay analyzing two poems by Adrienne Rich, "Aunt Jennifer's Tigers" and "Mathilde in Normandy." The paper uses **MLA documentation style** and cites three outside sources.

See 10a

Student's
name and
page number
are on every
page

Cathy Thomason

Composition 102

Dr. Alvarez-Goldstein

9 May 2001

Assertive Men and Passive Women: A Comparison → Center title

of Adrienne Rich's "Aunt Jennifer's Tigers" and → Double-space

"Mathilde in Normandy"

Adrienne Rich began her poetic career in the 1950s
as an undergraduate at Radcliffe College. The product of a
conservative Southern family, Rich was greatly influenced
by her father, who encouraged the young poet to seek — Background
higher standards for her work. However, her early work
shows evidence of Rich's future struggle with this
upbringing. Although she used styles and subjects that
gained approval from both her father and the almost all-
male literary world, some of her early works suggest an
inner struggle with the status quo of male dominance
(Bennett 178). "Aunt Jennifer's Tigers" and "Mathilde in — Thesis
Normandy" clearly reflect this struggle. statement

Both "Aunt Jennifer's Tigers" and "Mathilde in
Normandy" tell the story of women living in the shadow of
men's accomplishments. The central figures of the two — Paragraph
poems display their creativity and intelligence through a summarizes
similarities
traditional female occupation, embroidery. Although the between two
poems
poems are set in different time periods ("Mathilde in
Normandy" in the Middle Ages and "Aunt Jennifer's Tigers"

in the 1950s), their focus is the same: both are about women who recognize their subordinate positions but are powerless to change their situations. The difference between the two, however, lies in the fact that Mathilde does not suffer the inner conflict that Aunt Jennifer does.

"Aunt Jennifer's Tigers" is the story of a woman trapped in a conventional and apparently boring marriage. Her outlet is her needlework; through her embroidery, she creates a fantasy world of tigers as an escape from her real life. In 1972, in her essay "When We Dead Awaken," Rich said, "In writing this poem, composed and apparently cool as it is, I thought I was creating a portrait of an imaginary woman" (469). What she later discovered was that Aunt Jennifer was probably typical of many married women in the 1950s. These women, Rich observed, "didn't talk to each other much in the fifties—not about their secret emptiness, their frustrations . . ." (470).

Standing in opposition to the timid and frustrated Aunt Jennifer are the tigers in the first stanza:

> Aunt Jennifer's tigers prance across a screen,
>
> Bright topaz denizens of a world of green.
>
> They do not fear the men beneath the tree;
>
> They pace in sleek chivalric certainty. (lines 1–4)

Unlike Aunt Jennifer, the tigers move with confidence and "chivalric certainty." They are not dominated by men, as Aunt

**Identifying tag introduces quotation**

**Parenthetical documentation**

**Long quotation indented 10 spaces (1″) from left-hand margin; no quotation marks necessary**

**(First reference to lines of poetry includes word *lines;* subsequent references do not.)**

Thomason 3

Jennifer is. According to Claire Keyes, this stanza contains the dominant voice (24). Furthermore, Pope, Byars, and Gillette indicate that, although Aunt Jennifer is not assertive or forceful, her creations—the tigers—are. In other words, Aunt Jennifer's work is more interesting than she is. Even so, the tigers are a part of Aunt Jennifer's imagination, and they show there is more to Aunt Jennifer than her existence as a housewife would suggest.

"Mathilde in Normandy" is based on the folktale that William the Conqueror's wife, Queen Mathilde, created the Bordeaux Tapestry to tell the story of the Norman invasion of England (Keyes 24). The men in this poem are as powerful as the men who dominate Aunt Jennifer, showing their masculinity in their attack on another country. Although Rich acknowledges Mathilde's position as a woman who may never see her husband again—"Say what you will, anxiety there too / Played havoc with the skein" (21–22)—Mathilde, unlike Aunt Jennifer, has no problem with the notion that women should stay home. According to the speaker, "Yours was a time when women sat at home" (17). Therefore, Mathilde does not suffer inner turmoil about her role in life as a subordinate wife.

Mathilde is separated from her husband's world because she is female and considered unable to fight, to compete in a male world. Aunt Jennifer, however, is held back from the male world by a different barrier:

Short quotation run in with text; slash separates two lines of poetry

471

Thomason 4

> Aunt Jennifer's fingers fluttering through her wool
>
> Find even the ivory needle hard to pull.
>
> The massive weight of Uncle's wedding band
>
> Sits heavily upon Aunt Jennifer's hand. (5–8)

Her marriage is not a happy one; her wedding band holds her down (Keyes 23). Thus, in accepting her role as housewife, Aunt Jennifer is denied a satisfying existence. She is reduced to maintaining a household for a husband who dominates all aspects of her life. Even Aunt Jennifer's pursuit of art is made difficult by her marriage. The "weight" of her wedding band makes it difficult to embroider.

For Mathilde, life is objectionable only because she fears that her husband and the men of the kingdom will not return. She identifies with her husband's cause and accepts the fact that the life men lead is dangerous. Unlike Mathilde, Aunt Jennifer sees her marriage as imprisonment; she will be free only when she dies:

> When Aunt is dead, her terrified hands will lie
>
> Still ringed with the ordeals she was mastered by.
>
> The tigers in the panel that she made
>
> Will go on prancing, proud and unafraid. (9–12)

Aunt Jennifer's hands are "terrified," overwhelmed by the power that her husband, and society, have over her. Aunt Jennifer, who is "mastered" by her situation, stands in opposition to the tigers, who flaunt their independence,

Thomason 5

forever "prancing, proud and unafraid." Mathilde's
experience with male power is also terrifying. She is in the
vulnerable position of being a queen whose husband and
court are away at war. If her husband does not return, she
can be subjugated by another man, one wishing to take
over the kingdom.

Both "Aunt Jennifer's Tigers" and "Mathilde in
Normandy" present stories of women bound to men.
Although both poems suggest that conventional
relationships between men and women are unsatisfactory,
Mathilde does not struggle against her role as Aunt
Jennifer does. As Claire Keyes points out, although these
poems are "well mannered and feminine on the surface,"
they "speak differently in their muted stories" (28). Although
only "Aunt Jennifer's Tigers" openly criticizes the status
quo, both poems reflect the inner conflicts of women and
express their buried desires subtly.

Conclusion

Thomason 6

Works Cited

Bennett, Paula. "Dutiful Daughter." My Life a Loaded Gun: Female Creativity and Feminist Politics. Boston: Beacon, 1986. 171–76.

Keyes, Claire. The Aesthetics of Power: The Story of Adrienne Rich. Athens: U of Georgia P, 1986.

Pope, Deborah, Thomas B. Byars, and Meg Boerema Gillette. "On 'Aunt Jennifer's Tigers.'" Modern American Poetry Site (MAPS). Ed. Cary Nelson. Urbana: U of Illinois at Urbana-Champaign, 2002. 14 Apr. 2003 <http//www.english.uiuc.edu/maps/poets/m_r/rich/tiger.htm>.

Rich, Adrienne. "Aunt Jennifer's Tigers." Poems: Selected and New. New York: Norton, 1974. 81.

---. "Mathilde in Normandy." Poems: Selected and New. New York: Norton, 1974. 94–95.

---. "When We Dead Awaken." Ways of Reading: An Anthology for Writers. Ed. David Bartholomae and Anthony Petrowsky. Boston: Bedford, 1993. 461–76.

Chapter **44**

# Designing Documents and Web Sites

In many college writing situations, the **format** of your paper—specifying how you use headings, how you construct tables and charts, and how you arrange information on the title page—is defined by the discipline in which you are writing. Although formatting conventions may differ from discipline to discipline, the basic principles of document design remain the same. This chapter presents general guidelines for designing documents (papers, letters, reports, and so on) and Web sites, as well as specific advice for designing all your written work so it is easy to read and understand.

## 44a   Understanding Document Design

Computers offer writers a world of design possibilities: the ability to manipulate text, to use different typefaces, to insert headings, to add graphics, and to use color. These possibilities, however, increase the choices that you must make every time you write. Should you, for example, use several different typefaces? Should you insert a picture into a document? Should you use color to attract a reader's attention?

**Document design** refers to the principles that help you determine the most effective way of designing a piece of written work—a research paper, memo, report, business letter, or résumé, for example—so it communicates its ideas clearly and effectively. A well-designed document has a visual format that emphasizes key ideas and is easy on the eye. Although formatting guidelines—for example, how tables and charts are constructed and how information is arranged on a title page—may differ from discipline to discipline, all well-designed documents share the same general characteristics:

- An effective format
- Clear headings
- Useful lists
- Helpful visuals

## (1) Creating an Effective Visual Format

An effective document contains visual cues that help readers locate and understand the information on the page, making it easier to read. For example, wide margins can be used to give a page a balanced, uncluttered appearance, and white space can break up a long discussion. In addition, type size and typeface can make a word or phrase stand out on a page.

*Margins* Margins frame a page and prevent it from appearing overcrowded. Because long lines of text can overwhelm readers and make a document difficult to read, a page should have margins of at least one inch all around. If the material you are writing about is highly technical or unusually difficult, use wider margins—one and a half inches. Keep in mind that specific assignments often have specific requirements for margins. Before you prepare a document, consult the appropriate style sheet.

Except for documents such as flyers and brochures, where you might want to isolate blocks of text for emphasis, you should **justify** (uniformly align, except for paragraph indentations) the left-hand margin. You can either leave a ragged edge on the right, or you can justify your text so all the words are aligned evenly at the right margin. (A ragged edge is preferable because it varies the visual landscape of your text, making it easier to read.)

*White Space* *White space* is the area of a page that is left blank. Used effectively, white space can isolate material and thereby focus a reader's attention on it. You can use white space around a block of text—a paragraph or a section, for example—or around visuals such as charts, graphs, and photographs. White space can eliminate clutter, break a discussion into manageable components, and help readers process information more easily.

*Typeface and Type Size* Your computer gives you a wide variety of typefaces and type sizes (measured in *points*) from which to choose. **Typefaces** are distinctively designed sets of letters, numbers, and punctuation marks that usually have the name of their designer or a historical name. Choose a typeface that is suitable for your purpose and audience. In your academic writing, avoid fancy or elaborate typefaces—such as script or 𝔬𝔩𝔡 𝔈𝔫𝔤𝔩𝔦𝔰𝔥, for example—that call attention to themselves and distract readers. Select a typeface that is simple and direct—Courier, Times New Roman, or Arial, for example. In other kinds of writing—such as Web pages and flyers—decorative typefaces may be used to help you emphasize a point or attract a reader's attention.

You also have a wide variety of **type sizes** available to you. For most of your academic papers, use a 10- or 12-point type (headings will sometimes be larger). Advertisements, brochures, and Web pages frequently require a great variety of type sizes. Keep in mind, however, that point size alone is not a reliable guide for size. For instance, 12-point type in **Chicago** is much larger than 12-point type in Courier or Arial condensed light.

*Line Spacing* Line spacing refers to the amount of space between the lines of a document. If the lines are too far apart, the text will be seen to lack cohesion; if the lines are too close together, the text will appear crowded and be difficult to read. The type of writing you do sometimes determines line spacing. For example, the paragraphs of business letters are usually single spaced and separated by a double space, and the paragraphs of academic papers are usually double spaced.

## (2) Using Headings

Used effectively, headings not only act as signals that help readers process information, but they also break up a text, making it inviting and easy to read. Different academic disciplines have different requirements concerning headings. For this reason, consult the appropriate style manual before inserting headings in a paper.

Headings perform three functions in a document:

- *Headings tell readers that a new idea is being introduced.* In this way, headings tell readers what to expect in a section before they actually read it.
- *Headings emphasize key ideas.* By isolating an idea from the text around it, headings help readers identify important information.
- *Headings indicate the organization of information in a text.* Headings use various typefaces and type sizes (as well as indentation) to indicate the relative importance of ideas. For example, the most important information in a text will be set off as first-level headings and have the same typeface and type size. The next most important information will be set off as second-level heading, also with the same typeface and type size.

*Number of Headings* The number of headings you use depends on the document. A long, complicated document will need more headings than a shorter, less complicated one. Keep in mind that too few headings may not be of much use, but too many headings will make your document look like an outline.

*Phrasing* Headings should be brief, informative, and to the point. They can be single words: *Summary* or *Introduction,* for example. Headings can also be phrases (always stated in **parallel** terms): *Traditional Family Patterns, Alternate Family Patterns, Modern Family Patterns.* They can also be questions (*How Do You Choose a Major?*) or statements *(Choose Your Major Carefully).*

See 24a

*Indentation* Indenting is one way of distinguishing one level of heading from another. The more important a heading is, the closer it is to the left-hand margin. In other words, first-level headings are justified left, second-level headings are indented five spaces, and third-level headings are indented another two or three spaces. Headings and subheadings may also be *centered,* placed *flush left, indented,* or *run into the text.*

*Typographical Emphasis* You can emphasize important words in headings by using **boldface,** *italics,* or ALL CAPITAL LETTERS. Used in moderation, these distinctive typefaces make a text easier to read. Used excessively, however, they slow readers down.

*Consistency* Headings at the same level should have the same format—the same typeface, type size, and spacing. In addition, if one first-level heading is boldfaced and centered, all other first-level headings must be boldfaced and centered. Using consistent patterns in this way reinforces the connection between content and ideas and makes a document easier to understand.

**Note:** Never separate a heading from the text that goes with it: if a heading is at the bottom of one page and the text that goes with it is on the next page, move the heading onto the next page so readers can see the heading and the text together.

### Sample heading formats

**Flush Left, Boldfaced, Uppercase and Lowercase**
   **Indented, Boldfaced, Uppercase and Lowercase**
      *Indented, italicized, lowercase paragraph heading run into the text and ending with a period.*

> *Or*
>
> **Centered, Boldfaced, Uppercase and Lowercase**
> Flush Left, Underlined, Uppercase and Lowercase
>     Indented, underlined, lowercase paragraph heading ending
> with a period.
>         ALL CAPITAL LETTERS, CENTERED

## (3) Constructing Lists

A list makes information easier to understand by breaking long discussions into a series of key ideas. By isolating individual pieces of information this way and by providing visual cues, such as bullets or numbers, a list directs readers' eyes to important information on a page.

### CONSTRUCTING EFFECTIVE LISTS

When constructing lists, you should follow these guidelines.

- *Indent each item on a list.* Each item on a list should be indented (just as the items on this list are) so that it stands out from the text around it.

- *Set off items in a list with numbers or bullets.* Use **bullets** when items are not organized according to any particular sequence or priority (the members of a club, for example). Use **numbers** when you want to indicate that items are organized according to a sequence (the steps in a process, for example) or priority (the things a company should do to decrease spending, for example).

- *Introduce a list with a complete sentence.* Do not simply drop a list into a document; introduce it with a complete sentence (followed by a colon) that tells readers what the list contains and why you are including it in your discussion.

- *Use parallel structure.* Lists are easiest to read when all items are **parallel** and about the same length.

  See
  24a

  A number of factors can cause high unemployment:

  - a decrease in consumer spending

  - a decrease in factory orders

  - a decrease in factory output

*continued on the following page*

479

*continued from the previous page*

- *Punctuate correctly.* If the items on a list are fragments (as they are in the previous example), begin each item with a lowercase letter and do not end it with a period. However, if the items on a list are complete sentences (as they are in the example below), begin each item with a capital letter and end it with a period.

Here are the three steps we must take to reduce our spending:

1. We must cut our workforce by 10%.
2. We must use less-expensive vendors.
3. We must decrease overtime payments.

## (4) Using Visuals

**Visuals,** such as tables, graphs, diagrams, and photographs, can not only help you communicate complex ideas but can also help you attract readers' attention. You can create your own tables and graphs by using applications in software packages like *Excel, Lotus,* or *Word.* In addition, many stand-alone graphics software packages enable you to create complex charts, tables, and graphs that contain three-dimensional effects. Instead of creating your own visuals, you can photocopy or scan diagrams and photographs from a print source or download them from the Internet or from CD-ROMs or DVDs. Remember, however, that if you use a visual from a source, you must use appropriate **documentation**.

See Chs. 10–12

### Visuals and copyright

**Copyright** gives an author the legal right to control the copying of his or her work—both text and visuals. The law makes a clear distinction between visuals used in documents for school and visuals used in documents that will be published. In general, you may use graphics from a source—print or electonic—as long as your instructor gives you permission to do so and as long as you document the source, just as you would any other source. If you use visuals in documents that will be published, however, you must obtain permission in writing from the person or organization that holds the copyright. Sometimes, the copyright holder will grant permission without charge, but most of the time there will be a fee. (Some software packages, especially those that contain "clip art," include permission fees in the cost of the software package.) Remember, it is your responsibility to determine whether or not permission is required.

*Tables* Tables present data in a condensed, visual format—arranged in rows and columns. Tables most often contain numerical data, although occasionally they contain words as well as numbers. When you plan your table, make sure you include only the data that you will need; discard information that is too detailed or difficult to understand. Keep in mind that tables may distract readers, so include only those necessary to support your discussion. The following table reports the writer's original research and therefore needs no documentation.

McVay 3

As the following table shows, the Madison location now employs more workers in every site than the St. Paul location.

Table 1                                                        Heading

Number of Employees at Each Location                           Descriptive caption

| | Location | |
|---|---|---|
| Employees | Madison | St. Paul |
| Plant | 461 | 254 | Data |
| Warehouse | 45 | 23 |
| Outlet Stores | 15 | 9 |

Because the Madison location has grown so quickly, steps must be taken to. . . .

481

*Graphs* Like tables, graphs present data in visual form. Whereas tables present specific numerical data, graphs convey the general pattern or trend that the data suggest. Because graphs tend to be more general (and therefore less accurate) than tables, they are frequently accompanied by tables. The following is an example of a bar graph reproduced from a source.

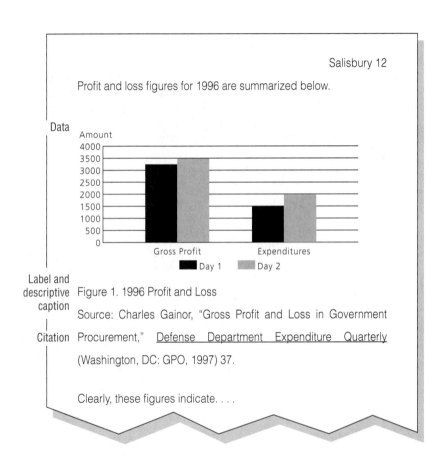

Salisbury 12

Profit and loss figures for 1996 are summarized below.

Data

Label and descriptive caption — Figure 1. 1996 Profit and Loss

Citation — Source: Charles Gainor, "Gross Profit and Loss in Government Procurement," <u>Defense Department Expenditure Quarterly</u> (Washington, DC: GPO, 1997) 37.

Clearly, these figures indicate. . . .

*Diagrams* A diagram enables you to focus on specific details of a mechanism or object. Diagrams are often used in scientific and technical writing to clarify concepts while eliminating paragraphs of detailed and confusing description. The following diagram, which illustrates the ancient Greek theater, serves a similar purpose in a literature paper.

Dixon 10

The design of the ancient Greek theater is similar to that of a present-day sports stadium, as Figure 2 illustrates.

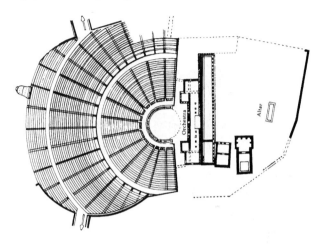

Fig. 2. The Theater of Dionysus at Athens, from W. B. Worthen, The Harcourt Brace Anthology of Drama, 3rd Edition (Fort Worth: Harcourt, 2000) 16.

Label and descriptive caption

Citation

This design, with its tiered seats, enabled the audience to view the actors onstage as well as. . . .

*Photographs* Photographs enable you to show exactly what something or someone looks like—an animal in its natural habitat, a work of fine art, or an actor in costume, for example. Although computer technology that enables you to paste photographs directly into a text is widely available, use it with restraint. Not every photograph will support or enhance your written text; in fact, an irrelevant photograph distracts readers. The following photograph of Mark Twain helps readers understand the student writer's point.

Robes 3

In the later years of his life, Twain was seen more as a personality than as a writer. Figure 3 shows him in a characteristic
pose.

Label and
descriptive
caption

Fig. 3. Mark Twain, <u>On Porch with Kitten, Mark Twain and His</u>
<u>Times,</u> 17 April 1999, U of Virginia, 18 June 2000 <http://
etext.virginia.edu/railton/index2html>.

The white suit he wears in this photograph. . . .

## ✓checklist Using visuals

- ✓ Use a visual only when it contributes something important to the discussion, not for embellishment.
- ✓ Use the visual in the text only if you plan to discuss it in your paper (place the visual in an appendix if you do not).

✓ Introduce each visual with a complete sentence.
✓ Follow each visual with a discussion of its significance.
✓ Leave wide margins around each visual.
✓ Place the visual as close as possible to the section of your document in which it is discussed.
✓ Label each visual appropriately.
✓ Document each visual borrowed from a source.

## 44b  Designing a Web Site

Because many colleges and universities provide students with a full range of Internet services, you may have the opportunity to create a Web page—or even a full Web site. You may even be asked to do so as part of the requirements for a course. Like other documents, Web pages are subject to specific conventions of document design.

Essentially, there are two ways to create Web pages. You can create a Web page from scratch using HTML (hypertext markup language), the programming language used to convert standard documents to World Wide Web hypertext documents. Or (and this is by far the easier way), you can use Web page creation software packages that are commercially available. This software automatically converts text and graphics into HTML so they can be posted on the Web.

### (1) Creating a Basic Web Page

If you have never created a Web site, you might begin by building a personal home page. **Personal home pages** usually contain information about how to contact the author, a brief biography, and links to other Web sites. Later, when you become more proficient, you can expand this home page into a full **Web site** (a group of related Web pages). Basic Web pages contain only text, but more advanced Web pages include photographs, animation, and even film clips. You can get ideas for your Web page by examining other Web pages and determining what appeals to you. Keep in mind, however, that although you may borrow formatting ideas from a Web site, it is never acceptable to plagiarize a site's content.

See 9b

### Web sites and copyright

As a rule, assume that any material on a Web site is copyrighted unless the author makes an explicit statement to the contrary. This means you must receive written permission if you are going to reproduce this material on your Web site. The only exception to this rule is the **fair use doctrine,** which allows the use of copyrighted material for the purpose of commentary, parody, or research and education. The amount of a particular work you use is also a consideration. You can quote a sentence of an article from the *New York Times* on your Web site for the purpose of commenting on it, but you must get permission from the *New York Times* to reproduce the article in its entirety. The purpose of your use—that is, whether or not you are using it commercially—is important as well: commercial use of any portion of the article always requires permission. As of now, however, you do not have to get permission to provide a link from your own Web site to the article on the *New York Times*'s Web site. (The material you quote in a research paper for one of your classes falls under the fair use doctrine and does not require permission.)

To create a simple Web page from scratch, you will need to know a few of the most basic HTML tags. (**Tags** are codes that tell your Web browser how to display text and images.) If you have a document you want to turn into a Web page, you must code it by placing the proper HTML tags where they are needed.

### Basic HTML tags

<HTML> Indicates the beginning of an HTML document

<BODY> Indicates the start of a document's body text

<P>, </P> Indicates begin paragraph and end paragraph, respectively

<H1>, <H2>, <H3>, <H4> Heading tags, from largest to smallest

<A HREF= "(Web address here)"> Tag used to create a link to another Web page

> </A> Ends linked text
>
> <BR> Indicates a line break
>
> <B> Indicates that the word following will appear in bold
>
> </B> Indicates the end of a word that will appear in bold
>
> </BODY> Indicates the end of a document's body text
>
> </HTML> Indicates the end of a document

If you examine a coded Web page, you will notice it begins with an <HTML> tag at the top and ends with an </HTML> tag at the bottom. Within the document, <BODY> and </BODY> tags indicate the beginning and end of a document's text, and paragraph <P> and heading <H> tags organize body text into headings, subheadings, and paragraphs.

Once you have mastered simple text-only pages, you can move on to design Web pages that include tables, charts, photographs, animation, and even film clips. One way to learn how to do this is to examine the HTML codes for your favorite Web pages. Do this by clicking on *view* in your browser's main menu (at the top of your computer screen) and selecting *page source* from the pull-down menu. Your browser will display the HTML code for the page you are viewing. You can "save" the source code in a word processing document and borrow it later as you create pages of your own.

## (2) Organizing Information

Before moving on to create a full Web site, sketch a basic plan on a piece of paper. Consider how your Web pages will be connected and what links you will provide to other Web sites. Your home page should provide an overview of your site and give readers a clear sense of what material the site will contain. Beginning with the home page, users will navigate from one piece of information to another.

As you plan your Web site, consider how your pages will be organized. If your site is relatively simple, you can arrange pages so one page leads sequentially to the next. For example, your personal Web site could begin with a home page and then progress to a page that presents your interest in sports, then to one that presents your volunteer work, and finally to your résumé. If your site is relatively complicated, however, you will have to group pages according to their order of importance or their relevance to a particular category. *The Brief Handbook's* Web site, for example, presents information under various headings—*Careers, Events and Resources,* and *Practice Quizzes,* for example (see Figure 1). Each of these headings contains links to other pages, which in turn link to more pages.

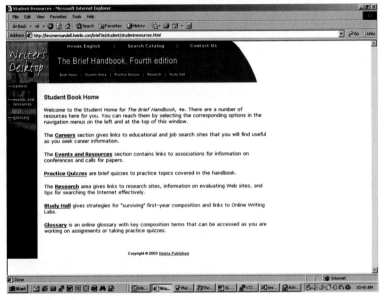

**Figure 1** *Page from* The Brief Handbook's *Web site*

When you design your Web site, you should lay out text and graphics so they present your ideas clearly and logically. Because your home page is the first thing readers will encounter, it should be clear and easy to follow. Present related items next to each other, and use text sparingly. Make sure you identify related items by highlighting them in the same color or by using the same type-face or graphic. Remember, however, that using too many graphics or elaborate typefaces will confuse readers.

## (3) Providing Links

Your home page will contain buttons or links. **Buttons**—graphic icons such as arrows or pictures—enable readers to move from one page of a Web site to another. **Links** (short for hyperlinks)—words or URLs highlighted and underlined in blue—enable readers to navigate from one site to another. Keep in mind that when you provide a link, you are directing people to the Web site to which the link refers. For this reason, you should make sure the site is up and running and the information that appears there is both relevant and reliable.

## (4) Proofreading Your Text

Before you post your site on the Web, proofread the text of your Web pages just as you would any other document. (Even if you run a spell check and a grammar check, you should still proofread carefully.) Then, make sure you have provided both *begin* and *end* tags. If you have included links on your Web site, be sure you have entered the full URL (beginning with *http://*). If you have used a colored background or text, be sure you have avoided color combinations that make your pages difficult to read (purple on black, for example). Finally, make certain you have acknowledged all material—graphics as well as text—that you have borrowed from a source.

## (5) Posting Your Web Site

Once you have designed a Web site, you will need to upload, or **post,** it so you can view it on the Web. Most commonly, Web pages are posted with FTP (File Transfer Protocol) software programs. Recent versions of the most popular Internet browsers also contain software for posting pages on the Web.

To get your site up on the Web, transfer your files to an **Internet server,** a computer connected to the Internet. Your Internet service provider will instruct you on how to use FTP to transfer your files. Once your site is up and running, you will instantly be able to see if you have made any mistakes in coding. These errors will be apparent as soon as you view your pages on the Web.

Your next step is to publicize your new Web site. Even though many search engines automatically search for new Web sites, you should give formal notification that you have launched a new site. Most search engines have links to pages where you can register new sites. Alternatively, you can access Web sites that automatically send your information to a number of Web sites. (By doing this, you do not have to repeat the same information each time you register. You can find these sites by doing a keyword search of the phrase "site registration.")

## ✓ checklist  Designing a Web site

✓ Decide what content and design features appeal to you.
✓ Consider how you want your site to be organized.
✓ Draw a basic plan of your site.
✓ Lay out text and graphics so they present your ideas clearly and logically.
✓ Supply clear and informative links.
✓ Make sure all your links are active.
✓ Proofread your text.
✓ Make sure your site looks the way you want it to.
✓ Make sure you have acknowledged all material that you have borrowed from a source.
✓ Post your site to an Internet server.
✓ Notify search engines that your site is up and running.

# Chapter 45

# Writing for the Workplace

## 45a Writing Business Letters

Business letters should be brief and to the point, with important information placed early in the letter. Be concise, avoid digressions, and try to sound as natural as possible.

The first paragraph of your letter introduces your subject and mentions any pertinent previous correspondence. The body of your letter presents the facts readers need in order to understand your points. (If your ideas are complicated, present your points in a bulleted or numbered list.) Your conclusion should reinforce your message.

See 44a3

Single-space within paragraphs, and double-space between paragraphs. Proofread carefully to make sure there are no errors in spelling or punctuation. Most often business letters use **block format,** with all parts of the letter aligned with the left-hand margin.

---

**http://kirsznermandell.heinle.com**

### Sending messages by fax and e-mail

The standards for electronic messages are the same as those for any other form of business correspondence.

**Faxes** Remember that faxes are often received not by an individual but at a central location, so include a cover sheet that contains the recipient's name and title, the date, the company and department, the fax and telephone numbers, and the total number of pages faxed. In addition, supply your own name and telephone and fax numbers. (It is also a good idea to call ahead to alert the addressee that a fax is coming.)

**E-mail** Although e-mail can be quite informal, you should treat an e-mail message as if it were a standard business letter. Include a salutation and a subject line, and be sure to state your purpose and to present your ideas clearly and succinctly. Avoid slang and imprecise diction, and proofread carefully. Also keep in mind that e-mail composed at work is the property of the employer, who has the legal right to access it. Finally, never forward a business e-mail to another person or to an electronic bulletin board, such as a newsgroup or listserv, unless you have the writer's permission.

Writing for the Workplace

✳ *Sample Letter—Block Format*

Heading   6732 Wyncote Avenue
Houston, TX 77004
May 3, 2002

Inside   Mr. William S. Price, Jr., Director
address   Division of Archives and History
Department of Cultural Resources
109 East Jones Street
Raleigh, NC 27611

Salutation   Dear Mr. Price:

Thank you for sending me the material I requested about pirates in colonial North Carolina.

Body   Both the pamphlets and the bibliography were extremely useful for my research. Without your help, I am sure my paper would not have been so well received.

I have enclosed a copy of my paper, and I would appreciate any comments you may have. Again, thank you for your time and trouble.

Complimentary
close   Sincerely yours,

Written
signature   *Kevin Wolk*

Typed   Kevin Wolk
signature

Copy sent   cc: Dr. N. Provisor, Professor of History
Additional   Enc.: Research paper
data

**492**

## 45b   Writing Letters of Application

When you apply for employment, your primary objective is to obtain an interview. The **letter of application** summarizes your qualifications for a specific position.

Begin your letter of application by identifying the job you are applying for and stating where you heard about it—in a newspaper, in a professional journal, on the Internet, or from your school's job placement service, for example. Be sure to include the date of the advertisement and the exact title of the position. End your introduction with a statement that expresses your ability to do the job.

In the body of your letter, provide the information that will convince your reader of your qualifications—for example, relevant courses you have taken and pertinent job experience. Be sure to address any specific points mentioned in the advertisement. Above all, emphasize your strengths, and explain how they relate to the specific job for which you are applying.

Conclude by saying that you have enclosed your résumé. State that you are available for an interview, noting any dates on which you will not be available.

**?** ✳ *Sample Letter of Application*

| | |
|---|---|
| Heading | 246 Hillside Drive |
| | Urbana, IL 61801 |
| | October 20, 2002 |
| | kr237@metropolis.105.com |
| Inside address | Mr. Maurice Snyder, Personnel Director |
| | Guilford, Fox, and Morris |
| | 22 Hamilton Street |
| | Urbana, IL 61822 |
| Salutation | Dear Mr. Snyder: |

My college advisor, Dr. Raymond Walsh, has told me that you are interested in hiring a part-time accounting assistant. I believe that my academic background and my work experience qualify me for this position.

**Body** — I am presently a junior accounting major at the University of Illinois. During the past year, I have taken courses in taxation, trusts, and business law. I am also proficient in Lotus and ClarisWorks. Last spring, I gained practical accounting experience by working in our department's tax clinic.

Double-space →

After I graduate, I hope to get a master's degree in taxation and then return to the Urbana area. I believe that my experience in taxation as well as my familiarity with the local business community would enable me to contribute to your firm.

Single-space →

I have enclosed a résumé for your examination. I will be available for an interview any time after midterm examinations, which end October 25. I look forward to hearing from you.

Complimentary close — Sincerely yours,

Written signature — *Sandra Kraft*

Typed signature — Sandra Kraft

Additional data — Enc.: Résumé

## 45c    Designing Print Résumés

A résumé lists relevant information about your education, your job experience, your goals, and your personal interests.

There is no single correct format for a résumé. You may decide to arrange your résumé in **chronological order** (see page 496), listing your education and work experience in sequence (beginning with the most recent), or in **emphatic order** (see page 497), beginning with the material that will be of most interest to an employer (for example, important skills). Whatever a résumé's arrangement, it should be brief—one page is sufficient for an undergraduate—easy to read, and logically organized.

### Print résumés

Use strong action verbs to describe your duties, responsibilities, and accomplishments.

| | | |
|---|---|---|
| accomplished | achieved | supervised |
| communicated | collaborated | instructed |
| completed | implemented | proposed |
| performed | organized | trained |

Note: Use past tense for past positions and present tense for current positions.

KAREN L. OLSON

SCHOOL
3312 Hamilton St. Apt. 18
Philadelphia, PA 19104
215-382-0831
olsonk@durm.ocs.drexel.edu

HOME
110 Ascot Ct.
Harmony, PA 16037
412-452-2944

EDUCATION

DREXEL UNIVERSITY, Philadelphia, PA 19104
Bachelor of Science in Graphic Design
Anticipated Graduation: June 2002
Cumulative Grade Point Average: 3.2 on a 4.0 scale

COMPUTER SKILLS AND COURSE WORK

HARDWARE
Operate both Macintosh computer and PCs.

SOFTWARE
*Adobe Illustrator, Photoshop,* and *TypeAlign; QuarkXPress; CorelDRAW; Micrografx Designer*

COURSES
Corporate Identity, Environmental Graphics, Typography, Photography, Painting and Printmaking, Sculpture, Computer Imaging, Art History

EMPLOYMENT EXPERIENCE

UNISYS CORPORATION, Blue Bell, PA 19124
June–September 1999, Cooperative Education
Graphic Designer. Designed interior pages as well as covers for target marketing brochures. Created various logos and spot art designed for use on inter-office memos and departmental publications.

CHARMING SHOPPES, INC., Bensalem, PA 19020
June–December 1998, Cooperative Education
Graphic Designer/Fashion Illustrator. Created graphics for future placement on garments. Did some textile designing. Drew flat illustrations of garments to scale in computer. Prepared presentation boards.

*THE TRIANGLE.* Drexel University, Philadelphia, PA 19104
January 1999–present
Graphics Editor. Design all display advertisements submitted to Drexel's student newspaper.

DESIGN AND IMAGING STUDIO, Drexel University, Philadelphia, PA 19104
October 1997–June 1999
Monitor. Supervised computer activity in studio. Answered telephone. Assisted other graphic design students in using computer programs.

ACTIVITIES AND AWARDS

*The Triangle,* Graphics Editor: 1998–present
Kappa Omicron Nu Honor Society, vice president: 1997–present
Dean's List: Spring 1996, fall and winter 1997
Graphics Group, vice president: 1997–present

REFERENCES AND PORTFOLIO

Available upon request.

✳ *Sample Résumé: Emphatic Order* ❓

# Michael D. Fuller

SCHOOL
27 College Avenue
University of Maryland
College Park, MD 20742
(301) 357-0732
mful532@aol.com

HOME
1203 Hampton Road
Joppa, MD 21085
(301) 877-1437

Restaurant Experience

McDonald's Restaurant, Pikesville, MD. Cook.
Prepared hamburgers. Acted as assistant manager for two weeks while manager was on vacation. Supervised employees, helped prepare payroll and work schedules. Was named employee of the month. Summer 1998.

University of Maryland, College Park, MD. Cafeteria busboy.
Cleaned tables, set up cafeteria, and prepared hot trays. September 1999–May 2000.

Other Work Experience

University of Maryland Library, College Park, MD. Reference assistant. Filed, sorted, typed, shelved, and catalogued. Earnings offset college expenses. September 1998–May 1999.

Education

University of Maryland, College Park, MD (sophomore).
Biology major. Expected date of graduation: June 2002.
Forest Park High School, Baltimore, MD.

Interests

Member of University Debating Society.
Tutor in University's Academic Enrichment Program.

References

Mr. Arthur Sanducci, Manager
McDonald's Restaurant
5712 Avery Road
Pikesville, MD 22513

Mr. William Czernick, Manager
Cafeteria
University of Maryland
College Park, MD 20742

Ms. Stephanie Young, Librarian
Library
University of Maryland
College Park, MD 20742

# 45d  Designing Scannable Résumés

Many employers now request scannable résumés that they will download into a database for future reference. If you have to prepare such a résumé, you must format it accordingly. Because scanners will not pick up columns, bullets, or italics, do not use them in a scannable résumé. In addition, do not use shaded or colored paper, which will make your résumé difficult to read. (**NOTE:** If you are sending your résumé as an e-mail attachment to be downloaded into a database, use the guidelines discussed here. If it will be stored as a print document, follow the guidelines in **45c.**)

Whereas in a print résumé you use specific action verbs (*edited company newsletter*) to describe your accomplishments, in a scannable résumé you also use key nouns (*editor*) that can be entered into a company database. These words will help employers find your résumé when they carry out a keyword search for applicants with certain skills. (To facilitate a keyword search, some applicants include a Keyword section on their résumés.) In addition, a scannable résumé may include a separate section that lists skills. For example, if you wanted to emphasize your computer skills, you would include terms such as *WordPerfect, FileMaker Pro,* and *PowerPoint.*

**http://kirsznermandell.heinle.com**

**?**

### Posting a résumé

Increasingly, résumés are posted on electronic bulletin boards or on Web sites such as Monster.com, and frequently, these résumés contain hyperlinks to other sites. (These links are underlined and highlighted in blue.) For example, your name could be a link to your home page, which might include a biographical sketch as well as pictures and a short video clip. Or, a company's name in your résumé's Work Experience section could be a link to the company's Web site. Presently, the majority of résumés are still submitted on paper, but electronic résumés are gaining in popularity, and many experts believe the paper résumé will soon be a thing of the past.

## ❋ Sample Résumé: Scannable

Constantine G. Doukakis
2000 Clover Lane          Phone: (817) 735-9120
Fort Worth, TX 76107      E-Mail: Douk@aol.com

Employment Objective: Entry-level position in an organization that will enable me to use my academic knowledge and the skills that I learned in my work experience.

Education:

University of Texas at Arlington, Bachelor of Science in Civil Engineering. June 2000. Major: Structural Engineering. Graduated Magna Cum Laude. Overall GPA: 3.754 on a 4.0 base.

Scholastic Honors and Awards:

Member of Phi Eta Sigma First-Year Academic Honor Society, Chi Epsilon Civil Engineering Academic Society, Tau Beta Pi Engineering Academic Society, Golden Key National Honor Society.

Jack Woolf Memorial Scholarship for Outstanding Academic Performance.

Cooperative Employment Experience:

Dallas-Fort Worth International Airport, Tarrant County, TX, Dec. 1998 to June 1999. Assistant Engineer. Supervised and inspected airfield paving, drainage, and utility projects as well as terminal building renovations. Performed on-site and laboratory soil tests. Prepared concrete samples for load testing.

Dallas-Fort Worth International Airport, Tarrant County, TX, Jan. 1999 to June 1999. Draftsperson in Design Office. Prepared contract drawings and updated base plans as well as designed and estimated costs for small construction projects.

Johnson County Electric Cooperative, Cleburne, TX, Jan. 1998 to June 1998. Junior Engineer in Plant Dept. of Maintenance and Construction Division. Inspected and supervised in-plant construction. Devised solutions to construction problems. Estimated costs of materials for small construction projects. Presented historical data relating to the function of the department.

Key Words:

Organizational and leadership skills. Written and oral communication skills. IBM microcomputer hardware. DOS, Windows 2000, and MacOs. Word, Excel, FileMakerPro, PowerPoint, WordPerfect, and various Internet client software. Computer model development.

# 45e   Writing Memos

Memos communicate information within an organization. A memo can be short or long, depending on its purpose.

Begin your memo with a purpose statement that presents your reason for writing the memo. Follow this statement with a summary section that tells readers what to expect in the rest of the memo. Then, in the body of your memo, present your support: the detailed information that supports the main point of your memo. If your memo is short, use bulleted or numbered lists to emphasize information. If it is long—more than two or three paragraphs—use headings to designate the various sections of the memo (*Summary, Background, Benefits,* and so on). End your memo with a statement of your conclusions and recommendations.

### Sample Memo

TO: Ina Ellen, Senior Counselor
FROM: Kim Williams, Student Tutor Supervisor
SUBJECT: Construction of a Tutoring Center
DATE: November 10, 2002

Opening component

This memo proposes the establishment of a tutoring center in the Office of Student Affairs.

Purpose statement

BACKGROUND
Under the present system, tutors must work with students at a number of facilities scattered across the university campus. As a result, tutors waste a lot of time running from one facility to another and are often late for appointments.

NEW FACILITY
I propose that we establish a tutoring facility adjacent to the Office of Student Affairs. The two empty classrooms next to the office, presently used for storage of office furniture, would be ideal for this use. We could furnish these offices with the desks and file cabinets already stored in these rooms.

Body

BENEFITS
The benefits of this facility would be the centralizing of the tutoring services and the proximity of the facility to the Office of Student Affairs. The tutoring facility could also use the secretarial services of the Office of Student Affairs.

RECOMMENDATIONS
To implement this project we would need to do the following:

Conclusion

1. Clean up and paint rooms 331 and 333
2. Use folding partitions to divide each room into five single-desk offices
3. Use stored office equipment to furnish the center

I am certain these changes would do much to improve the tutoring service. I look forward to discussing this matter with you in more detail.

# 45f Writing E-Mail

In many workplaces, virtually all internal (and some external) communications are transmitted as e-mail. Although personal e-mail tends to be quite informal, business e-mail observes the conventions of standard written communication. The following guidelines can help you communicate effectively in an electronic environment.

---

## ✓checklist Writing e-mail

✓ Write in complete sentences. Avoid the slang, imprecise diction, and abbreviations that are commonplace in personal e-mail.

✓ Use an appropriate tone. Address readers with respect, just as you would in a standard business letter.

✓ Include a subject line that clearly identifies your content. If your subject line is vague, your e-mail may be deleted without being read.

✓ Make your message as short as possible. Because most e-mails are read on the screen, long discussions are difficult to follow.

✓ Use short paragraphs, and leave an extra space between paragraphs.

✓ Use lists and internal headings to make your message easier to read and understand.

✓ Take the time to edit your e-mail after you have written it. Delete excess words and phrases.

✓ Proofread carefully before sending your e-mail. Look for errors in grammar, spelling, and punctuation.

✓ Make sure that your list of recipients is accurate and that you do not send your e-mail to unintended recipients.

✓ Do not send your e-mail until you are absolutely certain your message says exactly what you want it to say.

✓ Do not forward an e-mail unless you have the permission of the sender.

✓ Watch what you write. Keep in mind that e-mail written at work is the property of the employer, who has the legal right to access it, even without your permission.

---

http://kirsznermandell.heinle.com

## Opening e-mail attachments

Be careful opening attachments. E-mail attachments can contain viruses, so only open attachments from people you know. In addition, make sure you keep your virus-scanning software current.

### Voice mail

Like e-mail, voice mail can present challenges. The following tips will help you deliver a voice-mail message clearly and effectively.

- *Try to organize your message before you deliver it.* Long, meandering, or repetitive messages will frustrate listeners.
- *State the subject of your message first.* Then, fill in the details.
- *Speak slowly.* Many experts advise people to speak much more slowly than they would in normal conversation.
- *Speak clearly.* Enunciate your words precisely so a listener will understand your message the first time. Be sure to spell your name.
- *Give your phone number twice—once at the beginning and again at the end of your message.* No on wants to replay a voice-mail message just to get a phone number.
- Don't forget to state the date and time of your call.

# Chapter 46

# Making Oral Presentations

At school and on the job, you may sometimes be called on to make an oral presentation. In a college course, you might be asked to explain your ideas, to defend your position, or to present the results of your research. At work, you might be asked to discuss a process, propose a project, or solve a problem. Although many people are uncomfortable about giving oral presentations, the guidelines that follow can make the process easier and less stressful.

## 46a  Getting Started

Just as with writing an essay, the preparation phase of an oral presentation is as important as the speech itself. The time you spend on this phase will make your task easier later on.

*Identify Your Topic*  The first thing you should do is to identify the topic of your speech. Sometimes you are given a topic; at other times, you have the option of choosing your own. Once you have a topic, you should decide how much information, as well as what kind of information, you will need.

*Consider Your Audience*  The easiest way to determine what kind of information you will need is to consider the nature of your audience. Is your audience made up of experts or of people who know very little about your topic? How much background information will you have to provide? Can you use technical terms, or should you avoid them? Do you think your audience will be interested in your topic, or will you have to create interest? What opinions or ideas about your topic will the members of your audience bring with them?

**Audience**

An **expert audience** is made up of people who have intimate knowledge of your particular field or subject.
A **collegial audience** is made up of people who share the same frame of reference as you do.
A **general audience** is made up of people who have no specific knowledge of your topic or field.
A **mixed audience** is made up of people who have varying degrees of knowledge about your topic or field.

*Consider Your Purpose* Your speech should have a specific purpose that you can sum up concisely—for example, *to suggest ways to make registration easier for students.* To help you zero in on your purpose, ask yourself what you are trying to accomplish with your presentation. Are you trying to inform? to instruct? to stimulate an exchange of ideas? to get support for a project? to solicit feedback? to persuade? It is good idea to keep this purpose statement in front you on an index card to keep you focused as you plan your speech.

*Consider Your Constraints* How much time do you have for your presentation? (Obviously a ten-minute presentation requires more information and preparation than a three-minute presentation.) Do you already know enough about your topic, or will you have to do research? Where will you go to find information? Would you go to the library? the Internet? somewhere else?

## 46b Planning Your Speech

At the planning phase, you focus your ideas about your topic and develop a thesis; then, you decide what specific points you will discuss and divide your speech into a few manageable sections.

*Develop a Thesis Statement* Before you actually begin to plan your speech, develop a thesis statement that clearly and concisely presents your main idea—the key idea you want to communicate to your audience. For example, the student who wrote the purpose statement above came up with this thesis statement for her speech: *The university needs to implement a three-step plan to make registration easier for students.* If you know a lot about your topic, you can develop a thesis on your own. If you do not, you will have to gather information and review it before you can decide on a thesis. As you plan your speech, remember to refer to your thesis to make sure you stay on track.

***Decide on Your Points*** Once you have developed a thesis, you can decide what points you will discuss. Unlike readers, who can reread a passage until they understand it, listeners must understand information the first time they hear it. For this reason, speeches usually focus on points that are clear and easy to follow. Frequently, your thesis statement states or strongly implies these points: *There are three steps that the university should take to make registration easier for students.*

***Gather Support*** You cannot expect your listeners to accept what you say on face value. You must supply details, facts, and examples to convince listeners that what you are saying is both accurate and reasonable. You can gather supporting material in the library, on the Web, or from your own experience. No matter how much support you supply, however, you should expect listeners to ask questions and be prepared to answer them.

***Outline the Individual Parts of Your Speech*** Every speech has a beginning, a middle, and an end. Your **introduction** should introduce your subject, engage your audience's interest, and state your thesis—but it should *not* present an in-depth discussion or a summary of your topic. The **body,** or middle section, of your speech should present the points that support your thesis. It should also include the facts, examples, and other information that will clarify your points and help convince listeners your thesis is reasonable. As you present your points, use strong topic sentences to lead listeners from one point to another: *The first step, The second step,* and so on. Your **conclusion** should bring your speech to a definite end and reinforce your thesis. Because an audience remembers best what it hears last, this section is extremely important. In your conclusion, restate your thesis and reaffirm how your speech supports it.

## 46c   Preparing Your Notes

Most people use notes of some form when they give a speech. Each system of notes has advantages and disadvantages.

506

*Full Text* Some people like to write out the full text of their speech and refer to it during their presentation. If the type is large enough, and if you triple-space, such notes can be useful. One disadvantage of using a full text of your speech is that it is easy to lose your place and become disoriented; another is that you may find yourself simply reading your speech. In either case, you not only stop relating to your audience but also lose their interest.

*3×5 Cards* Some people write parts of their speech—for example, a list of key points or definitions—on 3×5 note cards. Cards are portable, so they can be rearranged easily. They are also small, so they can be placed inconspicuously on a podium or a table. With some practice, you can learn to use note cards effectively. You have to be careful, however, not to become so dependent on the cards that you lose eye contact with your audience or begin fidgeting with the cards as you give your speech.

*Outlines* Some people like to refer to an outline when they give a speech. As they speak, they can glance down at the outline to get their bearings or to remind themselves of a point they may have forgotten. Because an outline does not contain the full text of a speech, the temptation to read is eliminated. However, if for some reason you draw a blank, an outline gives you very little to fall back on.

*Visual Aids* Finally, some people like to use visual aids—such as overhead projectors, slides, or computer presentation software like Microsoft's *PowerPoint* to keep them on track.

See 46d

## 46d  Preparing Visual Aids

As you plan your speech, decide whether you want to use some type of visual aid. Visual aids such as overhead transparencies, posters, or *PowerPoint* can reinforce important information and make your speech easier to understand. They can also break the monotony of a speech and help focus an audience's attention.

For a simple speech, a visual aid may be no more than a definition or a few key terms, names, or dates written on the board. For a more complicated presentation, you might need charts, graphs, diagrams, or photographs—or even objects. The major consideration for including a visual aid is whether it actually adds something to your speech. If a poster will help your listeners understand some key concepts, then by all means use one. However, if it will do little to highlight the information in your speech, then do not use it. Finally, if you are using equipment such as a slide projector or a laptop, make sure you know how to operate it—and have a contingency plan just in case the equipment does not work the way it should. For example, it is a good idea to back up a *PowerPoint* presentation with overhead transparencies just in case the computer at school or at work will not open your files.

If possible, visit the room in which you will be giving your speech, and see whether it has the equipment you need. Some college classrooms are equipped with overhead projectors or computer interfaces; at other schools, you have to make arrangements in advance for equipment.

Finally, make sure that whatever visual aid you use is large enough for everyone in your audience to see. Printing or typing should be neat and free of errors, and graphics should be clearly labeled and easy to see. A slide from a *PowerPoint* presentation appears below.

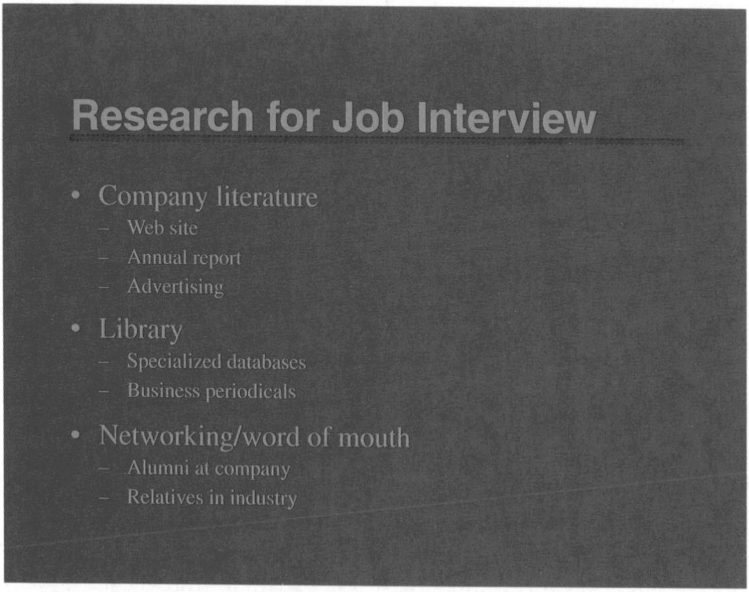

**Figure 1** *Sample* PowerPoint *slide*

# Preparing Visual Aids

## Using Visual Aids in Your Presentations

| Visual Aid | Advantages | Disadvantages |
|---|---|---|
| *Computer presentations* | • Clear<br>• Easy to read<br>• Professional<br>• Graphics and animated effects<br>• Portable (disk or CD-ROM) | • Special equipment needed<br>• Expertise needed<br>• Special software needed<br>• Software might not be compatible with all computer systems |
| *Overhead projectors* | • Transparencies are inexpensive<br>• Transparencies are easily prepared with computer or copier<br>• Transparencies are portable<br>• Transparencies can be written on during presentation<br>• Projector is easy to operate | • Transparencies can stick together<br>• Transparencies can be placed upside down.<br>• Some projectors are noisy<br>• Transparencies must be placed on projector by hand<br>• Speaker must avoid power cord to projector during presentation |
| *Slide projector* | • Colorful<br>• Professional<br>• Projector is easy to use<br>• Slides can be reversed during presentation<br>• Portable (slide carousel) | • Slides are expensive to produce<br>• Special equipment needed for lettering and graphics<br>• Dark room needed for presentation<br>• Slides can jam in projector |
| *Posters or flip charts* | • Low-tech and personal<br>• Good for small-group presentations<br>• Portable | • May not be large enough to be seen in some rooms<br>• Artistic ability needed<br>• May be expensive if prepared professionally<br>• Must be secured to an easel |
| *Chalkboards or whiteboards* | • Available in most presentation rooms<br>• Easy to use<br>• Easy to erase or change information during presentation | • Difficult to draw complicated graphics<br>• Handwriting must be legible<br>• Must catch errors as you write<br>• Cannot face audience when writing or drawing<br>• Very informal |

---

## ✓checklist Designing visual aids

✓ Do not put more than three or four major points on a single visual.
✓ Use single words or short phrases, not sentences or paragraphs.
✓ Use bulleted or numbered lists.
✓ Use drawings and photographs only when they are large enough and clear enough to be seen.

*continued on the following page*

*continued from the previous page*

✓ Limit the number of visuals. For a three- to five-minute presentation, five or six visuals are usually enough.

✓ Use the same color type and the same typeface and type size for comparable material.

✓ Use color to enhance your presentation. Use contrasting colors for backgrounds so lettering or graphics stand out.

✓ Use type that is large enough for your audience to see (36-point type for major headings and 18-point type for text).

✓ Do not use elaborate graphics or special effects just because your computer software enables you to do so (this is especially relevant for users of *PowerPoint*).

## 46e    Rehearsing Your Speech

There is a direct relationship between how thoroughly you prepared and how effective your speech is. For this reason, practice your speech often—at least five times—and make sure you practice delivering your speech with your visuals. (You want to discover problems with your visuals now and not during your presentation.) Do not try to memorize your entire speech, but be sure you know it well enough so you can move from point to point without constantly looking at your notes.

If possible, rehearse your speech in the actual room you will be using, and try standing at the back of the room to make sure your visuals can be seen clearly. You should also practice in front of friends, and get some constructive criticism about both the content and the delivery of your speech. Another strategy is to use a tape recorder to help you rehearse. When you play back the tape, you can hear whether you are pronouncing your words clearly and whether you are saying "uh" or "you know" throughout your presentation. Finally, time yourself. Make certain your three-minute speech actually takes three minutes to deliver.

## 46f    Delivering Your Speech

The most important part of your speech is your delivery. Keep in mind that a certain amount of nervousness is normal, so try not to focus on your nervousness too much. Channel the nervous energy into your speech, and let it work for you. While you are waiting to begin, take some deep breaths and calm down. Once you get to the front of the room, do not start right away. Take the time to make sure everything you will need is there and all your equipment is positioned properly.

Before you speak, make sure both feet are flat on the floor and you are facing the audience. When you begin speaking, pace yourself. Speak slowly and clearly, and look at the entire audience, one person at a time. Make sure you speak *to* your audience, not *at* them. Even though your speech is planned, it should sound natural and conversational. Speak loudly enough for everyone in the room to hear you, and remember to vary your pitch and your volume so you do not speak in a monotone. Try using pauses to emphasize important points and to give listeners time to consider what you have said. Finally, sound enthusiastic about your subject. If you appear to be bored or distracted, your audience will be too.

Your movements should be purposeful and natural. Do not pace or lean against something. Move around only when the need arises—for example, to change a visual, to point to a chart, or to distribute something. Never turn your back to your audience; if you have to write on the board, make sure you are angled toward the audience. Try to use hand movements to emphasize points, but do not play with pens or notecards as you speak, and do not put your hands in your pockets. Also, resist the temptation to deliver your speech from behind a podium or a table: come around to the front and address the audience directly.

Finally, dress appropriately for the occasion. How you look will be the first thing that listeners notice about you. (Although shorts and a T-shirt may be appropriate for an afternoon in the park, they are not suitable for a presentation.) Dressing appropriately not only demonstrates your respect for your audience but also shows that you are someone who deserves to be taken seriously.

## (✓checklist) Delivering your speech

✓ Take your time before you begin.
✓ Make sure your visuals are positioned properly.
✓ Make sure equipment is operating properly.
✓ Position yourself effectively.
✓ Stand straight.
✓ Speak slowly and clearly.
✓ Maintain eye contact with the audience.
✓ Use natural gestures.
✓ Face the audience at all times.

*continued on the following page*

**511**

*continued from the previous page*

✓ Do not block your visuals.
✓ Try to relax.
✓ Do not get flustered if something unexpected happens.
✓ If you forget something, don't let your audience know. Work it in later.
✓ Do not sit down immediately after your speech. Leave time for questions.

# ESL

**47 English for Speakers of Other Languages    515**

**47a** Nouns   516
**47b** Pronouns   519
**47c** Verbs   521
**47d** Adjectives and Adverbs   530
**47e** Prepositions   532
**47f** Word Order   535
**47g** Eliminating Wordiness   537
**47h** Commonly Confused Words   538

# PART 13

## ❓ Frequently Asked Questions

**Chapter 47** **English for Speakers of Other Languages   515**
- Why can't I write *clothings* and *informations*❓   517
- What is the difference between *a* and *the*❓   517
- What is a double negative❓   525
- If several adjectives modify one noun, which adjective goes first❓   531
- How do I know which preposition to use❓   533
- Does the subject of a sentence always come before the verb❓   535

| **URLs** | *Visit the following sites for answers to more FAQs* |
|---|---|

**The ESL Study Hall (George Washington U.)**
*http://home.gwu.edu/~meloni/eslstudyhall/*

**Dave Sperling's ESL (Eng. as a Second Language) Cafe**
*http://www.eslcafe.com/*

# English for Speakers of Other Languages

## ✓checklist English language basics

✓ **In English, words may change their form according to their function.** In some languages, words do not change form, or they change form according to rules different from those of English. For example, in English, verbs change form to communicate whether an action is taking place in the past, present, or future; in Chinese, however, other words may be added to the sentence to indicate when the action took place (yesterday, last month, ten years ago), but the verb itself does not change form to indicate past tense action.

✓ **In English, context is extremely important to understanding function.** Sometimes it is impossible to identify the function of an English word without noting its context. In the following sentences, for instance, the very same words can perform different functions according to their relationships to other words:

Juan and I are taking a <u>walk</u>. (*Walk* is a noun, a direct object of the verb *taking*, with an article, *a*, attached to it.)
If you <u>walk</u> instead of driving, you will help conserve the earth's resources. (*Walk* is a verb, the predicate of the subject *you*.)

Jie was <u>walking</u> across campus when she met her chemistry professor. (*Walking* is part of the verb, predicate of the subject *Jie*.)
<u>Walking</u> a few miles a day will make you healthier. (*Walking* is a noun, the subject of the verb *will make*.)
Next summer we'll take a walking tour of southern Italy. (*Walking is an adjective describing tour*.)

✓ **Spelling in English is not <u>perfectly</u> phonetic and sometimes may seem illogical.** In many languages that use a phonetic alphabet or syllabary, such as Japanese, Korean, or Persian script, words are spelled exactly as they are pronounced. <u>Spelling</u> in English may be related more to the history of the word and its origins in other languages than to the way the word is pronounced. Therefore, learning to spell correctly is often a matter of

See
Ch. 34

*continued on the following page*

*continued from the previous page*

See ESL
47f

See
1a3

memorization, not sounding out the word phonetically. For example, "ough" is pronounced differently in the words *tough, though,* and *thought.*

✓ Word order **is extremely important in English sentences.** For example, word order may indicate which word is the subject of the sentence and which is the object, or whether the sentence is a question or a statement.

✓ Writing in American English is more direct and more concise than writing in many other languages. Although it may seem rude to do so in your native culture, explaining your main points immediately in an essay or other piece of writing is valued in English. Most American English instructors will require that you state a **thesis** at the beginning of your essay instead of waiting to reveal the points you wish to convey. The material that supports your thesis should then follow in a linear fashion. By avoiding formality, unnecessary repetition, and overly complex sentence structures, you will keep your readers interested in your writing.

## 47a   Nouns

Writer's
Resource
CD-ROM

See
A1

A *noun* names things: people, objects, places, feelings, ideas. Nouns can be quite different in different languages. In some languages, nouns have gender; that is, they may be **masculine** or **feminine.** In Spanish, for example, the word for *moon* (*la luna*) is feminine, whereas the word for *sun* (*el sol*) is masculine. In English, however, nouns do not have gender. In other languages, there is no difference between the singular and plural forms of nouns. In Japanese, for instance, one person is *hito,* and many people are still *hito.* In English, however, most nouns have different forms for singular and plural number (such as singular *star* and plural *stars*), but there are exceptions to this rule. In some languages (including English), nouns may be used as adjectives: "She ate a cheese sandwich."

### (1) Singular, Plural, and Noncount Nouns

In English, nouns may have **number;** that is, they may change in form according to whether they name one thing or more than one

# Nouns

thing. If a noun names one thing, it is a *singular* noun; if a noun names more than one thing, it is a **plural** noun.

See 34b7

To change most singular nouns to plural, add -*s* or -*es* to the singular form. For example, *pencil* changes to *pencils*, and *bench* changes to *benches*.

However, many nouns in English are irregular. To change an irregular noun from singular to plural, you will need to change the spelling of the word instead of just adding -*s* or -*es* to the end of the word. For example, *mouse* changes to *mice*, *tooth* changes to *teeth*, and *child* changes to *children*.

Some English nouns do not have a plural form. These are called **noncount nouns** because what they name cannot be counted. (**Count nouns** name items that can be counted, such as *woman* or *desk*.)

To avoid confusion, consult a dictionary in order to determine if a noun takes a regular plural form or an irregular plural form and to determine if a noun is a count or a noncount noun.

### Noncount nouns

The following commonly used nouns are noncount nouns. These words have no plural forms. Therefore, you should never add -*s* to them.

?

| | |
|---|---|
| advice | homework |
| clothing | information |
| education | knowledge |
| equipment | luggage |
| evidence | merchandise |
| furniture | revenge |

## (2) Using Articles with Nouns

English has two type of articles, indefinite and definite. Use an indefinite article (*a* or *an*) with a noun when readers are not familiar with the noun you are naming—for example, when you are introducing a noun for the first time. To say, "Jatin entered *a* building" signals to the audience that you are introducing the idea of the building into your speech or writing for the first time. The building is unspecific, or indefinite, until it has been identified.

?

English for Speakers of Other Languages

The indefinite article *a* is used when the word following it (which may be a noun or an adjective) begins with a consonant or with a consonant sound: *a tree, a onetime offer*. The indefinite article *an* is used if the word following it begins with a vowel (*a, e, i, o,* or *u*) or with a vowel sound: *an apple, an honor*.

Use the definite article (*the*) when the noun you are naming has already been introduced, when the noun is already familiar to readers, or when the noun to which you refer is specific. To say, "Jatin entered *the* building" signals to readers that you are referring to the same building you mentioned earlier. The building now has become specific and may be referred to by the definite article.

**Using articles with nouns**

There are three main exceptions to the rules governing the use of articles with nouns.

1. A **plural noun** does not require an **indefinite article:** "I love horses," not "I love <u>a</u> horses." (A plural noun does, however, require a definite article when you have already introduced the noun to your readers or when you are referring to a specific plural noun: "I love <u>the</u> horses in the national park near my house.")

2. A **noncount noun** may or may not require an article: "Love conquers all," not "<u>A</u> love conquers all" or "<u>The</u> love conquers all." "A good education is important," not "Good education is important." "The homework is difficult" or "Homework is difficult," not "<u>A</u> homework is difficult."

3. A **proper noun,** which names a particular person, place, or thing, sometimes takes an article and sometimes does not. When you use an article with a proper noun, do not capitalize the article unless the article is the first word of the sentence.

"<u>The</u> Mississippi River is one of the longest rivers in the world," not "Mississippi River is one of the longest rivers in the world." "Teresa was born in <u>the</u> United States," not "Teresa was born in United States." "China is the most populous nation on earth," not "<u>The</u> China is the most populous nation on earth."

### (3) Using Other Determiners with Nouns

**Determiners** are words that function as <u>adjectives</u> to limit or qualify the meaning of nouns. In addition to articles, nouns may be identified by other determiners that function in ways similar to articles, such as **demonstrative pronouns, possessive nouns** and **pronouns, numbers** (both **cardinal** and **ordinal**), and other words indicating number and order.

See
A4

## Using other determiners with nouns

1. **Demonstrative pronouns** (*this, that, these, those*) communicate
   - The relative nearness or farness of the noun from the speaker's position. Use *this* and *these* for things that are near; use *that* and *those* for things that are far: *this* book on my desk, *that* book on your desk, *these* shoes on my feet, *those* shoes in the closet.
   - The number of things indicated. Use *this* and *that* for singular nouns, *these* and *those* for plural nouns: *this* (or *that*) flower in the vase, *these* (or *those*) flowers in the garden.
2. **Possessive nouns** and **possessive pronouns** (*Ashraf's, his, their*) show who or what the noun belongs to: *Maria's* courage, *everybody's* fears, the *country's* natural resources, *my* personality, *our* groceries.
3. **Cardinal** numbers (*three, fifty, a thousand*) indicate how many of the noun you mean: *seven* continents, *twelve* apples, a *hundred* lakes. **Ordinal** numbers (*first, tenth, thirtieth*) indicate in what order the noun appears among other items: *third* planet from the sun, *first* date, *tenth* anniversary.
4. Words other than numbers may indicate **amount** (*many, few*) or **order** (*next, last*) and function in the same ways as cardinal and ordinal numbers: *few* opportunities, *last* chance.

## 47b Pronouns

Writer's
Resource
CD-ROM

See
A2

Any English noun may be replaced by a <u>pronoun</u>. For example, *doctor* may be replaced by *he* or *she*, *books* by *them*, and *computer* by *it*. The English language uses more pronouns than most other languages. In Japanese, for example, it is common to repeat the noun again and again without using a pronoun replacement, but such repetition would sound odd to a native speaker of English. (Note that a pronoun, like the noun it replaces, must agree with the verb in number.)

## (1) Pronoun Reference

**See 19c**

**Pronoun reference** is very important in English sentences, where the noun the pronoun replaces (the **antecedent**) must be easily identified. For this reason, you should place the pronoun as close as possible to the noun it replaces so the noun to which the pronoun refers is clear. Sometimes, however, this is impossible. In such cases, it is best to use the noun itself instead of replacing it with a pronoun.

Unclear: When Tara met Emily, <u>she</u> was nervous. (Does *she* refer to Tara or Emily?)

Clear: When Tara met Emily, <u>Tara</u> was nervous.

Unclear: Stefano and Victor love <u>his</u> DVD collection. (Whose DVD collection—Stefano's, Victor's, or someone else's?)

Clear: Stefano and Victor love <u>Emilio's</u> DVD collection.

## (2) Pronoun Placement

Never use a pronoun immediately after the noun it replaces. For example, do not say, "Most of my classmates they are smart"; instead, say, "Most of my classmates are smart." The only exception to this rule occurs with an **intensive pronoun**. An intensive pronoun ends in *-self* and emphasizes the preceding noun or pronoun: "Marta *herself* was eager to hear the results."

**See A2**

## (3) Indefinite Pronouns

Unlike personal pronouns (*I, you, he, she, it, we, they, me, us, him, her,* and *them*), **indefinite pronouns** do not refer to a particular person, place, or thing and, therefore, do not require an antecedent. **Indefinite pronoun subjects** (*anybody, nobody, each, either, someone, something, all, some*), like personal pronouns, must agree in number with the sentence's verb.

**See 15a4**

Incorrect: <u>Nobody have</u> failed the exam.

Correct: <u>Nobody has</u> failed the exam. (*Nobody* is a singular subject and requires a singular verb.)

**520**

### (4) Appositives

Appositives are nouns or noun phrases that identify or rename an adjacent noun or pronoun. An appositive usually follows the noun it explains or modifies but can sometimes precede it. The **case** of a pronoun in an appositive depends on the case of the word it describes.

See
19b3

> My parents, <u>Mary and John</u>, live in Louisiana. (*Mary and John* identify *parents.*)

> The event organizers, <u>William and I</u>, attended the banquet. (*William and I* identifies *the event organizers.*)

> <u>One of the brightest stars in the sky</u>, Alpha Centauri is the closest star to the sun. (*One of the brightest stars in the sky* identifies *Alpha Centauri.*)

If an appositive is not necessary to the meaning of the sentence, use commas to set off the appositive from the rest of the sentence. If an appositive is necessary to the meaning of the sentence, no commas should be used.

> His aunt <u>Trang</u> is in the hospital. (*Trang* is necessary to the meaning of the sentence because it identifies which aunt is in the hospital.)

> Akta's car, a <u>1994 Jeep Cherokee</u>, broke down last night, and she had to walk home. (*1994 Jeep Cherokee* is not necessary to the meaning of the sentence.)

# 47c Verbs

Writer's
Resource
CD-ROM

See
A3

Though <u>verbs</u> in all languages perform similar functions, they differ in form and usage from language to language perhaps more than any other part of speech or grammatical unit.

Although all languages use verbs to express *states of being*, many languages use two different verbs to describe permanent and impermanent states of being—for example, *ser* and *estar* in Spanish. Other languages use two different verbs to describe animate and inanimate objects—for instance, *aru* and *iru* in Japanese. With its single verb *be*, English is in this respect simpler than many other languages.

Languages may also differ in the ways they use verbs to communicate *action*. In Arabic, verbs change form to communicate whether the action they describe is complete or not. In Japanese, verbs can be conjugated to communicate the speaker's feelings about the action of the verb—for example, whether the action was overdone. Again, because English communicates such concepts in other ways, the forms of its action verbs are simpler in these contexts than those in other languages.

## (1) Person, Number, and Tense

See 15a

English verbs change their form according to *person, number,* and *tense.* The verb in a sentence must <u>agree</u> with the subject in person and number. Person refers to *who* or *what* is performing the action of the verb (for example, *I, you,* or *someone else*). Number refers to *how many* people or things are performing the action (one or more than one). Using the correct person and number in the verbs in your sentences is very important in communicating the meanings you intend.

See 18b

<u>Tense</u> refers to *when* the action of the verb takes place—in the past, present, or future. The tense of the verb changes the form of the verb. For example, adding *-ed* to many English verbs creates a past tense and places the action of the verb in the past. One problem that many nonnative speakers of English have with English verb tenses results from the large number of irregular verbs in English: for example, the first-person singular present tense of the verb *be* is not "I be" but "I am," and the first-person singular past tense of the verb *to fight* is not "I fighted" but "I fought."

## (2) Auxiliary Verbs

To create various tenses of both regular and irregular verbs in English, **auxiliary verbs** (also known as helping verbs) are used. Auxiliary verbs include forms of the verbs *be, have,* and *do* (Julio *is taking* a vacation," "I *have been* tired lately," "He *does* not *need* a license") and also verbs such as *would, should,* and *can* ("We *should conserve* more of our resources," "You *can succeed* if you try"), which are known as **modal auxiliaries**. Such auxiliary verbs are necessary because English verbs do not change their form, as verbs in other languages do, to express ideas such as the probability, desirability, or necessity of the action described by the verb.

The auxiliary verbs *be, have,* and *do* change form to agree with the subject; the main verb remains in present tense or past tense.

I <u>am</u> ready to go to the meeting.
They <u>were</u> ready to go to the meeting.

Mr. Chuen <u>has</u> lived in that house for eight years.
They <u>have</u> lived near downtown for only one year.

Ms. Trepagnier <u>does</u> not like the opera.
My brothers <u>do</u> not want to see a Broadway musical.

Modal auxiliaries—*should, would, can, may, might*—never change form.

I <u>can</u> paint the props, and then Myria and Emma <u>can</u> set them up tomorrow.

Mr. Lam and Ms. Boyer <u>might</u> be able to attend, but Mr. Esposito <u>might</u> not be able to make it.

Roisin <u>would</u> enjoy law school, but his brothers probably <u>would</u> not.

## (3) Forming Verb Tenses

The following examples demonstrate how to form various verb tenses. The verb used to illustrate the various tenses is *eat,* which is an irregular verb. The past tense of *eat* is *ate,* and the past participle is *eaten.*

Use the **simple present tense** for something that happens regularly or that is a fact.

I <u>eat</u> lunch at noon every day.

Use the **simple past tense** to refer to an action completed in the past. To form the simple past tense, add *-d* or *-ed* to regular verbs. <u>Irregular verbs</u>, like *eat,* have special past tense forms.

I <u>ate</u> lunch at noon yesterday.

Use the **simple future tense** to refer to an action that will occur in the future. To form the simple future tense, add *will* before the present tense verb form.

I <u>will eat</u> lunch at noon tomorrow.

Use the **present perfect tense** to refer to an action that began at an unspecified time in the past and may or may not be completed. To form the present perfect tense, add *have* to the past participle form of the verb.

I <u>have eaten</u> lunch.

Use the **past perfect tense** to refer to an action that occurred at a particular time in the past, often before another action. To form the past perfect tense, add *had* to the past participle form of the verb.

I <u>had</u> already <u>eaten</u> lunch when my mother arrived.

Use the **future perfect tense** to refer to an action in the future that will occur before another action in the future. To form the future perfect tense, add *will have* before the past participle form of the verb.

I <u>will have eaten</u> lunch when the meeting starts.

Use the **present progressive tense** to refer to an action that is occurring at the time it is expressed in speech or writing. To form the present progressive tense, add a form of the present tense verb *be* before the verb, and add *-ing* to the present tense form of the verb.

I <u>am eating</u> lunch right now.

Use the **past progressive tense** to indicate a continuous activity in the past or an action occurring in the past at the same time as another action in the past. To form the past progressive tense, add a form of the past tense verb *be* before the verb, and add *-ing* to the present tense form of the verb.

I <u>was eating</u> lunch when someone knocked on the door.

Use the **future progressive tense** to indicate a continuing action in the future. To form the future progressive tense, add a form of the future tense verb *be* before the verb, and add *-ing* to the present tense of the verb.

I <u>will be eating</u> lunch when the package is delivered tomorrow.

Use the **present perfect progressive tense** to indicate an action continuing from the past into the present and possibly into the future. To form the present perfect progressive tense, add *have been* before the verb, and add *-ing* to the present tense of the verb.

I <u>have been eating</u> lunch at noon every day for three years.

Use the **past perfect progressive tense** to indicate that a past action continued until another action occurred. To form the past perfect progressive tense, add *had been* before the verb, and add *-ing* to the present tense of the verb.

I <u>had been eating</u> lunch at noon every day until my work schedule changed.

Use the **future perfect progressive tense** to indicate that an action will continue until a certain future time. To form the future perfect progressive tense, add *will have been* before the verb, and add *-ing* to the present tense of the verb.

On December 8, I <u>will have been eating</u> lunch at noon every day for four years.

**Note:** Only auxiliary verbs, not the verbs they "help," change form to indicate person, number, and tense. (Modal auxiliaries, however, never change form to indicate tense, person, or number.)

> had     go
> We ~~have~~ to ~~went~~ downtown yesterday.

(Remember that only the auxiliary verb *had* should be in the past tense.)

## closeUP

### Choosing the simplest verb tense

Some nonnative speakers of English use verb tenses that are more complicated than they need to be. Such speakers may do this because their native language uses more complicated tenses where English does not or because they are nervous about using simple tenses and "overcorrect" their verbs into complicated tenses.

Specifically, nonnative speakers tend to use progressive and perfect verb forms instead of simple verb forms. To communicate your ideas clearly to an English-speaking audience, choose the simplest possible verb tense.

## (4) Negative Verbs

The meaning of a verb may be made negative in English in a variety of ways, chiefly by adding the words *not* or *does not* to the verb (is, *is not*; can ski, *can't* ski: drives a car, *does not* drive a car).

Nonnative speakers (and some native speakers of English) sometimes use double negatives. A **double negative** occurs when the meaning of a verb is negated not just once but twice in a single sentence. In some languages, a double structure is actually required in order to negate a verb; for example, the French phrase *je ne sais pas* ("I don't know") uses the double structure *ne* + *pas* around the verb *sais*. However, a double negative is incorrect in English.

Henry doesn't have ^any friends at all. (*or* Henry ^has no friends at all.)

I looked for articles in the library, but there weren't none. (*or* I looked for articles in the library, but there weren't ^any.)

## (5) Transitive and Intransitive Verbs

Many nonnative speakers of English find it difficult to decide whether or not a verb needs an object or in what order direct and indirect objects should be placed in a sentence. Learning the difference between transitive verbs and intransitive verbs can help you with such problems.

A **transitive verb** is a verb that has a direct object: "My father asked a question" (subject + verb + direct object). In this example, *asked* is a transitive verb; it needs an object to complete its meaning. An **intransitive verb** is a verb that does not take an object: "The doctor smiled" (subject + verb). In this example, *smile* is an intransitive verb; it does not need an object to complete its meaning. Consult a dictionary to determine whether a verb is transitive or intransitive—that is, to determine whether or not it needs an object.

A transitive verb may be followed by a direct object or by both an indirect object and a direct object. (An indirect object is the noun that receives the action.) The indirect object may come before or after the direct object. If the indirect object follows the direct object, then the preposition *to* or *for* must precede the indirect object.

Keith wrote a letter. (verb + direct object)

Keith wrote his friend a letter. (verb + indirect object + direct object)

Keith wrote a letter to his friend. (verb + direct object + *to/for* + indirect object)

Some verbs in English look similar and have similar meanings, except that one is transitive and the other is intransitive—for example, *lie* is intransitive, *lay* is transitive; *sit* is intransitive, *set* is transitive; *rise* is intransitive, *raise* is transitive. Knowing whether a verb is transitive or intransitive will help you with troublesome verb pairs like these and help you place the words in a sentence in the correct order. It is also important to know whether a verb is transitive or intransitive because only transitive verbs can be used in the passive voice.

## (6) Voice

Verbs may be in either active or passive <u>voice</u>. When the subject of a sentence performs the action of the verb, the verb is in **active voice.** When the action of the verb is done to the subject, the verb is in **passive voice.** Because readers of English prefer active voice over passive voice, use active voice whenever possible. If you do, your sentences will be shorter and you will convey your intended meaning more directly.

See 18d

Karla and Miguel purchased the plane tickets. (active voice)

The plane tickets were purchased by Karla and Miguel. (passive voice)

## (7) Phrasal Verbs

Many verbs in English are composed of two or more words—for example, *check up on, run for, turn into,* and *wait on.* These verbs are called **phrasal verbs.** Knowing the definitions of the individual words that make up these verbs is not always enough to enable you to define the verbs accurately. The only way to learn the definitions of these phrasal verbs is to consult a dictionary and to pay close attention to the use of these verbs in speech and writing. It is important to become familiar with phrasal verbs and their definitions so you will recognize these verbs as phrasal verbs instead of simply as verbs that are followed by prepositions.

Sometimes the words that make up a phrasal verb can be separated from each other by a direct object. In these *separable* phrasal verbs, the object can come either before or after the preposition. For example, "Ellen *turned down* the job offer" and "Ellen *turned* the job offer *down*" are both correct. However, when the object is a pronoun, the pronoun must come before the preposition. Therefore, "Ellen turned *it* down" is correct; "Ellen turned down *it*" is incorrect.

Some phrasal verbs, however—such as *look into, make up for,* and *break into*—consist of words that can never be separated. With these *inseparable* phrasal verbs, you do not have a choice of where to place the object. It must always follow the preposition. For example, "Anna *cared for* her niece" is correct, but "Anna *cared* her niece *for*" is incorrect.

## Phrasal verbs

A phrasal verb is composed of a main verb and one or more prepositions. The following phrasal verbs are separable.

| Verb | Definition |
|------|------------|
| call off | cancel |
| carry on | continue |
| cheer up | try to make happy |
| clean out | clean the inside of |
| cut down | reduce |
| figure out | solve |
| fill in | substitute |
| find out | discover |
| give back | return something |
| give up | stop doing something or stop trying |
| leave out | omit |
| pass on | transmit |
| put away | place something in its proper place |
| put back | place something in its original place |
| put off | postpone |
| start over | start again |
| throw away/out | discard |
| touch up | repair |

The following phrasal verbs are inseparable.

| Verb | Definition |
|------|------------|
| come down with | develop an illness |
| come up with | produce |
| do away with | abolish |
| fall behind in | lag |
| get along with | be congenial with |
| get away with | avoid punishment |
| keep up with | maintain |
| look up to | admire |
| make up for | compensate |
| pass on | transmit |
| put up with | tolerate |
| run into | meet by chance |
| see to | arrange |
| show up | arrive |
| stand by | wait |
| stand up for | support |
| talk over | discuss |
| watch out for | be careful for |

## (8) Using Verbs as Nouns and Adjectives

When English verbs are used as **nouns** or **adjectives,** speakers of other languages may be confused—particularly if in their native language words do not change their function according to their position in a sentence. Two verb forms may be used as nouns: **infinitives,** which always begin with *to,* as in *to work, to sleep, to eat,* and **gerunds,** which always end in *-ing,* as in *working, sleeping, eating.*

To bite into this steak requires better teeth than mine. (infinitive used as a noun)

Cooking is one of my favorite hobbies. (gerund used as a noun)

Sometimes, a gerund and infinitive of the same verb are interchangeable. For example, "He continued *to sleep*" and "He continued *sleeping*" convey the same meaning. However, this is not always the case. Saying, "Marco and Lisa stopped *to eat* at Julio's Café" is not the same as saying, "Marco and Lisa stopped *eating* at Julio's Café." In this example, the meaning of the sentence changes depending on whether a gerund or infinitive is used.

**Present participles**, which also end in *-ing,* and **past participles,** which usually end in *-ed, -t,* or *-en,* as in *worked, slept,* and *eaten,* are frequently used as adjectives.

See 18a1

Some people think raw fish is healthier than cooked fish. (past participle used as an adjective)

According to the Bible, God spoke to Moses from a burning bush. (present participle used as an adjective)

A **participial phrase** is a group of words consisting of the participle plus the pronoun, noun, or noun phrase that functions as the direct object, indirect object, or complement of the action being expressed by the participle. To avoid confusion, the participial phrase must be placed as close as possible to the noun it modifies.

Jeffrey saw Lori skating at the park. (The participial phrase is used as an adjective that modifies *Lori.*)

The hikers fined for littering were banned from the park for seven days. (The participial phrase is used as an adjective that modifies *hikers.*)

Having visited San Francisco last week, Jim and Lynn showed us pictures from their vacation. (The participial phrase is used as an adjective that modifies *Jim and Lynn.*)

**Note:** When a participial phrase falls at the beginning of a sentence, a comma is used to set it off. When a participial phrase is used in the middle of a sentence, commas should be used only if the phrase is *not* essential to the meaning of the sentence. No commas should be used if the participial phrase is essential to the meaning of the sentence.

# 47d   Adjectives and Adverbs

Writer's
Resource
CD-ROM

See
Ch 20

Adjectives and adverbs are modifiers that describe or provide additional information about other words in a sentence—adjectives provide information about nouns, and adverbs provide information about verbs, adjectives, and other adverbs.

**Adjectives** generally describe nouns. A book might be *large* or *small, red* or *blue, expensive* or *cheap.* Unlike adjectives in other languages, English adjectives change their form only to indicate degree (*fast, faster, fastest*). In English, adjectives do not have to agree in number or gender with the nouns they describe (as they must in French and German, for example).

**Adverbs** in English are easily identified; nearly all end in *-ly* (*calmly, loudly, rapidly*), except for a small number of "intensifiers," such as *very, rather,* and *quite.* Adverbs generally describe verbs. A person may walk *slowly* or *quickly, shyly* or *confidently, elegantly* or *clumsily.* Adverbs also may modify adjectives (*very* blue eyes, *truly* religious man) or other adverbs (answer *rather stupidly,* investigate *extremely thoroughly*).

## (1) Position of Adjectives and Adverbs

In Arabic and in Romance languages such as French, Spanish, and Italian, **adjectives** generally *follow* the nouns they describe. In English, however, adjectives usually appear *before* the nouns they describe. In English, one would not say, "*Cars red and black* are involved in more accidents than *cars blue, green, or white.*" Instead, one would say, "*Red and black cars* are involved in more accidents than *blue, green, or white cars.*"

**Adverbs** may appear before or after the verbs they describe, but they should be placed as close to the verb as possible: not "I *told* John that I couldn't meet him for lunch *politely,*" but "I *politely told* John that I couldn't meet him for lunch" or "I *told* John *politely* that I couldn't meet him for lunch." When an adverb describes an adjective or another adverb, it usually comes *before* that adjective or adverb: "The essay has *basically sound* logic"; "You must express yourself *absolutely clearly*." Never place an adverb between the verb and the direct object.

**Incorrect:** Rolf drank quickly the water.

**Correct:** Rolf drank the water quickly (or, Rolf quickly drank the water).

**Incorrect:** Suong took quietly the test.

**Correct:** Suong quietly took the test (or, Suong took the test *quietly*).

**Note:** To avoid confusion about whether to use an adjective or an adverb, remember that adjectives modify nouns, and adverbs modify verbs, adjectives, and other adverbs. An adjective always follows a form of the verb *be* if the adjective modifies the subject of the sentence. For example, "I was *careful*" (not "I was *carefully*").

## (2) Order of Adjectives

A single noun may be described by more than one adjective, perhaps even by a list of adjectives in a row. Given a list of three or four adjectives, most native speakers of English would arrange them in a sentence in the same order. If shoes are to be described as *green* and *big*, numbering *two*, and of the type worn for playing *tennis*, most native speakers of English would say, "two big green tennis shoes." Generally, the adjectives most important in completing the meaning of the noun are placed closest to the noun.

**Order of articles, adjectives, and other determiners**                    **?**

1. articles (*a, an, the*), demonstrative pronouns (*this, that, these, those*), or possessive nouns or pronouns (*his, our, Maria's, everybody's*)
2. amounts (*one, five, many, few*) and order (*first, next, last*)
3. personal opinions (*nice, ugly, crowded, pitiful*)
4. sizes and shapes (*small, tall, straight, crooked*)
5. ages (*young, old, modern, ancient*)
6. colors (*red, blue, dark, light*)
7. nouns functioning as adjectives to form a unit with the noun (*soccer* ball, *cardboard* box, *history* class)

## (3) Use of Adjectives and Adverbs to Indicate Degree

Adjectives can be used with nouns to indicate degree. Degree indicates relative quality, quantity, or manner. The **comparative** degree is used when two items are compared. To form the comparative of an adjective, you sometimes add *-er* to the adjective (*nicer, shorter*) and sometimes place the word *more* before the adjective (*more comprehensive, more significant*). The **superlative** degree is used when more than two items are compared. To form the superlative, you sometimes add *-est* to the adjective (*nicest, shortest*) and sometimes place the word *most* before the adjective (*most comprehensive, most significant*).

See 20c

Use *-er* and *-est* to create comparative and superlative forms of one-syllable adjectives. With all adjectives that have more than two syllables (as well as some two-syllable adjectives, such as *pretty* and *deadly*), use *more* and *most* to indicate comparative and superlative degrees.

Maggie's dog is <u>smaller</u> than Hetal's dog. (comparative)

I think Maura's behavior is <u>more predictable</u> than Thao's behavior. (comparative)

Kimani is the <u>tallest</u> child in her kindergarten class. (superlative)

Neil and Paulette are the <u>most talented</u> players in the league. (superlative)

Adverbs, like adjectives, change their form to indicate degree. Add *-er* or *more* to the adverb to indicate comparative degree. Add *-est* or *most* to indicate superlative degree.

I drive <u>more slowly</u> in the rain than I do in clear weather. (comparative)

Of Paul's four children, Brandon <u>most easily</u> accomplished his goals. (superlative)

# 47e   Prepositions

Writer's Resource CD-ROM

See A6

In English, **prepositions** (such as *to, from, at, with, among, between*) give meaning to nouns by linking them with other words and other parts of the sentence. Prepositions convey several different kinds of information.

# Prepositions

- Relations to **time** (*at* nine o'clock, *in* five minutes, *for* a month)
- Relations to **place** (*in* the classroom, *at* the library, *beside* the chair) and **direction** (*to* the market, *onto* the stage, *toward* the freeway)
- Relations of **association** (go *with* someone, the tip *of* the iceberg)
- Relations of **purpose** (working *for* money, dieting *to* lose weight)

In English, certain prepositions that relate to time have specific uses with certain types of nouns, such as days, months, and seasons. For example, *on* is used with days and specific dates: *on* Monday, *on* September 13, 1977. *In* is used with months, seasons, and years: *in* November, *in* the spring, *in* 1999. To denote a particular part of the day, several different prepositions are used. It is correct to say "*in* the morning" and "*in* the afternoon." However, the preposition *at* is used to express other times of day, such as "*at* noon," "*at* night," and "*at* seven o'clock." These uses must be memorized.

## (1) Commonly Confused Prepositions

Some prepositions—such as *to, in, on, into,* and *onto*—are very similar to one another and are therefore easily confused. Below are basic definitions of these prepositions. If you are not sure which preposition to use, consult a dictionary for additional meanings of these prepositions.

### ✓checklist Commonly confused prepositions ?

✓ *To* is the basic preposition of direction. It indicates movement toward a physical place: "*to* the restaurant"; "*to* the meeting." *To* is also the preposition used to form the infinitive of a verb: "He wanted *to deposit* his paycheck before noon"; "Irene offered *to drive* Maria to the baseball game."

✓ *In* indicates that something is within the area of or within the boundaries of a particular space: "*in* the garden"; "*in* the winter"; "*in* the car."

✓ *On* indicates position above or being supported by something: "*on* the porch"; "*on* my lap"; "*on* the chair."

✓ *Into* indicates movement to the inside of or interior of something: "*into* the room"; "*into* the lake"; "*into* the box." Although *into* and *in* are sometimes interchangeable, note that *into* differs from *in* depending on whether the subject is stationary or moving. *Into* usually indicates movement, as in "I jumped *into* the water." *In* usually indicates a stationary position, as in "Mary is swimming *in* the water."

*continued on the following page*

*continued from the previous page*

✓ *Onto* indicates movement to a position on top of something: "jump *onto* the chair"; "fall *onto* the floor." Both *on* and *onto* can be used to indicate a position on top of something, and therefore they can be used interchangeably, but *onto* specifies that the subject is moving to a place from a different place or from an outside position.

## (2) Pronouns in Prepositional Phrases

See 19a2

Both native speakers of English and nonnative speakers of English sometimes have difficulty choosing which pronoun should follow a preposition. The pronoun that is the object of the preposition should be in the **objective case**.

Would you like to go to a movie with <u>me</u>? (not "Would you like to go to a movie with *I*?")

Would you like to eat lunch with Felix and <u>me</u>? (not "Would you like to eat lunch with Felix and *I*?")

Just between <u>you</u> and <u>me</u>, I think you won the contest. (not "Just between *you* and *I*, I think you won the contest.")

## (3) Prepositions in Idiomatic Expressions

In some languages, prepositions may be used in quite different ways, may exist in forms quite different from English, or may not exist at all. Therefore, speakers of those languages may have a lot of difficulty with English prepositions. Speakers of languages with prepositions very similar to those in English—especially Romance languages such as Spanish, French, and Italian—have a different problem: they may be tempted to translate their own languages' prepositional phrases directly into English.

### Prepositions in idiomatic expressions

| Common nonnative speaker usage | Native speaker usage |
|---|---|
| according *with* | according *to* |
| apologize *at* | apologize *to* |
| appeal *at* | appeal *to* |

| Common nonnative speaker usage | Native speaker usage |
|---|---|
| believe *at* | believe *in* |
| different *to* | different *from* |
| *for* least, *for* most | *at* least, *at* most |
| refer *at* | refer *to* |
| relevant *with* | relevant *to* |
| similar *with* | similar *to* |
| subscribe *with* | subscribe *to* |

# 47f Word Order

In English, word order is extremely important, contributing a good deal to the meaning of a sentence.

## (1) Standard Word Order

Like Chinese, English is an "SVO" language, one in which the most typical sentence pattern is "subject-verb-object." (Arabic, by contrast, is an example of a "VSO" language.) If you deviate from the SVO pattern, you may not communicate your ideas clearly. There are times, however, when writers in English do deviate from the SVO pattern.

## (2) Word Order in Questions

Word order in questions can be particularly troublesome for speakers of languages other than English, partly because there are so many different ways to arrange words when questions are formed in English.

**Word order in questions** **?**

- To create a yes/no question from a statement using the verb *be*, simply invert the order of the subject and the verb:

  <u>Rasheem is</u> researching the depletion of the ozone layer.

  <u>Is Rasheem</u> researching the depletion of the ozone layer?

*continued on the following page*

*continued from the previous page*

- To create a yes/no question from a statement using a verb other than *be*, use a form of the auxiliary verb *do* before the sentence without inverting the subject and verb:

  <u>Does</u> Rasheem want to research the depletion of the ozone layer?

  <u>Do</u> Rasheem's friends want to help him with his research?

  <u>Did</u> Rasheem's professors approve his research proposal?

- You can also form a question by adding a **tag question** (such as *won't he?* or *didn't I?*) to the end of a statement. If the verb of the main statement is *positive,* then the verb of the tag question is *negative;* if the verb of the main statement is *negative,* then the verb of the tag question is *positive:*

  Rasheem <u>is</u> researching the depletion of the ozone layer, <u>isn't</u> he?

  Rasheem <u>doesn't</u> intend to write his dissertation about the depletion of the ozone layer, <u>does</u> he?

- To create a question asking for information, use **interrogative** words (*who, what, where, when, why, how*), and invert the order of the subject and verb (note that *who* functions as the subject of the question in which it appears):

  <u>Who is</u> researching the depletion of the ozone layer?

  <u>What is Rasheem</u> researching?

  <u>Where is Rasheem</u> researching the depletion of the ozone layer?

## (3) Word Order in Imperative Sentences

**Imperative** sentences state commands. It is common for the subject of the sentence in an imperative sentence to be left out because *you* is understood to be the subject: "Go to school"; "Eat your dinner." Therefore, the word order pattern in an imperative sentence is often "verb-object," or "VO."

## (4) Word Order with Direct and Indirect Quotations

See 32a

<u>Direct quotations</u> use the exact words that the original writer or speaker used; consequently, the order of the words in a direct quotation cannot be modified. However, you can modify the placement of the *identifying tag,* the phrase that identifies the writer or

**536**

speaker you are quoting. The identifying tag can be placed *before, in the middle of,* or *after* the quotation. (Note that direct quotations are always placed within quotation marks.)

He said, "Before I return the shoes to the department store, I must find the receipt." (identifying tag before the quotation)

"Before I return the shoes to the department store," he said, "I must find the receipt." (identifying tag in the middle of the quotation)

"Before I return the shoes to the department store, I must find the receipt," he said. (identifying tag after the quotation)

With **indirect quotations,** which summarize what the speaker or writer said, quotation marks are not used. Because you are simply reporting to your audience what the speaker or writer said, not quoting directly, you may change the words the speaker or writer used so long as you retain the meaning of the source. With indirect quotations, it is often necessary to change the order of the words in the sentence as well as the pronouns and the verb tense used in the source.

Direct quotation: "Before I return the shoes to the department store, I must find the receipt."

Indirect quotation: He said that he needed to find the receipt for the shoes before he could return them to the department store.

## 47g   Eliminating Wordiness

In most cases, writing in English requires you to be concise and direct. The following suggestions will help you eliminate **wordiness** in your writing.

See 23a

### ✓checklist Eliminating wordiness

✓ Eliminate unnecessary determiners, including adjectives, adverbs, and prepositional phrases.

Wordy: I do not have a preference for any particular kind of car.
Concise: I do not prefer a particular car.

✓ Use simple tenses whenever possible.

Wordy: I have already visited the museum. (present perfect tense)
Concise: I already visited the museum. (simple past tense)

*continued on the following page*

*continued from the previous page*

✓ Change prepositional phrases into adjectives whenever possible.

Wordy: The team that finishes in first place will advance to the regional championship.

Concise: The first-place team will advance to the regional championship.

✓ Avoid unnecessary use of *it* and *there* as subjects of sentences.

Wordy: There is a road that extends directly from New Orleans to Baton Rouge.

Concise: A road extends directly from New Orleans to Baton Rouge.

✓ Condense long phrases into shorter phrases or a single word.

Wordy: at this point in time
Concise: *now* or *yet*
Wordy: It is obvious that
Concise: Obviously

## 47h  Commonly Confused Words

A number of word pairs in English have similar meanings. These word pairs can be confusing to nonnative English speakers because although the meanings of the two words may be similar, the ways in which the expressions are used in sentences are different.

### *No and Not*

*No* is an adjective; *not* is an adverb. Therefore, use *no* with nouns, and use *not* with verbs, adjectives, and other adverbs.

She has <u>no</u> desire to go to the football game.

Sergio's sisters are <u>not</u> friendly.

### *Too and Very*

*Too* is an intensifier. It is used to add emphasis in a sentence and to indicate excess: "It is <u>too</u> cold outside to go swimming." *Very* is also an intensifier. It means "greatly or intensely," but not to excess: "It <u>was</u> very cold outside, but not cold enough to keep us from playing in the backyard."

### Even, Even If, and Even Though

When used as an adverb, *even* is used to intensify or indicate surprise: "Greta felt <u>even</u> worse than she looked"; "<u>Even</u> my little brother knows how to figure that out!"

*Even if* is used in a sentence where there is a condition that may or may not occur: "<u>Even if</u> it rains tomorrow, I'm going to the park." *Even though* is similar in meaning to *although:* "<u>Even though</u> Christopher is a very fast runner, he did not make the national track team."

### A Few/A Little and Few/Less

*A few* and *a little* mean "not much," but "some" or "enough." *A few* is used with count nouns. *A little* is used with noncount nouns. "We have <u>a few</u> screws remaining from the project"; "There is <u>a little</u> bit of paint left in the can." *Few* and *little* mean "a small number." "<u>Few</u> singers are as talented as Kelly"; "I have <u>little</u> hope that this situation will change."

### Much and Many

Both *much* and *many* mean "a great quantity" or "to a great degree." Use *much* to modify noncount nouns: "<u>much</u> experience"; "<u>much</u> money." Use *many* to modify count nouns: "<u>many</u> people"; "<u>many</u> incidents."

### Most of, Most, and The Most

*Most* and *most of* have similar meanings. *Most of* means "nearly all." Use *most of* when the noun that follows is a specific plural noun. When you use *most of*, be sure to use the definite article *the* before the noun: "<u>Most of</u> the children had cookies for dessert."

*Most* is used for more general observations and means nearly all: <u>Most</u> houses in the United States have electricity.

*The most* is used for comparing more than two of something: "Thomas has <u>the most</u> jellybeans"; "Pedro is <u>the most</u> experienced of the engineers."

### Some and Any

*Some* denotes an unspecified amount or quantity that may be part of a larger amount. It can modify both count and noncount nouns: "<u>some</u> water"; "<u>some</u> melons." *Any* indicates an unspecified amount, which may be none, some, or all. It can modify both count and noncount nouns: "<u>any</u> person"; "<u>any</u> luggage."

# PART 14

## Appendixes

**A    Parts of Speech    543**
   **A1**   Nouns    543
   **A2**   Pronouns    543
   **A3**   Verbs    545
   **A4**   Adjectives    547
   **A5**   Adverbs    547
   **A6**   Prepositions    548
   **A7**   Conjunctions    549
   **A8**   Interjections    550

**B    Sentence Review    551**
   **B1**   Basic Sentence Elements    551
   **B2**   Basic Sentence Patterns    551
   **B3**   Phrases and Clauses    553
   **B4**   Types of Sentences    555

# PART 14

**URLs**    *Visit the following sites for answers to more FAQs*

**Ask a Grammar Expert (e-mailed responses to grammar questions)**
*http://www.grammarnow.com/*

**UIUC Writer's Workshop (Illinois)**
*http://www.english.uiuc.edu/cws/wworkshop/nounsdefined.htm*

**Jack Lynch's Guide to Grammar and Style (much on mechanics)**
*http://andromeda.rutgers.edu/~jlynch/Writing/contents.html*

**Elementary Rules of Composition from Strunk's *Elements of Style***
*http://www.bartleby.com/141/strunk.html#III*

**Sentence Craft (L. Behrens, UCSB)**
*http://www.writing.ucsb.edu/faculty/behrens/cid/index*

**Sentence Combining Basics (Bowling Green)**
*http://www.bgsu.edu/departments/writing-lab/
sentence_combining_b.html*

# Parts of Speech

The eight basic **parts of speech**—the building blocks for all English sentences—are *nouns, pronouns, verbs, adjectives, adverbs, prepositions, conjunctions,* and *interjections.* How a word is classified depends on its function in a sentence.

## A1   Nouns

Writer's
Resource
CD-ROM

**Nouns** name people, animals, places, things, ideas, actions, or qualities.

A **common noun** names any of a class of people, places, or things: *artist, judge, building, event, city.*

A **proper noun,** always capitalized, refers to a particular person, place, or thing: *Mary Cassatt, Crimean War.*

A **count noun** names something that can be counted: *five dogs, two dozen grapes.*

A **noncount noun** names a quantity that is not countable: *time, dust, work, gold.* Noncount nouns generally have only a singular form.

A **collective noun** designates a group thought of as a unit: *committee, class, family.* Collective nouns are generally singular unless the members of the group are referred to as individuals.

An **abstract noun** refers to an intangible idea or quality: *love, hate, justice, anger, fear, prejudice.*

**ESL Note:** For more information on nouns, **see 47a.**

## A2   Pronouns

Writer's
Resource
CD-ROM

**Pronouns** are words used in place of nouns or other pronouns. The word for which a pronoun stands is its **antecedent.**

If you use a quotation in your paper, you must document it.

**Note:** Although different types of pronouns may have exactly the same form, they are distinguished from one another by their function in a sentence.

A **personal pronoun** stands for a person or thing: *I, me, we, us, my, mine, our, ours, you, your, yours, he, she, it, its, him, his, her, hers, they, them, their, theirs.*

They made her an offer she couldn't refuse.

An **indefinite pronoun** does not refer to any particular person or thing, and so it does not require an antecedent. Indefinite pronouns include *another, any, each, few, many, some, nothing, one, anyone, everyone, everybody, everything, someone, something, either,* and *neither.*

Many are called, but few are chosen.

A **reflexive pronoun** ends with *-self* and refers to a recipient of the action that is the same as the actor: *myself, yourself, himself, herself, itself, oneself, themselves, ourselves, yourselves.*

They found themselves in downtown Pittsburgh.

An **intensive pronoun** emphasizes a preceding noun or pronoun. (Intensive pronouns have the same form as reflexive pronouns.)

Darrow himself was sure his client was innocent.

A **relative pronoun** introduces an adjective or noun clause in a sentence. Relative pronouns include *which, who, whom, that, what, whose, whatever, whoever, whomever,* and *whichever.*

Gandhi was the man who led India to independence. (introduces adjective clause)

Whatever happens will be a surprise. (introduces noun clause)

An **interrogative pronoun** introduces a question. Interrogative pronouns include *who, which, what, whom, whose, whoever, whatever,* and *whichever.*

Who was that masked man?

A **demonstrative pronoun** points to a particular thing or group of things. *This, that, these,* and *those* are demonstrative pronouns.

This is one of Shakespeare's early plays.

A **reciprocal pronoun** denotes a mutual relationship. The reciprocal pronouns are *each other* and *one another. Each other* indicates a relationship between two individuals; *one another* denotes a relationship among more than two.

Cathy and I respect <u>each other</u> for our differences; all people should respect <u>one another's</u> differences as we do.

**ESL Note:** For more information about pronouns, **see 47b.**

# A3  Verbs

A **verb** may express either action or a state of being.

Writer's
Resource
CD-ROM

He <u>ran</u> for the train. (physical action)

He <u>thought</u> about taking the bus. (emotional action)

Jen <u>became</u> ill after dinner. (state of being)

Verbs can be classified into two groups: *main verbs* and *auxiliary verbs.*

*Main Verbs* **Main verbs** carry most of the meaning in a sentence or clause.
Some main verbs are action verbs.

Emily Dickinson's work <u>anticipated</u> much of modern poetry.

Other main verbs function as linking verbs. A **linking verb** does not show any physical or emotional action. Its function is to link the subject to a **subject complement,** a word or phrase that renames or describes the subject. Linking verbs include *be, become,* and *seem* and verbs that describe sensations—*look, appear, feel, taste, smell,* and so on.

Carbon disulfide <u>smells</u> bad.

*Auxiliary Verbs* **Auxiliary verbs** (also called **helping verbs**), such as *be* and *have,* combine with main verbs to form **verb phrases.** Auxiliary verbs indicate tense, voice, or mood.

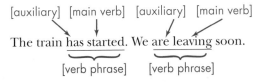

[auxiliary]  [main verb]   [auxiliary]  [main verb]

The train <u>has started</u>. We <u>are leaving</u> soon.

[verb phrase]       [verb phrase]

**545**

Certain auxiliary verbs, known as **modal auxiliaries,** indicate necessity, possibility, willingness, obligation, or ability.

| MODAL AUXILIARIES | | | |
|---|---|---|---|
| must | shall | might | need [to] |
| will | should | can | ought [to] |
| would | may | could | |

*Verbals* **Verbals,** such as *known* or *running* or *to go,* are verb forms that act as adjectives, adverbs, or nouns. A verbal can never serve as a sentence's main verb unless it is used with one or more auxiliary verbs (<u>is</u> going). Verbals include *participles, infinitives,* and *gerunds.*

*Participles* Virtually every verb has a present participle, which ends in *-ing* (*loving, learning*) and a past participle, which usually ends in *-d* or *-ed* (*agreed, learned*). Some verbs have **irregular** past participles (*gone, begun, written*). Participles may function in a sentence as adjectives or as nouns.

See
18a

Twenty brands of <u>running</u> shoes were on display. (Present participle serves as adjective modifying *shoes.*)

The <u>wounded</u> were given emergency first aid. (Past participle serves as subject.)

*Infinitives* An **infinitive**—the *to* form of the verb—may function as an adjective, an adverb, or a noun.

Ann Arbor was clearly the place <u>to be</u>. (Infinitive serves as adjective modifying *place.*)

Carla went outside <u>to think</u>. (Infinitive serves as adverb modifying *went.*)

<u>To win</u> was everything. (Infinitive serves as subject.)

*Gerunds* **Gerunds,** which like present participles end in *-ing,* always function as nouns.

<u>Seeing</u> is <u>believing</u>. (Gerunds serve as subject and subject complement.)

Andrew loves skiing. (Gerund is direct object of verb *loves*.)

**ESL Note:** For more information on verbs, **see 47c.**

## A4 Adjectives

Writer's
Resource
CD-ROM

**Adjectives** describe, limit, qualify, or in some other way modify nouns or pronouns.

**Descriptive adjectives** name a quality of the noun or pronoun they modify.

After the game, they were exhausted.

They ordered a chocolate soda and a butterscotch sundae.

When articles, pronouns, numbers, and the like function as adjectives, limiting or qualifying nouns or pronouns, they are referred to as determiners.

**ESL Note:** For more information on adjectives, **see 47d.**

## A5 Adverbs

Writer's
Resource
CD-ROM

**Adverbs** describe the action of verbs or modify adjectives or other adverbs (or complete phrases, clauses, or sentences). They answer the questions "How?" "Why?" "Where?" "When?" "Under what conditions?" and "To what extent?"

He walked rather hesitantly toward the front of the room. (walked *how?*)

Let's meet tomorrow for coffee. (meet *when?*)

Adverbs that modify adjectives or other adverbs limit or qualify the words they modify.

He pitched an almost perfect game yesterday.

*Interrogative Adverbs* The **interrogative adverbs** (*how, when, why,* and *where*) introduce questions.

Why did the compound darken?

See
3b2

*Conjunctive Adverbs* **Conjunctive adverbs** act as <u>transitional words</u>, joining and relating independent clauses.

See ESL
47d

### FREQUENTLY USED CONJUNCTIVE ADVERBS

| | | | |
|---|---|---|---|
| accordingly | furthermore | meanwhile | similarly |
| also | hence | moreover | still |
| anyway | however | nevertheless | then |
| besides | incidentally | next | thereafter |
| certainly | indeed | nonetheless | therefore |
| consequently | instead | now | thus |
| finally | likewise | otherwise | undoubtedly |

**ESL Note:** For more information on adverbs, **see 47d.**

## A6    Prepositions

Writer's
Resource
CD-ROM

A **preposition** introduces a noun or pronoun (or a phrase or clause functioning in the sentence as a noun), linking it to other words in the sentence. The word or word group that the preposition introduces is its **object.**

```
              prep   obj           prep      obj
They received a postcard from Bobby telling about his trip
prep obj
to Canada.
```

### FREQUENTLY USED PREPOSITIONS

| | | | |
|---|---|---|---|
| about | across | against | among |
| above | after | along | around |
| as | despite | of | throughout |
| at | down | off | to |
| before | during | on | toward |
| behind | except | onto | under |

## Conjunctions

| | | | |
|---|---|---|---|
| below | for | out | underneath |
| beneath | from | outside | until |
| beside | in | over | up |
| between | inside | past | upon |
| beyond | into | regarding | with |
| by | like | since | within |
| concerning | near | through | without |

**ESL Note:** For more information on prepositions, **see 47e.**

# A7 Conjunctions

Writer's Resource CD-ROM

**Conjunctions** connect words, phrases, clauses, or sentences.

*Coordinating Conjunctions* **Coordinating conjunctions** (*and, or, but, nor, for, so, yet*) connect words, phrases, or clauses of equal weight.

The choice was difficult: chicken <u>or</u> fish. (*Or* links two nouns.)

Thoreau wrote *Walden* in 1854, <u>and</u> he died in 1862. (*And* links two independent clauses.)

*Correlative Conjunctions* Always used in pairs, **correlative conjunctions** also link items of equal weight.

<u>Both</u> Hancock <u>and</u> Jefferson signed the Declaration of Independence. (Correlative conjunctions link nouns.)

<u>Either</u> I will renew my lease, <u>or</u> I will move. (Correlative conjunctions link independent clauses.)

| CORRELATIVE CONJUNCTIONS | |
|---|---|
| both . . . and | neither . . . nor |
| either . . . or | not only . . . but also |
| just as . . . so | whether . . . or |

**549**

*Subordinating Conjunctions* Words such as *since, because,* and *although* are subordinating conjunctions. They introduce adverb clauses and thus connect the sentence's independent (main) clause to a dependent (subordinate) clause to form a **complex sentence**.

See
21a2

Although people may feel healthy, they can still have medical problems.

It is best to diagram your garden before you start to plant.

## A8  Interjections

*Interjections* **Interjections** are words used as exclamations to express emotion: *Oh! Ouch! Wow! Alas! Hey!* They may be set off by commas or, for greater emphasis, by an exclamation point.

# Sentence Review

## B1 Basic Sentence Elements

Writer's
Resource
CD-ROM

A **sentence** is an independent grammatical unit that contains a subject and a predicate and expresses a complete thought.

The quick brown fox jumped over the lazy dog.

It came from outer space.

A **simple subject** is a noun or noun substitute (*fox, it*) that tells who or what the sentence is about. A **simple predicate** is a verb or verb phrase (*jumped, came*) that tells or asks something about the subject. The **complete subject** of a sentence includes the simple subject plus all its modifiers (*the quick brown fox*). The **complete predicate** includes the verb or verb phrase and all the words associated with it—such as modifiers, objects, and complements (*jumped over the lazy dog, came from outer space*).

## B2 Basic Sentence Patterns

Writer's
Resource
CD-ROM

A **simple sentence** consists of at least one subject and one predicate. Simple sentences conform to one of five patterns.

**Subject + Intransitive Verb (s + v)**

     s          v
The price of gold rose.

     s    v
Stock prices may fall.

Here, the verbs *rose* and *may fall* are **intransitive**—that is, they do not need an object to complete their meaning.

**Subject + Transitive Verb + Direct Object (s + v + do)**

     s      v       do
Van Gogh created *The Starry Night.*

     s     v   do
Caroline saved Jake.

Here, the verbs *created* and *saved* are **transitive**—they require an object to complete their meaning. In each case, a **direct object** indicates where the verb's action is directed and who or what is affected by it.

**Subject + Transitive Verb + Direct Object + Object Complement (s + v + do + oc)**

This pattern includes an object complement that describes or renames the direct object.

  s    v          do   oc
I found the exam easy. (Object complement *easy* describes direct object *exam*.)

       s      v    do    oc
The class elected Bridget treasurer. (Object complement *treasurer* renames direct object *Bridget*.)

**Subject + Linking Verb + Subject Complement (s + v + sc)**

      s      v   sc
The injection was painless.

     s      v       sc
Tony Blair became prime minister.

See A3

Here, a **linking verb** (*was, became*) connects a subject to a **subject complement** (*painless, prime minister*), a word or phrase that describes or renames the subject. In the first sentence, the complement is a **predicate adjective** that describes the subject; in the second, the complement is a **predicate nominative** that renames the subject. The linking verb is like an equal sign, equating the subject with its complement (*Tony Blair = prime minister.*)

**Subject + Transitive Verb + Indirect Object + Direct Object (s + v + io + do)**

The **indirect object** tells to whom or for whom the verb's action was done.

     s    v    io      do
Cyrano wrote Roxanne a poem. (Cyrano wrote a poem for Roxanne.)

    s    v   io   do
Hester gave Pearl a kiss. (Hester gave a kiss to Pearl.)

# B3　Phrases and Clauses

## (1) Phrases

Writer's
Resource
CD-ROM

A **phrase** is a group of related words that lacks a subject or predicate or both and functions as a single part of speech. It cannot stand alone as a sentence.

A **verb phrase** consists of a **main verb** and all its auxiliary verbs. (Time is *flying*.) A **noun phrase** includes a noun or pronoun plus all related modifiers. (I'll climb *the highest mountain*.)

A **prepositional phrase** consists of a **preposition**, its object, and any modifiers of that object.

See A6

They discussed the ethical implications of the animal studies.

He was last seen heading into the sunset.

A **verbal phrase** consists of a **verbal** and its related objects, modifiers, or complements. A verbal phrase may be a **participial phrase,** a **gerund phrase,** or an **infinitive phrase.**

See A3

Encouraged by the voter turnout, the candidate predicted a victory. (participial phrase)

Taking it easy always makes sense. (gerund phrase)

The jury recessed to evaluate the evidence. (infinitive phrase)

An **absolute phrase** usually consists of a noun and a participle, accompanied by modifiers. It modifies an entire independent clause rather than a particular word or phrase.

Their toes tapping, they watched the auditions.

## (2) Clauses

A **clause** is a group of related words that includes a subject and a predicate. An **independent** (main) **clause** may stand alone as a sentence, but a **dependent** (subordinate) **clause** cannot. It must always be combined with an independent clause to form a **complex sentence**.

See 21a2

[Lucretia Mott was an abolitionist]. [She was also a pioneer for women's rights.] (two independent clauses)

[Lucretia Mott was an abolitionist] [who was also a pioneer for women's rights]. (independent clause, dependent clause)

[Although Lucretia Mott was known for her support of women's rights], [she was also a prominent abolitionist]. (dependent clause, independent clause)

Dependent clauses may be adjective, adverb, or noun clauses.

**Adjective clauses,** sometimes called **relative clauses,** modify nouns or pronouns and always follow the nouns or pronouns they modify. They are introduced by relative pronouns—*that, what, which, who,* and so forth—or by the adverbs *where* and *when.*

Celeste's grandparents, who were born in Romania, speak little English. (Adjective clause modifies the noun *grandparents.*)

The Pulitzer Prizes are prestigious awards that are presented for excellence in journalism. (Adjective clause modifies the noun *awards.*)

*Sophie's Choice* is a novel set in Brooklyn, where the narrator lives in a pink house. (Adjective clause modifies the noun *Brooklyn.*)

**Adverb clauses** modify verbs, adjectives, adverbs, entire phrases, or independent clauses. They are always introduced by subordinating conjunctions.

Mark will go wherever there's a party. (Adverb clause modifies *will go,* telling *where* Mark will go.)

Because 75 percent of its exports are fish products, Iceland's economy is heavily dependent on the fishing industry. (Adverb clause modifies independent clause, telling *why* the fishing industry is so important.)

**Noun clauses** function as subjects, objects, or complements. A noun clause may be introduced by a relative pronoun or by *whether, when, where, why,* or *how.*

What you see is what you get. (Noun clauses are subject and subject complement.)

They wondered <u>why it was so quiet</u>. (Noun clause is direct object.)

To <u>whom it may concern</u>: (Noun clause is object of preposition.)

# B4   Types of Sentences

Writer's
Resource
CD-ROM

## (1) Simple, Compound, Complex, and Compound-Complex Sentences

A **simple sentence** is a single independent clause. A simple sentence may consist of just a subject and a predicate.

<u>Jessica</u> <u>fell</u>.

Or, a simple sentence can be expanded with different kinds of modifying words and phrases.

Jessica and her younger sister Victoria almost immediately fell hopelessly in love with the very mysterious Henry Goodyear.

A **compound sentence** consists of two or more simple sentences (independent clauses) linked by a coordinating conjunction (preceded by a comma), by a semicolon (alone or with a transitional word or phrase), by correlative conjunctions, or by a colon.

See
21a1

    Independent clause            Independent clause
[The moon rose in the sky], <u>and</u> [the stars shone brightly].

           Independent clause
[José wanted to spend a quiet afternoon fishing and reading];

           Independent clause
<u>however,</u> [his friends surprised him with a new set of plans].

A **complex sentence** consists of an independent clause along with one or more dependent clauses.

See
21a2

    Independent clause            Dependent clause
[It was hard for us to believe] [that anyone could be so cruel].

           Dependent clause
[Because the program had been so poorly attended in the past],

    Independent clause            Dependent clause
[the committee wondered] [whether it should be funded this year].

See
21a3   A **compound-complex sentence** is a compound sentence—made up of at least two independent clauses—that also includes at least one dependent clause.

Dependent clause                    Independent
[Because driving a cab can be so dangerous], [my mother always

clause                  Dependent clause                  Independent
worried] [when my father had to work late], and [she could rarely

clause
sleep more than a few minutes at a time].

## (2) Declarative, Interrogative, Imperative, and Exclamatory Sentences

Sentences can also be classified according to their function.

**Declarative sentences,** the most common type, make statements: *World War II ended in 1945.*

See ESL
47f2   **Interrogative sentences** pose questions, usually by inverting standard subject-verb order (often with an interrogative word) or adding a form of *do: Is Maggie at home? Where is Maggie? Does Maggie live here?*

See ESL
47f3   **Imperative** sentences express commands or requests, using the second-person singular of the verb and generally omitting the pronoun subject *you: Go to your room. Please believe me. Stop that.*

**Exclamatory sentences** express strong emotion and end with an exclamation point: *The killing must stop now!*

# INDEX

Page numbers in blue refer to definitions.

A, *an*, 362, 517–518
*A few, a little and few, less,* 539
*A little,* comparative and superlative forms, 325
*A little and few, less, a few,* 539
*A lot,* 362, 417
*A lot of, lots, lots of,* 368
*A number, the number,* 291
*A while, awhile,* 363
Abbreviations
  acronyms, 380, 432
  of dates, 433
  editing misused abbreviations, 433–435
  at end of sentence, 379
  misuse of, 432
  in MLA documentation, 433
  of numbers, 433
  of organization names, 432
  with periods, 379
  postal abbreviations, 380
  of technical terms, 432
  of temperatures, 433
  of times of day, 433
  titles of persons, 432
  without periods, 380
*-able, -ible,* 419
Absolute phrases, 387, 553
Abstract nouns, 543
Abstract words, 354
Abstracts of journal articles, 449
Academic courses and departments
  abbreviation of, 434
  capitalization of, 423
*Accept, except,* 362, 416
Accuracy
  of Internet sources, 159
  of supporting evidence, 84
Acronyms, 380, 432
Active reading skills, 449–451
Active voice
  definition of, 316
  for emphasis, 339–340
  preference for, 527
  shift to passive voice from, 295–296
  uses of, 316
AD, capitalization of, 433
*Ad hominem* (argument to the person), 89

Addition, transitional words and phrases signaling, 66
Addresses
  commas in, 389
  numerals for, 437
Adjective(s)
  as subject complement, 322
  capitalization of those formed from proper nouns, 423–424
  cautions on, 323
  comparative and superlative forms of, 323–325, 532
  compound adjectives, 430
  coordinate adjectives, 383
  definition of, 322, 530, 547
  descriptive adjectives, 547
  double negatives, 326
  for ESL students, 530–532
  illogical comparatives and superlatives, 325
  in informal speech, 323
  in series, 383
  order of, 531
  position of, 530
  predicate adjectives, 552
  use of, 322
  verbs used as, 529–530
Adjective clauses, 345, 554
Adverb(s)
  comparative and superlative forms of, 323–325, 532
  conjunctive adverbs, 329, 548
  definition of, 530, 547
  double negatives, 326
  for ESL students, 530–532
  illogical comparatives and superlatives, 325
  interrogative adverbs, 547
  position of, 530–531
  use of, 323
Adverb clauses, 554
*Advice, advise,* 362
*Advise, advice,* 362
*Affect, effect,* 362, 416
Agreement
  definition of, 288
  pronoun-antecedent agreement, 292–294
  subject-verb agreement, 288–292

Aircraft, italics for titles of, 426
*All ready, already,* 362, 417
*All right, alright,* 362, 417
*Allusion, illusion,* 362
Almanacs, 137
*Already, all ready,* 362, 417
*Alright, all right,* 362, 417
AltaVista, 152
Ambiguous antecedents, 320
American Psychological Association. *See* APA style
*Among, between,* 362–363
Amount, words indicating, 519
*Amount, number,* 363
*An, a,* 362, 517–518
Analogy, 73, 356
Analyzing your assignment, 6
*And/or,* 363
Annotating, 450–451
Antecedent(s)
  agreement between pronouns and, 292–294, 320–321
  ambiguous antecedent, 320
  compound antecedents, 292–293
  definition of, 292, 543
  indefinite pronouns, 293
  nonexistent antecedent, 320–321
  not needed for indefinite pronouns, 520
  of pronouns, 520, 543–544
  relative pronouns, 292
  remote antecedent, 320
  *who, which, that,* 321
Antithesis, 92
antonyms, 360
*Any, some,* 539
*Any way, anyway,* 417
APA style
  checklists, 235–237
  content notes, 235
  in-text citations, 225–229
  manuscript guidelines, 235–237
  for numbers and numerals, 436
  reference list, 229–234, 237
  sample research paper, 237–248

557

Apostrophe(s)
contractions, 396
forming plurals, 397
misuse of, 395–396
omitted letters, 396
omitted numbers, 396
possessive case, 394–396
Appositives
case of pronouns in, 319,
521
colon introducing, 405
commas with, 521
dash setting off, 407
definition of, 319, 405, 521
for eliminating repetition,
344
placement of, 521
as sentence fragment, 282
Argument, 91
Argument to ignorance, 89
Argument to the people, 89
Argument to the person (ad
hominem), 89
Argumentative essays
audience of, 92
checklists, 94, 101
computer used for, 93
conclusion, 95
credibility of, 94
evidence in, 93
fairness of, 94
introduction, 95
organizing, 94–95
planning, 91–93
refuting of opposing
arguments, 92–93, 95
sample essay, 96–101
thesis for, 91–92
thesis statement, 95
transitional words and
phrases with, 96
Argumentative thesis,
91–92
Arise, principal parts, 308
Articles
definite articles, 517–518
indefinite articles,
517–518
with noncount nouns,
518
with nouns, 517–518
order of, 531
with plural nouns, 518
with proper nouns, 518
Artistic movements,
capitalization of, 422
Artworks, italics for titles of,
426
As, comparisons with
pronouns and, 318
As, like, 363
As . . . as . . ., 363

Ask Jeeves, 152
Assertions, 93
At, to, 363
Atlases, 137
Audience
of argumentative essays,
92
checklist, 6
collegial audience, 505
of essay, 5–6
of essay exam answers,
453
expert audience, 505
general audience, 505
identifying, 5–6, 69
mixed audience, 505
of oral presentation,
504–505
of paragraph, 69
Audiocassette recordings
APA style, 234
Chicago style, 257
CSE style, 271
MLA style, 195
Auxiliary verbs, 522–523,
545–546
Awake, principal parts, 308
Awhile, a while, 363

Bad, badly, 363
Bad, comparative and
superlative forms,
325
Badly, bad, 363
Badly, comparative and
superlative forms,
325
Balanced sentences, 339
Bandwagon fallacy, 89
Base form of verbs, 307–310
Basic English. See English for
speakers of other
languages
Basis for comparison, 53
BC, capitalization of, 433
BCE, capitalization of, 433
Be
incorrect use of, 298
principal parts, 308
Beat, principal parts, 308
Begging the question, 89
Begin, principal parts, 308
Being as, being that, 363
Being that, being as, 363
Bend, principal parts, 308
Beside, besides, 363
Bet, principal parts, 308
Between, among, 362–363
Bias
choice of evidence, 86
definition of, 85
detecting, 85–86

sexist or racist statements,
85
slanted language, 85
tone of writing, 86
writer's stated beliefs, 85
Biased language
avoiding, 356–358
offensive labels, 356–357
sexist language, 294,
357–358
Bible. See Sacred books and
figures
Bibliographic databases,
132–133, 139–141
Bibliographies (reference
works), 131
Bibliography. See also
Working bibliography
APA style, 229–234, 237,
246
Chicago style, 250–261,
262, 266
CSE style, 268–272, 275
MLA style, 187–203, 206,
219–220, 474
working bibliography,
108–109
Biographical reference
books, 131
Bite, principal parts, 308
Block format for business
letters, 491–492
Blow, principal parts, 308
Body
of oral presentations, 506
of research paper, 123
Body paragraphs, 15
Bookmarks, 155
Books
APA style for citing,
229–230
Chicago style for citing,
251–253
CSE style for citing,
269–270, 272
italics for titles of, 426
for library research,
137–138, 142–143, 449
MLA style for works-cited
list, 187–191, 196
quotation marks for
chapters or sections of,
402
Boolean operators/search,
134, 151–152
Brackets
with comments within
quotations, 408–409
within parentheses, 409
Brainstorming, 9–10, 454
Brand names, capitalization
of, 423

*Break,* principal parts, 308
*Bring,* principal parts, 308
*Bring, take,* 364
British spellings, 416
Browsing in library, 129–130
*Build,* principal parts, 308
Bullets for lists, 479
*Burst,* principal parts, 308
Business
  databases, 139–130
  search engines, 154
  Web sites, 161
Business letters, 406, 491–492
Businesses
  abbreviation of, 434
  capitalization of, 423
Buttons, **488**
*Buy,* principal parts, 308

Calendar, 441–442
Call number of book, 137
*Can, may,* 364
*Capital, capitol,* 364
Capitalization
  editing misused capitals,
    424–425
  first word of sentence, 421
  poetry, 421
  proper nouns, 421–424
  single letters in special
    constructions, 424
  words in titles, 424
*Capitol, capital,* 364
Cardinal numbers, 519
Cartoons, MLA style, 195,
    198
Case
  appositives, 319, 521
  comparisons with *than* or
    *as,* 318
  in compound
    constructions, 318
  objective case of
    pronouns, 317
  possessive case of
    pronouns, 317, 318
  of pronouns, 317–319
  subjective case of
    pronouns, 317
  *we* and *us* before noun,
    319
  *who* and *whom,* 318–319
Catalogs. *See* Online catalogs
*Catch,* principal parts, 308
Cause and effect
  checklists, 61, 75
  definition of, **72**
  paragraph, 72
  thesis statement, 19
  transitional words and
    phrases introducing,
    67

writing cause-and-effect
    essays, 39, 50–53
Cause-and-effect essays, 39,
    50–53
CBE style *See* CSE style
CD recordings
  APA style, 234
  Chicago style, 257
  MLA style, 195
CD-ROMs, 134–135, 361
CE, capitalization of, 433
*Center around,* 364
Centuries, capitalization of,
    425
*-ch,* plurals of words ending
    in, 420
Chalkboards, 509
Checklists
  analyzing your
    assignment, 6
  APA documentation style,
    235–237
  argumentative essays, 94,
    101
  audience, 6
  Chicago documentation
    style, 261–262
  commas, 383, 386
  concluding paragraph, 80
  conference with
    instructor, 26
  credibility, 94
  critical thinking, 90
  CSE documentation style,
    273
  e-mail, 502
  English for speakers of
    other languages,
    515–516, 533–534
  essays, 5, 6, 14, 17, 20,
    26–28, 61
  fairness, 94
  formal outline, 120–121
  highlighting, 450
  Internet, 155, 157–160
  interviews, 144–145
  introductory paragraph, 78
  library sources, 126, 127,
    138
  literature, 461–464
  MLA style, 205–206
  note taking, 114
  oral presentations, 509–12
  outline, 20, 120–121
  paragraphs, 62, 75, 78, 80
  paraphrasing a source,
    118
  patterns of development,
    61, 75
  photocopies and
    computer printouts,
    115

plagiarism avoidance,
    174–175
prepositions, 533–534
punctuation of adjectives
    in series, 383
purpose of essay, 5
reading literature,
    461–462
research process,
    106–107, 114, 115, 117,
    118, 120–121, 124
restrictive and
    nonrestrictive
    modifiers, 386
revising, 26–28, 78, 80,
    124
revising comma splices
    and fused sentences,
    285
revising paragraphs, 27,
    78, 80
revising research paper,
    124
revising sentence
    fragments, 282
revising sentences, 27
revising whole essay, 26
revising words, 27
sexist language
    elimination, 358
study skills, 447–448
summarizing a source,
    117
surveys, 146
thesis statement, 17
topic choice, 106–107
topic tree, 14
typing research paper,
    235–236, 261
visual aids design,
    509–510
visuals, 484–485
Web site design, 490
wordiness, 537–538
Chemistry style manual,
    276
Chicago style
  bibliography, 250–261,
    262, 266
  checklists, 261–262
  endnotes and footnotes,
    250, 262, 265
  manuscript guidelines,
    261
  sample research paper,
    262–266
*Choose,* principal parts, 308
Choppy sentences, revising,
    331–332
Chronological order
  of paragraph, **64**
  of résumés, 495, 496

# INDEX

Circulating collection, 129
Circumlocution, **342–343**
Citation-sequence format, 267–268
*Cite, site,* 364
Clarity, hyphens for, 431
Classification. *See* Division and classification
Classification paragraphs, 74
Clause(s). *See also* Dependent clauses; Independent clauses
  adjective clauses, 554
  adverb clauses, 554
  as sentence opening, 334
  comma between dependent and independent clause, 393
  comma between phrase and, 393
  definition of, **553**
  eliminating adjective clauses, 345
  noun clauses, 554–555
  relative clauses, 554
Clichés, **355**
*Climactic, climatic,* 364
*Climatic, climactic,* 364
*Cling,* principal parts, 308
Clipped forms, **351,** 380
Closed-ended questions, 144
Clustering, **10,** 11
*Coarse, course,* 364
Coherence
  arrangement of details in paragraph for, 64–65
  definition of, **64**
  of paragraph, 64–68
  between paragraphs, 68
  parallel structure for, 67
  repeating key words and phrases for, 67–68
  transitional words and phrases for, 65–67
Coined compounds, **431**
Collaborative brainstorming, **10**
Collaborative revision, **25**
Collective nouns
  collective noun subjects, agreement with, 290
  definition of, **290, 543**
  pronoun-antecedent agreement, 293
  subject-verb agreement, 290–291
College writing, 352
Collegial audience, **505**
Colloquial diction, **351–352**

Colon(s)
  complete sentence following, 405
  editing misused colons, 406
  with examples, explanations, or summaries, 378
  with explanatory material, 405
  for emphasis, 337
  in publisher information in works-cited list, 406
  with independent clauses, 377, 405
  with lists or series, 283, 393, 405
  with long prose passages and poetry, 401
  quotation following, 405, 406
  quotation marks with, 402
  after salutations in business letters, 406
  separating minutes from hours, 406
  separating titles from subtitles, 406
Columbia Online Style (COS) for, 203–205
*Come,* principal parts, 308
Comic strips, MLA style, 195
Comma(s)
  with absolute phrases, 387
  after abbreviation in sentence, 379
  with appositives, 521
  checklists, 383, 386
  with contradictory phrases, 387
  with dependent clauses, 384
  with direct quotations, 388, 393
  editing misused commas, 389–391
  for preventing misreading, 389
  with identifying tag, 165–166, 388, 399
  in addresses, 389
  in complex sentences, 330
  in compound sentences, 329, 329–330
  in compound-complex sentences, 331
  in dates, 389
  with independent clauses, 329, 377
  with introductory elements, 384–385
  with items in series, 377, 382–383

with nonessential items, 378
with nonrestrictive modifiers, 385–386
between phrase and clause, 393
quotation marks with, 402
with *that* and *which,* 386
with titles or degrees following name, 388
with transitional words and phrases, 385, 387, 392
with verbal and prepositional phrases, 384
Comma splices, **285–287,** 392
Common knowledge, **170**
Common nouns, **543**
Comparative forms of adverbs and adjectives, 323–325, 532
Comparison and contrast
  basis for comparison, 53
  checklists, 61, 75
  definition of, **72**
  in introductory paragraph, 77
  paragraphs, 72–73
  point-by-point comparison, 54
  subject-by-subject comparison, 54
  thesis statement, 19
  transitional words and phrases signaling, 66
  writing comparison-and-contrast essays, 39, 53–56
Comparison-and-contrast essays, 39, **53–56**
Complement(s)
  colon not used to separate verbs and their complements, 406
  comma not used in compound complements, 390–391
  object complements, 552
  subject complements, 322, 545, 552
*Complement, compliment,* 364
Complete predicate, **551**
Complete subject, **551**
Complex sentences, **330,** 344, 553–554, **555**
*Compliment, complement,* 364
Compound adjectives, hyphens in, **430**
Compound complement, 390–391

**560**

Compound-complex sentences, **331, 556**
Compound fractions, 431
Compound nouns
definition of, **420**
plurals of, 420
Compound numerals, hyphens in, 431
Compound objects, 318, 390–391
Compound predicates, 390
Compound sentences, **329**–330, 332, **555**
Compound subjects
comma not used in, 390
for eliminating repetition, 344
subject-verb agreement, 289–290
Compound words
coined compounds, 431
definition of, **429**
hyphen for dividing, 429–431
as two separate words, 430
Computer. *See also* Internet; Web sites
argumentative essay, 93
drafting, 122
editing and proofreading, 33–34
electronic dictionaries, 361
formal outline, 21, 121
generating ideas, 10
grammar checkers, 32
note taking, 114
*PowerPoint* for visual aids, 507–508
revising, 25, 125
spell checkers, 32, 417, 420
study skills and, 446
working bibliography, 108–109
Computer presentations, 509
Computer printouts in research process, 115
Computer software
APA style for citing, 234
italics for titles of, 426
Concession, transitional expressions signaling, 67
Concise sentences, 341–345
Concluding paragraph
cautions on, 79
checklist, 80
definition of, **15, 78**
examples of, 78–79
strategies, 79
Conclusion
argumentative essays, 95

oral presentations, 506
research paper, 123
transitional words and phrases introducing, 67
Conclusion of syllogism, **87**
Concrete words, **354**
Conditional statements, 315
Conference with instructor, 25–26
Conjunction(s)
with complex sentences, 330, 550
with compound sentences, 329–330
coordinating conjunctions, 287, 329, 344, 377, **549**
correlative conjunctions, 330, 347, **549**
definition of, **549**
in sentence fragment, 283
rambling sentences and, 344
subordinating conjunctions, 283, 287, 330, 550
Conjunctive adverbs, 329, **548**
Connotation, **353**
*Conscience, conscious,* 364
*Conscious, conscience,* 364
Content notes. *See also* Endnotes
APA style, 235
MLA style, 202–205, 218
superscript indicating, 202
*Continual, continuous,* 364
*Continuous, continual,* 364
Contractions, 396
Contradictory phrases, commas with, 387
Contrast. *See* Comparison and contrast
Controversial statements, 77–78
Convenient sample, **145**
Coordinate adjectives, **383**
Coordinate elements, **382**–383
Coordinating conjunctions
with compound sentences, 329
definition of, **549**
with independent clauses, 287, 329, 377
rambling sentences and, 344
Coordination in sentences, **331**

Copyright
fair use doctrine and, 486
visuals and, 480–481
Web sites and, 486
Correlative conjunctions, 330, 347, **549**
Correspondence. *See* Letters (correspondence)
COS. *See* Columbia Online Style (COS) for
*Cost,* principal parts, 308
*Could of, should of, would of,* 365
*Council, counsel,* 365
Council of Science Editors. *See* CSE style
*Counsel, council,* 365
Count nouns, **517, 543**
*Couple of,* 365
*Course, coarse,* 364
Credibility
of argumentative essays, 94
checklist, 94
of Internet sources, 159
of library sources, 142
*Criterion, criteria,* 291, 365
Critical thinking
checklist, 90
deductive reasoning, 87
detecting bias, 85–86
evaluating supporting evidence, 84–85
fact distinguished from opinion, 83–84
inductive reasoning, 86–87
inference in, 87
kinds of supporting evidence, 84
logical fallacies, 88–89
logical reasoning, 86–87
Cross-references, 408
CSE style
checklists, 273
citation-sequence format, 267–268
documentation in text, 267–268
manuscript guidelines, 273
name-year format, 268
reference list, 268–272, 275
sample research paper, 274–275
Cumulative sentences, **338**
Currency
of Internet sources, 160
of library sources, 142

Dangling modifiers
  creating dependent
    clause to revise, 303
  creating new subject to
    revise, 303
  definition of, 302
  and passive voice, 303
  revising, 302–303
Dash(es)
  editing overused dashes,
    407
  with examples,
    explanations, or
    summaries, 378
  for emphasis, 337
  for interruption, 407
  for introducing summary,
    407
  with nonessential items,
    378, 406–407
  with quotation marks, 403
Data, 365
Databases
  APA style for citing, 234
  definition of, 132
  in library research,
    132–135, 139–141
  MLA style for citing,
    195–196
Dates
  abbreviation of, 433
  commas in, 389
  numerals for, 437
  parentheses around, 408
  question marks for
    questionable dates,
    381
Days of week
  abbreviation of, 433
  capitalization of, 422
DC, abbreviation of, 434
DDC. See Dewey Decimal
  Classification System
  (DDC)
Deadwood, 341–342
Deal, principal parts, 308
Debatable topic, 91
Decimals, 437
Declarative sentences, 333,
  556
Deductive reasoning, 87
Definite articles, 517–518
Definition(s)
  faulty predication and,
    298
  formal definition, 58
  in dictionary, 359–361
  in introductory
    paragraph, 77
  italics for terms being
    defined, 427
Definition essays, 39, 59–61

Definition (pattern of
    development)
  checklists, 61, 75
  paragraph, 74–75
  thesis statement, 19
  writing definition essays,
    39, 58–61
Demonstrative pronouns,
  519, 544
Denotation, 353
Dependent clauses
  comma between
    independent clause
    and, 393
  comma setting off, 384
  definition of, 553
  at end of sentence,
    391
  as mixed construction,
    297–298
  relocating misplaced
    dependent clauses, 301
  for revising dangling
    modifiers, 303
  as sentence fragment,
    281, 283
  verb tense in, 313
Description
  checklists, 61, 75
  definition of, 70
  paragraph, 70–71
  thesis statement, 18
  writing descriptive essays,
    39, 42–45
Descriptive adjectives, 547
Descriptive essays, 39, 42–45
Design
  of documents, 475–485
  of visual aids, 507–510
  of Web sites, 485–490
Determiners, 519, 531, 547
Dewey Decimal Classification
  System (DDC),
  129–130
Diagrams, 482–483
Dialogue, quotation marks
  with, 398
Diction. See also Word choice
  appropriate level of,
    351–352
  pretentious diction, 355
Dictionaries
  electronic dictionaries,
    361
  sample entry, 359
  specialized dictionaries,
    131, 136
  unabridged dictionaries,
    136
  use of, 359–361
Different from, different than,
  365

Different than, different from,
  365
Dig, principal parts, 308
Direct discourse, 297
Direct object, 551–552
Direct quotations. See also
  Quotation(s)
  commas with, 388, 393
  shifts between direct and
    indirect discourse, 297
  word order with,
    536–537
Discreet, discrete, 365
Discrete, discreet, 365
Discussion lists, 156
Diseases, capitalization of,
  425
Disinterested, uninterested,
  365
Dissertations, MLA style for,
  190–191
Dive, principal parts, 308
Division and classification
  checklists, 61, 75
  definition of, 74
  paragraphs, 74
  thesis statement, 19
  writing division-and-
    classification essays, 39,
    56–58
Division-and-classification
  essays, 39, 56–58
Division paragraphs, 74
Do, principal parts, 308
Document design
  checklist, 484–485
  definition of, 475
  headings, 477–479
  line spacing, 477
  list of style manuals in
    various disciplines,
    276–277
  lists, 479–480
  margins, 476
  type face and type size,
    476–477
  visual format, 476–77
  visuals in, 480–485
  white space, 476
Documentation
  APA style, 225–248
  Chicago style, 250–267
  CSE style, 267–275
  definition of, 182
  MLA style, 182–220
  of statistics, 173
Documents, capitalization of,
  422
Doesn't, don't, 365
Dogpile, 153
Dominant impression, 42
Don't, doesn't, 365

Double negatives, 326,
525–526
Drafting
computer used for, 122
essays, 21–24
research paper, 121–125
sample final draft, 35–38
sample first draft, 22–24
sample second draft with
instructor's comments,
28–31
in writing process, 21–24
writing rough draft,
22–24
*Drag,* principal parts, 308
Drama
italics for titles of plays,
426
MLA style for
parenthetical
references to plays, 185
MLA style for works-cited
list, 189–190
numerals for divisions of
plays, 437
periods for marking
divisions in plays, 380
reading, 462
*Draw,* principal parts, 308
*Drink,* principal parts, 308
*Drive,* principal parts, 308
DVDs, 134–135

*e.g.,* 365, 434
*Eat,* principal parts, 308
Editing
abbreviations, 433–435
capitalization, 424–425
colons, 406
commas, 389–391
computer used for, 33–34
dashes, 407
definition of, 31
essays, 31–38
grammar checkers for, 32
question marks, 381
quotation marks, 403–404
research paper, 125
semicolons, 393
spell checkers for, 32, 417,
420
title for essay, 33
in writing process,
31–38
Education databases, 140
*Effect, affect,* 362, 416
Either/or fallacy, 88
Electronic addresses,
149–150, 158, 160, 380,
429
Electronic dictionaries, 361

Electronic sources
APA style for citing, 228,
232–234
Chicago style for citing,
257–260
Columbia Online Style
(COS) for, 203–205
CSE style for citing, 272
evaluation of, 158–161,
199
italics for titles of, 426
MLA style for
parenthetical
references to, 186–187
MLA style for works-cited
list, 195–202
for research paper, 105,
132–135
Ellipses, 166–167, 409–411
E-mail
APA style for citing, 233
attachments to, 503
Chicago style for citing,
258
interviews, 144
MLA style for citing, 198
sentence fragments in,
284
in workplace, 491,
502–503
writing, 156, 491, 502–503
Embedding in sentences, 332
*Emigrate from, immigrate to,*
365–366
*Eminent, imminent,* 366
Emotions, writing to express,
4
Emphasis
active voice for, 339–340
balanced sentences, 339
colon or dash for, 337
cumulative sentences,
338
exclamation points for,
381
italics for, 428
parallelism for, 338
periodic sentences, 338
repetition for, 339
transitional expressions
for, 337
word order and, 336–338
Emphatic order, of résumés,
495, 497
Emphatic sentences,
336–340
Encyclopedias, 131
End punctuation
exclamation points, 381
periods, 379–380
question marks, 381

Endnotes. *See also* Content
notes
Chicago style, 250–261,
262, 265
definition of, 250
English for speakers of other
languages
adjectives, 530–532
adverbs, 530–532
checklists, 515–516,
533–534
commonly confused
words, 538–539
eliminating wordiness,
537–538
nouns, 516–519
prepositions, 532–535
pronouns, 519–521
verbs, 521–530
word order, 535–537
*Enthused,* 366
Entry word of dictionary, 359
Equivocation, 88
*-er,* as comparative form, 324
ESL. *See* English for speakers
of other languages
Essay(s)
argumentative essays,
91–101
audience of, 5–6
body paragraphs, 15
cause-and-effect essays,
39, 50–53
checklists, 5, 6, 14, 17, 20,
26–28, 61
comparison-and-contrast
essays, 39, 53–56
concluding paragraph, 15
definition essays, 39, 58–61
descriptive essays, 39,
42–45
division-and-classification
essays, 39, 56–58
drafting, 21–24
editing and proofreading,
31–38
exemplification essays, 39,
45–48
in-class essays, 459
introductory paragraph,
15, 76–78
narrative essays, 39–42
outline for, 19–21
planning, 3–12
process essays, 39, 48–50
purpose of, 4–5
quotation marks for titles
of, 401
revising, 24–31
sample final draft, 35–38
sample first draft, 22–24

sample second draft with instructor's comments, 28–31
shaping, 12–21
thesis statement, 14–19
thesis-and-support essay, 14–19
title for, 33
writing process for, 3–38
Essay exams
brainstorming for, 454
key words in exam questions, 454
planning answers, 452–454
sample answer, 456–459
thesis statement and list of points, 454–455
writing and revising, 455–456
*-est*, as comparative form, 324
*etc.*, 366, 434
Ethnic groups, capitalization of, 423
Etymology of words, 360
Euphemisms, 353
Evaluation
Internet sources, 158–161, 199
library sources, 141–143
*Even, even if, even though,* 539
Events, capitalization of, 422
*Every day, everyday,* 366, 417
*Every one, everyone,* 366
*Everyday, every day,* 366, 417
*Everyone, every one,* 366
Evidence
accuracy of, 84
in argumentative essays, 93
choice of, as biased, 86
definition of, 93
evaluating, 84–85
kinds of, 84
oral presentations, 506
relevance of, 85
representativeness of, 85
sufficiency of, 84
Examples
colon for setting off, 378
dash for setting of, 378
as supporting evidence, 84
transitional words and phrases signaling, 19
Exams. *See* Essay exams
*Except, accept,* 362, 416
*Excite,* 152
Exclamation point(s)
with quotation marks, 403
uses of, 381

Exclamatory sentences, 556
Exemplification
checklists, 61, 75
definition of, 71
paragraph, 71
thesis statement, 18
writing exemplification essays, 39, 45–48
Exemplification essays, 39, 45–48
Expert audience, 505
Expert testimony, 84
Explanations
colon introducing, 378, 405
dash for setting of, 378
*Explicit, implicit,* 366
Exploratory research, 107

*-f* or *-fe,* plurals of words ending in, 419
Fair use doctrine, 486
Fairness of argumentative essays, 94
*Fall,* principal parts, 308
Fallacies, 88–89
False analogy, 89
*Farther, further,* 366
Faulty parallelism, 347–348
Faulty predication, 298–299
Faxes, 491
Feminine nouns, 516
*Fewer, less,* 366
Fiction, reading, 461
*Fight,* principal parts, 308
Figures of speech, 356
Films
APA style, 234
Chicago style, 257
italics for titles of, 426
MLA style, 194
*Find,* principal parts, 308
Fine-tuning your thesis, 119
*Firstly (secondly, thirdly, . . .),* 366
Flame, 158
Flip charts, 509
*Fly,* principal parts, 308
Focused freewriting, 8
Focused research, 110–112
Footnotes, Chicago style, 250, 262
Foreign words and phrases
italics for, 427
Latin expressions, 434
plurals of, 291, 420
subject-verb agreement, 291
*Forget,* principal parts, 308
Formal definition, 58
Formal diction, 351

Formal outline, 19, 21, 24, 120–121, 120
Fractions
compound fractions, 431
numerals for, 437
Freewriting, 7–8
*Freeze,* principal parts, 308
FTP (file transfer protocol), 157
Full-text databases, 133
Fused sentences, 285–287, 392
Future perfect progressive tense, 313, 525
Future perfect tense, 312, 524
Future progressive tense, 312, 524
Future tense, 311, 523

Gender of nouns, 516
General audience, 505
General words, 353
Geographical regions, capitalization of, 422
Geology style manual, 276
Gerund(s), 529, 546–547
Gerund phrases, 553
*Get,* principal parts, 308
*Give,* principal parts, 308
Glossary of usage, 362–373
*Go,* principal parts, 308
GoHip, 153
*Good,* comparative and superlative forms, 325
*Good, well,* 366–367
Google, 153
Gopher, 156
*Got to,* 367
Government agencies, capitalization of, 423
Government documents
APA style for citing, 230
Chicago style for citing, 256
in library research, 141
MLA style for parenthetical references to, 186
MLA style for works-cited list, 191
style manual, 276
Grammar checkers, 32
Graphs, 213, 482
*Grow,* principal parts, 308

*Hang (execute),* principal parts, 308
*Hang (suspend),* principal parts, 308
*Hanged, hung,* 367
Hasty generalization, 88
*Have,* principal parts, 308

*He, she,* 367
Headings in document design, 477–479
*Hear,* principal parts, 309
Helping (auxiliary) verbs, 522–523, 545–546
Highlighting, 450
Historical documents, 427
Historical periods and events, capitalization of, 422, 425
Holidays
 abbreviation of, 433
 capitalization of, 422
Home pages, 148, 196, 485
Homophones, 416
*Hopefully,* 367
Hotbot, 153
HTML tags, 486–487
Humanities. *See also* Literature
 Chicago documentation style, 250–266
 databases, 139–130
 MLA style, 182–220
 search engines, 154
 style manual, 277
 Web sites, 161
*Hung, hanged,* 367
Hyperlinks, 488–489
Hypertext links, 148
Hyphen(s)
 for breaking word at end of line, 429
 for clarity, 431
 for dividing compound words, 429–431
 for dividing electronic addresses (URLs), 429
 in coined compounds, 431
 in compound adjectives, 430
 in compound numerals, 431
 with prefixes and suffixes, 430–431
 suspended hyphens, 430

*I,* capitalization of, 424
*i.e.,* 367, 434
*-ible, -able,* 419
Ideas
 brainstorming, 9–10
 clustering, 10
 developing in writing, 7–12
 generating, 7–10
 grouping, 12–14
 topic tree, 12–14, 13
Identification numbers, 438

Identifying tag, 165–166, 388, 398–399
Idiomatic expression, prepositions in, 534–535
Idioms, 361
*If, whether,* 367
*Illusion, allusion,* 362
*Immigrate to, emigrate from,* 365–366
*Imminent, eminent,* 366
Imperative mood, 314
Imperative sentences, 333, 536, 556
*Implicit, explicit,* 366
*Imply, infer,* 367
*In,* 533
Inappropriate language, 354–355
In-class essays, 459
Indefinite articles, 517–518
Indefinite pronouns
 antecedents not needed for of, 520
 definition of, 544
 possessive case of, 394
 pronoun-antecedent agreement, 293, 294
 subject-verb agreement, 290, 520
Indentation
 of headings, 478
 of lists, 479
 of long prose passages, 400
 of poetry, 401
Independent clauses
 colon separating, 377, 405
 comma between dependent clause and, 393
 comma for setting off, 329, 377
 as comma splice, 285–287, 392
 coordinating conjunction between, 287, 329, 377
 definition of, 553
 as fused sentence, 285–287, 392
 as mixed construction, 297–298
 revising with periods, 285–286
 revising with semicolons, 286
 as run-on sentence, 285
 semicolon for setting off, 286, 329, 377, 387, 392
 sentence fragments attached to, 282–283
 subordinating conjunctions with, 287

with transitional word or phrase, 286, 377, 387, 392
In-depth questions, 11
Indicative mood, 314
Indirect discourse, 297
Indirect object, 552
Indirect questions, 390
Indirect quotations, 297, 390, 403, 537. *See also* Quotation(s)
Inductive reasoning, 86–87
*Infer, imply,* 367
Inference, 87
Infinitive(s), 313–314, 529, 546
Infinitive phrases, 553
Inform, writing to, 4
Informal diction, 351–352
Informal outline, 19, 20
Infoseek, 153
*Inside of, outside of,* 367
Instant messaging, 157
Institutions, capitalization of, 423
Instructions in process essays, 48
Instructors' comments, 25–26, 28–31
Intensive pronouns, 544
Interjection(s)
 capitalization of, 424
 comma with, 388
 definition of, 550
 exclamation points with, 381
Interlibrary loans, 141
Internet. *See also* Web sites
 bookmarks, 155
 checklists, 155, 157–160
 definition of, 147
 electronic address, 149–150, 158, 160, 429
 e-mail, 156, 491, 502–503
 evaluating Internet sources, 158–161
 FTP (file transfer protocol), 157
 gopher, 156
 instant messaging, 157
 introduction, 147–148
 IRCS, 157
 keyword search, 150–152
 listservs, 156
 MOOS, 157
 MUDS, 157
 netiquette, 157–158
 newsgroups, 156
 plagiarism and, 171–172
 posting a résumé, 498
 posting a Web site, 489
 search engines, 148–155

strategies if you cannot connect, 149–150
subject search, 150, 151
telnet, 157
World Wide Web, 148–155
Internet servers, 489
Interrogative adverbs, 547
Interrogative pronouns, 544
Interrogative sentences, 556
Interruption, dash for, 407
Interviews
Chicago style, 256–257
conducting, 144–145
MLA style, 193–194
*Into*, 533
Intransitive verbs, 526–527, 551
Introduction
argumentative essays, 95
oral presentation, 506
research paper, 122–123
Introductory paragraph
cautions about, 78
checklist, 78
definition of, 15, 76
examples of, 76–78
revising, 78
strategies, 76–78
Intrusive modifiers, 302
Inverted subject-verb order, 291, 334–335
IRCS, 157
*Irregardless, regardless*, 367
Irregular verbs, principal parts of, 307–310
*Is when, is where*, 298, 368
*Is where, is when*, 298, 368
ISP (Internet service provider), 148
Italics
for elements spoken of as themselves, 397, 427
for emphasis, 428
for foreign words and phrases, 427
MLA style on, 428
for terms being defined, 427
for titles and names, 426–427
underlining for, 401, 428
*It's, its*, 368, 416
*Its, it's*, 368, 416

Jargon, 354
Journal, 7
Journalism style manual, 276
Journalistic questions, 10, 12
Justifying margins, 476

*Keep*, principal parts, 309

Key words and phrases, repeating for coherence, 67–68
Keyword search
Internet, 150–152
online catalog, 127, 128
online databases, 134
*Kind of, sort of*, 368
*Know*, principal parts, 309

Languages, capitalization of, 423
Latin expressions, abbreviation of, 434
Law
databases, 140
search engines, 154
style manual, 276
*Lay, lie*, 310, 368
*Lay*, principal parts, 309, 310
LC. *See* Library of Congress Classification System (LC)
*Lead*, principal parts, 309
*Least*, as superlative form, 324
*Leave, let*, 368
Legal cases, capitalization of, 422
*Lend*, principal parts, 309
*Less, a few, a little and few*, 539
*Less*, as comparative form, 324
*Less, fewer*, 366
*Let*
leave, 368
principal parts, 309
Letters (alphabet)
apostrophes for omitted letters, 396
capitalization of single letters, 424
doubling final consonants, 418
*ie/ei* combinations, 418
parentheses around, 408
silent *e* before suffix, 418
silent letters, 415
vowels in unstressed positions, 415
*y* before suffix, 419
Letters (correspondence)
APA style for citing, 232
application letters, 493–494
business letters, 406, 491–492
Chicago style for citing, 256
MLA style for citing, 194

Letters of application, 493–494
Letters to the editor
APA style, 232
MLA style, 197
Library catalogs. *See* Online catalogs
Library of Congress Classification System (LC), 130
*Library of Congress Subject Headings*, 127–128
Library sources
books, 137–138, 142–143, 449
browsing, 129–130
call number of book, 137
CD-ROMs and DVDs, 134–135
checklists, 126, 127, 138
circulating collection, 129
Dewey Decimal Classification System (DDC), 129–130
electronic resources, 132–135
evaluating, 141–143
exploratory library research, 126–135
focused library research, 135–141
government documents, 141
interlibrary loans, 141
Library of Congress Classification System (LC), 130
online catalogs, 126–128, 137–138
online databases, 132–135, 139–141
periodical articles, 138–141, 449
periodicals, 138–139, 142–143
reference works, 129, 131, 136–137
research outside the library, 144–146
special collections, 141
special library services, 141
study skills and, 445–446
tracking down missing source, 138
vertical files, 141
Web site of library, 128
Web sites for, 135–136
*Lie, lay*, 310, 368
*Lie (recline)*, principal parts, 309, 310

*Lie (tell an untruth)*, principal parts, 309
*Like, as,* 363
Limiting modifiers, 300
Line spacing in document design, 477
Linking verbs, 292, 298, 322, 545
 agreement with, 292
Links, 488–489
Lists
 colon introducing, 283, 393, 405
 constructing, 479–480
 parallelism in, 347
 punctuation of, 408, 480
 sentence fragment as, 283
Listservs, 156
Literary movements, capitalization of, 422
Literature
 checklists on reading and writing about, 461–464
 reading, 460–462
 sample student papers, 464–474
 writing about, 462–474
Logical fallacies, 88–89
Logical order, of paragraph, 65
Logical reasoning, 86–87
Long prose passages
 colon introducing, 406
 indentation of, 400
 quotation marks for, 400
 quotation marks for quotes and titles within, 403
*Loose, lose,* 368
*Lose, loose,* 368
*Lots, lots of, a lot of,* 368
*Lots of, a lot of, lots,* 368
Lycos, 153

Magazine articles. *See* Periodical articles
Magellan, 153
Main verbs, 545
Major premise of syllogism, 87
*Make,* principal parts, 309
*Man,* 368
*Many,* comparative and superlative forms, 325
*Many, much,* 539
Mapping, 10, 11
Maps
 CSE style, 272
 MLA style, 198
Margins in document design, 476

Masculine nouns, 516
Mathematics style manual, 277
*May, can,* 364
*May be, maybe,* 369
*Maybe, may be,* 369
Measurement
 abbreviation of units of, 434–435
 numerals for, 437
*Media, medium,* 291, 369
Medicine
 capitalization of medical terms, 425
 databases, 140
 search engines, 154
 style manual, 277
*Medium, media,* 291, 369
Memos, 500–501
Mentors, 447
Metacrawler engines, 153
Metaphors, 356
Metasearch engines, 153
*Might have, might of,* 369
*Might of, might have,* 369
Minor premise of syllogism, 87
Misplaced modifiers. *See also* Modifier(s)
 definition of, 300
 placing modifying words precisely, 300–301
 relocating misplaced dependent clauses, 301
 relocating misplaced phrases, 301
 revising, 302
Mixed audience, 505
Mixed constructions, 297–298
MLA style
 abbreviations in, 433
 breaking URL at end of line, 429
 checklists, 205–206
 content notes, 202–205, 218
 ellipses, 410
 manuscript guidelines, 205–206
 for measurement units, 435
 for numbers and numerals, 436–438
 parenthetical references in text, 182–187
 sample student paper, 206–220, 468–474
 underlining for italics, 401, 428
 works-cited list, 187–202, 206, 219–220, 474

writing for literature, 468–474
Modal auxiliaries, 522–523, 546
Modifier(s). *See also* Adjective(s); Adverb(s)
 dangling modifiers, 302–303
 intrusive modifiers, 302
 limiting modifiers, 300
 misplaced modifiers, 300–301
 nonrestrictive modifiers, 385–386
 restrictive modifiers, 385–386, 389
 squinting modifiers, 300–301
Money
 numerals for, 437
 symbol for, 435
Months
 abbreviation of, 433
 capitalization of, 422
Monuments, capitalization of, 422
Mood
 definition of, 314
 imperative mood, 314
 indicative mood, 314
 shifts in, 296
 subjunctive mood, 314–315
MOOS, 157
*More,* as comparative form, 324
*Most, most of, the most,* 539
*Most,* as superlative form, 324
Motion pictures. *See* Films
Movies *See* Films
*Mt.,* abbreviation of, 434
*Much,* comparative and superlative forms, 325
*Much, many,* 539
MUDS, 157
Music style manual, 277

Name(s). *See* People's names; Proper nouns
Name-year format, 268
Narration
 checklists, 61, 75
 definition of, 70
 paragraph, 70
 thesis statement, 18
 writing narrative essays, 39–42
Narrative essays, 39–42
Narrowing of focus, 19
Nationalities, capitalization of, 423
Natural sciences. *See* Science

# INDEX

Negative verbs, 525–526
Neologisms, **354**–355
Netiquette, **157**–158
News, search engines for, 154
Newsgroups
APA style for citing, 233
description of, 156
MLA style for citing, 198
Newspaper(s), titles of, 426
Newspaper articles
APA style for citing, 231,
233–234
Chicago style for citing,
255–256, 259
CSE style for citing, 271
MLA style for citing,
192–193, 196, 201
quotation marks for titles
of, 401
*No,* comma with, 388
*No, not,* 538
*No.,* abbreviation of, 433
Non sequitur (does not
follow), 88
Noncount nouns, **517**, 518,
**543**
Nonessential items
circumlocution, 342–343
comma or commas for
setting off, 378,
385–388
dash for setting off, 378,
406–407
deadwood, 341–342
eliminating, 341–343
nonrestrictive modifiers,
385–386
parentheses for setting
off, 378, 407–408
utility words, 342
Nonexistent antecedents,
320–321
Nonprint sources
APA style for citing, 234
Chicago style for citing,
257
CSE style for citing,
271–272
Nonrestrictive modifiers,
**385**–386
Nonstandard diction, **352**
Northern Light, 153
*Not, no,* 538
Note cards
for oral presentation, 507
for taking notes, 113, 114
Note taking, 112–115
Notes for oral presentations,
506–507
Noun(s)
abstract nouns, 543

and words indicating
amount or order, 519
articles with, 517–518
with cardinal numbers,
519
collective nouns, 290–291,
293, 543
common nouns, 543
compound nouns, 420
count nouns, 517, 543
definition of, **516**, **543**
demonstrative pronouns
with, 519
determiners with, 519,
531, 547
for ESL students, 516–519
gender of, 516
noncount nouns, 517,
518, 543
number of, 516–517
with ordinal numbers, 519
plurals of, 394–395,
419–420
possessive case of,
394–395
possessive nouns, 519
proper nouns, **421**–424,
**543**
verbs used as, 529–530
*we* and *us* before, 319
Noun clauses, **554**–555
Noun phrases, 345, **553**
Number. *See also* Plurals;
Singular nouns
*Number, amount,* 363
Number
definition of, **297**,
**516–517**
of nouns, 516–517
pronoun-antecedent
agreement, 292–294
shifts in, 297
subject-verb agreement,
288–292, 522
Numbers
abbreviation of, 433
apostrophes for omitted
numbers, 396
cardinal numbers, 519
for lists, 479
numerals versus spelled-
out numbers, 436
ordinal numbers, 519
parentheses around, 408
question marks for
questionable numbers,
381
Numerals
for addresses, 437
compound numerals,
431

conventional uses of,
437–438
for dates, 437
for decimals, 437
for divisions of written
works, 437
for fractions, 437
for identification
numbers, 438
for measurements before
abbreviation or
symbol, 437
for percentages, 437
for ratios, 438
for scores, 438
spelled-out numbers
versus, 436
for statistics, 438
for sums of money, 437
for times of day, 437

*O,* capitalization of, 424
*-o,* plurals of words ending
in, 420
*O.K., okay, OK,* 369
Object(s)
colon not used to separate
verbs or prepositions
and, 406
direct object, 551–552
indirect object, 552
of preposition, 548
Object complements, 552
Objective case of pronouns,
317, 534
Objectivity
of Internet sources, 160
of library sources, 142
Observing, and planning
essay, 7
Offensive labels, 356–357
*OK, O.K., okay,* 369
*Okay, OK, O.K.,* 369
*On,* 533
Online, 148
Online catalogs, **126**–128,
137–138
Online databases, **132**–135,
139–141
*Onto,* 534
Open-ended questions, 144
Opinion
in concluding paragraph,
79
definition of, **83**
fact distinguished from,
83–84
Oral presentations
audience of, 504–505
body of, 506
checklists, 509–12

conclusion, 506
constraints on, 505
delivering, 510–512
full text of, 507
getting started, 504–505
introduction, 506
notes for, 506–507
outline of, 507
planning, 505–506
points of, 506
purpose of, 505
rehearsing, 510
supporting evidence in, 506
thesis statement, 505–506
topic of, 504
visual aids for, 507–510
Order, words indicating, 519
Order of words. *See* Word order
Ordinal numbers, 519
Organizations
abbreviation of, 432
capitalization of, 423
Outline
checklist, 20
definition of, **19**
formal outline, **19**, 21, 24, 120–121
informal outline, **19**, 20
oral presentation, 507
parallelism in, 347
research paper, 120–21
sentence outline, 206–209
*Outside of, inside of,* 367
Overhead projectors, 509

Page header, **235**
Paired items, parallelism with, 346–347
Pamphlets, MLA style for citing, 191
Paragraphs
arrangement of details in, 64–65
audience of, 69
body paragraphs, 15
cause-and-effect paragraphs, 72
checklists, 62, 75, 78, 80
chronological order of, 64
classification paragraphs, 74
coherence between, 68
coherent paragraphs, 64–68
comparison-and-contrast paragraphs, 72–73
concluding paragraph, 15
definition of, **62**

definition paragraphs, 74–75
descriptive paragraphs, 70–71
division paragraphs, 74
exemplification paragraphs, 71
introductory paragraph, 15, 76–78
key words and phrases in, 67–68
logical order of, 65
main idea of, 69
narrative paragraphs, 70
patterns of development of, 70–75
process paragraphs, 71–72
purpose of, 69
revising, 27
spatial order of, 64
topic sentences of, 62–64
transitional words and phrases in, 65–67
unified paragraphs, 62–64
well-developed paragraphs, 68–69
when to paragraph, 62
Parallelism
coherent paragraphs, 67
definition of, **67, 346**
for emphasis, 338–339
items in series, 346
in lists, 347, 479
in outlines, 347
paired items, 346–347
repeating key words, 348
revising faulty parallelism, 347–348
in sentences, 338–339, 346–348
Paraphrases
checklist, 118
definition of, **117**
example of, 117–118
identifying tag with, 165
integrating, 168
MLA style for parenthetical references, 183
Parentheses
brackets within, 409
with letters and numbers, 408
with nonessential items, 378, 407–408
Parenthetical references in text
APA style, 225–229
CSE style, 267–268
definition of, **182**

MLA style, 182–187
punctuating with, 183, 408
Participial phrases, **529–530**, 553
Participle(s)
of regular and irregular verbs, 307–310
participial phrases, 529–530, 553
past participles, 307–310, 314, 529, 546
present participles, 307–310, 314, 529, 546
tense of, 314
Part-of-speech labels in dictionary, 360
Parts of speech, **534–550**. *See also specific parts of speech,* such as Noun(s)
*Passed, past,* 369
Passive voice
and dangling modifiers, 303
definition of, **316**
eliminating passive constructions in rambling sentences, 345
preference of active voice versus, 527
shift to active voice from, 295–296
uses of, 316, 340
*Past, passed,* 369
Past participles, **307–310**, 314, 529, 546
Past perfect progressive tense, **313**, 524–525
Past perfect tense, **312**, 524
Past progressive tense, **312**, 524
Past subjunctive, **315**
Past tense
definition of, **311**
form of regular and irregular verbs, 307–310
uses of, 523
Patterns of development, 18, 39–61, 70–75
People's names
capitalization of, 421–422
in direct address, 388
titles following, 388, 421–422, 432
*Percent, percentage,* 369
*Percentage, percent,* 369
Percentages
numerals for, 437
symbol for, 435
Perfect tenses, 310, **311–312**, 523–524

Period(s)
for abbreviations,
379–380
for divisions of written
works, 380
for ending a sentence,
379
for marking divisions in
electronic address, 380
for revising comma splice
or fused sentences,
285–286
quotation marks with, 402
Periodic sentences, **338**
Periodical(s)
in library research,
138–139, 142–143
italics for titles of, 426
Periodical articles
APA style for citing, 231
Chicago style for citing,
254–255, 259–260
CSE style for citing, 270,
272
in library research,
138–141, 449
MLA style for citing,
191–192, 196–197, 200
quotation marks for titles
of, 401
Periodical indexes, **139–141**
Person
definition of, **296**
shifts in, 296
of verbs, 522
Personal home pages, 196,
485
Personal organizer, 441–442
Personal pronouns
definition of, **544**
possessive case of, 395
Personification, **356**
Persuasive writing, 4–5
*Phenomenon, phenomena,* 369
Philosophic movements,
capitalization of, 422
Photocopies in research
process, 115
Photographs, 483–484
Phrasal verbs, 527–528
Phrase(s). *See also* Foreign
words and phrases;
Prepositional phrases;
Transitional words and
phrases
absolute phrases, 387, 553
as sentence opening, 334
comma between clause
and, 393
definition of, **553**
gerund phrases, 553
infinitive phrases, 553

key phrases, 67–68
noun phrases, 553
participial phrases,
529–530, 553
relocating misplaced
phrases, 301
revising wordy phrases,
343
verb phrases, 553
verbal phrases, 384, 553
Physics style manual, 277
Places
abbreviation of, 434
capitalization of, 422
Plagiarism
avoiding, 169–175
causes of accidental
plagiarism, 170
checklist for avoiding,
174–175
definition of, **169**
differentiating your
words and ideas from
those of source,
173–174
documentation of
statistics, 173
enclosing borrowed words
in quotation marks,
171
imitation of source's
syntax and phrasing,
172–173
and Internet sources,
171–172
Planning
argumentative essays,
91–93
essay exam answers,
452–454
essays, 3–12
oral presentation,
505–506
in writing process, 3–12
Plays. *See* Drama
Plurals
apostrophes for forming,
397
articles with, 518
compound nouns, 420
count versus noncount
nouns, 517
foreign words, 291, 420
forming, 397, 419–420,
517
nouns, 395, 419–420,
516–517
possessive case of plural
nouns, 394–395
subject-verb agreement,
288
*Plus,* 369

Poetry
capitalization in, 421
ellipses indicating
omission in, 411
italics to titles of long
poems, 426
MLA style for
parenthetical
references to, 185
MLA style for works-cited
list, 189–190
numerals for divisions of
long poems, 437
periods for marking
divisions in long
poems, 380
quotation marks for titles
of short poems,
401–402
quotation marks with
passages from, 401
reading, 461–462
slashes with, 401, 409
Point-by-point comparison,
54
Popular publications, **142–143**
Possessive case
compound nouns or
groups of words, 395
personal pronouns, 318,
395
plural nouns, 394–395
pronouns, 317, 318, 395
singular nouns, 394
two or more items, 395
Possessive nouns, 519
Possessive pronouns, 519
Post hoc fallacy, 88
Postal abbreviations, 380
Posters, 509
Posting
résumés, 498
Web site, **489**
*PowerPoint,* 507–508
*Precede, proceed,* 369
Predicate(s). *See also* Verb(s)
complete predicate, 551
faulty predication,
298–299
simple predicate, 551
Predicate adjectives, **552**
Predicate nominative, **552**
Prediction in concluding
paragraph, 79
Prefixes, hyphens with,
430–431
Preposition(s)
checklist, 533–534
colon not used to separate
objects and, 406
commonly confused
prepositions, 533–534

definition of, **532, 548**
for ESL students,
532–535
in idiomatic expression,
534–535
list of frequently used
prepositions,
548–549
object of, 548
pronouns in prepositional
phrases, 534
uses of, 533
Prepositional phrases
comma setting off, 384
definition of, **553**
as mixed construction,
297–298
pronouns in, 534
wordiness of, 345
Present participles, 307–310,
314, 529, 546
Present perfect participles,
314
Present perfect progressive
tense, **313,** 524
Present perfect tense, **312,**
523
Present progressive tense,
**312,** 524
Present subjunctive, **315**
Present tense
definition of, 311
subject-verb agreement,
288
uses of, 311, 523
in writing about
literature, 295
Pretentious diction, **355**
Previewing (active reading),
**449**
Primary sources, 111–112
*Principal, principle,* 369–370,
416
Principal parts of verbs,
307–310
*Principle, principal,* 369–370,
416
Print résumés, 495–497
Print sources, **105.** *See also*
Books
*Proceed, precede,* 369
Process
checklists, 61, 75
definition of, **71**
paragraph, 71–72
thesis statement, 18
writing process essays, 39,
48–50
Process essays, 39, 48–50
Process explanation, **48**
Progressive tenses, 310,
**312–313**

Pronoun(s)
agreement between
antecedents and,
292–294, 520
ambiguous antecedent,
321
antecedents of, 520,
543–544
appositives, 319, 521
case of, 317–319
comparisons with *than* or
*as,* 318
demonstrative pronouns,
519, 544
for ESL students, 519–521
in prepositional phrases,
534
indefinite pronouns, **290,**
293, 294, 394, 520, 544
intensive pronouns, 544
interrogative pronouns,
544
nonexistent antecedent,
320–321
objective case of, 317, 534
personal pronouns, 395,
544
placement of, 520
possessive case of, 317,
318
possessive pronouns, 519
pronoun reference and,
520
reciprocal pronouns, 545
reflexive pronouns, 544
relative pronouns, 283,
287, 330, 544
remote antecedent, 320
revising reference errors,
320–321
shifts in person and
number, 296–297
substituting pronoun to
eliminate repetition,
343
*we* and *us* before noun,
319
*who, which, that,* 321
*who* and *whom,* 318–319
Pronoun-antecedent
agreement
collective noun
antecedents, 293
compound antecedents,
292–293
indefinite pronoun
antecedents, 293, 294
Pronunciation
in dictionary, 359–360
homophones, 416
words often pronounced
carelessly, 416

Proofreading
computer used for, 33–34
definition of, **32**
essays, 32–38
grammar checkers for, 32
research paper, 125
spell checkers for, 32, 417,
420
Web site text, 489
in writing process, 32–38
Proper nouns
abbreviation of, 432–434
articles with, 518
capitalization of, 421–424
definition of, **543**
plurals of, 419
Proprietary databases, **133**
Prose. *See also* Literature
long prose passages, 400,
403, 406
MLA style for
parenthetical
references to, 185
*Prove,* principal parts, 309
Punctuation marks
apostrophe, 394–397
brackets, 408–409
colon, 405–406
comma, 382–391
dash, 406–407
ellipses, 409–410
exclamation point, 381
parentheses, 407–408
period, 379–380
question mark, 381
quotation marks, 398–404
semicolon, 392–393
slash, 409
Purpose
checklist, 5
definition of, 4
determining, 4–5, 69
of essay exam answers, 453
of essays, 4–5
of oral presentation, 505
of paragraphs, 69

Question(s)
closed-ended questions,
144
in interviews, 144
in introductory
paragraph, 76–77
in-depth questions, 11
indirect questions, 390
journalistic questions, 10,
12
open-ended questions,
144
pronoun case in, 319
rhetorical questions, 333
tag questions, 388

word order in, 535–536
Question mark(s)
  at end of direct question,
    381
  at end of sentence after
    abbreviation, 379
  editing misused question
    marks, 381
  for questionable dates
    and numbers, 381
  with quotation marks, 403
*Quotation, quote,* 370
Quotation(s)
  brackets setting off
    comments within,
    408–409
  colon introducing, 405,
    406
  comma with direct
    quotation, 388, 393
  direct quotations, 297,
    388, 393, 536–537
  editing misused
    quotation marks,
    403–404
  identifying tag with,
    165–166, 388, 398–399
  in concluding paragraph,
    79
  in introductory
    paragraph, 76
  in research paper,
    118–119
  indirect quotations, 297,
    390, 403, 537
  integrating, 165
  interrupted quotation,
    286
  long quotations, 167
  MLA style for
    parenthetical
    references, 183
  of long prose passages,
    400
  of poetry, 401, 409, 411
  omissions within, 166–167
  shifts between direct and
    indirect discourse, 297
  substitutions or additions
    within, 166
  within quotations, 403
  word order with direct
    and indirect
    quotations, 536–537
  words used in special
    ways, 402
Quotation books, 137
Quotation marks
  with colon, 402
  with comma, 402
  with dash, 403
  with dialogue, 398

editing misused quotation
    marks, 403–404
  enclosing borrowed words
    in, 171
  exclamation point with,
    403
  for long prose passages,
    400
  with other punctuation
    marks, 402–403
  with period, 402
  for poetry, 401
  with question mark, 403
  for quotation within
    quotation, 403
  with semicolon, 402
  setting off quoted speech
    or writing, 398–399
  single quotation marks,
    403
  for titles of works,
    401–402, 403, 426
*Quote, quotation,* 370

Races, capitalization of,
    423
Racist statements, 85
Radio programs
  italics for titles of, 426
  MLA style, 194, 198
  quotation marks for
    episodes of, 402
*Raise, rise,* 370
Random sample, 145
Ratios, numerals for, 438
*Read,* principal parts, 309
Reading
  active reading, 449–451
  literature, 460–462
  planning essay and, 7
Reading sources in research
    process, 111
*Real, really,* 370
*Really, real,* 370
*Reason is because, reason is
    that,* 299, 370
Reciprocal pronouns, 545
Recordings
  ALA style, 234
  Chicago style, 257
  CSE style, 271
  MLA style, 195
Red herring, 89
Reference lists. *See also*
    Bibliography
  APA style, 229–234, 237,
    246
  CSE style, 268–272, 275
Reference works
  APA style for citing, 230
  in library research, 129,
    131, 136–137

MLA style for citing, 191,
    201
Reflexive pronouns, **544**
Refutation of opposing
    arguments, 92–93, 95
*Regardless, irregardless,* 367
Regionalisms, **352**
Regular verbs, principal parts
    of, 307
Rehearsing a speech, 510
Relative clauses, **554**
Relative pronouns
  in complex sentences, 330
  definition of, **544**
  with independent clauses,
    287
  list of, 330
  in sentence fragment, 283
  subject-verb agreement,
    292
Relevance of supporting
    evidence, 85
Religions, capitalization of,
    423
Remote antecedents, 320
Repetition
  deleting redundancy,
    343
  eliminating unnecessary
    repetition, 343–344
  for emphasis, 339
  substituting pronoun to
    eliminate, 343
Research paper
  APA style, 237–248
  Chicago style, 262–266
  CSE style, 274–275
  MLA style, 206–220
  shaping research paper,
    122–123
Research process
  avoiding plagiarism,
    169–175
  body of research paper,
    123
  checklists, 106–107, 114,
    115, 117, 118, 120–121,
    124
  conclusion of research
    paper, 123
  drafting, 121–124
  editing and proofreading,
    125
  exploratory research, 107
  final draft of research
    paper, 125
  focused research, 110–112
  integrating source
    material into writing,
    123–124, 164–169
  Internet sources, 147–163
  interviews, 144–145

introduction of research
paper, 122–123
library sources, 126–146
note taking, 112–119
outlining, 120–21
paraphrasing sources,
117–118
photocopies and
computer printouts,
115
primary sources, 111–112
quoting sources, 118–119
reading sources, 111
research outside the
library, 144–146
research question, 107
revising research paper,
124–125
secondary sources,
111–112
summarizing sources,
116–117, 118
summary of and schedule
for, 105–6
tentative thesis, 110
thesis statement, 119
title of research paper,
125
topic choice in, 106–107
working bibliography,
108–109
Research question, 107
*Respectably, respectfully,
respectively,* 370
*Respectfully, respectively,
respectably,* 370
*Respectively, respectably,
respectfully,* 370
Restrictive modifiers,
385–386, 389
Résumés
posting, 498
print résumés, 495–497
scannable résumés,
498–499
Revising
agreement errors,
288–294
awkward or confusing
sentences, 295–299
checklists, 26–28
choppy sentences,
331–332
collaborative revision, 25
comma splices, 285–287
computer used for, 25,
125
dangling modifiers,
302–303
essay, 24–31
essay exam answers,
455–456

faulty parallelism,
347–348
faulty predication,
298–299
formal outline for, 24
fused sentences, 285–287
instructors' comments for,
25–26, 28–31
intrusive modifiers, 302
misplaced modifiers,
300–301
mixed constructions,
297–298
paragraphs, 27
parallelism, 347–348
rambling sentences,
344–345
research paper, 124–125
sentence fragments,
281–284
sentences, 27, 281–303
thesis statement, 17
unwarranted shifts,
295–297
words, 28
wordy phrases, 343
in writing process, 24–31
Rhetorical questions, 333
*Ride,* principal parts, 309
*Ring,* principal parts, 309
*Rise,* principal parts, 309
*Rise, raise,* 370
Rough drafts. *See* Drafting
*Run,* principal parts, 309
Run-on sentences, 285

*-s*
plurals of words ending
in, 420
possessive case of nouns
ending in, 394
Sacred books and figures
capitalization of, 423
italics not used for, 427
MLA style for
parenthetical
references to Bible,
185
numerals for divisions of
Bible, 437
periods for marking
division of Bible, 380
Sample for survey, 145
*Say,* principal parts, 309
Scholarly publications,
142–143
Science
CSE documentation style,
267–275
databases, 139–130
style manuals, 276–277
Web sites, 162

Scores, numerals for, 438
Search engine, 148–155
Search Engine Watch, 154
Search operators, 151–152
Seasons, capitalization of,
425
Secondary sources, 111–112
*See,* principal parts, 309
*Seed* endings, 419
Semicolon(s)
editing misused
semicolons, 393
in compound sentences,
329–330
with independent clauses,
329, 377, 387, 392
with items in series, 377,
383, 392–393
quotation marks with, 402
revising comma splice or
fused sentence, 286
Sentence(s). *See also*
Subject(s) of
sentence(s)
balanced sentences, 339
basic elements of, 551
basic patterns of, 551–552
breaking up strings of
compound sentences,
332–33
capitalization of first word
of, 421
combining choppy simple
sentences, 331–332
complex sentences, 330,
344, 553–554, 555
compound sentences,
329–330, 332, 555
compound-complex
sentences, 331, 556
concise sentences,
341–345
coordination in, 331
cumulative sentences,
338
declarative sentences,
333, 556
definition of, 551
embedding in, 332
emphatic sentences,
336–340
exclamatory sentences,
556
faulty predication in,
298–299
following long sentence
with short sentence,
332
imperative sentences, 333,
536, 556
incomplete or illogical
comparisons in, 299

interrogative sentences, 556

length of, 331–332

maintaining boundaries of, 282

mixed constructions in, 297–298

openings for, 334

parallelism in, 338–339, 346–348

period at end of, 379

periodic sentences, 338

rambling sentences, 344–345

revising, 27, 281–303

run-on sentences, 285

simple sentences, 551–552, 555

subordination in, 331–332

topic sentence, 62–64

types of, 555–556

unwarranted shifts in, 295–297

varied sentences, 329–335

verb tenses in, 313–314

word order in, 291, 334–338

Sentence fragments

attaching to independent clause, 282–283

definition of, 281

deleting subordinating conjunction or relative pronoun, 283

as lists, 283

revising, 281–284

in speech or e-mail, 284

supplying missing subject or verb for, 284

Sentence outline, 206–209

Sequence, transitional expressions signaling, 66

Series

adjectives in, 383

colon introducing, 405

commas separating items in, 377, 382–383

of coordinate elements, 382–383

parallelism with items in, 346

of questions in introductory paragraph, 76–77

of quotations in introductory paragraph, 76

semicolons separating items in, 377, 383, 392–393

*Set, sit,* 310, 370

*Set (place),* principal parts, 309, 310

Sexist language, 294, 357–358

Sexist statements, 85

*-sh,* plurals of words ending in, 420

*Shake,* principal parts, 309

*Shall, will,* 370

Shaping

essays, 12–21

research paper, 122–123

thesis statement for, 18–19

in writing process, 12–21

*She, he,* 367

Ships, italics for titles of, 426

Short stories

MLA style for works-cited list, 189–190

quotation marks for titles of, 401

*Should of, would of, could of,* 365

*Shrink,* principal parts, 309

*sic,* 408

Silent *e* before suffix, 418

Silent letters, 415

Similes, 356

Simple predicate, 551

Simple sentences, 551–552, 555

Simple subject, 551

Simple tenses, 310, 311, 523

*Since,* 370

*Sing,* principal parts, 309

Single quotation marks, 403

Singular nouns

plural forms of, 291, 517

possessive case, 394

subject-verb agreement, 288

*Sink,* principal parts, 309

*Sit,* principal parts, 309, 310

*Sit, set,* 310, 370

*Site, cite,* 364

Slang, 352, 404

Slanted language, 85

Slash(es)

with poetry, 401, 409

separating one option from another, 409

Slide projector, 509

*Sneak,* principal parts, 309

*So,* 371

Social sciences

APA documentation style, 225–248

Chicago documentation style, 250–266

databases, 139–130

Web sites, 162

Software programs. *See* Computer software

*Some,* comparative and superlative forms, 325

*Some, any,* 539

*Some time, sometime, sometimes,* 371

Songs, quotation marks for titles of, 401–402

*Sort of, kind of,* 368

Source material, integrating into research paper, 123–124, 164–169

Spacecraft, italics for titles of, 426

Spatial order of paragraph, 64

*Speak,* principal parts, 309

Special library collections, 141

Specific words, 353

Speeches. *See* Oral presentations

*Speed,* principal parts, 309

Spell checkers, 32, 417, 420

Spelling

*-able* and *-ible* suffixes, 419

American and British spellings, 416

doubling final consonants, 418

for ESL students, 515–516

homophones, 416

*ie/ei* combinations, 418

one word or two words, 417

plurals, 419–420

rules, 417–420

*seed* endings, 419

silent *e* before suffix, 418

silent letters, 415

spell checkers, 32, 417, 420

vowels in unstressed positions, 415

words often pronounced carelessly, 416

*y* before suffix, 419

*Spin,* principal parts, 309

Sports search engines, 154

*Spring,* principal parts, 309

Squinting modifiers, 300–301

*-ss,* plurals of words ending in, 420

*St.,* abbreviation of, 434

Stability, of Internet sources, 161

*Stand,* principal parts, 309

*Stationary, stationery,* 371

*Stationery, stationary,* 371

Statistics

documentation of, 173
numerals for, 438
as supporting evidence,
84
*Steal*, principal parts, 309
Streets, abbreviation of, 434
*Strike*, principal parts, 309
Structures, capitalization of,
422
Student essays. *See* Essay(s)
Student research paper. *See*
Research paper
Study skills
active learning outside
the classroom,
444–445
active reading skills,
449–451
checklist, 447–448
college services and, 445
essay exams, 452–459
library use, 445–446
lifelong learning, 447
making contacts with
students, staff, and
instructors, 446–447
mentors and, 447
priority on studying,
442–443
technology use, 446
time management,
441–442
understanding school and
course requirements,
443
Style manuals in different
disciplines, 276–277.
*See also* APA style;
Chicago style; CSE
style; MLA style
Subject-by-subject
comparisons, 54, **73**
Subject complements, 322,
**545**, 552
Subject guide, **150**, 151
Subject headings, 127–128,
**134**
Subject search
Internet, 150, 151
online catalog, 127–128
online databases, 134
Subject(s) of sentence(s). *See
also* Sentence(s)
agreement between verbs
and, 288–292, 522
collective noun subjects,
290–291
complete subject, 551
compound subjects joined
by *and*, 289
compound subjects joined
by *or*, 289–290

creating new subject to
revise dangling
modifier, 303
indefinite pronoun
subjects, 290
inverted subject-verb
order, 291, 334–335
separating verb from, 335
simple subject, 551
singular subjects with
plural forms, 291
verbal phrases as, 384
words between verb and,
288–289
Subject-verb agreement
collective noun subjects,
290–291
compound subjects joined
by *and*, 289
compound subjects joined
by *or*, 289–290
foreign plurals, 291
indefinite pronoun
subjects, 290
inverted subject-verb
order, 291
linking verbs, 292
present tense verbs, 288
relative pronouns, 292
separating subject from
verb., 335
singular subjects with
plural forms, 291
words between subject
and verb, 288–289
Subjective case of pronouns,
317
Subjunctive mood, 314–315
Subordinating conjunctions
in complex sentences,
330
definition of, **550**
with independent clauses,
287
list of, 330
in sentence fragment,
283
Subordination in sentences,
**331–332**
Successful students. *See* Study
skills
Sufficiency
of library sources, 141
of supporting evidence,
84
Suffixes
*-able* and *-ible* suffixes, 419
hyphens with, 430–431
silent *e* before, 418
*y* before, 419
Summaries
colon for setting off, 378

dash for setting of, 378,
407
integrating into writing,
168
MLA style for
parenthetical
references, 183
of sources, **116–117**, 118
transitional words and
phrases introducing,
67
Superlative forms of adverbs
and adjectives,
323–325, 532
Superscript, **202**
Supporting evidence. *See*
Evidence
*Supposed to, used to*, 371
Surveys, 145–146
Suspended hyphens, **430**
*Swear*, principal parts, 309
Sweeping generalization, 88
*Swim*, principal parts, 309
*Swing*, principal parts, 309
Syllogism, **87**
Symbols, abbreviation of, 435
Synchronous
communication, **157**
Synonyms, **360**
Synthesis, **168–169**

Tables
APA style for citing, 229,
247–248
in document design,
481–482
Tag questions, 388
Tags, **486–487**
*Take, bring*, 364
*Take*, principal parts, 309
*Teach*, principal parts, 309
Technical terms
abbreviation of, 432
quotation marks not used
for, 404
Television programs
APA style, 234
italics for titles of, 426
MLA style, 194
quotation marks for
episodes of, 402
Telnet, 157
Temperatures, abbreviation
of, 433
Tense
choosing simplest verb
tense, 525
perfect tenses, 310,
311–312, 523–524
progressive tenses, 310,
312–313, 524–525
shifts in, 295

simple tenses, 310, 311,
523
use of, in sentences,
313–314
of verbs, 522
Tentative thesis, 110
*Than,* comparisons with
pronouns and, 318
*Than, then,* 371
*That,* comma with, 386
*That, which, who,* 321, 371,
386
*The,* as definite article, 518
*The number, a number,* 291
*Their, there, they're,* 371
*Theirself, themselves, theirselves,*
371
*Theirselves, theirself, themselves,*
371
*Themselves, theirselves, theirself,*
371
*Then, than,* 371
*There, they're, their,* 371
*There is, there are,* 336
Thesaurus, 360–361
Thesis
argumentative thesis,
91–92
definition of, 14
tentative thesis, 110
Thesis-and-support essay,
14–15
Thesis statement
argumentative essays, 95
checklist, 17
essay exam answers,
454–455
essays, 14–19
oral presentation,
505–506
pattern of development
and, 18–19
research paper, 119
revising, 17
word choice, 15, 16, 17
*They're, their, there,* 371
Thinking critically. *See*
Critical thinking
*Throw,* principal parts, 309
*Till, until, 'til,* 371
Time
prepositions relating to,
533
transitional words and
phrases signaling, 66
Time management,
441–442
Times of day
abbreviation of, 433
colon separating minutes
from hours, 406
numerals for, 437

Titles of persons
abbreviation of, 432
capitalization of, 421–422
comma with title
following name, 388
Titles of works
capitalization of important
words in, 424
colon separating subtitle
from, 406
essays, 33
italics for, 426–427
quotation marks for,
401–402, 403, 426
research papers, 125
single quotation marks
for, 403
student papers, 404
*To, at,* 363
*To, too, two,* 372
*To,* use of, 533
Tone of writing, 86
*Too, two, to,* 372
*Too, very,* 538
Topic
argumentative essays, 91
debatable topic, 91
of essay, 6–7
of oral presentation, 504
research topic, 106–7
Topic sentence, 62–64
Topic tree, 12–14, 13
Trains, italics for titles of, 426
Transitional words and
phrases
argumentative essays, 96
comma setting off, 385,
387, 392
in compound sentences,
329
definition of, 65
for emphasis, 337
examples of, 329
with independent clauses,
286, 377, 387, 392
in paragraph, 65–67
purposes of, 66–67
semicolon before, 329
Transitive verbs, 526–527,
551–552
*Try and, try to,* 372
*Try to, try and,* 372
*Two, to, too,* 372
*-Type,* 372
Type face and type size,
476–477

Unabridged dictionaries, 136
Underlining for italics, 401,
428
*Uninterested, disinterested,* 365
*Unique,* 372

Unity
definition of, 62
of paragraph, 62–64
topic sentences, 63–64
*Until, 'til, till,* 371
URLs, 149–150, 160, 380,
429
*US*
abbreviation of, 434
before noun, 319
Usage glossary, 362–373
Usage labels in dictionary,
361
*Used to, supposed to,* 371
Usenet system, 156
Utility words, 342, 354
*Utilize,* 372

Varied sentences, 329–335
Verb(s). *See also* Predicate(s)
agreement between
subjects and, 288–292,
522
auxiliary verbs, 522–523,
545–546
colon not used to separate
objects or
complements and,
406
definition of, 545
faulty predication,
298–299
for ESL students, 521–530
in dependent clauses, 313
in résumés, 495
integrating source
material into writing,
164
intransitive verbs,
526–527, 551
irregular verbs, 307–310
linking verbs, 292, 298,
322, 545
main verbs, 545
modal auxiliaries,
522–523, 546
mood of, 296, 314–315
negative verbs, 525–526
number of, 522
person of, 522
phrasal verbs, 527–528
present tense verbs, 288
principal parts of,
307–310
regular verbs, 307
separating subject from,
335
shifts in mood, 296
shifts in tense, 295
shifts in voice, 295–296
tenses of, 295, 310–314,
522, 523–525

transitive verbs, 526–527, 551–552
use of, as nouns and adjectives, 529–530
voice of, 295–296, 316, 527
words between subject and, 288–289
Verb phrases, **553**
Verbal(s), **546**
Verbal phrases, 384, **553**
Vertical files, 141
*Very, too,* 538
Videotapes
Chicago style, 257
CSE style, 272
MLA style, 194
Visuals
checklist, 509–510
copyright and, 480–481
design of, for oral presentation, 507–510
in document design, 480–485
oral presentations, 507
Voice
dangling modifiers and passive voice, 303
definition of, **316**
eliminating passive constructions in rambling sentences, 345
emphasis through active voice, 339–340
preference of active versus passive voice, 527
shifts in, 295–296
uses of active and passive voice, 316
Voice mail, 503
Vowels
*ie/ei* combinations, 418
in unstressed positions, 415

*Wait for, wait on,* 372
*Wait on, wait for,* 372
*Wake,* principal parts, 309
*We,* before noun, 319
*Wear,* principal parts, 309
*Weather, whether,* 372
Web browser, 148
Web page, **148**
Web sites. *See also* Internet
checklist on design of, 490
Chicago style for citing, 258
and copyright, 486
creating basic Web page, 485–487

definition of, **148, 485**
designing, 485–490
evaluation of, 158–161, 199
for library research, 135–136
library's own Web site, 128
links for, 488–489
list of useful Web sites, 161–163
organizing information for, 487–488
posting, 489
proofreading text for, 489
Webbing, **10,** 11
WebCrawler, 153
Week days, capitalization of, 422
*Well,* comparative and superlative forms, 325
*Well, good,* 366–367
Well-developed paragraphs, **68–69**
*Were, we're,* 372
*We're, were,* 372
*Whether, if,* 367
*Whether, weather,* 372
*Which,* comma with, 386
*Which, who, that,* 321, 371, 386
White space in document design, 476
Whiteboards, 509
*Who,* case of, 318–319
*Who, that, which,* 321, 371, 386
*Who, whom,* 318–319, 372–373
*Whom,* case of, 318–319
*Whom, who,* 318–319, 372–373
*Who's, whose,* 373
*Whose, who's,* 373
*Will, shall,* 370
Word(s). *See also* Dictionaries; Foreign words and phrases; Noun(s); Spelling; Verb(s); *and other parts of speech*
as sentence opening, 334
careless pronunciation of, 416
commonly confused words, 538–539
ending in *-f* or *fe,* 419
ending in *-o,* 420
ending in *-s, -ss, -sh, -ch, -x, -z,* 420
ending in *-y,* 419
hyphen for breaking word at end of line, 429

plurals of, 419–420
quotation marks for words used in special ways, 402
revising, 28
*seed* endings of, 419
spelling as one word or two words, 417
Word choice
abstract words, 354
appropriate level of diction, 351–352
argumentative thesis, 92
avoiding biased language, 356–358
avoiding inappropriate language, 354–355
clichés, 355
clipped forms, 351, 380
college writing, 352
colloquial diction, 351–352
concrete words, 354
connotation, 353
denotation, 353
euphemisms, 353
figures of speech, 356
formal diction, 351
general words, 353
informal diction, 351–352
jargon, 354
neologisms, 354–355
nonstandard diction, 352
offensive labels, 356–357
pretentious diction, 355
regionalisms, 352
sexist language, 294, 357–358
slang, 352, 404
specific words, 353
thesis statement, 15, 16, 17
Word order
adjectives, 531
articles, 531
climactic word order, **337**
determiners, 531
with direct quotations, 536–537
emphasis through, 336–338
for ESL students, 535–537
experimenting with, 337–338
in imperative sentences, 536
with indirect quotations, 537
inverting, 291, 334–335
in questions, 535–536
separating subject from verb, 335
standard word order, 535

Wordiness
  checklist, 537–538
  circumlocution, 342–343
  deadwood, 341–342
  eliminating, 341–343,
    537–538
  revising wordy phrases,
    343
  utility words, 342
Working bibliography,
  108–109. *See also*
  Bibliography
Workplace
  business letters, 406,
    491–492
  e-mail, 491, 502–503
  letters of application,
    493–494
  memos, 500–501
  résumés, 495–499
  voice mail, 503
Works-cited list. *See also*
  Bibliography
  argumentative essays, 101
  MLA style, 187–203, 206,
    219–220, 474
  publisher information in,
    406
World Wide Web, 148–155.
  *See also* Internet; Web
  sites

*Would of, could of, should of,*
  365
*Wring,* principal parts, 309
*Write,* principal parts, 309
Writing
  about literature, 462–474
  business letters, 491–492
  cause-and-effect essays,
    39, 50–53
  comparison-and-contrast
    essays, 39, 53–56
  concise sentences,
    341–345
  definition essays, 39,
    58–61
  descriptive essays, 39,
    42–45
  division-and-classification
    essays, 39, 56–58
  e-mail, 491, 502–503
  emphatic sentences,
    336–340
  essay exams, 452–459
  essays, 3–38
  exemplification essays, 39,
    45–48
  freewriting, 7–8
  in-class essays, 459
  letters of application,
    493–494
  memos, 500–501

narrative essays, 39–42
  paragraphs, 62–80
  process essays, 39, 48–50
  résumés, 495–499
  varied sentences, 329–335
  for workplace, 491–503
Writing process
  drafting, 21–24
  editing and proofreading,
    31–38
  planning, 3–12
  revising, 24–31
  shaping, 12–21
  stages in, 3

*-x,* plurals of words ending
  in, 420

*-y*
  before suffix, 419
  *-er* and *-est* after, 324
  plurals of words ending
  in, 419
Yahoo, 153
Yearbooks, **137**
*Yes,* comma with, 388
*Your, you're,* 373
*You're, your,* 373

*-z,* plurals of words ending in,
  420

# CREDITS

*Pages 4, 63, 339:* From "Aria: A Memoir of a Bilingual Childhood" from HUNGER OF MEMORY by Richard Rodriquez. Copyright © 1982 by Richard Rodiquez. Reprinted by permission of Georges Borchardt, Inc., for the author.

*Page 149:* Screen capture of Netscape Netcenter Web site. Copyright Netscape Communications Corporation. Screenshot used with permission.

*Page 151:* Screen capture of Google Web site. Reprinted by permission of Google.

*Page 359:* Excerpt from THE AMERICAN HERITAGE DICTIONARY, Second Edition. Copyright © 1991 by Houghton Mifflin Company. Reprinted by permission from THE AMERICAN HERITAGE DICTIONARY, Second College Edition.

*Page 464:* "The True Blue American" by Delmore Scwartz from SELECTED POEMS: SUMMER KNOWLEDGE. Copyright © 1959 by Delmore Scwartz. Reprinted by permission of New Directions Publishing Corp.

*Page 488:* Screen capture of Heinle Web site. Copyright © 2002 Heinle Publishers. Reprinted with permission of Thomson Learning: www.thomsonrights.com. Fax 800/730-2215.

# FREQUENTLY ASKED QUESTIONS

## Chapter 1    Writing Essays  3
- How do I find ideas to write about?  7
- How do I arrange ideas into an essay?  12
- How do I construct an outline?  19
- How do I revise a draft?  24
- How do I find a title for my paper?  33
- What should my finished paper look like?  35

## Chapter 2    Essay Patterns across the Disciplines  39
- How do I decide which pattern to use to structure my essay?  39
- How do I organize a comparison-and-contrast essay?  54

## Chapter 3    Writing Paragraphs  62
- When do I begin a new paragraph?  62
- What transitional words and phrases can I use to make my paragraphs flow?  66
- How do I know when I have enough information to support my paragraph's main idea?  68
- What is the best way to set up a comparison-and-contrast paragraph?  72
- How do I write a good introduction for my paper?  76
- How do I write an effective conclusion?  78

## Chapter 4    Thinking Critically  83
- What is critical thinking?  83
- How do I tell the difference between a fact and an opinion?  83
- How do I detect bias in an argument?  85
- What is an inference?  87
- What is a logical fallacy?  88
- What is a non sequitur?  88
- How do I recognize post hoc reasoning?  88

## Chapter 5    Writing Argumentative Essays  91
- How do I know if a topic is suitable for argument?  91
- What can I do to make sure I have an argumentative thesis?  92
- How should I deal with opposing arguments?  92
- How can I make sure I am being fair?  94
- How should I organize my argumentative essay?  95

## Chapter 6    The Research Process  105
- How do I plan a research project?  105
- How do I keep track of my sources?  108
- What format should I use for taking notes?  114
- What is the difference between a paraphrase and a summary?  117
- When should I quote the source?  119

## Chapter 7    Using and Evaluating Library Sources  126
- Why should I use the library's electronic resources? Why can't I just use the Internet?  132
- What online databases should I use?  140
- How do I evaluate the books and articles that I get from the library?  141
- What is the difference between a scholarly publication and a popular publication?  143

## Chapter 8  Using and Evaluating Internet Sources  147
- What is the best way to do a keyword search?  150
- How do I choose the right search engine?  152
- How can I evaluate the information on a Web site?  158
- How do I know if I can trust an anonymous Web source?  159

## Chapter 9  Integrating Sources and Avoiding Plagiarism  164
- How do I avoid saying "he said" or "she said" every time I use a source?  164
- What exactly is plagiarism?  169
- Is there anything I do not have to document?  170
- How can I make sure that readers will be able to tell the difference between my ideas and those of my sources?  173

## Chapter 10  MLA Documentation Style  182
- What is MLA style?  182
- How do I list the sources I use in my paper?  187
- How do I document sources I get from the Internet?  195
- How do I type a works-cited list?  206
- What should an MLA paper look like?  210

## Chapter 11  APA Documentation Style  225
- When should I use APA documentation?  225
- How do I cite a work that has more than two authors?  226
- How do I cite an article I found on the Internet?  232
- How do I arrange the works in an APA reference list?  237
- What should an APA paper look like?  237

## Chapter 12  Chicago, CSE, and Other Documentation Styles  250
- When should I use Chicago-style documentation?  250
- What should a Chicago-style paper look like?  262
- When should I use CSE documentation?  267
- What should a CSE-style paper look like?  274
- What other documentation styles are there?  276

## Chapter 13  Revising Sentence Fragments  281
- What exactly is a sentence fragment?  281
- How do I turn a fragment into a complete sentence?  282
- Are sentence fragments ever acceptable?  284

## Chapter 14  Revising Comma Splices and Fused Sentences  285
- What are comma splices and fused sentences, and how are they different from run-on sentences?  285
- How do I revise a comma splice or a fused sentence?  285

## Chapter 15  Revising Agreement Errors  288
- What do I do if a phrase like *along with* comes between the subject and the verb?  289
- If a subject has two parts, is the verb singular or plural?  289
- Do subjects like *anyone* take singular or plural verbs?  290
- Can I use *they* and *their* to refer to words like *everyone*?  294

## Chapter 16  Revising Awkward or Confusing Sentences  295
- What is the difference between direct and indirect discourse?  297
- How do I correct an incomplete or illogical comparison?  299

## Chapter 17 Revising Misplaced and Dangling Modifiers 300
- What are misplaced modifiers, and how do I revise them? 300
- What are dangling modifiers, and how do I revise them? 302

## Chapter 18 Using Verbs Correctly: Form, Tense, Mood, and Voice 307
- What is an irregular verb? 307
- What is the difference between *lie* and *lay*? 310
- Which is correct, "I wish I were" or "I wish I was"? 315
- What is the passive voice? 316
- Is active voice always better than passive voice? 316

## Chapter 19 Using Pronouns Correctly 318
- Is *I* always more appropriate than *me*? 318
- How do I know whether to use *who* or *whom*? 318
- What is an antecedent? 320
- When should I use *who, which,* and *that*? 321

## Chapter 20 Using Adjectives and Adverbs Correctly 322
- What is the difference between an adjective and an adverb? 322
- How do I know when to use *more* and when to use an *-er* ending? 324
- How do I know when to use *most* and when to use an *-est* ending? 324
- What's wrong with *most unique*? 325
- Why is a double negative wrong? 326

## Chapter 21 Writing Varied Sentences 329
- How do I combine choppy sentences to make my writing "flow"? 331
- What do I do if I have a whole string of compound sentences? 332
- What should I do if every sentence starts with *I* or another subject? 334

## Chapter 22 Writing Emphatic Sentences 336
- Is it OK to start a sentence with *there is* or *there are*? 336
- Is repeating words and phrases ever a good idea? 339
- When can I use passive voice? 340

## Chapter 23 Writing Concise Sentences 341
- How can I tell which words I really need and which can be cut? 341
- How do I edit a long, rambling sentence? 344

## Chapter 24 Using Parallelism 346
- What is parallelism? 346
- How can I use parallelism to improve my writing? 347
- How can I correct faulty parallelism? 347

## Chapter 25 Choosing Words 351
- How formal should I be in my college writing? 352
- How do I know whether I am using exactly the right word? 353
- What is a cliché? 355
- What is sexist language and how can I avoid it? 357

## Chapter 26 Using a Dictionary 359
- What kind of dictionary should I use? 359
- Should I use a thesaurus? 360
- Is an electronic dictionary better than a print dictionary? 361

## Chapter 27    A Glossary of Usage  363
- Is *criteria* singular or plural?  365
- Which is correct, *everyday* or *every day*?  366
- What is the difference between *imply* and *infer*?  367

## Chapter 28    Using End Punctuation  379
- Do abbreviations always include periods?  380
- How are periods used in electronic addresses?  380

## Chapter 29    Using Commas  382
- Do I need a comma before the *and* that comes between the last two items in a series?  382
- How do I use commas with *that* and *which*?  386
- How do I use commas with *however* and *for example*?  387
- Should I always use a comma before *and* and *but*?  390

## Chapter 30    Using Semicolons  392
- When do I use a semicolon?  392
- Do I introduce a list with a semicolon or a colon?  393

## Chapter 31    Using Apostrophes  394
- How do I form the possessive if a singular noun ends in *-s*?  394
- How do I form the possessive if a plural word ends in *-s*?  394
- What is the difference between *its* and *it's*?  396

## Chapter 32    Using Quotations Marks  398
- When do I use quotation marks with titles?  401
- Does punctuation go inside or outside quotation marks?  402
- What if a quotation is inside another quotation?  403

## Chapter 33    Using Other Punctuation Marks  405
- When do I use a colon to introduce a quotation?  406
- When should I use parentheses?  407
- How do I show that I have deleted words from a quotation?  409

## Chapter 34    Spelling  415
- Why is English spelling so hard?  415
- Do I still need to proofread if I run a spell check?  417
- Are there any spelling rules I can memorize?  417
- How do I find the correct spelling of a word if I don't know how to spell it?  420

## Chapter 35    Capitalization  421
- Is the first word of a line of poetry always capitalized?  421
- Are *east* and *west* capitalized?  422
- Are *black* and *white* capitalized when they refer to race?  423
- Which words in titles are not capitalized?  424
- Are the names of seasons capitalized?  425

## Chapter 36    Italics  426
- What kinds of titles are italicized?  426

**Chapter 37   Hyphens  429**
- Should I use a hyphen to divide a URL at the end of a line?  429
- Where do I put the hyphen when I have to divide a compound noun?  429

**Chapter 38   Abbreviations  432**
- Is it OK to use abbreviations for technical terms?  432
- Are abbreviations like *e.g.* and *etc.* acceptable in college writing?  434

**Chapter 39   Numbers  436**
- When do I spell out a number, and when do I use a numeral?  436

**Chapter 40   Ten Habits of Successful Students  441**
- What strategies can I use to help me manage my time?  441
- What is the best way to study?  442
- What college services can help me?  445

**Chapter 41   Developing Active Reading Skills  449**
- What kinds of highlighting symbols should I use?  450
- How do I take marginal notes?  450

**Chapter 42   Writing Essay Exams  452**
- How do I organize an essay exam answer?  454
- What should I look for when I reread my answer?  455
- What does an effective essay exam answer look like?  456

**Chapter 43   Writing About Literature  460**
- Do I put a title in quotation marks or underline it?  464
- What does a paper about literature look like?  466

**Chapter 44   Designing Documents and Web Sites  475**
- What is document design?  475
- Should I use headings in my paper?  477
- Should I use numbers or bullets when I make a list?  479
- What kinds of visuals should I use in my paper?  480

**Chapter 45   Writing for the Workplace  491**
- How do I write a letter to apply for a job?  494
- What should a résumé look like?  496–497
- Should I post my résumé on a Web site?  498

**Chapter 46   Making Oral Presentations  504**
- What kind of notes should I use?  506
- Should I use visual aids?  507

**Chapter 47   English for Speakers of Other Languages  515**
- Why can't I write *closings* and *informations*?  517
- What is the difference between *a* and *the*?  517
- What is a double negative?  525
- If several adjectives modify one noun, which adjective goes first?  531
- How do I know which preposition to use?  533
- Does the subject of a sentence always come before the verb?  535

# CONTENTS

**PART 1**
**Writing Essays and Paragraphs 1**

**1 Writing Essays 3**
a Understanding the Writing Process 3
b Planning 3
c Shaping 12
d Drafting and Revising 21
e Editing and Proofreading 31

**2 Essay Patterns across the Disciplines 39**
a Writing Narrative Essays 39
b Writing Descriptive Essays 42
c Writing Exemplification Essays 45
d Writing Process Essays 48
e Writing Cause-and-Effect Essays 50
f Writing Comparison-and-Contrast Essays 53
g Writing Division-and-Classification Essays 56
h Writing Definition Essays 58

**3 Writing Paragraphs 62**
a Writing Unified Paragraphs 62
b Writing Coherent Paragraphs 64
c Writing Well-Developed Paragraphs 68
d Patterns for Paragraph Development 70
e Writing Introductory and Concluding Paragraphs 76

**PART 2**
**Critical Thinking and Argumentation 81**

**4 Thinking Critically 83**
a Distinguishing Fact from Opinion 83
b Evaluating Supporting Evidence 84
c Detecting Bias 85
d Understanding Inductive and Deductive Reasoning 86
e Recognizing Logical Fallacies 88

**5 Writing Argumentative Essays 91**
a Planning an Argumentative Essay 91
b Using Evidence and Establishing Credibility 93
c Organizing an Argumentative Essay 94
d Writing an Argumentative Essay 96

**PART 3**
**The Research Process 103**

**6 The Research Process 105**
a Choosing a Topic 106
b Doing Exploratory Research and Formulating a Research Question 107
c Assembling a Working Bibliography 108
d Developing a Tentative Thesis 110
e Doing Focused Research 110
f Taking Notes 112
g Fine-Tuning Your Thesis 119
h Outlining, Drafting, and Revising 120

**7 Using and Evaluating Library Sources 126**
a Doing Exploratory Library Research 126
b Doing Focused Library Research 135
c Evaluating Library Sources 141
d Doing Research Outside the Library 144

**8 Using and Evaluating Internet Sources 147**
a Understanding the Internet 147
b Using the World Wide Web for Research 148
c Using Other Internet Tools 155
d Evaluating Internet Sources 158
e Useful Web Sites 161

**9 Integrating Sources and Avoiding Plagiarism 164**
a Integrating Source Material into Your Writing 164
b Avoiding Plagiarism 169

**PART 4**
**Documenting Sources: MLA Style 177**

**10 MLA Documentation Style 182**
a Using MLA Style 182
b MLA Manuscript Guidelines 205
c Sample MLA-Style Research Paper 206

**PART 5**
**Documenting Sources: APA and Other Styles 221**

**11 APA Documentation Style 225**
a Using APA Style 225
b APA Manuscript Guidelines 235
c Sample APA-Style Research Paper 237

**12 Chicago, CSE, and Other Documentation Styles 250**
a Using Chicago Style 250
b Chicago-Style Manuscript Guidelines 261
c Sample Chicago-Style Research Paper (Excerpts) 262
d Using CSE (formerly CBE) Style 267
e CSE Manuscript Guidelines 273
f Sample CSE-Style Research Paper (Excerpts) 274
g Using Other Documentation Styles 276

**PART 6**
**Five Common Sentence Errors 279**

**13 Revising Sentence Fragments 281**
a Attaching the Fragment to an Independent Clause 282
b Deleting the Subordinating Conjunction or Relative Pronoun 283
c Supplying the Missing Subject or Verb 284